Liberty and Justice
for All

OTHER BOOKS BY RONALD C. WHITE, JR.

American Christianity: A Case Approach,
coeditor with Louis B. Weeks, and Garth M. Roselle

Partners in Peace and Education,
coeditor with Eugene Fisher

The Social Gospel: Religion and Reform in Changing America,
coauthor with C. Howard Hopkins

An Unsettled Arena: Religion and the Bill of Rights,
coeditor with Albright G. Zimmerman

Liberty and Justice for All

RACIAL REFORM AND THE SOCIAL GOSPEL (1877–1925)

Ronald C. White, Jr.

THE RAUSCHENBUSCH LECTURES,
NEW SERIES, II

1817

HARPER & ROW, PUBLISHERS, SAN FRANCISCO

New York, Grand Rapids, Philadelphia, St. Louis
London, Singapore, Sydney, Tokyo, Toronto

The Rauschenbusch Lectures are sponsored by Colgate-
Rochester Divinity School/Bexley Hall/Crozer Theological
Seminary, Rochester, NY.

LIBERTY AND JUSTICE FOR ALL: *Racial Reform and the Social Gospel
(1877–1925).* Copyright © 1990 by Ronald C. White, Jr. All
rights reserved. Printed in the United States of America.
No part of this book may be used or reproduced in any manner
whatsoever without written permission except in the case of
brief quotations embodied in critical articles and reviews.
For information address Harper & Row, Publishers, Inc.,
10 East 53rd Street, New York, NY 10022.

FIRST EDITION

Library of Congress Cataloging-in-Publication Data

White, Ronald C., Jr.
    Liberty and justice for all : racial reform and the social gospel
(1877–1925) / Ronald C. White, Jr.—1st ed.
        p.   cm.—(The Rauschenbusch lectures ; new ser., 2)
    Includes bibliographical references.
    ISBN 0–06–069361–4
    1. Afro-Americans—History—1877–1964.   2. United States—Race
relations.   3. Afro-Americans—Civil rights.   4. Race relations—Religious aspects—
Christianity.   5. Social gospel.   6. United States—
History—1865–1921.   I. Title.   II. Series.
E185.61.W595   1990
973'.0496073—dc20   89–45550
                                                                                        CIP

90 91 92 93 94 HAD 10 9 8 7 6 5 4 3 2 1

This edition is printed on acid-free paper that
meets the American National Standards Institute Z39.48 Standard.

For

C. Howard Hopkins
Historian of the Social Gospel
Mentor and Colleague
Friend

Contents

Foreword

Many fine studies of the Social Gospel have enriched our understanding of the reform movements that blossomed into progressivism nearly a century ago. And in recent years the explosion of scholarship in Afro-American history has provided new information and perspectives on race relations and civil rights activism during the same era. Curiously, however, little previous research has focused on the interconnections between these two movements. The reason for this puzzling fact seems to become clear, though, when one reads assertions by prominent historians that social Christianity "ignored the Negro," "said nothing with real meaning about racial injustices," and "did little to help the cause of the emancipation of the Black American." Presumably, therefore, little has been written about the Social Gospel and racial reform because there is little to write.

Nothing could be more wrong, as Ronald C. White demonstrates in this important and pathbreaking book. Not only did many prominent advocates of the Social Gospel participate in movements for racial reform; they also provided dynamic leadership in such important institutions for black education, civil rights, and economic welfare as the American Missionary Association, the NAACP, and the National Urban League—the last two having been founded during this era. Nor should this involvement come as a surprise. An earlier generation of Christian social activists had generated an abolitionist movement that helped achieve emancipation and equal rights for freed slaves and laid the foundations of black education in the 1860s. A century later, Martin Luther King, Jr., and other black religious leaders electrified the world with their crusade for racial justice. It would be surprising if this impulse of social Christianity had disappeared during the intervening decades. Most assuredly it did not, as this rich and rewarding study makes abundantly clear.

Part of the reason for the myopia of previous scholars toward the
race-relations activism of the Social Gospel has been their narrowness
of focus on the urban North. As Ronald White demonstrates, a significant Social Gospel movement also existed among black churches and
southern white churches. In this book we learn of the work of black
clergymen like Alexander Walters and Francis Grimké and of southern
whites like Edgar Gardner Murphy and Willis D. Weatherford, as well
as of such notable northern Social Gospel leaders as Washington Gladden. We emerge from this study with a broader understanding of the
meaning and significance of social Christianity.

The story is not a simple one of crusaders for racial justice battling
the forces of evil and reaction. The interplay of black and white, of
North and South, of radical, liberal, and conservative ideology produced a variety of approaches to the racial problems of those years. By
the early twentieth century these approaches had sorted themselves
into two principal philosophies, associated with Booker T. Washington
and W. E. B. Du Bois: one emphasizing education, uplift, and gradualism; the other emphasizing protest, activism, and civil rights. Social
Gospelers found themselves in both camps. Some of them moved from
a radical position in their early careers to the meliorist, gradualist approach in later years; others moved in a different direction. While some
tried to mediate between the conflicting forces, a number tried to pursue both strategies. The history of racial reform during those decades
from 1875 to 1925 is a complex, confusing one of shifting alliances and
competing philosophies. Because the Social Gospel movement reflected
these kaleidoscopic patterns, historians have previously failed to understand its complexities or have ignored the whole matter. That fact
helps explain their misleading generalizations about a lack of Social
Gospel commitment to racial concerns. Ronald White unravels these
complexities without oversimplifying them in this stimulating study
that sheds new light on an important but neglected subject. In the
process he also broadens the horizons of our understanding of race
relations in the United States today.

James M. McPherson
Princeton University

Preface

"Liberty and justice for all"—these words, which conclude the pledge of allegiance to the flag of the United States of America, have resounded across the nation since their first public presentation in 1892. Penned at the beginning of the Progressive Era, the pledge invoked for Americans of that day the dreams of the martyred president, Abraham Lincoln. On January 1, 1863, President Lincoln had signed the Emancipation Proclamation, decreeing that over 3 million black men, women, and children "are, and henceforward shall be, free."[1]

One hundred years after the Emancipation Proclamation, in the summer of 1963, more than 200,000 Americans gathered in front of the Lincoln Memorial to hear Martin Luther King, Jr., proclaim, "I have a dream." In spelling out his dream, this young black Baptist minister wove together motifs from both Christian and civil Scriptures and songs to call America to redeem Lincoln's promise of freedom for all.

This book is about some of what happened between Abraham Lincoln's proclamation and the dream of Martin Luther King, Jr. Civil War and civil rights are such momentous sagas in our history that the years in between are often largely forgotten. This book tells the story of some of the people and movements in the period 1877–1925 who dared to keep the dream alive.

For the people in this story the foundation of their dream was a prophetic understanding of the Christian faith. Central to the aspirations and achievements of 1863 and 1963 were Christian individuals, movements, and institutions. Abolitionists in the nineteenth century and civil rights workers in our own time who prayed and protested constituted the backbone of dynamic movements seeking full equality for all Americans. This is the story of a courageous minority in continuity with this stream who often bucked both culture and church to speak up and live out the ideals of both civil and Christian creeds.

The original impetus for this study was questions asked by a young pastor beginning ministry at the height of Martin Luther King's civil rights campaign. How had America arrived at such a predicament? What had the churches done, or not done, in the period immediately preceding the King years? Were there any resources or precedents in the earlier story that could be helpful in the present crisis?

For two decades I have been seeking answers to these questions. If, as my son Bradley says, "half of your life is in that book," it is because the questions have multiplied and they admit to no easy answers. Over time I learned to look in unconventional places for some of the answers, found myself unsatisfied with earlier versions of this manuscript, and through the help of many friends slowly began to ask some better questions.

In seeking resources I turned early to a dynamic religious and social movement known, from the first years of the twentieth century, as the Social Gospel. This movement has been characterized as "America's most unique contribution to the great ongoing stream of Christianity."[2] But when asking questions about the relation of the Social Gospel to racial reform, I heard almost one answer: the Social Gospel was not involved. I discovered that existing scholarship had largely ignored the role of Social Gospel leaders in relation to race and reform. This omission had occurred in histories of both race relations and the Social Gospel. David M. Reimers's judgment that when the Social Gospelers "turned their attention to problems of industrialization and urbanization, they turned away from concern for the Negro" has been cited again and again in a variety of standard studies.[3]

Other scholars have made essentially the same judgment. George M. Fredrickson maintained that "for the most part, Gladden and other northern proponents of 'social Christianity' ignored the Negro."[4] Thomas F. Gossett observed that "whereas the social gospel ministers spoke out openly and fearlessly against other injustices of society, they said nothing with real meaning about racial injustices."[5] Preston N. Williams concluded that "the Social Gospel from its beginning until 1920 had done little to help the cause of the emancipation of the Black American."[6] Finally, Robert Moats Miller spoke for many when he observed:

> If the years between Jamestown and Fort Sumter saw an element of American Protestantism slowly challenge the entrenched institution of slavery, the years between Appomattox and Versailles saw the churches almost completely mired on the muddy and rut-pocked road to racial equality. Hopkins, May, and others devoted isolated sentences, not chapters or books, to Protestantism's fight for racial justice. The story does not deserve much fuller treatment.[7]

But the story does deserve fuller treatment. Gladden and other proponents of the Social Gospel did not ignore racial reform. On the contrary, many of them were active in church missionary societies fostering black education, progressive movements ameliorating racial injustice, and biracial ventures in reform begun in the new century. While some indeed embraced a conservative approach, others eventually adopted more militant strategies, joined the NAACP, and responded positively to a changing and more assertive black leadership.

Some of the traditional judgments about the Social Gospel and racial reform will indeed be confirmed in this book. Many leaders were preoccupied with a cluster of issues relating to the city and labor and consequently neglected racial reform. They were as insensitive to the deterioration in race relations as were many other progressives. But others surmounted the prevailing racism of their age and used the social message of Christianity to challenge caste. This book focuses primarily on these leaders. I examine their ideas and their strategies and the movements that emanated from both.

In the course of my research I have discovered again and again that the relationship between the Social Gospel and racial reform is more multifaceted than previously suggested. To place the complex story in perspective, this book reaches backward to the connections with pre–Civil War abolitionism and forward to the ecumenical interracial movements growing out of World War I. A central discovery in the research is how much this is a story of movement and change.

I believe that during the quarter century after 1898 many Social Gospel leaders participated in fresh experiences, changed their minds, and became involved in new movements of racial cooperation and reform. This book looks at persons recognizable as primary leaders in the traditional histories of the Social Gospel. But it also considers many other, lesser figures for whom race was a primary concern. To this researcher's surprise, many of these persons were southerners. A significant cadre were women. The story is complex, involving change, development, regression, and growth.

In the spirit of the Rauschenbusch lectureship, this book is addressed both to the scholarly community and to the churches. It is my hope that the story has been told in a way that will interest persons of all persuasions who are concerned about the promise and the pledge of "liberty and justice for all."

The invitation to deliver the 1984-1985 Rauschenbusch Lectures provided the catalyst to turn twenty years of research and writing into lectures and finally into this volume. The Rauschenbusch Lectures were established in 1931 to honor the prophet of the American Social Gospel. Credit for reinvigorating the lecture series in recent years is due Leonard I. Sweet, then dean of Colgate Rochester–Bexley Hall–Crozer Seminary. His conviction that the new lecture series ought to focus on the Social Gospel, and his encouragement at a difficult time, is deeply appreciated. I am honored to be numbered with those who have delivered these lectures over the past six decades. Walter Rauschenbusch continues to be a formative influence in my own pilgrimage.

In the course of these years a number of awards have helped make possible this study. I wish to acknowledge a Research Grant from Princeton University, a Ford Foundation Dissertation Fellowship in Ethnic Studies, a Faculty Fellowship from Rider College, as well as special released time granted by President Edward B. Lindaman of Whitworth College and President Thomas G. Gillespie of Princeton Theological Seminary. The invitation from President Arnold Come to be a visiting professor of church history at San Francisco Theological Seminary and the Graduate Theological Union at Berkeley provided time for transforming an earlier conceptual framework. After the Rauschenbusch Lectures the opportunity to be a University Fellow at Princeton University afforded the opportunity to cast separate lectures into an expanded study. The unparalleled setting and working conditions at the Huntington Library in San Marino, California, has been a balm in Gilead and a boon to trying to write this story whole.

Many persons have helped in the course of my research. I am indebted to the directors and staffs of the following libraries and institutions: American Baptist Historical Society, housed in the library of the Colgate Rochester–Bexley Hall–Crozer Theological Seminary; Amistad Research Center, Tulane University; Negro Collection, Atlanta University; Bowdoin College Library; Colorado College Library; Columbia University Library; Drew University Library; Emory University Library; Quaker Collection, Haverford College Library; Rutherford B. Hayes Library, Fremont, Ohio; Huntington Library; Kansas State Historical Library; Manuscript, Newspaper, and Stack and Reader Divisions of the Library of Congress; Los Angeles Public Library; New York Public Library, including the Newspaper Annex and the Schomburg Library; Southern Historical Collection, University of North Carolina Library; Ohio State Historical Society; Presbyterian Historical Society; Robert E. Speer Library, Princeton Theological Seminary; Firestone Library, Princeton University; Burke Library Union Theological Seminary (New York); Whitworth College Library; and Divinity School and University Library, Yale University. In addition, I received generous assistance from the staffs of the First Congregational Church, Columbus, Ohio, and the Central Congregational Church, Topeka, Kansas.

Teachers, colleagues, students and friends have helped refine the direction of this study over the years. I thank John F. Wilson, Arthur S. Link, James M. McPherson, and Horton Davies, all of Princeton University, for their counsel and encouragement in the beginning stages of my work. At Rider College, Albright G. Zimmerman and C. Howard Hopkins extended encouragement and opportunity. At Whitworth College, F. Dale Bruner read an early version of this study, and Ronald G. Frase and Duncan S. Ferguson offered continuing encouragement.

Three persons have continued in conversation in recent years as expansion, refinement, and succeeding drafts have emerged. James M. Washington has challenged me about the role of the black Social Gospelers in the story. In asking new questions about them and the interaction between blacks and whites, I have discovered more than I was told I could find when I first began my work. This is a growing edge of my own research, and I am aware that others need to help expand this part of the story. Robert T. Handy has been unfailing in his promptness and thoroughness in reading various drafts of this study. Respected by a generation of American church historians, he has given me both his careful scholarship and his affirmation. Finally, Jim McPherson has taught me about abolitionism, black education, and reform. Through many conversations—in both his home and on the tennis courts—I have benefited from both his questions and his insights. I am grateful to him for his Foreword to this study.

My association with Harper & Row has been unfailingly congenial and productive. John Loudon and Georgia Hughes have helped me walk through the doors to publication. Wendy Chiu, production editor, and Craig Noll, my copy editor, have been immensely helpful.

I dedicate this book to the first historian of the Social Gospel. C. Howard Hopkins's *Rise of the Social Gospel in American Protestantism, 1865–1915*, published in 1940, has stood the test of time. In 1976 it was my privilege to be a coauthor with Howard of *The Social Gospel: Religion and Reform in Changing America*. Out of a profound sense of gratitude to a scholar and a friend, I offer this dedication.

Introduction

This introduction is provided mainly for those who pause at the entrance to this story and ask the question, What is the Social Gospel? At the popular level the words *Social Gospel* have become part of everyday language. Along with such words as *puritan* or *fundamentalist*, the phrase *Social Gospel* has become so overused or misused as to obscure its generic or historic meaning. It is sometimes used as a label or a libel, depending on the point of view of the speaker.

The Social Gospel as a historical movement grew to maturity in the half century between the end of the Civil War and the end of World War I.[1] The rise of the Social Gospel paralleled and penetrated the political and humanitarian movement known as progressivism. Historian Carl Degler has summed up its contribution in this way: "The acceptance of the social gospel spelled the transformation of American Protestantism."[2]

The Social Gospel was a variegated movement that defies easy definition. In this introduction I present a skeletal sketch that will receive bones and flesh as the more detailed story of the Social Gospel and racial reform is told.

Toward the end of the Progressive Era, the Social Gospel was defined by Shailer Mathews, one of its leading adherents, as "the application of the teaching of Jesus and the total message of the Christian salvation to society, the economic life, and social institutions . . . as well as to individuals."[3] Christianity has manifested social dimensions throughout its history. What is here identified as the Social Gospel was basically an indigenous movement growing within the matrix of American Protestantism.[4] Interacting with the changing problems of an increasingly industrialized and urbanized nation, the Social Gospel launched a crusade for social justice in many areas of American life.

The crusade recruited ministers and laypersons who advocated their points of view as pastors, educators, editors, and directors of reform organizations. The story of the embracing of a Social Gospel has a familiar if plaintive refrain. Personal encounter with human misery that, upon reflection, is seen to be not an individual problem but one of society is always a starting point. For example, Washington Gladden, called the Father of the Social Gospel, was invited to speak to a meeting of the unemployed not long after he arrived in Springfield, Massachusetts, a city that had been hard hit by the industrial depression that followed the panic of 1873. Shaken by the stories of the unemployed, Gladden invited these men to come to North Congregational Church the following Sunday. The men resisted at first because they told Gladden his church was made up of the employers of the city. But they came, and the dialogue sparked by Gladden's messages had the practical result of the church's setting up an employment bureau that found jobs for men out of hope. In 1876 these talks were printed as *Working Men and Their Employers*, the first of a cascade of Gladden books about a Social Gospel.

Walter Rauschenbusch, who became the most prominent theologian of the movement, was likewise turned around early in his ministry by terrible human problems of poverty, unemployment, bad housing, disease, and crime that he encountered as pastor of the Second German Baptist Church in the "Hell's Kitchen" district of New York City from 1886 to 1897. He wrote an article entitled "Beneath the Glitter" for a city paper in which he tried to describe the human tragedies happening within his parish day by day. Rooted in German pietism and prepared for a traditional ministry of preaching and the care of souls, Rauschenbusch now concluded that "Hell's Kitchen is not a safe place for saved souls."[5]

Reverdy C. Ransom described his experiences when he first came to Allegheney City, Pennsylvania, in 1888. "My first vision of the need for social service came to me as my wife and I almost daily went through the alleys and climbed the dark stairways of the wretched tenements" where his people lived. But if Ransom embraced a Social Gospel because of experiences similar to Rauschenbusch and Gladden, he faced other experiences that were dissimilar. Ransom and many black pastors in post–Civil War America took responsibility for the whole life of their people. Living in a society where nearly all social institutions soon became strictly segregated, black churches became the central institutions in black America. Although black religion has sometimes been depicted as "other worldly," in point of fact the racism within American society helped focus black pastors and lay leaders on a this worldly ministry. Many black churches became "institutional church-es," that is, they offered a whole range of services denied blacks in the dominant white society. The histories of the Social Gospel have been of a white story, but it is clear that it was a black and white story. William N. DeBerry, Francis G. Grimké, George E. Haynes, Kelly Miller, Henry Hugh Proctor, Mary Church Terrell, Alexander Walters, Ida B. Wells-Barnett and many other black pastors and laity participated in broad Social Gospel ministries, including racial reform. What is more, there are clear linkages between white and black leaders in both church and reform organizations.[6]

If the experiences of Gladden, Rauschenbusch, Haynes, Ransom, and others made them acutely aware of social evil, these experiences were also a catalyst sending them back to the sources of their faith for a message and a strategy. The Social Gospel was not simply a response to the conditions of urban, industrial America but was part of an on-going, vibrant theological tradition.

The central core of this tradition was a growing appreciation of the meaning of social salvation. The concern was not simply for the indi-vidual and his or her soul, or even for the church, but for all of society. This message was rooted in a dynamic understanding of the kingdom of God. The kingdom was not simply spiritual, if that term meant being invisible or coming at the end of history; it was not simply individual, although personal commitment to the Lord of the kingdom was preached. Rather, they visualized the kingdom as taking shape in the present world whenever men and women responded to Christ's call for righteousness, love, and justice.

In addressing the Baptist Congress in 1889, Rauschenbusch declared clearly that there were two main objectives of the Christian faith. One mandate was recognized, but the second was not. Christians agreed on the mandate to change individual lives. "But I claim that that is only one-half of the object of Christianity, that the other half is to bring in the kingdom of God, and that the efforts of the Christian Church ought to be directed in a like measure to the accomplishment of that last object."[7]

In focusing on the kingdom of God, advocates of the Social Gospel stressed the immanence of God. The implication was that all areas of life might be sanctified and must be related to Christ's kingly rule. Jesus' teachings delineated the value content of the kingdom. Above all, Christ was the prophetic Lord who called men and women into the common life to struggle with every form of social evil rather than being simply the comforting Savior of an individualistic religion.

Rauschenbusch liked to emphasize that the Social Gospel was not a new gospel. He believed that he and others were recovering a social emphasis present in the Scriptures as well as in different periods of the history of the church. This social emphasis was being worked out in interesting combination with pietism in Christian socialist circles in Germany. In England the writings of Frederick Denison Maurice and Charles Kingsley subsequently influenced both the Christian socialist movement and the Episcopal church in this country. The seeds of the Social Gospel can be found also in the evangelical voluntary societies nourished by the revivalism in pre–Civil War America. For revivalist Charles G. Finney it was quite a natural step from the "anxious bench" of the revival meeting to the activities of the antislavery movement. Many a later Social Gospel advocate was reared under the influence of abolitionist and antislavery ideas and strategies.

After the Civil War, the socialization of American Protestantism was stimulated by the rise of the so-called New Theology in the 1880s. Building on the thinking of Horace Bushnell, the New Theology was propagated by such men as Theodore Thorton Munger, pastor of the United Congregational Church on the New Haven green; Newman Smyth, minister of Center Church, New Haven; and Professor William Jewett Tucker of Andover Theological Seminary. The New Theology, or Progressive Orthodoxy, as it was called sometimes, sought to distance itself from what it deemed the static individualism of the older ortho-doxy and to "ally itself with all movements for bettering the condition of mankind."[8]

In discussing theological foundations, we perhaps should remind ourselves again that the Social Gospel is a phenomenon difficult to de-fine or contain. To define the Social Gospel as liberal is to miss the diversity of the movement. Not all liberals were Social Gospelers, and not all Social Gospelers were liberal. An important segment of the So-cial Gospel was indeed a product of the theological liberalism known as the New Theology. On the other hand, the theology of Walter Raus-chenbusch was rooted also in an evangelical piety that he never forgot. It is little known that he edited a volume of gospel songs with Ira D. Sankey, who was well known as evangelist Dwight L. Moody's collab-orator. Francis J. Grimké, taught by Charles Hodge at Princeton Semi-nary, prided himself in his conservative Presbyterian adherence to biblical preaching and strict morality. Called the "black puritan" by his congregation, Grimké was a prophet thundering against the racism within his own denomination and in the nation. Charles Stelzle, Presbyterian founder of New York's Labor Temple, attended Moody Bible Institute. Stelzle was liberal on social issues but was really quite conservative in much of his theology.

Today *liberal* and *evangelical* are terms often used in opposition. Kenneth Cauthen insists that these terms must be used jointly to describe Rauschenbusch. *Evangelical liberal* is an apt term for Rauschenbusch, Grimké, and some others for whom the person and work of Jesus Christ were foundational, but who at the same time sought a faith that could be believed by intelligent moderns.[9] Rauschenbusch, Gladden, Lyman Abbott, and other Social Gospelers were liberal for their day in that they accepted the validity of a historical-critical approach to the Bible and did not draw back from Darwinian theories of evolution. On the other hand, many liberals on theological questions remained quite conservative in their understanding of society and did not become involved in the activism of social Christianity.

An important distinction can be made between the Social Gospel at the turn of the century and its pre–Civil War antecedents. The Social Gospelers marched forth equipped not only with the New Theology but with the methods and results of the new social sciences that were being incorporated into college curricula in the 1880s and 1890s. Several key leaders in our story were early sociologists who, armed with the new sociology and anthropology, challenged traditional theories of race and inferiority. In addition they used sociological theory in implementing strategies for social change.

Theology and sociology were merged to give content to what became the watchwords of the Social Gospel: "the fatherhood of God and the brotherhood of man." In the kingdom, all were the children of God and thus sisters and brothers to each other. The apostle Paul's description of the interdependent members of the one body was the biblical basis appealed to for this reality. In the new social sciences, society was portrayed as organic or solidaristic, a conception congruent with the familial relationships within the kingdom. From both sources, then, the organic model displaced individualistic interpretations of society.

The popular acceptance and usage of the term *Social Gospel* seems to have occurred around the turn of the century. Iowa pastor Charles O. Brown described Henry George's *Wealth and Poverty* as "a new social gospel" in 1886. W. D. P. Bliss used the words on the front page of the first issue of the *Dawn* in 1889. The phrase was spread abroad by a communitarian experiment in Georgia, "the Christian Commonwealth

Colony," which began publishing a magazine in 1898 called the *Social Gospel*. The colony disbanded in 1900, but the title of the magazine helped consolidate the popular usage of the term. *Social Gospel* continued to be interchanged at times with the more generic term *social Christianity*, or *progressive Christianity*.[10]

I do want to insist that the Social Gospel does not simply equal social concern. Many people in that era were indeed concerned about individuals caught in the web of urban blight, just as many persons today are concerned about social problems. I argue that the Social Gospel was a watershed movement that understood that "Hell's Kitchen is not a safe place for saved souls." They saw that the problem was not the poor but poverty. They came to understand that social problems were systemic, to use a recent word. The question in their day was, "Do you take the slum out of the person, or the person out of the slum?" Many of the Social Gospelers started with the first answer, but their urban, industrial, racial experiences did not allow them to stay there.[11]

Social concern expressed itself in charity. It came in, after the fact, to help men and women in gospel mission centers and homes for girls. The Social Gospel decided to act—before the fact—by challenging structures that precipitated unemployment, poverty, and misery. The need was not charity but justice. Charity deals with individuals, but justice deals with unjust social conditions.

It must also be argued that the Social Gospel was the bridge to more modern understandings of social justice and subsequent corporate strategies of reform. The traditional conservative tendency is to mark off social concern as an important but definitely secondary priority. The Social Gospel, responding to what it repeatedly labeled the "crisis" of modern industrialized urban society, called for a dynamic understanding of social salvation.

These definitions are operative in the discussions that follow. For the most part, the persons described display not simply an interest in racial reform but a theological affinity with the cluster of ideas born out of an understanding of social salvation. In almost every case, interest in racial reform is either preceded by or accompanied by interest in several other reform issues. It may come as a surprise to some that a significant number of the persons in this story have as many evangelical as liberal tendencies. I have been interested to learn that the combination of evangelical and liberal ideas in this period (for example, interest simultaneously in Bible study, foreign missions, and racial reform in

YMCA circles) was more possible and acceptable than it often has been in the recent past.

The Social Gospel did not begin as a highly organized movement. Rather, it was a network of movements operating in different contexts. Individuals connected with the Social Gospel worked through ongoing religious and secular organizations. From time to time, they established study and action groups of their own. There never was, however, an official organization representing the Social Gospel.

Denominationally, the Social Gospel was influential within a wide range of both white and black denominations. Among whites the influence was greatest in the traditional Anglo-American denominations: the Baptist, Congregational, Methodist, Episcopal, and Presbyterian churches. It was also prevalent among Unitarians and Quakers. Among blacks the Social Gospel could be found in black denominations such as the National Baptist, African Methodist Episcopal, and African Methodist Episcopal Zion churches as well as in smaller church bodies. Some of the most important black leaders were members of virtually all white denominations. In this context, black pastors developed their prophetic calling in part by the need to challenge the racism within their own denomination.

The acceptance of the Social Gospel into the institutions of American religious life occurred with the organization of the Federal Council of Churches in 1908. The Federal Council owed much of its original momentum to the fact that precisely in these years the Social Gospel was reaching its full maturity. In the second decade of the century the energy of individuals and movements was translated into the council and into newly created denominational social action agencies.[12]

In breaking down the barriers between the sacred and the secular, the leaders of the Social Gospel cooperated with others involved in the urgent tasks of reform. In many reform organizations they found themselves working side by side with persons caught up in the idealism of progressivism. Indeed Richard Hofstadter called progressivism "a phase in the history of the Protestant conscience, a latterday Protestant revival."[13] Whether at the American Economic Association or the Southern Sociological Congress, exponents of the Social Gospel shared the platform with other progressives.

Political progressivism is associated with the presidencies of Theodore Roosevelt and Woodrow Wilson. Lyman Abbott, Congregational minister and editor of the *Outlook,* was a chaplain to Roosevelt's progressivism. In 1909, after Roosevelt had left office, he became an editor of the *Outlook*. Wilson's Presbyterian roots and Christian idealism are well known. The racial policies of both Roosevelt and Wilson are a part of the story of the Social Gospel's engagement with racial reform.

Within the Social Gospel there never was unanimity on goals or tactics. Often, as in the story of racial reform, the individuals committed to the Social Gospel found themselves divided. The narrative of their differing perceptions of the race issue is filled with conflict and ambiguity. To begin with the Lake Mohonk Conference on the Negro Question and to move back and forth over half a century is to become aware, however, of growth and change. In trying to understand the myriad stories within the story, one becomes much more acutely aware not only of the historical precedent but of the continuing realities in our own striving toward racial justice.

Part One

RETREAT FROM RECONSTRUCTION, 1877–1897

CHAPTER 1

"The Negro Question"

There is no Negro problem—only the problem of humanity.
                                                    —LYMAN ABBOTT

So far as the peaceful and Christian solution of the race problem is concerned, indeed, I am inclined to think that the only education required is that of the *white* race. The hate, the oppression, the injustice are all on our side.

                                        —ALBION WINEGAR TOURGÉE

In early June 1890 a group of eighty delegates, leaders in philanthropy, education, journalism, and religion, met at the Lake Mohonk Mountain House in Ulster County, New York, to discuss "the Negro Question." It seemed an unlikely time for such a meeting. In the years since the end of Reconstruction, white leaders had been losing interest in the aspirations of black Americans. Nearly all were convinced that Reconstruction had been a tragedy, producing sectional sores that only time and lowered voices could heal.[1]

Actually, the conference of 1890 was the beginning of a new forum for a series of meetings held each year at Albert K. Smiley's famous hotel. Smiley, a Quaker, had made the Lake Mohonk Mountain House, opened in 1870, not only a popular resort but a center for conferences on current issues. Annual conferences on Indian affairs had met there beginning in 1883. At the last session, former president Rutherford B. Hayes had expressed the "hope that the day may soon come when that other weaker race" would have such an annual assembly. As Smiley told the delegates as they gathered on June 4, "That remark caused the founding of this conference."[2]

The place for the conference was conducive to a gathering concerned with both religion and reform. A report by a contemporary referred to Lake Mohonk as a church.[3] Daily public worship went hand in hand with vigorous discussion of reform issues. A biographical study of the Smiley brothers describes their "concern and involvement in education, business, ground adornment and land use, Indian affairs, international arbitration, Negro affairs, and religious endeavors" as "illustrative of the social gospel in action."[4]

As the first action of the conference, Hayes was unanimously elected chairman. Hayes represented in his own career the mixed messages of the conference. He had been elected president in 1877 in a disputed contest with his Democratic opponent, Samuel J. Tilden. Hayes received a minority of the popular vote but won the electoral battle months later in the House of Representatives only when he agreed to end the policies of Reconstruction in the South. This political retreat created a climate wherein the gains by blacks in the years after the Civil War were first eroded and then reversed. But if ever after he was associated with the retreat from Reconstruction, in the decade after his presidency Hayes devoted himself to the cause of Negro education.

Hayes set the tone for the conference in his opening remarks. He told the delegates, "We seek conscientiously to avoid whatever is sectarian, or that smacks of partisanship or sectionalism."[5] This tone was reflected for the most part in the meetings of June 4 through 6. Hayes was followed by General Samuel Chapman Armstrong, founder of Hampton Institute and mentor of Booker T. Washington, who spoke on the topic "Industrial Schools for the Negroes." Succeeding meetings reiterated the benefits of religion, education, hard work, thrift, and patience in the cause of what the delegates called, in the parlance of the day, black uplift.

All of the delegates were white. George Washington Cable, renowned literary figure, had written Smiley trying to secure an invitation for Booker T. Washington and several other black leaders, but his efforts were unsuccessful. Cable subsequently decided not to attend the conference.[6] William Hayes Ward, editor of the New York Independent, commented in his report for his popular weekly periodical that future conferences should include representative black leaders.[7] But the absence of blacks was accepted without mention by nearly all of the delegates in attendance. Lyman Abbott, editor of the Christian Union and successor to Henry Ward Beecher as pastor of the influential Plymouth Congregational Church of Brooklyn, defended the lack of invitations to blacks by using the analogy of patients not being invited to participate in a consultation with their doctors.[8]

All of the people invited were not present. Special efforts had been made to invite southern church and educational leaders, but these efforts were not particularly successful.[9] Some of those not able to attend sent letters of support. The only letter read in its entirety was from Bishop Atticus Green Haygood of Georgia. On Thursday evening,

June 5, James M. Buckley, editor of the influential Methodist publication the *New York Christian Advocate,* called to the attention of those assembled the significance "to the welfare of the Negro" of the recent election of Haygood as a bishop in the Methodist Episcopal Church, South. Buckley described Haygood, for the past decade general agent of the John F. Slater Fund and a primary source of support for Negro education in the South, as having taken "the most advanced position" on the Negro question.[10] At other times and places, Haygood spoke out more forcefully, but his admonition to those at Lake Mohonk was a call for patience.

> Many white people North are unduly impatient. Many white people South are unduly anxious. Many colored people do not sufficiently realize how much has been done for them and achieved by them to be patient with conditions that cannot be changed at once, or to be happy in the hopes that are born of gratitude to the God who has led them.[11]

Most at Lake Mohonk were receptive to this call for patience.

Lyman Abbott voiced to the conference on Thursday his present feeling that perhaps there was no Negro problem. The comment was really two-edged, part sarcasm, and partly a shift in Abbott's own thinking.

Abbott was responding to some remarks that had been made during the Wednesday morning discussion period. Judge Albion Winegar Tourgée, who had lived both in the South and the North, had said categorically, "I do not hesitate to say that the colored people of the South have accomplished more in twenty-five years, from an industrial point of view, than any people on the face of the earth ever before achieved under anything like such unfavorable conditions." Abbott was more than a little annoyed at the judge's optimism, but especially at the position Tourgée seemed to be assigning blacks. Rather cynically, Abbott retorted, "I began to think that the Negro was the one who marched at the head of the procession and that the Anglo-Saxon brought up the rear."[12]

In the remarks that followed, Abbott alluded to the existing divisions in society, whether political, social, economic, religious, or racial, and pointed to a common humanity as the answer to those divisions. In this sense, he said, "there is no Negro problem—only the problem of humanity." Instead of divisions, Abbott wanted the conferees to focus on "Man—man born of God, made in his image, and with an immortal future before him. With a free field and an open racecourse, let every man find his own place by his own courage, energy, and enterprise."[13]

The problem of humanity could best be handled by the action of the "new humanity."

Abbott also took exception to Tourgée's earlier remarks that blacks were not welcome in northern churches. He told those assembled that in the church of which he was pastor, black faces were seen and welcomed Sunday after Sunday.

As the conference reconvened on Thursday evening, Abbott's comments did not go unanswered. His fellow New York editor, James Buckley, noted that if there was no Negro problem, the people gathered at Smiley's hotel should not be there. Then followed, in the midst of what had been a rather bland day, some sparks that ignited the evening's session. The exchange was recorded in the official minutes.

DR. BUCKLEY: I wonder what would be the effect if about seventy-five Negro families were to be scattered throughout Plymouth Church. My conviction is that consternation would be the result, and that a large number of persons would pass away unless these seventy families were thrown out.

DR. ABBOTT: Send them along, and we will see.

DR. BUCKLEY: You know that I cannot do it. Therefore you speak with great confidence. If I had a magic wand, I would put them all there next Sunday.[14]

The next morning, as a mighty thunderstorm advanced along the valley of the Mohonk, Albion W. Tourgée unleashed his own thunderbolts against Abbott and all who spoke like him. Tourgée was white, not black, but his address, "The Negro's View of the Race Problem," was a militant and at times blunderbuss attempt to give the delegates a radically different perspective.

When Smiley had invited Tourgée, he told Tourgée that "the object of the conference is the uplifting of the Negro thru his Christianization and education."[15] Tourgée knew something about Christianization and education of blacks. A layman in the Methodist Episcopal Church, he was a man who had expressed these concerns in a variety of positions. His greatest talent was exhibited in his writings. Already the author of more than a dozen works of fiction, Tourgée was about to receive great prominence for his critical novel *Murvale Eastman: Christian Socialist*. Nearing completion in serial form in the *Chicago Advance*, the book was published in the latter part of 1890. Showing understanding of the evils of modern industrial life, Tourgée presented a piece of "serious social analysis, which in this instance obviously reflected and contributed to the Social Gospel movement."[16]

Standard accounts of the Social Gospel have given some recognition to Tourgée's importance in making the Christian social novel "the Social Gospel's most spectacular and eventually successful secular medium."[17] These studies have neglected, however, to link Tourgée's major writings, which continued to be about blacks, to this same Social Gospel.

Tourgée's writings on black Americans developed out of his own experience in the South. Having grown up in the North and after participating in the Civil War on the Union side, Tourgée settled in Greensboro, North Carolina, in October 1865. Over the course of the next fourteen years, he was deeply involved in the Reconstruction South in various roles as politician, editor, code commissioner, and judge. To his enemies, he was the carpetbagger personified, and he obliged them by naming his Greensboro home "Carpet-Bag Lodge," where Tourgée's black friends were always welcome.

In 1879, as Tourgée was ending his southern residence, his first important novel, A Fool's Errand, was being readied for anonymous publication "By One of the Fools." Compared favorably to Uncle Tom's Cabin, Tourgée's Fool's Errand became an immediate best-seller. In this story of the clash between Radical Republicans and the racist South, the hero is subjected to verbal attacks by his neighbors and a plot against his life by the Klan. Although not autobiographical in every sense, many of the incidents bear a striking resemblance to events in Tourgée's life, including the Klan plot.[18] Through the leading figure, Comfort Servosse, of French Huguenot background (as was Tourgée), we come to understand how slavery had corrupted the moral character of the slaveholder. Now that slavery was ended, blacks had to be educated and given a degree of political equality.[19] At the conclusion of the novel Servosse heads north again, the fool's unfruitful errand at an end. In the summer of 1879 Tourgée, the self-identified "fool," left the South for good.

Early in 1890 Tourgée aroused wide interest with the publication of Pactolus Prime; or, The White Christ. The story of a black bootblack in Washington, D.C., the plot provided the vehicle to discuss such topics as race pride, Christian hypocrisy, emigration to Africa, imperialism, current black economic progress, and Tourgée's major concern, national education of blacks. Strident and uncompromising, the book was both roundly applauded and soundly denounced. A dominant southern response was best articulated by Joel Chandler Harris. "What shall we say of such a writer? Is he a monomaniac or simply a refugee from his race?"[20]

Tourgée was not a refugee from his race as he attempted to bring a different point of view to Lake Mohonk. As Rutherford B. Hayes recorded in his private diary concerning Tourgée: "He is an orator—pungent—dramatic—original and daring. He rebuked the Churches—the North—the South—and stood for the Negro."[21]

The judge began by putting into perspective his own understanding of the relation of religion and politics. In this one area, Tourgée found an ally in Lyman Abbott, who had said on the previous day that his politics and religion were always mixed. The conference had self-consciously attempted to discourage political discussion and resolutions about specific legislation. Speaking to this attitude, Tourgée told the conferees that "when Christianity quits the field of political relations or politics discards the tents of Christian philosophy, I have little use for either."[22]

Early in his speech, Tourgée met head on the standard southern rejoinder, echoed more and more in the North, that the South knew the Negroes best because it had held them in bondage for twelve generations. After first reaffirming his own credentials as an expert on the situation in the South, the judge was far more perceptive than most of his contemporaries when he countered, "If history teaches anything, it is that the gulf between the master and the slave is the hardest of all social chasms to span, and the master's estimate of the bondman's interest, character, and rights, the farthest possible from the bondman's notion of the same."[23]

Tourgée could be biting as well as perceptive. He was both when he described what all the talk at the conference seemed to be saying about Christianization and education. The emphasis was on industrial training with a de-emphasis of political rights. Tourgée's own paraphrase of the advice being given blacks was, "Praise God and make money." His own advice dealt, as expected, with education, but he said little about the education of blacks. "So far as the peaceful and Christian solution of the race problem is concerned, indeed, I am inclined to think that the only education required is that of the *white* race. The hate, the oppression, the injustice are all on our side." There was a white problem, not a black problem, with which conferees needed to deal. "Even we who are met here to discuss the Negro, to deplore his infirmities, to magnify our charity, to extol our own excellences and determine what ought to be done with and for him," he went on, "do not regard his opinion about the matter as at all important. We do not ask him what he thinks of his own condition."[24]

To drive home his point, Tourgée became personal just once. He responded to Lyman Abbott's remark that there was no Negro problem by asking, "I wonder if the man who made the statement ever tried to apply the Christ-rule in the relations of the races in this Christian land?" He asked everyone in the room to try to think what it would be like to have in his veins the blood of a race that some Christians said was under a divine curse. "Did you ever think, sir, how much it would take to hire anyone in this audience to assume the burden of a black skin for a lifetime?"[25]

Tourgée sat down at 11 A.M. By 11 P.M., after some resolutions that failed to take seriously the sense and direction of Tourgée's remarks, the First Lake Mohonk Conference on the Negro Question adjourned.

The Lake Mohonk Conference is significant, then, not so much for what it produced as what it represented. Chairman Rutherford B. Hayes symbolized a perplexing combination of compromise and commitment. The focus on education was an unwritten assent to a prevailing climate of opinion that eschewed controversial political discussion. The dominant emphasis on industrial education indicated the sphere of progress held out for blacks. Lyman Abbott, as a leader of the forces of social Christianity, was typical of an element within that group who were prophetic and sensitive in championing many peoples and causes, but they were often contradictory in failing to understand blacks and their white advocates who sought immediate, not deferred, racial justice. The total absence of blacks made the entire conference operate from the outset in a climate of paternalism. And finally, there was Judge Tourgée, former carpetbagger turned literary militant, a lonely white trying to tell other whites about the so-called Negro's view of the race problem.

CHAPTER 2

Reappraisal in the North

Some of us started twenty-five years ago with the idea that the black man was as good as the white man, and not that the color of the skin made any difference; but the color of the skin and the kink of the hair did mean something.

—LYMAN ABBOTT

If Lake Mohonk was most important as a mirror of the period, it occurred at a time when the fate of black Americans was at a crossroads. A generation removed from the Civil War and the institution of slavery, it was the season for reappraisal of "the Negro question" in the North. Recoiling from what most deemed to be the ill-conceived overkill of Reconstruction policies, northern leaders looked longingly for a reduction of intersectional tensions. Encouraged by the New South rhetoric of advancement via industrialization, accompanied by the continuing growth of education for blacks, most northern leaders were still talking progress on "the Negro question" in the 1880s.

But the strategies for progress were changing. A retreat from Reconstruction was in the air. Reappraisal was the mood. And the trend was to fall back from reform to accommodation. Reform strategies were based within a tradition of agitation for equal rights accomplished either through legislation or by direct action. The term *accommodation* is used here to describe a posture of acceptance of the subservient place of blacks in society, coupled with gradual, nonpolitical attempts to ameliorate the race's condition within the existing framework. Most northern leaders followed this path, although the retreat was by no means always orderly or without variation.

In the retreat from reform to accommodation, 1890 was a transition year. The Negro question was ebbing as a national political issue in direct relation to a ground swell of state legislation, sustained by the courts at all levels, aimed at making Jim Crow a legal nonperson throughout the South. After a period of some fluidity and uncertainty in the seventies and eighties, white supremacy was consolidated in the nineties and early 1900s by legal and illegal means. Disfranchisement through various property and literacy barriers was first enacted by Mississippi in 1890. Poll taxes and white primaries were added to complete the disfranchisement process in other southern states. A state law in 1887 first codified the separation of whites and blacks on trains, but at the turn of the century these Jim Crow laws were proliferated to include every conceivable place where whites and blacks might come together.[1]

Coinciding with legal changes was an outbreak of violence against blacks. Tables 1 and 2 chart the horror of lynching that occurred right in the midst of the Progressive Era.

As the tables show, from 1891 through 1901, more than 100 persons were lynched each year. The peak was 1892, when 226 persons were lynched, of whom 155 were black. Although the number of lynchings decreased after 1892, the percentage of black deaths among the total rose steadily. Lynching was a national problem, but the overwhelming number of black deaths, 95.5 percent, occurred in South.[2]

Statistics can never capture the terror of lynch law. All blacks were meant to feel the fear of "Judge Lynch" as white supremacy cowed law-abiding blacks and fair-minded whites alike.

Were there no political or legal means to turn back this rising tide of discrimination and violence? For many, a most promising opportunity to assist blacks was offered by the Blair Education Bill that made its way through the legislative process in the 1880s. First introduced in 1881 by Senator Henry W. Blair of New Hampshire, chairman of the Senate Education and Labor Committee, the measure provided for national aid for education by the federal government's spending $77 million over an eight-year period, this money to be at least matched by state expenditures. The money was to be divided among the states, according to illiteracy percentages. The bill was national in scope, but because of the varying proportions of illiteracy, 75 percent of the money would go to the South—and blacks composed 70 percent of the southern illiteracy rolls. Segregated schools were countenanced in the bill, but both federal and state money had to be spent equally for the education of each child without the distinction of race or color.[3]

The Blair Bill passed the Senate in 1884, 1886, and 1888 but each time was buried in committee by the powerful House leadership. Now in 1890, for the first time in sixteen years, the Republican party controlled both houses of Congress as well as the presidency and seemingly was in a position to pass the bill. These hopes were not to be realized, as the tenuous Senate alliance of northern Republicans and southern Democrats cracked enough to allow the defeat of the Blair Bill in March 1890. Although talk continued of reviving the Blair Bill or something similar, such a measure never really had a chance again.

There was still one more opportunity for national legislative action. In the same month as the Lake Mohonk conference, Henry Cabot Lodge of Massachusetts, making his first major speech in the House of Representatives, led the fight for a Federal Elections Bill. It called for supervision of such elections by federal circuit courts upon request by a certain number of voters. From the beginning, southern opponents

Table 1.   Persons Lynched in the United States. 1889–1918

Year	Total	White	Black	Year	Total[a]	White	Black
1889	175	80	95	1904	86	7	79
1890	91	3	88	1905	65	5	60
1891	194	67	127	1906	68	4	64
1892	226	71	155	1907	62	3	59
1893	153	39	114	1908	100	8	92
1894	182	54	128	1909	89	14	75
1895	178	68	110	1910	90	10	80
1896	125	46	79	1911	71	8	63
1897	162	38	124	1912	64	3	61
1898	127	24	103	1913	48	1	47
1899	109	22	87	1914	54	5	49
1900	101	12	89	1915	96	43	53
1901	135	27	108	1916	58	7	51
1902	94	10	84	1917	50	2	48
1903	104	17	87	1918	67	4	63

Source: National Association for the Advancement of Colored People, *Thirty Years of Lynching* (New York, 1919), 29.

[a]Totals exclude victims of riots in 1906 in Atlanta and in 1917 in East St. Louis, Illinois.

Table 2.   Five-Year Summaries of Lynchings in the United States, 1889–1918

Years	Grand Total[a]	White			Black			
		Total	% Male	Female	Total	%	Male	Female
1889–1893	839	260	32.2 258	2	579	67.8	571	8
1894–1898	774	230	29.7 221	9	544	70.3	529	15
1899–1903	543	88	16.2 88	0	455	83.8	451	4
1904–1908	381	27	7.0 27	0	354	93.0	348	6
1909–1913	362	36	10.2 36	0	326	89.8	320	6
1914–1918	325	61	18.8 61	0	264	81.2	253	11
	3,224	702	21.8 691	11	2,522	78.2	2,472	50

Source: National Association for the Advancement of Colored People, *Thirty Years of Lynching*, 30.

[a]Totals exclude victims of riots in 1906 in Atlanta and in 1917 in East St. Louis, Illinois.

pointed to the feared specter of federal intervention and thus labeled the measure the Force Bill. The bill passed the House in July after vigorous debate and was sent to the Senate. The bill was debated in the Senate, but because of political compromise involving tariff and silver legislation, it never came to a vote and was dead by the end of the year.[4]

If reappraisal among whites was a sign of their own retreat from Reconstruction radicalism, it was also a response to new leadership among blacks. In February 1895, Frederick Douglass died. This former slave who became the leading black abolitionist symbolized the tradition of protest and agitation for racial reform. On September 18, 1895, Booker T. Washington gave a principal address at the Cotton States and International Exposition in Atlanta. He was already well known, but what became known as the Atlanta Compromise Address "catapulted Washington into national fame and recognition" as the new leader of his people.[5]

By his own recounting, Washington believed a change in strategy away from Douglass's forceful protests was needed. The Atlanta address provided the forum for Washington to state his platform. He saw his task as speaking for a generation of blacks living in a new situation. Born a slave, Washington reached his twenty-first birthday in 1877, the year that marked the end of Reconstruction. Douglass's political agitation helped destroy slavery, but from the viewpoint of Washington, "the long and bitter political struggle in which he had engaged against slavery had not prepared Mr. Douglass to take up the equally difficult task of fitting the Negro for the opportunities of freedom." Washington believed this critique was true of other leaders of Douglass's generation as well. "I felt that millions of Negroes needed something more than to be reminded of their sufferings and of their political rights."[6]

Educated at Hampton Institute in Virginia, Washington became the founding principal of Tuskegee Institute in Alabama in 1881. During the next years Washington created an institution that was the rival of Hampton, the difference being that Tuskegee had an all-black faculty and staff. De-emphasizing politics, Washington fostered a philosophy of industrial education that, he believed, would lead to gradual economic uplift.

The Atlanta exposition speech put into words the evolving Washington philosophy. Early on, he gave public recognition to a reappraisal of Reconstruction.

Ignorant and inexperienced, it is not strange that in the first years of our new life we began at the top instead of at the bottom; that a seat in Congress or the state legislature was more sought than real estate or industrial skill; that the political convention or stump speaking had more attraction than starting a dairy farm or a truck garden.[7]

Washington went on to tell his own people to begin where they were. For most blacks this advice meant beginning at the bottom.

Washington's power as a leader resided in part in his ability to communicate his philosophy by the use of homespun metaphors. To make his point here he utilized a metaphor that was repeated far and wide: "Cast down your bucket where you are."[8] Blacks and whites alike appropriated this metaphor to mean that blacks should make a beginning where beginnings were possible—in agriculture, mechanics, commerce, and domestic service. Washington included in his list "the professions," but such careers now came last instead of first.

The Tuskegee principal's professed concern was for the masses. He feared that in the leap from slavery to freedom there was the temptation to focus on the few who would become doctors, business leaders, or ministers. But this emphasis would be at the expense of the masses. "Our greatest danger is that . . . we may overlook the fact that the masses of us are to live by the production of our hands, and fail to keep in mind that we shall prosper in proportion as we learn to dignify and glorify common labor and put brains and skill into the common occupations of life." In Washington's way of thinking, he was not so much putting down the quest for excellence as he was elevating work as the means to economic advancement.[9]

If Washington conceded the errors of Reconstruction in the South, thirty years after the end of the war he now told blacks and whites that their mutual self-interest lay in working together in the New South. To blacks he said, "It is in the South that the Negro is given a man's chance in the commercial world." To whites he appealed again to "cast down your bucket where you are," encouraging their investment "among the 8 million negroes you know, whose loyalty and love you have tested." Loyalty would be the badge by which blacks would win a place in the American dream. In times of economic uncertainty he described blacks as ready to work without strikes and labor wars. An economic realist who was concerned about the inroads that immigrants might make on black labor, Washington appealed eloquently to the need for an interlocking loyalty.

As we have proved our loyalty to you in the past, nursing your children, watching by the sickbeds of your mothers and fathers, and often following them with tear-dimmed eyes to their graves, so in the future, in our humble way, we shall stand by you with a devotion that no foreigner can approach, ready to lay down our lives, if need be, in defense of yours; interlacing our industrial, commercial, civil, and religious life with yours in a way that shall make the interests of both races one.[10]

This loyalty was to be part of an alliance between northern leadership—primarily business, philanthropic, and religious leaders—the New South white leadership, and blacks. Washington presented himself as a man whites could trust and blacks could follow.

Washington ended his plea with a qualification intended to assuage the fears of white America. He broached the issue of social relations by creating another metaphor that was destined to be quoted and remembered: "In all things that are purely social we can be as separate as the fingers, yet one as the hand in all things essential to mutual progress."[11]

The response to the Atlanta exposition address was overwhelming. Many papers printed the text of the speech in full. President Grover Cleveland spoke for many when he said: "I thank you with much enthusiasm for making the address. I have read it with intense interest, and I think the Exposition would be fully justified if it did not do more than furnish the opportunity for its delivery."[12]

The northern religious press joined in the general enthusiasm. Lyman Abbott's growing respect for Washington was reflected in comments in the *Outlook*, "No words spoken during the entire course of the Exposition produced so notable an effect as his." The Methodist *New York Christian Advocate* printed the text in its entirety and praised the speech. The Presbyterian *Interior* offered its commendation.[13]

Not every response of the religious press was positive or uncritical. H. T. Johnson of the AME *Christian Recorder* was noncommittal at first and then said that Washington's views were incorrect. William Hayes Ward of the *New York Independent* tempered his praise, offering the opinion that Washington "did not say at Atlanta all he felt." For Ward the work at Tuskegee was not finally as important as the path of higher education.[14]

On the heels of this address opportunities flowed in for Washington to speak all over the country. In lectures, from pulpits, and in newspaper articles, he proclaimed a black agenda that would strive for racial uplift by self-consciously shifting from the rhetoric of agitation to the reasoned appeal for accommodation. The Atlanta Compromise Address became the platform for race relations agreed upon by the majority of whites and blacks. Basking in the enthusiastic response to his remarks,

Washington now moved to solidify his own position as the leader of his people. He became the key black leader with white business leaders, philanthropists, and ministers. He held the keys of patronage by which he could open certain doors for aspiring blacks.

The Tuskegee philosophy is important for our story because it became the basic reference point for men and women allied with the developing Social Gospel. Whether the Washingtonian strategies were applauded, grudgingly accepted, or criticized, they formed the parameters for most discussions of the race question for a least the next decade. A recent generation of scholars has presented Washington mainly as an accommodator. It is not surprising that most whites who became involved in the race question followed a similar strategy of accommodation. But it would be a mistake to see the Washington strategy as all of one piece. He was not called the Wizard of Tuskegee for nothing. His admirers, black and white, represented a spectrum of opinion, some of it at variance with the Washingtonian philosophy and strategy. In the pages that follow it will be important to notice signs that some whites were willing to criticize Washington as they searched for more viable strategies of racial reform.

As the race question receded nationally and Jim Crow became a reality sectionally, what were the reactions of the emerging leaders of what was called in these years social Christianity? The way to begin to answer this question is to assay some representative responses on a spectrum from right to left: from accommodation to ameliorism, and then to reform and radicalism.

The burden of our study is to try to understand the men and women who attempted to bring a reforming impulse to the race problem. But before we can begin that task, we need to encounter two well-known leaders of social Christianity, the first of whom represents the silence, and the second the supposed racism with which the whole movement has been brushed.

Walter Rauschenbusch is the best-known leader of the Social Gospel. His silence on the race issue is in part responsible for our misreading the larger story of the Social Gospel and racial reform. Many secondary studies of religion and race have pursued the implicit line of reasoning: if Rauschenbusch was silent on the race issue, then the rest of the Social Gospel was probably silent also.

When Rauschenbusch did speak about the race issue in the early years it was usually in the context of speaking about immigration. At the turn of the century many progressives were calling for a limit in this country's open-door policy of immigration. Early in his pastorate Rauschenbusch addressed the Baptist Congress and called for keeping the doors open. Taking a position at variance from some of his Social Gospel and progressive friends, he asserted that the mixing of peoples of different ethnic backgrounds in America was a healthy and desirable policy.[15]

Rauschenbusch did not speak extensively about "the Negro question" until 1913, five years before his death. We will examine those remarks in their chronological sequence in chapter 13.

As we attempt to understand Rauschenbusch's silence, it is necessary to be aware of the special set of factors that shaped his life. Born in 1861, considerably later than Lyman Abbott (1835), Washington Gladden (1836), and Josiah Strong (1847), with whom he is often grouped, Rauschenbusch did not experience the trauma of the Civil War or Reconstruction. The seventh in a line of ministers, Rauschenbusch was raised within a close-knit German community in Rochester, New York. Except for various years of study in Germany and eleven years as a pastor in New York City, he spent all his life in Rochester. Educated at the University of Rochester and Rochester Theological Seminary, he returned to teach in the German department of the seminary in 1897, being elected professor of church history in 1902. A remarkable aspect of Rauschenbusch's career was that he became deaf in 1888. In the days before hearing aids were perfected, Rauschenbusch relied upon lip reading and a secretary to continue his pastoral and teaching career.[16]

The forging of the Social Gospel first came out of his contact with human tragedy in the parish and in the city. His experiences forced him back to his sources—the Bible, theology, and church history. Here he discovered the kingdom of God as central for both thought and action. In the early years of his ministry Raushenbusch wrote about the possibility of recovering the centrality of the kingdom of God for theology and ministry. For seventy-five years his manuscript "The Righteousness of the Kingdom" was lost, until an enterprising scholar found its scattered chapters in the American Baptist Society Archives in the early 1960s. We now believe Rauschenbusch was literally commissioned to write this study, as a participant in the Brotherhood of the Kingdom, a fellowship of local pastors.[17]

Rauschenbusch spent considerable time describing the state of Americana religion. He believed that the heritage of recent revivalism had reduced the Chrsitian vision to conversion one by one. Out of his experience in Hell's Kitchen he responded, "It is not enough to christianize individuals; we must christianize societies, organizations, nations, for they too have a life of their own which may be made better or worse." His study of the Bible had taught him the reality of what biblical scholars called the corporate personality. "Christ addressed Capernaum and Bethsaida as responsible personalities. He lamented over Jerusalem as a whole."[18]

The young Rauschenbusch proclaiamed a revolutionary Christianity as the answer to the present crisis in society. The foundation of this revolution was the kingdom of God, which was both personal and social.

> This then is the program of the Christian revolution: the Kingdom of God on earth. It includes a twofold aim: the regeneration of every individual to divine sonship and eternal life, and the victory of the spirit of Christ over the spirit of this world in every form of human society and a corresponding alteration in all the institutions formed by human society.[19]

The words are not as eloquent as in later writings, but the commitment to the kingdom of God became the *cantus firmus* of Rauschenbusch's continuing theology.

Rauschenbusch is important for our story even in his silence, for his formulation of the Social Gospel was referred to by those who used his motifs for their own theological reflection about the race problem. It is also important to remember, however, that in these early years Rauschenbusch was not yet the recognized theological leader of the Social Gospel. Known and respected, his national fame did not come fully until 1907 with the publication of *Christianity and the Social Crisis.*

If Rauschenbusch is remembered for his silence, Josiah Strong is remembered by some as a racist and imperialist. In the 1880s and 1890s people were talking more about Strong than Rauschenbusch. Strong created a sensation in 1885 with the publication of *Our Country.* Two decades before Rauschenbusch's *Christianity and the Social Crisis,* Strong addressed "the social questions" of the day—intemperance, socialism, wealth, and the city. In the process *Our Country* became one of the first of many best-selling volumes for the developing Social Gospel. The book also helped engender a discussion about the superiority of the "Anglo-Saxon race" that gave Strong the reputation of being racist and imperialist.

Strong was born in 1847 in Naperville, Illinois. Educated at Lane Seminary in Cincinnati, he served Congregational churches in Wyoming and Ohio. In 1881 he became secretary of the Congregational Home Missionary Society for work in Ohio, Kentucky, West Virginia, and western Pennsylvania. In 1884, Strong became the pastor of the Central Congregational church in Cincinnati. While in this position he wrote *Our Country*.[20]

Strong addressed many of the themes that home missions had been dealing with for decades: immigration, Romanism, education, and Mormonism. All of these issues were related to the growing importance of the West in the life of the nation. But it was his treatment of the social questions that made it a tract for the Social Gospel. It is difficult to say exactly why any book catches on, but *Our Country* spoke to both the peril and the opportunity facing American society. He challenged his readers to respond with a Christian social vision.

In the next-to-last chapter Strong discussed "The Anglo-Saxon and the World's Future." Having told his readers that "we are living in extraordinary times," he now proclaimed that the ushering in of an era of Christian progress would be done by what he labeled "the Anglo-Saxon race." With a brandishing of facts and statistics, Strong argued that Anglo-Saxons were superior to other peoples and even that Americans were superior to the English. He did admit that these virtues, rooted in a creative and aggressive spirit, could be misused, and for this reason he insisted on the necessity of Anglo-Saxon partnership with the ethics of Protestant Christianity. But his convictions were clear: "In my own mind, there is no doubt that the Anglo-Saxon is to exercise the commanding influence in the world's future."[21]

Strong's insistence on the superiority of the "Anglo-Saxon race" has been remembered. It strikes the modern reader as curious that he would speak of an ethnic group as a race, but this way of speaking was quite common at the time. Strong was a man who respected the natural and social sciences. He cited Darwin continually in this chapter. And yet he was laboring under an understanding of race that was discredited within his lifetime.

Strong's comments on race fed his chauvinist and expansionist ideas. Enamored of the social sciences, Strong used statistics to portray the great waves of immigration that would transform America. He said that the center of Anglo-Saxon civilization was shifting from Great Britain to America. What would happen as various races and peoples populated America in the next century? These peoples would be "Anglo-Saxonized."

But manifest destiny extended beyond this continent to the whole world. Strong spoke about the competition between superior and inferior races. In this competition America's destiny was to extend its Christian civilization around the globe. Strong was confident. "Is there

room for reasonable doubt that this race . . . is destined to dispossess
many weaker races, assimilate others, and mold the remainder, until,
in a very true and important sense, it has Anglo-Saxonized mankind?"[22]
In these remarks Strong sounds a theological triumphalism as well as a
political jingoism.

We must remember that Strong was speaking in a charged atmosphere, saying nothing different from what many other progressives
were saying. Unlike many progressives he was arguing not simply for
the expansion of American institutions but rather for the spread of
Christian values as part of the missionary outreach of the church. Although sometimes it seemed that for Strong, American and Christian
values were synonymous, at other times he critiqued America in light
of Christian values. Dorothea Muller argues that Strong, in distinction
from many progressives, was campaigning for Christian values to undergird the political expansionism that most were coming to accept as
America's destiny. From this perspective, Muller argues that "Strong
thought of a unique nationalism inspired by the principles of social
Christianity."[23]

If this chauvinism was acceptable to white progressives, it was not
acceptable to some black leaders. Alexander Crummel, rector of St.
Luke's Church in Washington, D.C., answered Strong in 1888. Crummel had served twenty years in Liberia on the faculty of Liberia College.
He returned to the United States in the 1870s and was recognized as a
leading black intellectual and churchman. His answer to Strong came
in an address to the Episcopal Church Congress, an informal forum
begun in 1874 to discuss social issues. In warming to his topic, "The
Race Problem in America," Crummel took on Strong and the trajectory
of *Our Country*. He criticized Strong's call for a solution to the race
problem by assimilation. "Dr. Strong evidently forgets that the principle of race is one of the most persistent of all things in the constitution
of man." Crummel saw the problem of America from a different vantage point. "It is the nation which is on trial. The Negro is only the
touch-stone. By this black man she stands or falls."[24]

But Strong could sound a very different note from that heard in *Our
Country*. Invited to address the American Missionary Association at its
annual meeting in Detroit in 1895, he tried to apply the new "social
consciousness" to the question of race. To the AMA, which had committed itself to working with both blacks and native Americans, Strong
asked whether there were then three races? "No," he replied, they are
"all one family, all blood relatives. The blood of Jesus Christ has made
them brothers."[25]

He spoke of the need for the new social consciousness to manifest itself in the race problem in a spirit of interdependence. This viewpoint, Strong reminded his listeners, was rooted in the reality that "different races of men are members of one great social organism."[26]

Strong, like many of his peers, was contradictory in his writings and remarks. Like many others he spoke with more empathy and understanding when asked to address himself to the specifics of the race question. The remarks of 1895 do indicate a change from his book of 1885. New experiences brought even more changes in Strong's thinking on race in the coming decades.

Among those who sought to grapple constructively with the race question, conservatives had long supported the various movements for colonization. The American Colonization Society (ACS), founded in 1816, became the chief agency of colonization, transporting freed blacks to Liberia. The first settlers arrived in 1820, and Liberia became an independent nation with a constitution in 1847. For the most part, the leaders of the Social Gospel were not involved in the colonization movement. They joined with the majority of Americans in recognizing that blacks were in America to stay. Social Gospel roots in the antislavery movement had been abolitionist and not colonizationist. A notable exception was Henry Codman Potter. His leadership in the temporary resurgence of the ACS in the early 1890s is one of the little-known dramas of this period.[27]

Potter was best known as an energetic, fair-minded Episcopalian. First as a New York City pastor and then as bishop, he gave prophetic leadership to the problems of labor and industry. Responding to the strikes, riots, and dissensions of the 1880s, Bishop Potter wrote a landmark pastoral letter in 1886. In it he envisioned a more human social community that would come "when capitalists and employers of labor forever dismissed the fallacy, which may be true enough in the domain of political economy, but is essentially false in the domain of religion, that the labor and the laborer are alike a commodity, to be bought and sold."[28] These thoughts were translated into action the next year with the organization of the Church Association for the Advancement of the Interests of Labor. CAIL's methods ranged from prayers and sermons to the use of the ballot, labor mediation, and finally the formation of sweatshop or tenement committees agitating for an end to injustices suffered by labor. CAIL, whose early success owed much to Potter, has been called by C. Howard Hopkins "the most remarkable organization in the half century of social Christianity's growth, with the exception of the Federal Council of Churches."[29]

Potter was concerned about the race question for many years, although his biographers have neglected this side of his reform interests. In 1871 he became a lifetime director of the American Colonization Society and was elected a vice-president in 1886. By a set of surprising and interlocking circumstances, Bishop Potter found himself propelled into the leadership of the ACS in the early nineties, just as its fortunes took a dramatic turn.[30]

The ACS declined in influence after 1865. By 1890 over 14,000 blacks had traveled to Liberia under society auspices, but only 1,130 of these had emigrated since 1872. Now the deteriorating racial situation, plus the beginnings of economic depression, made numbers of blacks ready to respond to a variety of alternatives. Henry M. Turner, a bishop in the African Methodist Episcopal Church who had been associated with the ACS since the late 1870s, was whipping up excitement for Africa. At this time the ACS was still the only agency providing money and a ship to get there, but it was experiencing financial troubles.[31]

Enthusiasm peaked in 1892 when groups of blacks from such faraway places as Arkansas and the Indian Territory (Oklahoma) prepared to come to New York to sail for Africa. The usual ACS-chartered ship carried fifty passengers. On February 20, 1892, a total of 186 blacks from Oklahoma arrived, followed on February 22 by thirty four more would-be emigrants from Arkansas. Because of a leader's fraud, lack of communication, and misunderstanding, both groups had come unannounced and unwanted. With other passengers expected, there were now nearly three hundred passengers waiting for some fifty places.[32]

In addition to these developments, the ACS was in the midst of its own internal crisis. President John H. B. Latrobe, who had held office since 1853, died in September 1891. Secretary William Coppinger, who had overseen the sailing arrangements for years, died on February 11, just days before the ACS was besieged with African emigrants.

Looking about for a new president, a man who would have the respect of blacks and whites, the society decided upon Bishop Potter at its annual meeting in January 1892. Traveling in Europe at the time and for a long while not knowing that he had been chosen president, Potter was willing to accept the office on the condition that the society was ready to embark upon new purposes and procedures. Bishop Turner was offered the position of secretary but declined.[33]

Later that fall President Potter addressed the society concerning the future. Replying to criticism that the ACS was an anachronism, he confessed that he had sometimes been plagued with such thoughts himself. The purposes that guided the organization in its early years needed to evolve. The ACS should not be about colonization because of the dim outlook for blacks in America but should focus on emigration because of the bright outlook for blacks in Africa. A new day was dawning. The "Dark Continent" was being opened, first by David Livingstone, and recently by many others. For this new day, the ACS needed new goals. There had to be an end to "indiscriminate colonization." This kind of colonization had been predicated upon getting rid of America's racial problem rather than upon a fundamental, positive interest in Africa's future. The policy had not really been helpful to Liberia, and it did not inspire confidence in the United States. In conclusion Potter offered a perspective for the future: "The motto of this Society needs henceforth to be: *multum non multa:* in the matter of those whom it sends to the Liberian coasts, 'not quantity but quality.'"[34]

At the January 1893, annual meeting, this new purpose was spelled out. The heart of the five points of the "Future Policy of the Society" was that the selection of quality people to meet Liberia's specific needs would enable and stimulate Liberia "to depend less and less upon others, and more and more upon herself."[35] Potter's vision and energy undergirded this attempt to relate the ACS to present realities in Africa.

As a means of implementing this new policy, the ACS changed its publication format at the end of 1892, replacing the *African Repository* with a semiannual *Liberia Bulletin*. The new journal presented more reliable information about Liberia, including as well sophisticated articles from many sources about the good future of all of Africa. The periodical became more substantive and less apologetic.

Despite Potter's more progressive and realistic intentions, the revival of interest in colonization was short lived, and measurable results were few. Unfortunately, the change in goals intersected the financial panic of 1893, which severely crippled opportunities to implement these goals. The temporary surge in applicants was occurring just as concern for blacks was reaching its nadir in the last decade of the century. However one assesses Potter's intentions, he was unable to attract sufficient white philanthropic backing or long-term black enthusiasm. The cry of "back to Africa" was not dead, but the ACS as an appropriate vehicle of this scheme was dying. The ACS continued in existence, but after its brief resurgence in 1892–1893, it was obsolete and finally died in 1910. African emigration continued through other independent channels but did not attract the quality blacks Potter hoped to enlist to build a self-sufficient Africa.

A more dominant and influential tendency was to adopt an accommodationist posture toward the continuing presence of blacks in America. When and where discussion of the race question continued, various northern leaders fell back from earlier equalitarian demands for political and civil rights. Although they continued to express concern for blacks, the focus now shifted to black education and economic uplift.

One of the more prominent national leaders reflecting this shift was Lyman Abbott. In the estimation of Henry Sloane Coffin, "Lyman Abbott was unquestionably the foremost doctor of the church in America in his time, and one of the half dozen most potent teachers of Christianity in our national history."[36] Usually grouped along with Walter Rauschenbusch, Washington Gladden, and Josiah Strong among the leading cadre of Social Gospelers, "Abbott's position as a publicist enabled him to wield a broader influence" than the others, according to his biographer.[37] As editor of the *Christian Union*, one of the first religious periodicals to attempt to come to terms with the new industrial situation, Abbott's views did gain wide circulation. From 1887 to 1899 Abbott served simultaneously as minister of Plymouth Congregational Church of Brooklyn. In 1893 the *Christian Union* became the *Outlook*, the change of name reflecting a greater desire to move from more constricted religious concerns to social, political, and literary subjects, all the time retaining a religious impetus. In that year its circulation numbered 30,000. By 1898 its circulation exceeded 100,000, which indicates the tremendous influence of the paper and its editor.

By the 1890s Abbott had reappraised the substance and perimeters of "the Negro question" and adopted a position of gradualism. At the core of Abbott's gradualism was a changed bearing toward the South. The way that Abbott's views had come almost full circle in the span of twenty-five years is intriguing.

Born in Massachusetts in 1835 and growing to maturity on the eve of the Civil War, Abbott said that an antislavery impulse was one of three factors that led him toward the Christian ministry. Writing many years later in his *Reminiscences*, Abbott explained that he had perceived four political options on the issue; he had been antislavery but not abolitionist, which he considered too radical.[38]

During the war years, Abbott served a Congregational church in Terre Haute, Indiana. From the beginning, Abbott was a minister who related religion to the political and social questions of the day. Prior to Abraham Lincoln's preliminary announcement about emancipation in 1862, Abbott publicly urged such a measure.[39] Southern loyalties were strong in Terre Haute, however, and it was here that the young New

Englander got his first real experience of the emotions surrounding the issue of slavery and race.

At the close of the war Abbott resigned from his church to accept the newly created position of executive secretary of the American Union Commission, shortly to become the American Freedmen's Union Commission (AFUC). In the 1866–1867 school year, approximately one-third of the northern teachers in the South were financed by this amalgamated league of nondenominational societies. Looking back on this assignment, Abbott reflected that it "seemed to me to offer a rare opportunity to take some part both in an individual and a social gospel."[40] Abbott meant that he had the privilege of personal contact with individuals who were being helped but that the work of the commission was intended to help change the structures of the South, especially the educational structures, so as to help a whole people.

The executive secretary was enthusiastic about the firstfruits of the work. In a paper prepared for the International Antislavery Conference in Paris in 1867, Abbott asserted that the "rapid and very marked" progress by blacks in education refuted "slavery's accusation of idleness and incapacity."[41]

The AFUC forbade segregation in its schools in the South. Abbott recognized that many children would want to attend schools with schoolmates of their own race, but when questioned specifically by southern whites, he affirmed the plank in the AFUC constitution that schools must be open to all. Any exclusion due to color was "inherently wrong." In an editorial entitled "Equal Rights" for the *American Freedman*, in which he spoke out strongly against discrimination, Abbott went on to say that the best friends of blacks did not speak in terms of inferiority. At the moment, according to Abbott, the capacity of blacks was unknown: only opportunity would prove what that capacity was. Any talk of superiority by whites therefore rested on a shaky foundation.[42]

With the passing of a quarter century, Abbott believed that he and many other white northerners had been overenthusiastic about solving "the southern question." In more youthful days as the war was drawing to a close, he had said: "We have not only to conquer the South—we have also to convert it. We have not only to occupy it by bayonets and bullets—but also by ideas and institutions."[43] Now, in 1890, Abbott's position was that "the Negro problem must be worked out by the Negroes and the white men of the South with the aid of the north, not by the north or federal government over the heads of the Negroes and the white men."[44]

This statement reflects Abbott's basic retreat from reform to accommodation in these transitional years. It is important to understand that his sentiments do not represent a lessening of interest in "the Negro question." They do suggest, however, a scaling down of the heights to which blacks ought rightly to aspire at the end of the nineteenth century. There is thus an accommodation to what Abbott would say are new realities in both North and South.

What was the basis of Abbott's withdrawal from reform to accommodation? First, his posture of gradualism grew out of an overriding concern for the healing of sectional divisions. A principal factor behind this change of mind was a distrust of the results of Reconstruction, coupled with a readiness to trust the good intentions of new leaders in the South. Looking backward, Abbott believed that Reconstruction failed because of the interference of carpetbag rule with home rule. "Since the War and Reconstruction," Abbott asserted, "the white man in the South has shown himself the friend of the slave."[45]

Second, Abbott looked with hope to the apostles of the New South. These leaders, according to Abbott, admitted the evils of slavery and were ready to build a new society that would be better for both black and white. Abbott was a guest of honor when Henry W. Grady, editor of the *Atlanta Constitution*, delivered his famous "New South" address before the New England Society of New York on December 21, 1886. Abbott applauded the speech in the next edition of the *Christian Union* and printed excerpts from it.[46]

It was in this context that Abbott saw more evil than good in the Federal Elections Bill of 1890. He editorialized in the *Christian Union* throughout the summer of 1890 against northern pressure on what should be properly a southern political affair. Counseling restraint, Abbott argued that if the "Force bill were to be passed, the inevitable result will be an incitement of race antagonism and a delay in progress."[47] Opposition to the Federal Elections Bill illustrates just how far Abbott had traveled along the road from reform to accommodation on the race question.

CHAPTER 3

Beyond Accommodation
to Reform

We are learning that it is not well to make one single concession to the
caste of prejudice. The right way is to fight against it vigorously and
persistently and never yield an inch.

TRUE

WILLIAM HAYES WARD

Justice is pictured blind, and her daughter, the Law, ought at least to
be color-blind.

—ALBION W. TOURGÉE,
PLESSY V. FERGUSON, 1896

In the midst of the reappraisal in the North, a courageous few bucked
the retreat from Reconstruction, a significant number of whom had
Social Gospel moorings. Never well organized, these intrepid individuals used pulpit, press, and reform organizations to speak up just
when crowds of former well-wishers were becoming silent.

If Lyman Abbott and the *Outlook* were increasingly the voices of
accommodation, there existed in New York another editor and religious
weekly that espoused a more vigorous ideology and strategy of racial
reform. William Hayes Ward and the *Independent* shared with Abbott
and the *Outlook* a common evangelical and abolitionist heritage and, by
the 1880s, were advancing similar Social Gospel themes and programs.
But in the arena of racial justice Ward advocated a more militant and
far-reaching program of reform. Ward and the *Independent* were significant opinion makers and molders at this time, but studies of both the
Social Gospel and race reform have not given adequate treatment to
either the editor or his weekly.

Founded in 1848, the *Independent* from the beginning had represented the vigorous antislavery wing of the Congregational church. Henry
C. Bowen, owner of the weekly, had begun his career in the silk company operated by Arthur Tappan, friend and financial benefactor of
Charles G. Finney and the cause of evangelical abolitionism. Ward

joined Bowen and the *Independent* in 1868 and was committed to the same reform ideals. Ward's New England ministerial forebears were deeply involved in the abolitionist movement. Before coming to the weekly, Ward had had served a Congregational parish and taught school. A noted biblical and Oriental scholar all his life (President Eliot had once offered him a chair in Assyriology at Harvard), he believed that his greatest usefulness to society could be through the field of journalism.[1]

Ward had been at Lake Mohonk. Disappointed in the all-white gathering, he dissented in an editorial from the overall tone of the meetings and called upon the conference to "make its influence felt among the more neglected or disputed lines of advance, and those that may influence legislation."[2] These words indicated the pattern of Ward's own involvement in "the Negro question." Eschewing the growing popularity of a strategy of accommodation, Ward believed in the efficacy of legislation and the necessity of agitation and force in backing just demands.

Following his own advice, Ward returned from Lake Mohonk to take up the cause of the Federal Elections Bill. On the day of the Lodge speech, an *Independent* editorial commented, "The facts clearly show that the time has come when Congress should exercise all the power needed to correct the monstrous abuses." As the bill was taken up by the Senate in early July, the coverage broadened. On July 10 the *Independent* argued for what it said was the heart of the bill by observing that blacks were no more free to vote in congressional elections than they were in state elections. To be sure, Bowen and Ward stood with the Republican party in what was for some strictly a partisan issue. More fundamentally, however, the *Independent* wanted black Americans to be assured "that so far as the power of Congress can go it will be exerted to secure to him the rights he had acquired under the Constitution of the United States." In September the *Independent* objected to the title "Force Bill," arguing that any beneficent enactment aimed at the suppression of wrongdoing must have force behind it. Cutting through to the marrow of the legislation, Ward preferred to title the federal elections measure "A Bill to Protect Human Rights."[3]

What stood behind support or criticism of the elections measure was the question of the basic posture now to be adopted toward the South. Even as his editorial counterpart, Lyman Abbott, called for restraint, Ward declared that restraint equaled caving in to the steady erosion of black rights in the South. While Abbott argued that the North was pushing the South, Ward believed it was the South itself, far from being persecuted, that was taking the initiative in undoing constitutional guarantees. Just as Abbott wanted to do away with rhetoric such as "the southern question," Ward editorialized, "The only 'Southern question' is that which is made by the South itself. It is not a question which the rest of the Union thrusts upon the South with the persistency of persecution. It is the South itself which thrusts it upon the country."[4]

An active Congregationalist, Ward was especially conscious of the racism within the churches. Accused by a friend of always viewing race relations in terms of ethics, Ward criticized church leaders for bending to social and cultural prejudices.

Ward was not above scolding the popular evangelist Dwight L. Moody for conducting general meetings in Chattanooga and New Orleans that were not open to blacks.[5] Ward campaigned against reunion talks in the 1880s between northern and southern Presbyterians because the plans included separate racial presbyteries and synods.[6] These talks came to nothing, but in 1904 the same issue was raised again in conversations that lated resulted in union between the northern Presbyterian church and the Cumberland Presbyterian church.[7]

The *Independent* devoted much more attention to the controversy among Congregationalists over the validity of separate or integrated associations of churches. The dispute centered in Georgia, but beginning in the late 1880s, it became a divisive issue in the national church. Ward and the *Independent* hammered away at this problem so much that one editorial concluded in exasperation, "We are weary of denouncing such wicked and unchristian conduct."[8] The solution of the problem was made all the more complicated by a Congregational polity that did not invest the national church with adjudicating powers.

All of these episodes in the 1880s and 1890s had a lesson in them for Ward, which he wanted others to learn. "Methodists tried to placate southern whites, but it doesn't work." The answer was not accommodation, but an even more vigorous defense of hard-won rights. In the midst of yet another comment on the continuing Georgia Congregational controversy, Ward reiterated his own platform: "We are learning that it is not well to make one single concession to the caste of prejudice. The right way is to fight against it vigorously and persistently and never yield an inch."[9]

Abbott and Ward were leading opinion makers in the developing Social Gospel because of their roles as editors of what were two of the leading religious periodicals of the day. Located in New York, they spoke both to and for a northern but also a national constituency. Often the chronicling of religious movements has focused on the ideas of key editors or theologians to the neglect of pastors and lay leaders involved in reform at the local level. This neglect has been true especially of leaders located in the South, Midwest, or West.

In this regard we turn now to the efforts of a young pastor in To-peka, Kansas, in the years just before he became a national figure. Charles M. Sheldon became known far and wide with the publication of *In His Steps* in 1897. The story of his involvement in racial reform, however, remains little known.[10]

Sheldon's early experience and education led him to embrace the Social Gospel. Raised in the Dakota Territory, Sheldon grew up with native Americans. These friendships bore fruit later, he said, in empa-thy for all who were the victims of racism and prejudice. His education at Brown University and Andover Theological Seminary helped him give words to the compassion that characterized his whole life and ministry. He took his seminary training while Andover was becoming known for its "evangelical liberalism." The emphasis in these years was on the immanence of God and the humanity of Jesus. Jesus revealed in his life, and not just in his death, divine love. Self-sacrificing love be-came the basis of Christian fellowship. The Progressive Orthodoxy, or the New Theology, emanating from Andover and other centers focused on ethical perfection.[11] Sheldon never thought of himself as a theologian and preferred throughout his life to emphasize the practical meaning of Jesus' life for the life of men and women.

Sheldon's first call was to serve the Congregational church in Water-bury, Vermont. After two years he was invited to come west to Topeka to assume the leadership of the recently formed Central Congregational Church, which began its congregational life meeting over a grocery store. Early on, Sheldon struggled with the perennial preacher's prob-lem: how to attract people, especially college students (at nearby Wash-burn College), to the Sunday evening services. His creative answer was to compose a sermon story each year, to be read chapter by chapter on successive Sunday nights. Each chapter ended with a problem or situ-ation sure to bring people back again the following Sunday for the resolution. He started reading *In His Steps* on October 4, 1896, the sev-enth in a series of sermon stories. As a cast of characters was intro-duced, each found himself or herself asking the central question of the story, What would Jesus do? The church was packed for these fall eve-nings, and the sermon story was serialized by the *Advance*, a Congre-gational weekly in Chicago, starting in November.

Sheldon attempted to publish *In His Steps* but was turned down by three publishers. Finally the *Advance* brought out an inexpensive book edition in 1897. Sheldon obtained copyright, but because the original serialization had been published without copyright, the book copyright was without value. This circumstance enhanced the distribution of the book. In the past century approximately forty publishers in the United States, fifteen in Great Britain, and twenty-seven in other countries have produced various editions. Total sales have always been difficult to calculate, but estimates range from 6 to 20 million volumes.[12]

Total sales do not calculate the influence of the book. In His Steps was the kind of book passed around from mother to grandfather to daughter. It was a nineteenth-century novel working out the implications of the cost of discipleship. Eric Goldman caught its true importance when he called it one of the thirteen books that have changed America.[13] A modern commentator on Sheldon has made the sage observation; "What the popular mind proposes, the sophisticated mind disposes."[14] Sheldon, if he is recognized at all today, has often been cast aside with the ultimate academic broadside: "popular." To do so is to miss the meaning, sometimes more subtle than appears at first glance, in his writings. The continuing interest in In His Steps can be measured in the present annual sales of approximately 100,000 volumes.

A series of experiences at the end of his first year in Topeka proved catalytic both for In His Steps and Sheldon's involvement in racial reform. In January 1890 a man knocked at Sheldon's door and asked for work. Sheldon could provide no work, but he never forgot the man's expression as he walked away in discouragement. It is exactly such an incident with which In His Steps begins. Stung by this experience and sensing the artificial barrier between pastor and people, Sheldon decided he needed to experience Topeka as a common person would. It was a bitterly cold winter in a time of economic depression. Dressed in old clothes, Sheldon walked into every store on Kansas Avenue, the main street of Topeka, seeking work but found none. For five days he searched in vain. Finally, on Saturday morning, he volunteered to work at the Santa Fe railroad yard and ended up being paid fifty cents.[15]

It was more than a story of individual need that gripped Sheldon. Looking back on that experience, Sheldon spoke of "the horrible blunder and stupidity of our whole industrial system that doesn't work according to any well established plan of a Brotherhood of men, but is driven by forces that revolve around some pagan rule of life called 'supply and demand.'"[16] Although today Sheldon is published and read by religious groups that see in him and his characters models of evangelical piety and discpleship and that in the same vein would distance themselves from any notion of a Social Gospel, it is important to understand just what is at stake behind the cast of individuals who people Sheldon's novels. Sheldon argues again and again for an understanding of the corporate nature of evil and the need for a Social Gospel large enough to change systems, not just individuals.

Staggered by his initial experience as an unrecognized laborer, Sheldon received permission from his church to live among eight social groups within the city in order to understand better their situation and concerns. The third week proved to have the most profound effect on Sheldon. He took lodgings in "Tennesseetown," a black section just across the street from his church. He intended to stay his customary week, but the people so provoked his empathy and imagination that he extended his stay for a second week and then a third.[17]

The residents of Tenesseetown were in Kansas as another result of the retreat from Reconstruction. When Rutherford B. Hayes was elected president in the Compromise of 1877, large numbers of blacks left the South seeking a better life. Thousands of blacks known as Exodusters passed through Topeka in search of new, cheap land in the West. Some stayed and settled in a location known ever after as Tennesseetown. In 1880 blacks constituted 24 percent of the population of Topeka.[18]

The newcomers faced many problems. The mayor of Topeka and public officials were not hospitable toward Tennesseetown. They refused to spend public funds to help the residents. The mayor went as far as to state that it would be better to spend the money to send them back to the South.

Young pastor Sheldon soon had other ideas. By living with the people, he experienced their conditions. Medical service was minimal. Educational opportunities were limited. Liquor and gambling and crime abounded.

Sheldon plunged into what he called the Christianization of Tennesseetown. He began by taking a careful sociological survey of the residents of Tennesseetown: their numbers, occupations, health, and general needs and wants. Sheldon was an advocate of the pastor's practicing "practical sociology." If he wanted to minister to the real needs of the parish. The results of this survey were published later in the Social Gospel journal the *Kingdom*. In addition, William Hayes Ward commended Sheldon's "admirable study" to the readers of the *Independent*.[19]

While living in Tennesseetown, Sheldon decided he would test the race prejudice of Topeka. He had a well-dressed black man go into three of the best restaurants in the city to find out what kind of treatment he would receive. Sheldon followed him and was pleased with what he observed. The same young man then applied for membership in the YMCA but was refused. He was told to set up a Negro association of his own. Sheldon did not miss making the point that the YMCA proved less Christian than the restaurants.[20]

After completing the survey, Sheldon called upon the members of Central Congregational to help him with a variety of projects. The largest response was from the young people. They started a reading room and a library. A nursery was set up for the children of working mothers. A community garden society was established. Adult classes were formed for the purpose of both manual and academic training.[21]

The project that was most gratifying to Sheldon and the Tennesseetown community was the organization of a kindergarten. In these years kindergartens were often not part of the public school system. Andrew Jordan, proprietor of the dance hall and speakeasy, agreed to lease the hall for the kindergarten. This was reported to be the first kindergarten for blacks west of the Mississippi. Opened in 1893, the school saw its enrollment rise to 210 by 1896. It continued in existence for over twenty years until taken over the city school board. Its accomplishments were widely acclaimed, for it won the silver medal at both the Jamestown and St. Louis expositions for the best exhibit presented by kindergartens, white or black.[22]

What can we say about Sheldon's approach to race and reform? In reading the accounts of the early years of Tennesseetown, both by Sheldon and others, we can observe a range of motives and actions. Education is offered by competent teachers. One of the public displays of this education, however, was teaching "little darky boys" to sing plantation songs. In reports of the projects the language of paternalism appears right alongside encouragement of blacks to assume responsibility for their own destiny. Sheldon continued to support the Second Colored Congregational church in Tennesseetown but also received some black children and adults into Central Church. In the first year of this new venture, one white family withdrew after the infusion of black children into the Sunday school.

More information about Sheldon's approach to racial reform can be found in his novels. In 1898 Sheldon wrote *The Redemption of Freetown,* which was really the story of the redemption of Tennesseetown. At the outset Sheldon told his readers that the story "is largely founded on actual facts known to very many besides myself." In the town of Merton the Reverend Howard Douglass experiences the problems of Freetown by taking up lodgings there, even as Sheldon did in Tennesseetown, Freetown is a section of Merton near the Emmanuel Church that Doug-

lass serves. Sheldon's story line is direct. Emmanuel is meant to call
forth the biblical image that God is with us. But the point is that the
Christian people of Emmanuel Church are not with the people of Freetown. On the contrary, Freetown "is cursed and criticized for the vice
and crime that flow out of it." But pastor Douglass asks, "How much
have the Christian people of this town ever done to check or remove
the source of that evil?"[23]

Sheldon nearly always begins with an assessment of the problem. A
first step is a social survey. The perceptive observer then discovers that
the problem is much larger than first imagined. In *In His Steps* Sheldon
consistently portrays the problems as more than the problems of individual sins. Thus, in constructing dialogue about his favorite issue of
temperance, he has Virginia say, "The saloon furnishes material to be
saved faster than the settlement or residence or rescue mission work
can save it." What is fascinating is the way the Rectangle, the local
tenement district, is spoken of many times as if it were a person—what
might be better called a corporate personality. Thus, as Virginia takes
the drunken prostitute Loreen up the street, we read: "The sight
seemed to impress the Rectangle seriously. It never took itself seriously
when it was drunk, but this was different." It is in the same spirit that
pastor Douglass bids his followers to deal with the source of the evil in
Freetown instead of dealing only with the symptoms.[24] The source is
not simply corrupt individuals but a whole social system.

If the problem was ultimately corporate, so was the solution. In *In
His Steps* we are told that various singers, Sunday school teachers, and
gospel visitors had made attempts to deal with the problems in the
Rectangle but that "the First Church of Raymond, as an institution, had
never really done anything."[25] To the extent that the problem is institutional, the solution must be institutional. In light of the problems of
Freetown, we are told that "the work to be done is so large that no one
church or person or organization can do it."[26] Sheldon encouraged the
writing of *Across the Way*, the history of the work of Central Church in
Tennesseetown, to demonstrate that it was the work not of a few key
individuals but of the whole Central Church.

If Sheldon often disparaged theological language and debate, his
own Christocentric theology is enunciated clearly as the solution to the
problem. Although Sheldon has left us little information about his days
at Andover, Daniel Day Williams's account of the so-called Andover
liberals who were Sheldon's teachers speaks of motifs heard again and
again in St. Charles of Topeka's novels. At the outset of *The Redemption
of Freetown* we hear that "it must be *ourselves*, the Christ in us, with the
unredeemed humanity near us, that must redeem" Freetown.[27]

This strong emphasis on the meaning of incarnation is heard later in the story when enthusiasm is increasing for various projects. Sheldon observed that it was not difficult to get money for the building needed, but "can we get the people?" The answer in both *In His Steps* and *The Redemption of Freetown* is that incarnation begins with gifts of money but ends up with people willing to live in inner city Chicago or in Freetown.

In 1896, the year that he began writing *In His Steps*, Sheldon paused to reflect upon the race issue in light of his experiences in Topeka. Aware of the importance of education, Sheldon observed that there was little incentive in education when young blacks could not get jobs in traditional occupations in business, labor, and education. Commenting on the white prejudice he encountered in his own congregation, highlighted by the withdrawal of one family, he was pleased that most white families remained with the congregation.

What can be said about the effectiveness of Sheldon's programs in Tennesseetown? Sheldon was often quite idealistic about his various programs, but in this case he admitted: "The caste prejudice which lies at the bottom of all this, is a thing which I, in my Puritan, Anglo-Saxon stupidity, have never been able to analyze." This admission notwithstanding, Thomas C. Cox has observed that Sheldon's approach "represented an efficient balance of Christian stewardship and Progressive reform." Cox notes a degree of paternalism underlying these efforts, but in his study of blacks in Topeka comments that "Sheldon's programs enhanced community participation and self-awareness to a noticeable degree." The efforts that Sheldon spearheaded put in place organizations that would continue to benefit the community.[28]

Sheldon's interest initially was in the Christianization of the blacks in Tennesseetown. He recognized that now his interest was broader. He became conscious of the liberties blacks did and did not enjoy in Kansas and across the nation. He was gratified that blacks did have equal rights with respect to theaters in Kansas, but he observed that race prejudice was "far from fading out." As a result of his experiences he now saw "the Negro question" from an altered perspective. "I do not have much hope of Christianizing the Negroes until we have Christianized the Anglo-Saxons." In concluding, he observed, "It is a present question with me now sometimes which race needs it the most."[29]

The spectrum of northern responses to "the Negro question" in these two decades was completed by an enigmatic figure who often found himself almost alone in his dogged militancy. Albion Winegar Tourgée had thundered his opinion at Lake Mohonk, and he continued to speak out and organize in the 1880s and 1890s. Critical of the retreat from Reconstruction, he had returned north to advocate reform tactics that placed him to the left of Ward. Tourgée proved to be uncompromising in his equalitarian goals.

He supported the Lodge Bill. But after writing and campaigning for national aid for education, he thrust himself into the debate over the Blair Bill on the side of the opposition. Tourgée testified before congressional committees on March 13, 1890, exactly one week before the decisive Senate vote was scheduled. He also lunched with President Benjamin Harrison, whom he and others had looked to as an ally in the struggle for black rights. On good terms with House Speaker Thomas B. Reed and Representative Harrison Kelley of Kansas, an outspoken equalitarian just elected to the House, Tourgée actually wrote two education bills introduced in the House by Kelley.[30]

Tourgée opposed the Blair Bill because, although money was to be given on the basis of illiteracy, states could distribute the money on a per capita basis. He could foresee a situation wherein blacks might number one-third of the population and two-thirds of the illiterates and yet receive only one-third of the money. In addition, he objected to administration of the bill by southern states which he did not trust. With Tourgée watching from the Senate gallery, the final vote was 31 to 37. A change of three votes would have passed the bill. There is evidence to show Tourgée's personal influence in the case of five votes against the measure.[31]

Tired of discussion and fruitless debate, Tourgée launched an equalitarian crusade in October 1891. In his weekly column in the prominent Chicago Republican newspaper the *Daily Inter Ocean*, Tourgée announced the formation of a new organization, the National Citizens Rights Association (NCRA). Envisioning the organization as a biracial pressure group, Tourgée's hope was expansive—his goal was 2 million members.

The initial response was encouraging. Hundreds of letters and applications poured in. The writers ranged from black leaders to the hardly literate black man from Chicago who wrote, "Please Don't let us alone for god knows I think Ever blackman in the worl loves you." Students at Oberlin announced a goal of five hundred for an NCRA chapter. The response of blacks from the South, often letters filled with evidences of suffering and fear, moved Tourgée to greater efforts.[32]

By the spring of 1892, over 100,000 members were claimed, but enthusiasm was leveling off. Tourgée had hoped to use his organization as a pressure group at the Republican convention that year, but these hopes were not fulfilled. The fiery orator was beset by problems in every hand. The crusade had never really caught on with blacks, who, Tourgée admitted, composed not more than 10 percent of the NCRA. Nearly all of these black members were from the South. Prominent black leaders, many of whom had hailed Tourgée in the past.[33] were now casting their lot with black-inspired organizations such as the Afro-American League.[34] In 1893 T. Thomas Fortune, editor of the *New York Age,* offered to make the *Age* the official organ of the NCRA. In an unexplained mistake, Tourgée refused to take up the offer, losing five thousand subscribers in the process. More important, he thereby lost a chance to gain new adherents in the East.[35] By early 1894 the NCRA was languishing. Various acts of resuscitation were tried, but by 1896 the organization was dead.

Despite attempts at black unity in these years, Tourgée was concerned precisely because blacks did not seem to be acting in concert. He wrote to Bishop Turner, opposing his emigration plans but also criticizing such divergent leaders as Washington and Fortune. Tourgée observed, "If the colored people will get together and demand one thing of God and that thing JUSTICE—the recognition and security of their rights—and then apply their united strength to secure and hold that place among the American people," they would have a much better opportunity to succeed.[36]

White support, as Tourgée had seen at Lake Mohonk, was on the wane for anything as disruptive as a crusade. The judge knew well what many white people thought of him, but he retorted in his usual way: "I am a 'fanatic' because I believe in the equal rights of all men, and in a God who is not partial to some of His children and cruel as an Aztec to others." In a typical change of a usual image, Tourgée continued, "You think God is on the side of the white man: I think the white man would best be careful that he is on the Lord's side."[37]

This is not to say that Tourgée did not influence white opinion in these years. In 1892, when the northern Methodist church passed a strong resolution denouncing unjust treatment of blacks, Ida B. Wells, black antilynching crusader, wrote to Tourgée, a Methodist layman, as "the one to whom, more than all others, . . . [belongs] the credit for awakening the sluggish conscience of the great M. E. Church."[38] After Tourgée spoke at a church meeting in Chicago, the Reverend Francis R. Rowley of the Baptist church wrote to thank Tourgée for greatly increasing his motivation to help "those denied their lawful rights."[39]

Tourgée's faith mirrored his personality—action was more important than theory or theology. In Tourgée's correspondence he was not reticent in correlating his active faith with his actions on the racial front.

Responding to Rowley, he said that his present understanding of his faith was that "the chief function of Christianity is to make the earthly conditions better, rather than to speculate upon or anticipate the heavenly ones." In writing to a Reverend R. E. Hull, he broke into lyric prose about the person and work of Christ.

> My Christ is not the easily comprehended piece of propriety and legerdemain which . . . has been depicted. To my mind Christ was as fierce and hot as the sands that scorched his feet and the sun which glared upon his head. He loved *man*—not pityingly and languishingly—but with an intense agonizing zeal which made him long to destroy the evil tendencies and unveil the healthful forces of human life.[40]

Tourgée's outspoken championing of racial justice continued to earn him the gratitude of large numbers of blacks. In 1893, during the summer of the World's Fair, the black men of Chicago organized and named a club in his honor, "because he was recognized as the Negro's best friend."[41] The Tourgée Club opened a clubhouse primarily for the entertainment of blacks visiting Chicago and the fair.

Tourgée could also be his own worst enemy. His conceit and lack of tact hampered the dissemination of his ideas and programs. A writer by vocation, his primary method of attacking racism was as a publicist. When founding a national organization, he lacked the skills of an organizer. And in Tourgée's dealings with blacks, he did not avoid the paternalism he criticized at Lake Mohonk. Genuinely desirous of stronger black solidarity, he also wanted blacks to continue to turn to him for counsel and leadership.

In all his efforts Tourgée looked to the social application of Christianity as the moral force, and the federal government as the political-legal power, to establish equal rights for blacks. Throughout his reform episodes, Tourgée never wavered on one point: It was fatuous to believe that the South could or would solve "the Negro question" if left strictly to its own devices. On the contrary, Tourgée believed that "when the South is once convinced that the country is determined that the Negro shall have his rights as a citizen, he will get them, but until that time he never will."[42]

But the South was not convinced. The South was hypersensitive about northern criticism, but when southern blacks were in trouble, they so often had no other place to turn but to the North.

In July 1890 Louisiana adopted a Jim Crow law requiring equal but separate accommodations for whites and blacks in public facilities and on railroads. Louis A. Martinet, editor of the *New Orleans Crusader*, immediately urged blacks to test the constitutionality of the law. The next year a "Citizens Committee to Test the Constitutionality of the Separate Car Law" was formed. In October, Martinet wrote to Judge Tourgée, "The revival of interest in the Jim Crow matter is owing to you more than anyone else." The citizens committee, Martinet wrote, would like Tourgée to be the leading counsel in a test case. Tourgée accepted, and the next month a letter from Martinet to Tourgée contained three pages of signatures of grateful black citizens of New Orleans.[43]

In 1892 Homer Adolph Plessy, a man of one-eighth African blood, was arrested for refusing to move from his seat in a railroad car reserved for whites. Tourgée and James C. Walker, a white criminal lawyer, argued the case against the Jim Crow law before the Criminal District Court for the Parish of New Orleans. Judge John H. Ferguson denied the arguments made in Plessy's behalf. The case was carried to the State Supreme Court and finally to the Supreme Court of the United States in late 1895 as *Plessy* v. *Ferguson.*

Tourgée carried the major burden of the case before the highest court. In his legal arguments he relied, more than he had before the Louisiana court, on the Thirteenth and Fourteenth amendments. He argued an affirmative rights position, stating that the Thirteenth and Fourteenth amendments bestowed a national citizenship on every person that no state could abrogate. Tourgée also brought to bear his own oratorical skill, which included a gift for the striking phrase.[44]

In the landmark decision announced in 1896, the court enunciated the "separate but equal" basis for segregation that helped buttress the legal basis of racial patterns in ensuing decades. The citizens committee and the blacks of America lost.

But looking backward through the prism of the civil rights years, we should not forget the eloquent dissent of Justice John Marshall Harlan. He declared, "The thin disguise of 'equal accommodations' will not mislead anyone, nor atone for the wrong this day done."[45] Judge Harlan, a former slaveholder, is often remembered for saying, "Our Constitution is color-blind." But Sidney Kaplan has pointed to the great similarity in language in the eloquent dissent of Harlan and the earlier argument of Tourgée. At the heart of his argument before the Court, Tourgée said, "Justice is pictured blind, and her daughter, the Law, ought at least to be color-blind."[46]

But justice was not color-blind in the 1880s and 1890s. The Supreme Court only codified what was happening on many fronts across the nation. The reality of the situation was not "separate and equal," as the court declared, but rather separate and unequal. It was this reality that scuttled the Lake Mohonk Conference on the Negro before it barely began. Another conference was held in 1891,[47] but that was the last venture. As a friend of Lake Mohonk remarked:

> It became at once apparent that it would be practically impossible for a conference held in the North, to which it would be difficult to get southern men to come, to do much to influence the separate states of the South towards an improvement in the condition of the Negro. Mr. Smiley is a man with whom speeches, however fine, pass for very little, unless they lead to something practical. He therefore decided, though reluctantly, to give up the Negro Conferences.[48]

Smiley realized that discussion could take place in the North, but practical action must take place in the South. It was in the South that more than 90 percent of black Americans lived. It was in the South that black Americans found themselves neither slave nor free, caught in the crossfire of forces determined to establish once and for all their place in legal and practical subservience in southern society.

It is thus to the South that we now turn. The larger story of race relations has been told from various perspectives, but the not insignificant story of religion, especially of an incipient social Christianity, needs to be brought into sharper focus.

CHAPTER 4

Dissenting Voices
in the South

The worst fault of the Southern people since the war in relation to the
Negro's education has not been that they themselves have done so little,
but that they have not more cordially cooperated with those who were
able to do great things and were trying hard to do them.
—ATTICUS GREENE HAYGOOD

Do we love *this neighbor* as ourselves? Do we run great risks both with
and for him? Do we give him our seat in God's house? Or do we tell
him to go to the gallery? When he makes his peace with God, does he
take the blessed cup and break bread with us or after us?
—GEORGE WASHINGTON CABLE

The mistake has often been made of assuming that during the last
decades of the nineteenth century no whites in the South were concerned about "liberty and justice for all." For a long time this assumption was part of one of the larger oversights in American history,
namely, that progressivism had not been present in the South. Even
after Arthur S. Link's seminal essay began to dispel this misreading of
the progressive map,[1] "the Negro question" remained for C. Vann
Woodward the exception: "The blind spot in the Southern progressive
record . . . was the Negro, for the whole movement in the South coincided paradoxically with the crest of the wave of racism."[2] There is no
disputing the fact that southern progressives were swept along by the
racist current, but there were notable exceptions who attempted to
swim upstream. Some of these leaders were part of an incipient social
Christianity.

A gradual reinterpretation of progressivism was based partly on the
distinction between the political and the humanitarian thrusts of the
movement. Political progressivism, offering relief to political injustices
via such means as the direct primary, initiative, and referendum, as
well as business regulation, offered no resistance to the structure and

ethos of white supremacy. When one turns to the humanitarian reformers, dealing with such issues as education, child labor, health, prisons,
and agriculture, one finds a progressive impulse more responsive to
racial injustices.

Even as attention has more recently focused on progressivism in the
South, there has been a historical lag in examining a corollary assumption that the Social Gospel was absent from the southern scene. Earlier
studies dealing with the Social Gospel consistently excluded the South.[3]
If the movement is defined narrowly as a response to the problems of
the city and of labor, it is now apparent that the South took important
strides in industrialization in the closing years of the century, which
were accompanied by many of the problems known in the North. If the
Social Gospel is defined more broadly, as concern for a whole series of
social problems wherein the solution was to deal with social systems
and not just individual victims, then problems more particularly southern, such as farm tenancy, illiteracy, the convict-lease system, and especially race relations need to be considered also.

In recent years the Social Gospel in the South has begun to be reas-
sessed. John L. Eighmy states, "For all the admitted resistance to religious liberalism, the new Protestant thought, especially the social
gospel, exerted important influence within southern church life."[4] Dewey W. Grantham, in his studies of southern progressivism, has asserted
that "there was an active social gospel in the South."[5] Wayne Flint, John
Patrick McDowell, Eighmy, and several others have pointed to the presence of the Social Gospel in denominational studies of southern Baptists and Methodists.[6] Much more work needs to be done to trace the
influence of the Social Gospel across the South in such divergent areas
as penal reform, agriculture, health, education, prohibition, and child
labor. And what about "the Negro question?"

Any reevaluation of the relationship of the Social Gospel and racial
reform in the South must be seen at the outset within the context of
the dominant and persistent pattern of racism within religious bodies
in the last decades of the nineteenth century. During this transitional
period between the end of Reconstruction and the beginnings of the
New South, the fundamental reality of caste evolved from the older
structure of slavery to the new structures of segregation. Religion had
been a bulwark of slavery, and so now it lent its not inconsiderable
moral strength to the reshaping of societal values. Religious leaders and
organizations exhibited attitudes and actions that were often indistin-
guishable from persons and agencies in other sections of southern
society.

Southern Baptists slightly outnumbered southern Methodists as the largest denomination in the South. In their own eyes Southern Baptists were making great progress in solving the southern problem. In fact, they said, blacks should be grateful for all of the aid they had received. "No people since the world began ever had so much or such efficient aid in their struggle from a savage life to a Christian civilization."[7] The optimism of the Southern Baptists seemed boundless. In 1891 the Home Mission Board of the Southern Baptist Convention stated that the "race problem . . . will be found of easy solution." Although recognizing that its own work was not yet as expansive or effective as it should be, these particular Southern Baptists were extremely confident about the future. "We do not hesitate to affirm our confident belief that an expenditure . . . of fifty thousand dollars a year for the next ten years will settle this race question forever."[8]

Actually, the positive influence of the Southern Baptist denomination on the race issue was extremely slight. With the vast majority of its members antagonistic to anything that smacked of social Christianity, Southern Baptists began their march to become by the mid-twentieth century the largest Protestant denomination in America by emphasizing the Bible, personal Christianity, and evangelism. At the same time, the Southern Baptists eschewed anything that ran counter to conservative cultural mores. A recent history of the social attitudes of Southern Baptists has demonstrated that the Social Gospel was present among an articulate minority of Baptists, but in its earliest influence it was directed toward such issues as temperance, labor, and agricultural reform and not toward race.[9]

Any meaningful Southern Baptist action toward blacks was hobbled by strong sectional feelings. In the early 1890s attempts at cooperation with northern Baptists in efforts to educate blacks in the South seemingly came to an agreement at the Fortress Monroe Conference of 1894. Some Southern Baptist state conventions refused to go along with the cooperative scheme. The end result was that any possible programs were left to the state conventions, and here the program ended.[10]

Black Baptists were not appreciative of these two white bodies making comity agreements about them without their participation and vote. Although black Baptists had been open to the initiatives of white Baptists, in these years of the advent of Jim Crow they were losing patience. Precisely during these years black Baptists evidenced stiffening resolve to the patterns of subservience under which they were expected to operate. At the annual meetings of the Southern Baptist Convention, black pastors in the host city customarily invited white Baptists to preach in their pulpits. When the convention met in Atlanta in 1892 and Washington, D.C., in 1895, black ministers decided to invite only those whites who would extend a reciprocal invitation to preach in their churches. Under those conditions no white ministers accepted.[11]

The black Baptist response to the Fortress Monroe agreements was "manifest more in action than in rhetoric." Reaction helped unify the often divided black leadership. In what James M. Washington has called "the other Atlanta Compromise," delegates from separate black organizations met in Atlanta in September 1895, to try to form a national denomination. Fresh from hearing Booker T. Washington's "Atlanta Compromise" address at the Cotton States Exposition, Baptists from across the country hammered out the framework for the National Baptist Convention. What now became the largest black church in America was a testimony to "the renewal of corporate self-confidence" among black Baptist leaders. Born precisely in the years when white and black Baptists "hurled invectives at one another," this new denomination consolidated the gains of blacks and became a forum for placing more demands upon whites.[12]

Southern Methodists took a more open stance toward church involvement in social issues. As a denomination, however, they were not much in advance of the Baptists on the issue of justice for blacks. The Methodist Episcopal Church, South, was formed in 1845 after a bitter controversy with their northern brothers and sisters over the right of the church to take direct action in the case of slavery. In the period of Reconstruction and thereafter, bitter feelings continued on the part of the southern Methodists in face of what they deemed to be intrusions on the part of the Methodist Episcopal Church, which came into the South after 1865 to work largely but not exclusively with blacks. For its own part the Methodist Episcopal Church, South, believed that it was discharging its obligations to its former slave constituents by giving its official blessing to the Colored Methodist Episcopal Church, established in 1870.[13] This verbal blessing was for the most part empty when it came to deeds. The General Conference of 1882 did vote to establish Paine Institute for black Methodists, but financial support for the institution did not prove forthcoming.

The various Methodist periodicals in the South provide a good index of the sentiment of Methodists during these years. The editors of the more prominent periodicals more often than not became the bishops of the church. The general organ of the Methodist Episcopal Church, South, was the *Nashville Christian Advocate*. In 1890 a new editor, Elijah Embree Hoss, came to the Nashville paper. Within months after assuming his post, Hoss went to great lengths to defend slavery against a northern editorial arguing that the present plight of blacks was but the natural result of being forced to live under generations of bondage. As a fraternal delegate to the 1892 General Conference of the northern Methodist Church, which passed a strong resolution aimed to prevent lynching and other injustices against blacks, Hoss criticized the resolution and the general attitudes of the northerners who stood up for blacks. In a typical editorial in 1895, Hoss defended the right of blacks to "life, liberty, and the pursuit of happiness" but then concluded that as far as he could see, blacks were going to remain the lowliest of workers for a long time to come.[14] In the aftermath of the race riot of 1898 in Wilmington, North Carolina, Hoss prognosticated about the future of blacks in the South.

> We have no trace of ill will against our colored fellow citizens. On the contrary, we wish to see them prosper in material and spiritual things. On every occasion we have, without stint, denounced all harsh and unjust methods of treating them. We are glad to see them get property, acquire knowledge, and advance in every way. But we record it as our sober judgment that they will not in a thousand years reach that level of intelligence and that stability of character which will make them the equals man for man of the white race. They will never again have a controlling influence in the Southern states. That question is settled.[15]

The story of the southern Presbyterians must be seen also within the context of denominational lines drawn over the issue of slavery. In 1837 Presbyterians split along Old School and New School lines. The division was forged over issues of theology and polity, but in addition the Old School party made common cause with proslavery sentiment in the South. Southern representation continued in both communions, but slavery divided the New Schoolers in 1858, and the outbreak of hostilities in 1861 finally rent the Old Schoolers. After the war the Presbyterian Church in the United States continued as a separate southern denomination and by 1890 embraced nearly 400,000 members. The record is clear that, with rare exceptions, the southern Presbyterians did little for blacks and almost nothing with them.[16] By the 1890s southern Presbyterian efforts were even less than in previous decades.[17]

This story of overt and silent racism was not the whole story. At this same time, and within these same churches, there existed a vocal minority committed to the cause of racial reform. Demonstrating different degrees of orthodoxy on the question of white supremacy, these persons were nevertheless dissenters from a society bent on undoing every vestige of Reconstruction. According to the vigor of their dissent, criticism or ostracism was their reward. Insofar as one can understand the basis of their dissent, it seems never to have been an isolated phenomenon related only to the issue of race but rather was part of a larger reform instinct that often can be staked out as part of an incipient southern social Christianity.

When Atticus Greene Haygood was elevated as bishop of the Methodist Episcopal Church, South, in 1890, his election was an encouragement to blacks and a testimony to the esteem in which he was held by whites. He was elected bishop as he was concluding nearly a decade of service as general agent of the John F. Slater Fund, a northern philanthropic endowment for black education. From 1880 until the early 1890s Haygood was the leading southern clerical leader working for and with the person whom he addressed fraternally in his most famous publication, *Our Brother in Black.*

During Haygood's early career in the church, there was nothing to distinguish his thinking and action from other southern ministers. Born in 1839, Haygood participated in the Civil War as a chaplain in the Confederate army. In the 1870s, already a church leader, he spoke out against the meddling of northern Methodists in southern affairs, particularly the South's handling of the race problem.[18] In 1876 he was elected president of Emory College, then located at Oxford, Georgia. From 1878 to 1882 he was at the same time editor of the *Wesleyan Christian Advocate.*

For reasons that are not altogether clear, Haygood underwent a decisive change in his position about blacks in 1880. This new attitude was enunciated in a Thanksgiving sermon delivered at Oxford: "The New South: Gratitude, Amendment, Hope." He echoed Henry W. Grady and others in expressing gratitude, not regret, for the new situation in which the South found itself. Haygood was grateful for the abolition of slavery, but his central theme was a call for a sober reappraisal of the South in all its strengths and weaknesses. Rising above the understandably defensive spirit of many, he spoke of a new way to his own people. "Let us of the South frankly recognize some of our faults and lacks, and try to reform and improve."[19]

Haygood's remarks were printed by the Methodist congregation at Oxford and read by the New York philanthropist George A. Seney. Without revealing his identity, Seney arranged to have ten thousand additional copies of the sermon printed. These copies brought Haygood to the attention of a national audience.[20]

Within two months Haygood was finishing *Our Brother in Black*. The author was under no illusions. On the night that he finished his book, he wrote to a friend, Eugene R. Hendrix, president of Central College in Missouri, who three decades later became the first president of the Federal Council of Churches. Reflecting on the New South sermon, the present, and the future, Haygood wrote:

> I rec'd scores of letters—nearly all from "the North" about Thanksgiving sermon. . . . Not a line from so-called "leaders" in the church. What is to become of us! It nearly breaks my heart to see men so blind and deaf—to their age—they stand—serenely winking at each other and back at 1844— While the very ground under their feet is going down—Fatuity.[21]

Our Brother in Black was aimed at a wide audience. There were criticisms of northern activism and hypocrisy, but also praise for northern benevolence personified in the representatives of the northern missionary societies. Discussing the vexing problem of northern school teachers in the South, Haygood ventured the opinion, "The worst fault of the Southern people since the war in relation to the Negro's education has not been that they themselves have done so little, but that they have not more cordially cooperated with those who were able to do great things and were trying hard to do them."[22]

Haygood had praise also for the South, or certainly the New South. The theme was sounded again and again of a new, progressive spirit and of the many changes that had taken place since 1865. Certainly this was Haygood's best estimate of the present situation, but his comments here and elsewhere were intended to encourage two groups that needed to be in closer cooperation. Haygood wanted to affirm and encourage those representatives of the New South honestly interested in the uplift of southern blacks. At the same time, he wanted to assure and encourage northern leaders that there was a new spirit and that their continued influence and financial resources would be welcome in the South.

On a number of points Haygood was certainly not new, but rather quite orthodox. He espoused what George M. Fredrickson has called "romantic racialism," meaning a belief in racial differences but not necessarily racial inferiority. Often this romantic racialism characterized blacks as possessing a warm emotional spirit, peculiarly open to Christianity. In his writings Haygood spoke of racial characteristics. He mentioned an inability of blacks to discipline and to organize their lives, particularly their labors. Their use of money could be compared to that of children who spent as if there were no tomorrow. What about the origin and permanence of these characteristics? "Their weaknesses are

perhaps partly in their blood; they may well be more in their antecedents."[23] Haygood seemed genuinely uncertain about this subject. In the
matter of the schoolhouse, Haygood believed that educational uplift
could and would be accomplished within a dual school system. This
policy would be best for both races and was quite openly a policy based
on the peculiar southern situation. No moral or theological principle
was at issue: "Right or wrong, wise or foolish, this is a fact."[24]

It was not the orthodox statements, however, that were appropriated
by the public, north and south, black and white. The very title *Our
Brother in Black* was an affront and a hope. Haygood was not thinking
in biological categories. Brotherhood was not so much scientific but a
reality that proceeded logically, whether Haygood or others liked it or
not, from the God who was Creator and Father. Haygood was not really
specific in pushing toward the implications of that brotherhood, apart
from the fact that he knew that a man needed to be educated in order
to be fully a man. But the Georgia Methodist, as he told his friend, was
ready to be a brother whatever the cost might be.

In the months that followed, Haygood was called "Nigger bishop"
(he was not yet a bishop) and "Nigger college president." Opposition
to Haygood's sentiments was voiced widely in white church meetings
and publications. Southern pulpits once open to him were now closed.[25]

In the late fall of 1881 a New England lecture tour brought a very
different response. In sixteen addresses Haygood reiterated themes
from *Our Brother in Black.* There were some criticisms of the North, as
at Tremont Temple in Boston when Haygood declared that it was northern pressure that forced upon blacks the ballot before they were able to
exercise the franchise responsibly. But the greater emphasis was a call
for a new intersectionalism to replace the bitter sectionalism of the recent past.[26] Partly through these contacts with northern church leaders,
educators, and philanthropists, Haygood was invited to become general
agent for the Slater Fund in 1882.

As general agent, Haygood was in the employ of a secular foundation, but the Slater resources were directed to black schools that had
been founded largely by northern Protestant denominations. Haygood's
own preferences for schools that were adding industrial education and
training to their curriculum helped to channel the flow of Slater money
in that direction. During these years major grants were given to the
fledgling Tuskegee Institute and its new president, Booker T. Washington. Regular grants were also given to Clark and Spelman in Atlanta
and Tougaloo in Mississippi. In 1891 in his final report to the Slater

Fund trustees, Haygood continued to think highly of this approach and to defend the progress blacks were making because of it.[27]

Within his own denomination Haygood was a vigorous advocate of the action of the General Conference of 1882 in establishing Paine Institute for black Methodists. After seven months of working in behalf of Paine "with small success," he asked in an address at Monteagle, Tennessee:

> Did the General Conference mean anything by the action it took on the subject of Negro education in Nashville, Tennessee, in May 1882? If so, what did it mean? It is incredible that we should have in this history a case of conscience like this: too much conscience to repudiate a duty, but not enough to do it—just enough to use good words.[28]

Later in the year Haygood pleaded for financial support for the new institution and rebuked his fellow white Methodists for their past and present inaction. Reviewing the beginnings of the Colored Methodist Episcopal Church, he reminded southern Methodists that their benevolence in turning over church facilities to the new black denomination was really only the disposal of properties that could not be used and were not worth selling. Surveying the thirteen years since the Colored Methodist Episcopal Church came into existence, Haygood concluded that almost no tangible aid had been afforded this fledgling institution. The attitude of white Methodists could only be compared to the Genesis story of Hagar and her son, Ishmael, being driven into the wilderness. The present judgment on white Methodists was that there were funds for white education but very little for the brother in black. Haygood called upon the white church to make its intentions clear. "We block the way of the colored church with our words." The solution was to get going or get out of the way and let others, even if they were from the North, lend a hand. "If we send 'Hagar' into the wilderness, we must not complain if God sends an angel to take her up. But it will be a shame forever to Abraham and all his house."[29]

This article touched off a series of rejoinders that filled the *Nashville Christian Advocate* pages for the next two months. Charles W. Miller, of Lexington, Kentucky, accused Haygood of the kind of exaggeration that was typical of the old abolitionism and the new negrophilism. Equating Haygood's posture with that of a recent northern Methodist missionary to the South, Miller stated that the southern church "does not desire to have any Gilbert Havenism on the Negro question thrust upon her." Another correspondent surely summed up the opinions of many when he said of Haygood: "He is an aggressive thinker and talker, and is sometimes less than just to himself, and sometimes unjust to his race and section. He has been severely criticized."[30]

Criticism did not deter Haygood from restating his beliefs. In 1889 *Our Brother in Black* was reissued, with a final section answering some of the questions and charges made in the intervening eight years. Not shying away from old issues, in the new chapter Haygood answered a frequent comment by saying, "If any shall answer me, 'If Northern people had only kept their hands off, Southern people would have done this work,' I must reply, and sorrowfully enough, 'You will have extraordinary difficulty in giving reasons for your belief.'"[31]

Depending on his audience, Haygood had a different emphasis. His letter to the Lake Mohonk Conference in 1890 tried to present to a largely northern group a positive view of what the South was doing. To some groups he defended the New South's efforts, but to other audiences he dissented from prevailing policies and programs. An inner consistency that grew within him from his years with the Slater Fund was the desire to heal the chasm between the two sections of the nation.

It is worth asking what kind of theological stance informed Haygood's reform interests. For the most part the Georgia Methodist was orthodox and rather uncomplicated. It is worth noting, though, how Haygood utilized the theological themes of a developing social Christianity when he attempted to relate theology to action. As the United States senator from Georgia, Patrick A. Walsh, observed, Haygood began from a creed of the fatherhood of God and the brotherhood of man. Haygood reiterated again and again that it was the brotherhood growing out of an appreciation of the kingdom of God that was the foundation for his solidarity with the oppressed brother in black. The other side of his commitment to a worldly religion can be seen in his frequent warnings against the kind of religion that was a ticket to heaven at the expense of involvement in the world. In this light he battled the holiness movement within his own denomination because he saw in it tendencies toward inwardness, legalism, and divisiveness.[32]

In addition to race relations and education, his reform interests included prohibition. In the 1880s he was a leading speaker at numerous prohibitionist meetings. Unlike some on the prohibitionist circuit his arguments did not turn on legalism or hatred of the liquor merchant. In common cause with progressives taking up this fight, Haygood focused on "the neglected classes" who were the victims of drink. From a religious perspective, he told an Augusta audience, the "occassional drunkard" was better than the "self-centered, self-satisfied Pharisee."[33] In 1887 he was one of two speakers on prohibition at the Evangelical Alliance Convention in Washington, D.C., the first of what have been called "the three most significant conferences ever held in the United States in the interest of social Christianity."[34]

Education, however, was the primary vehicle of reform for Haygood. His own self-understanding of his gifts can be seen in the exceptional act of turning down his ordination as a bishop in the Methodist Episcopal Church, South, in 1882, so that he might continue as president of Emory College and, in addition, take up the duties as Slater general agent. Committed to uplift by means of education, Haygood, as agent of the Slater Fund, was reluctant to push for racial reform in other spheres.

On balance, Haygood was a curious mixture of old and new on the race question. Joel Williamson is on the mark in describing Haygood as a paternalist. This attitude is explained in part by his background and mentors. Haygood was the son of a slaveowner noted for his kindness to his slaves. He was the protégé of Bishop George F. Pierce, who had admonished masters to treat their slaves well. Haygood had grown up in close intimacy with slaves, his own tutelage entrusted to a male slave. Williamson suggests that some white southerner leaders seemed to get an odd delight that one of their own was doing a job that they themselves did not want to do.[35]

But Haygood could also go beyond paternalism. Even though Haygood has been identified with the New South leaders, on the race question he was in the minority as over against the majority, led by Henry W. Grady, the leading spokesman for the New South. Paul Gaston is correct in showing that Grady and the majority, thinking of themselves as realists, involved themselves in intellectual contradictions that would surface by the end of the century. On the one hand they said they affirmed a real place for blacks in the New South. But despite their affirmation in the 1880s of the franchise and their support of industrial education, their deepest message was that blacks would always occupy the lower rungs in society. They would, in other words, always exist in a subservient condition.[36]

Haygood, on the other hand, envisioned a more open future. Industrial education was the beginning, but it was not the end as far as black possibilities. Haygood was a dissenter from the New South realism that consigned southern blacks forever to political subservience. Haygood was one of the few who thought "in terms of temporary political subservience and could imagine a different kind of racial pattern

existing at some time in the future."[37] He supported industrial education as a beginning but not as an end. He worked hard for Paine Institute as the Methodist expression of commitment to new possibilities for
blacks. His work on behalf of Paine set him against the sentiments of
Pierce and his own protégé and friend Bishop Warren A. Candler. Haygood was raising his voice just at the time as other voices were being
lowered. The "Nigger bishop" felt the full brunt of criticism from lifelong white friends in the South. Among blacks he was hailed as one
who understood their plight and aspirations. As for the North, especially among "early Protestant converts to the social gospel, Dr. Haygood by 1885 was considered to be the foremost friend of the Negro
among native Southerners."[38]

The most militant southern voice to be heard on the race question
in this period belonged to a churchman. George Washington Cable
achieved national literary fame for his writings on the Creoles of old
New Orleans. With the publication of Old Creole Days (1879), a book of
short stories, and The Grandissimes (1880), a novel, Cable became the
leading southern author in these years. Moving into the lecture circuits,
he was second probably only to Samuel Clemens in fame. Clemens and
Cable appeared together in some famous tours. Precisely at the point
of his greatest popularity, Cable jeopardized his literary and lecturing
career with his increasingly outspoken words about race relations to
both secular and church audiences.

Cable grew up in New Orleans in a slaveholding family. In an unpublished autobiographical statement, he described himself on the eve
of the Civil War as "reeking with patriotism of the strongest pro-slavery
type." In the years following the war, Cable was "unable to reconcile
the treatment of blacks with Christian principles." Through study of
the Scriptures and contemporary literature, participation in a debating
society, and personal contact with the freedmen, he began to question
his earlier assumptions.

In 1875, as a reporter for the New Orleans Picayune, he was assigned
to write a story on public schools in which black and white pupils sat
side by side. Later in the year, when a mass meeting was held in La-
fayette Square to protest this system, Cable wrote a letter to the New
Orleans Bulletin, a leading supporter of the rally. The published letter
was pragmatic in substance, decrying the emotional heat over the issue
and calling for the light of fair play and magnanimity. He wrote a second letter, but the editor declined to publish it.[39]

Cable's next public utterance on the subject was before the New Orleans Sunday School Association in 1881. It was not surprising that he spoke on this subject before a group of church workers, for the church had been the source of both frustration and liberation in the evolution of Cable's thinking. Cable was a Sunday school teacher in the Prytania Street Presbyterian Church in New Orleans. At age twenty-five he had been asked to take charge of the new mission school of the congregation, and this experience proved to be "a workshop for practical Christianity." He and his wife continued in this task for fifteen years. In 1882 he was elected a deacon in the church. In these years Cable was undergoing a shift in religious orientation because of the need for a clean break with a religious conservatism that in one era constructed a biblical defense for slavery and, after emancipation, adopted a continuing racist stance toward the rights of the freedmen. To the assembled Sunday school teachers Cable expressed his present convictions about white-black relations in terms of the parable of the Good Samaritan. The Samaritans were an inferior and outcast race as far as the Jews were concerned. And what about the black "Samaritans in their midst?" "Do we love *this neighbor* as ourselves?" Cable asked. "Do we run great risks both with and for him? Do we give him our seat in God's house? Or do we tell him to go to the gallery? When he makes his peace with God, does he take the blessed cup and break bread with us or after us?"[40]

The South's pride in Cable's literary success turned to wrath as a result of a commencement address he delivered at the University of Alabama in 1884. It was published the following January in the *Century Magazine* as "The Freedman's Case in Equity." The springboard for Cable's remarks was an incident that had occurred the previous year as he was traveling by train to Louisville. Cable witnessed an immaculately dressed black woman and her daughter compelled by law to be in the same car with a group of chained convicts. If she had been a nurse to a white child, she would have been riding instead in a nearly empty car reserved for whites only. The lesson of this incident was that the freedman was not actually free. In a direct attack on southern racial policy, Cable described the extralegal situation existing before the legal advent of Jim Crow. In the midst of talk about the New South,

> The adherent of the old regime stands in the way to every public privilege and place—steamer landing, railway platform, theater, concert hall, art display, public library, public school, courthouse, church, everything—flourishing the hot branding iron of ignominious distinctions.[41]

With these words Cable stepped beyond Haygood and others who as dissenters were still operating within the context of the separation of the races in public meeting places, including the school and the church. Although Cable mentioned the undoing of the Civil Rights Act of 1875 by the Supreme Court, the tenor of his remarks did not have to do with laws as much as with moral and ethical principles. Cable wanted to point up the hypocrisy of all talk of freedom when such bondage still existed. He believed that by speaking out strongly now he could sensitize and affirm "thousands of Southern-born white men and women . . . who see the wrong and folly of these things, silently blush for them, and withhold their open protests only because their belief is unfortunately stronger in the futility of their counsel than in the power of a just cause."[42]

Cable was now in the middle of a raging controversy. The *Century* received a flood of letters about his article, mostly from the South, and nearly all critical. As a response to this vast majority of the mail, the *Century* asked Henry W. Grady to reply to Cable. Grady's rambling remarks were not up to Cable's logic or prose but simply reiterated the conviction that the races would forever remain apart because of racial instinct and social custom.[43]

It should be noted that Cable's article apparently helped to elicit an article by Thomas U. Dudley, Episcopal bishop of Kentucky. Born and educated in Virginia, Dudley pleaded for changes in the midst of what he described as a worsening situation. He characterized segregation on trains and in public meeting places as "flagrant wrongs." Commending Cable and quoting from him throughout, Dudley culminated his own remarks with an attack upon the "cruel prejudice" of segregation in the churches. Dudley said he saw no problem in paying rent for pews or assigning seats for particular people, but such customs were something quite different from refusing entrance to a man because his face was black. Dudley appealed to the sacredness of the person as the theological foundation for action. "Your manhood is your right to enter—*if only your face is white.* Is this just? Is this equitable? Above all, is this Christian?"[44]

Later in 1885 what began as Cable's brief answer to Grady became a full essay and then a book, *The Silent South.* The title indicated another appeal to a body of southern people who agreed with Cable but who had been heretofore tragically silent. In this volume Cable took great pains to praise the South and speak of his fidelity to her virtues. He particularly wanted to set the record straight on the issue of civil rights and social privilege. Social equality was always a matter of personal

choice as opposed to a civil right based on impersonal law. "Social
Equality is a fool's dream. The present writer wants quite as little of it
as the most fervent traditionist of the most fervent South." Recognizing
Cable's traditional stance, however, some later critics have missed his
hidden agenda in emphasizing such distinctions. By identifying with
the white South's concern about social equality, he wished to emphasize
his central thrust for equality. He was afraid that some people "beg the
question of equity, and suppress a question of civil right by simply
calling it 'social intermingling.'"[45] Cable's strategy was to refrain from
quoting blacks directly, differing in this respect from Haygood. He did
not use specific examples that might add an undue emotional tone. He
emphasized moral principles as over against laws. Cable was hopeful
that this approach would encourage "the Silent South" to stand up and
to make its voice heard.

For a variety of reasons Cable left the South for New England in
1884, finally settling in Northampton, Massachusetts. Cable had been
an active Presbyterian, but Congregationalism was the branch of the
Reformed tradition that predominated in New England. Cable joined
the Edwards Congregational Church. He soon organized a Bible study
class within the congregation. In 1887 he was engaged to teach a weekly
class for Bible study on Saturday afternoons at the Tremont Temple in
Boston. The class prospered under Cable's leadership, so that it was
soon averaging two thousand participants each week. For fifteen
months he continued in this effort, but finally the difficulty of the weekly commuting forced him to give it up. In the meantime the Edwards
Church class was growing, so much that new quarters outside the
church had to be found. The city hall was secured, the class opened to
the entire community, and soon between four hundred and seven
hundred were attending each week.[46] Lyman Abbott took note of these
efforts by Cable and devoted an article in the *Christian Union* to "Mr.
Cable and His Church Work." Abbott commended the writer and
churchman for both his Bible study and humanitarian emphasis.[47]

Through these years Cable had hesitated to attack segregation in the
church because he believed many church people would support basic
rights for blacks but would never accept integrated churches. In 1889
his new denomination, the Congregational church, had to face up to
this issue. In the late 1880s separate white and black associations developed in Georgia and Alabama. In 1889 the all-white Georgia association asked for recognition at the triennial meeting of the National
Council of Congregational Churches. The more liberal Congregational
churches had been as straightforward as any on "the Negro question."

There were few Congregational churches in the South, but the Congregationalist American Missionary Association, in establishing new churches after the war, espoused a policy of open membership that produced numbers of mixed congregations. But now, in Georgia and Alabama, local southern custom was being wedded to the fundamental Congregational belief in the local autonomy of the churches. After vigorous debate separate delegations were recognized at the National Council meeting. Cable protested vehemently. In reply to the argument that it was better to keep the church together for the larger purpose of unity and harmony, he wrote:

> As in all such cases, so in this, we shall doubtless be told that an unflinching adherence to principle will result in jeopardizing the efficiency, even the existence, of a large number of churches. Our answer must be that in the scheme of the world's salvation, not the life, or numerical or financial prosperity of one or another church, but the maintenance and spread of the Divine Master's teachings *in their integrity* is the supreme necessity and command; and it is as true for a church as for the individual, "He that loveth his life loseth it."[48]

In 1892 in the next meeting the all-white Alabama association applied for recognition, but this time the National Council did not seat either delegation and advised the black and white associations to unite.[49]

Cable's words did not go unnoticed by blacks. After a speech on racism in the church and nation, Cable received a letter from a young W. E. B. Du Bois. The college student commended Cable. "I cannot refrain from writing you a word to express my deep appreciation for your recent Boston words in behalf of me and my people. In the midst of so much confusion and misapprehension, the clear utterance and moral heroism of one man is doubly welcome to the young Negro who is building a nation."[50]

After recommending that Booker T. Washington and other black leaders be invited to the Lake Mohonk Conference on the Negro Question in 1890, Cable received a letter from Washington thanking him for his efforts. "Were it possible for any action of yours to increase my respect and love for you, your position in this matter would certainly do so many fold."[51]

How do we understand the pilgrimage of Cable, who was esteemed by blacks and criticized by whites? Three observations are in order. First, Cable had the capacity to learn from his expanding experiences. His observations in the New Orleans schools in the 1870s first challenged his assumptions about the relations between blacks and whites. His provocative essay "The Freedman's Case in Equity" was triggered by an experience on the train to Louisville. A secret of his success as a novelist was that his short stories and novels were not simply written in the study but were created out of his interaction with real-life situations. The power in his words is his ability to get inside the experiences of his characters. Even in his early writings about the Creoles, he wrestled with the relationships between blacks and whites. In and through his characters we see Cable trying to understand white behavior toward blacks. The question Cable asked was, Why do whites need servile blacks? He saw behind the cries for white supremacy a deep fear when relationships were fluid or undefined. What whites really wanted, just as they wanted before the Civil War, was a relationship of master and servant. We hear in the words of Clemence, a slave character in *The Grandissimes*, that whites need servile blacks "fo' dey own cyumfut." Cable does not finally answer *why* whites need this mastery of blacks. But his probing went further than his contemporaries who reacted angrily against him.[52]

The second observation focuses on the Christian faith as the root of meaning in his life. These experiences forced Cable to reexamine his own purposes, which were deeply rooted in the Christian faith. Cable was a product of the Reformed tradition. Wherever he went, New Orleans or Northampton, he was deeply involved in a local congregation, either Presbyterian or Congregational. The center of his faith was the Bible. He returned to the Bible to wrestle with the proslavery and antislavery arguments he heard around him. He taught the Bible in what evidently was a compelling way, as the large crowds in Boston and Northampton demonstrated. But he went beyond proof text to the spirit of the text in interpreting the Bible for today. No less a Social Gospeler than Lyman Abbott commented on the power of Cable to link Bible study to contemporary life and problems.

Cable was a strict Presbyterian in his life-style. He did not smoke, drink, or gamble. Samuel Clemens (Mark Twain) put a portrait of Cable in his home in Hartford, but the two could not have been more different in life-style. We understand that Clemens was bothered by Cable's Puritan ways but recognized that this man was authentic and not the hypocrite that he was fond of satirizing.

Cable thus combined a rather orthodox theology and strict behavioral norms with what can only be called liberal views on race. This is an unusual combination in any age, but especially so at the end of the nineteenth century.

Third, it is important to chart Cable's pilgrimage from outrage to literary dissent to involvement in organizational reform. We can see his commitment to reform on two fronts: education and the church.

Although Cable tried to arrange an invitation for Booker T. Washington to attend the Lake Mohonk Conference, shortly thereafter he seems to have reevaluated the Washingtonian philosophy. Addressing the American Missionary Association later in 1890, Cable criticized black leaders who put in the mouths of their followers phrases such as: "All we want is education. All we want it for is to make ourselves better laborers and servants." He did not name names but rather invoked a litany of ideas that, although by then becoming commonplace among both blacks and whites, were most closely associated with Washington. "Give us but ample free schools, and we will waive all civil and political equality of rights and consent to be, not Americans, but only Africans in America."[53]

His disenchantment with Washington's approach is evident as well in his decision to decline invitations to speak in behalf of Tuskegee at Boston meetings in 1894 and 1897. As one scholar has noted, Cable thought "Washington was making compromises the Negro could not afford to make."[54]

The church was also making compromises. Cable not only had roots in the church but in these years finally surmounted his reluctance to speak to the church.[55] He had addressed the Sunday school teachers in New Orleans in the 1870s, but he stayed out of national church politics until moving to New England in the 1880s. Even as he was being criticized for abandoning a full-fledged literary career by dabbling in reform, it is now possible to see his involvement moving from words to actions. He threw himself into the debate about the seating of churches from Georgia and Alabama at the National Council of Congregational Churches.

His hopes for and criticisms of the church are reflected in his 1890 address to the American Missionary Association. He was particularly disturbed that so many in the North were content to accept uncritically the South's version of what it was doing to solve the southern problem. His own opinion was that the sum total of "the religious and educational work done by the Southern Protestant churches among the destitute millions of colored people of their states is positively too small to be counted." Distrustful of the acquiescence of black and white leaders to an accommodationist posture, Cable again championed full political equality for blacks.

He concluded his remarks with a call for the involvement of a politically energized church. The last sentence of his address summed up his longings: he wanted black citizens one day to be able to say, "It was the church of Christ that first brought us this deliverance."[56]

Throughout these years George Washington Cable spoke often of a "Silent South," a body of responsible citizens that would rise up to support the courageous few who had taken the lead on "the Negro question." The most apt commentary, however, on this silent force was contained in a letter from Albion W. Tourgée to a black leader in 1890: "Mr. Cable's 'Silent South' is a silent humbug—and always will be silent."[57] If Tourgée's terse evaluation of the silent followers was accurate, it is striking to realize that the voices of these articulate dissenters from southern racial policies fell silent also within the short span of a few years in the 1890s. With Jim Crow emerging and pressure from the North diminishing, there were casualties in the ranks of those who once supported the struggle for equality for black Americans.

George Washington Cable was a chief casualty. By 1890 he was more radical and equalitarian than other native southerners, but his voice was loudest just before he stopped speaking, after the early nineties. After the completion of his novel *John March, Southerner*, in 1894, Cable seldom mentioned "the Negro question," even though he lived for three more decades and continued to visit and write about the South. His interest in many reforms continued, but his silence about the race issue, probably the result of despair at not finding any solution in sight, has not been fully explained by himself or his biographers.

Atticus Greene Haygood was elected a bishop in 1890, but his diocese was faraway California. There was conjecture that his outspoken views on race relations was a chief reason behind his removal from the South. He moved his family to Los Angeles in 1891. His charge also included Mexico, and while traveling there, he contracted a disease that started a downward spiral of his health. He returned to the South in 1893 in a weakened condition and died in January 1896.

A measure of the esteem in which Haygood was held by blacks in the South was demonstrated in interracial services in his memory. Bishop Robert S. Williams of the Colored Methodist Episcopal Church participated in a service in which over 250 blacks joined with whites in an impressive tribute. The following month the largest church in Atlanta was "filled to overflowing" by blacks and whites. Henry H. Proctor, black pastor of the First Congregational Church, said succinctly, "He loved us, and we loved him." Professor Crogman of Clark University noted that "Bishop Haygood found the South discussing whether or not the Negro should be educated, and left it discussing how he should be educated." Crogman concluded, "He was our friend, the truest, bravest, staunchest, most pronounced friend that has yet arisen for us on Southern soil."[58]

Albion W. Tourgée, who liked to identify himself with the South, refused any retreat from radicalism. But in the end he was forced into inactivity as well. The most outspoken advocate of black rights, south and north, his efforts were not to know much success. And now he found himself impoverished and in ill health. A reprieve of sorts came in 1897, when he was appointed consul at Bordeaux, France, as a reward for past efforts for the Republican party. Tourgée received mail from the South expressing regret that Bordeaux was not even farther away and expressing the hope that George Washington Cable might soon join him there.[59]

Discouraged by the lack of any real solution to "the Negro question," he was not disinterested. In 1898 he followed with dismay reports of the race riot in Wilmington, North Carolina, which boiled up as the aftermath of a racially charged election. The nation had become accustomed to the lynching of the poor and, so it was said, criminal elements of the black population. At Wilmington the victims of a white attack were elected officials, law officers, newspaper editors, and prosperous businessmen. In faraway Bordeaux, Consul Tourgée read of what was transpiring at Wilmington and wrote to President McKinley, "Every day I have grown less and less hopeful with regard to the outcome."[60]

In all his struggles Tourgée had looked to Christian forces, if not always to the churches, to bring political and social salvation to blacks. Now Tourgée's disillusionment was rife as he speculated, as only he could, about the possibility of Christ's second coming being in the form of a black person. What would be the response of white America? In Tourgée's estimation it "would disintegrate and destroy the Christian churches of the United States. Then indeed, might it be written, 'He came to His own and His own received Him not.'"[61]

As this chapter has tried to make clear, the story of a growing racism in the South in the 1880s and 1890s was not the whole story. A vocal minority dissented from the societal rush to undo every hated aspect of Reconstruction. Committed to various aspects of racial reform, these individuals were nourished by an incipient Social Gospel.

CHAPTER 5

A Missionary Education Bridge

To the mass of the Southern people he is not yet regarded as a free man, but as a "freed Negro," and in every relation of life he is to be accorded, not the privileges of a man, but those of a Negro. They love the Negro, thousands of them with a tender regard, but they love him "in his place"; and that place is a position of servility to the white man.

—WILBUR PATTERSON THIRKIELD

It is a striking reality that men and women often need to travel hundreds or thousands of miles to discover social injustice in their own hometowns. I have sent students to Central America and South Africa and hear them say upon returning how much they learned about the United States. During the civil rights era of the 1950s and 1960s, northern and western students went south to stand up for liberty and justice for blacks. Labeled "outside agitators" in the South, they returned with new eyes to New Jersey and Illinois and California to become more involved in a whole series of social justice causes.

In comparing present and past, I have found myself asking the question, What is the pattern in all this? The appendix contains a biographical chart of persons related to the Social Gospel. It is striking that many of these persons who became involved in the race problem had one factor in common: they either lived or worked in the South at a formative point in their careers. More specifically, most of them became involved through the Negro education movement.

Missionary education was a bridge that connected the Social Gospel with the racial question. The traffic thereon helped educate northern Social Gospel leaders about the problems and aspirations of blacks at a time when more than 90 percent of black Americans were living below the Mason-Dixon Line. As northern men and women enlisted in the campaign to educate the freedmen, the teachers became the students in the schoolhouse of race. As whites were tutored about the race prob-

lem in the South, this education later bore fruit in quite different communities in the North.

It is helpful to understand early on some of the general patterns of
northern church involvement in the South. The story of this missionary
education campaign is meant to serve as a seedbed for the unfolding
biographies of men and women who become interested in racial reform.
Their subsequent patterns of involvement vary greatly, but in asking
the question of motivation, we are repeatedly drawn back to an early,
formative experience with missionary education.

The purpose of this chapter is not so much to retell the fascinating
but complex story of missionary education, which would be beyond the
scope of our present study, but rather to suggest the connections between missionary education and the Social Gospel. Both the major missionary society working in the South and two northern missionary
educators will be utilized as specific case studies. We will follow many
of the the individuals introduced here to their own northern communities, where the further stories of their involvement in racial reform
will be developed in the following decades in subsequent chapters.

It is important to remember how deeply Christian missionary forces
were involved in the beginnings of Negro education in the South. Within a decade after Appomattox, northern missionaries had established
more than a thousand schools in the South for the newly emancipated
freedmen. More than three thousand teachers journeyed south to participate in what for many was both a missionary venture and an educational crusade. Their newly founded schools varied in name and level
between elementary, secondary, and normal schools and academies,
colleges, and universities, but taken together they formed the basis of
education for blacks, especially higher education, until well into the
twentieth century. Missionary and freedmen's aid societies of northern
Protestant churches established more than one hundred institutions devoted to secondary and college education of blacks in the years following the Civil War. Most histories of black education have failed to deal
adequately with the role of these church societies. The stories of various
philanthropic enterprises, such as the George Peabody Fund (founded
in 1867), the John F. Slater Fund (1882), and the Anna T. Jeanes Fund
(1908), are more well known. James M. McPherson, in an important
study that attempts to adjust the balance sheet regarding Negro education, observes, "Before World War I the northern mission societies
founded largely by abolitionists were by far the most important contrib-
utors to Negro higher education."[1]

Leading the way was the American Missionary Association. Organized in 1846 by the union of abolitionist elements in three smaller Congregational societies, the AMA began its work in the South at Fortress Monroe, Virginia, in 1861. It established its first colleges—Fisk at Nashville, and Talladega in Alabama—in 1865. Methodists, Baptists, and Presbyterians made early and significant contributions also.

Within a very few years this early enthusiasm and growth were on the wane. The American Freedmen's Union Commission, an amalgamated league of nondenominational societies led for a while by Lyman Abbott, ceased to exist in 1869. The federal Freedmen's Bureau, many of whose schools were staffed by teachers from the churches, went out of business in 1870. What remained after dissolution and retrenchment were four freedmen's aid societies continuing to carry on major efforts: the American Missionary Association (nominally nondenominational but primarily Congregational), the Freedmen's Aid Society of the Methodist Episcopal Church, the American Baptist Home Mission Society, and the Committee on Missions to Freedmen of the Presbyterian Church in the U.S.A. In addition, there were smaller efforts by the Quakers and United Presbyterians.

Retrenchment did not mean permanent decline. By 1878 a new period of vigorous growth was beginning. Actually the decline was partly to be expected, for the initial crusade for education had been all-embracing, from elementary school through university education. As the states took over education for the lower grades, the societies turned their attention to their secondary schools and colleges. With the return to financial normalcy after the depression of 1873, the major mission societies experienced slow but steady growth in their budgets into the first decade of the twentieth century. By 1889, the combined budgets of the four largest societies surpassed the previous highest income of all the freedmen's aid societies in 1866. The long-term story was even more impressive. Countering the impression that missionary educators began "to melt away" with the collapse of Reconstruction, the records show that the number of colleges and secondary schools multiplied threefold, and the budgets for these societies multiplied more than fourfold by 1915.[2]

In reviewing the story, we must remember that some of the finest black institutions became independent of missionary support but continued to owe much to these same mission societies in terms of ideology, program, and staffing. This relationship was true for Berea College, Hampton Institute, and Atlanta University, schools set free from the American Missionary Association in the 1870s. It was true also for schools with such different histories as Howard University in Washington, D.C., and Leland University in New Orleans.

When schools were established, the question arose immediately about the organization of churches. In the early years the AMA organized churches in addition to schools. Its official policy, in both schools and churches, was openness to persons of both races. In this regard, it differed from its sister Congregational society, the American Home Missionary Society, which organized all-white churches in areas where the AMA was organizing mixed congregations. In actual practice, the Congregational churches founded by the AMA did not attract large numbers of blacks, who seemed more at home in the style of church life afforded by the Baptist and Methodist traditions. After the 1870s, the AMA focused its efforts more exclusively on education.[3]

The American Baptist Home Mission Society faced a different situation. More than half of black church members were Baptists, but nearly all became members of various black Baptist denominations. White northern Baptists contributed financial aid to black southern Baptists while at the same time concentrating their own efforts in the field of education.[4]

The Methodist Episcopal Church was the only northern denomination able to recruit large numbers of southern blacks. The Methodist Freedmen's Aid Society continued to focus on education, but parish efforts were initiated by the Missionary Society and the Church Extension Society. (It is important not to confuse the Methodist Episcopal Church with the Methodist Episcopal Church, South, the two splitting over the slavery issue in 1845.)[5]

Northern Presbyterians also organized black churches in the early years of Reconstruction. The first churches were made up of blacks who had formerly been members of white southern Presbyterian congregations. Much of the work centered in North Carolina. Black membership in the northern Presbyterian church increased from about five thousand in 1870 to approximately thirty thousand in 1915.[6]

Black Presbyterians and black Congregationalists never accounted for more than 1 percent of the total membership of their respective denominations.

The Protestant Episcopal church was the only major denomination with a significant constituency in the South that did not find itself divided by the war. In 1865 a Freedmen's Commission was established, but it was demoted to the status of a subcommittee in 1878. Funds were raised in the South for the work of the commission, but the size of the support was belied by the fact that almost all of it was given by three or four individuals. One must agree that "at no time was the Church solidly behind the Commission."[7]

The impact of the campaign to aid the freedmen spread beyond the foot soldiers who went south to teach. Even as many of the Social Gospelers were the products of an antislavery or abolitionist background, for more than a few these interests continued after the Civil War in the missionary march to the South. This involvement was of varying kinds. Sometimes it meant a direct involvement in the mission societies as teachers or administrators (the career of Lyman Abbott has already been mentioned in this regard). For others it meant serving as pastors in black or mixed congregations. For others it meant supporting these endeavors by serving on the boards and agencies of either the mission societies or the institutions they spawned. This support might mean attending a trustee meeting at Hampton, Atlanta, or Tuskegee. From time to time it involved delivering a commencement address or participating in a special conference.

A first exposure for many came through a unique enterprise of businessman and philanthropist Robert C. Ogden. A New York Presbyterian, Ogden served as president of the board of trustees of Hampton Institute in Virginia. In 1870 he began the practice of taking men and women from the North to the Hampton graduation exercises as his guests in a private railroad car. Later the railroad excursion was expanded to include Fisk and Tuskegee. Each year twenty-five individuals were exposed to black education. As we shall see, many of them returned to serve these same institutions in some governance capacity.

One way to measure the extent and breadth of this involvement is to take note of the many persons related to the Social Gospel who were elected trustees of five of the major black institutions in these years. The list in table 3 is partial, but even so it is suggestive of the broad range of Social Gospelers involved in black education. Some, as trustees of colleges in any era, attended meetings, made financial contributions, and probably did not do much more. But for most of these individuals this service meant an involvement at the very time that interest in black education in many circles in the North was waning.

One distinguished northerner who first went South on one of Robert C. Ogden's train excursions to Hampton Institute was Francis G. Peabody. A professor at Harvard, he was the first teacher of Christian social ethics in the United States. His book *Jesus Christ and the Social Question*, published in 1900, was one of the leading volumes in a whole series of Social Gospel books at the turn of the century. Peabody admitted that when he first visited Hampton he knew little about "the Negro question." Encouraged by Ogden, he became a trustee at Hampton and thus began his education. Many years later he authored *Education for Life: The Story of Hampton Institute*, written for the fiftieth anniversary of this pioneer black institution.

Peabody had learned much in the intervening years. Toward the end of the volume he took the measure of the black students and graduates he had come to know as a trustee. "The Negro race during the last half-century has proved itself capable, under favoring circumstances, of rapid self-development and, in some instances, of distinguished achievements in administrative leadership, in literature, or in art." Peabody noted that although opportunities had been meager for elementary education, "the reduction of illiteracy from 90 percent to 30 percent indicates a progress without parallel in history."[8]

Peabody asked, in conclusion, what the response of the South to this rapid progress would be. Noting the surge of migration to the North, he observed that if "industrial compensation and social justice are more accessible elsewhere," there was no need for blacks to remain

Table 3. Social Gospelers Serving as Trustees in Black Institutions

Institution	Trustee	Institution	Trustee
Atlanta University	Will Alexander	Fisk University	William H. Baldwin
	Amory H. Bradford		William N. DeBerry
	Henry Sloane Coffin		Robert R. Moton
	Chalres Cuthbert Hall		Maude Wilder Trawick
	Atticus G. Haygood		L. Hollingsworth Wood
	James Weldon Johnson		
	M. Ashby Jones	Hampton Institute	Charles Mead
	George L. Paine		Robert C. Ogden
	Willis D. Weatherford		Charles H. Parkhurst
	Richard R. Wright		Francis G. Peabody
			George F. Peabody
Howard University	Harlan Paul Douglass		Albert K. Smiley
	Francis J. Grimké		
	John Hurst	Tuskegee Institute	William H. Baldwin
	Benjamin F. Lee		Charles F. Dole
	Jesse E. Moorland		George A. Gordon
	Benjamin T. Tanner		Charles F. Mason
	Wilbur P. Thirkield		Robert C. Ogden
	Alexander Walters		George F. Peabody

Source: Catalogs from Atlanta, Fisk, Hampton, Howard, and Tuskegee, approximately 1890 to 1920. (Not every catalog was available for every year for each institution.)

in the South. Peabody, assessing all the problems, believed "the remedy is in the hands of the South." What should that remedy be? "It is in the substitution of encouragement for repression, of education for illiteracy, of ownership for dependence, and of statesmanship for politics."[9]

Another index of Social Gospel involvement in this missionary bridge is the people involved in the American Missionary Association, the leading missionary education society after Reconstruction. Among the officeholders were a cadre of Social Gospel leaders. The presidency of the AMA was a largely honorary office until 1902. In that year the president became part of the executive committee and thus was in a position to help give leadership to the organization. Washington Gladden had been elected president in 1901. With a new stature for the presidency in 1902, he was reelected and served in that post until 1904. His story will be told as a case study as chapter 9. Gladden was succeeded by Amory H. Bradford, a Congregational minister from Montclair, also a well-known Social Gospel leader.

At the annual meeting of the American Missionary Association the "annual" sermon was a high point. The person asked to preach to the annual meeting was not only a figure who enjoyed a national esteem but one who had demonstrated support for Negro education. In the list of these preachers in the years between 1895 and 1908, one is struck by how many are identified with the Social Gospel.

1895: William Hayes Ward
1896 (the Jubilee meeting): Lyman Abbott
1898: George A. Gordon
1901: Samuel Parkes Cadman
1903: Philip S. Moxom
1905: Charles M. Sheldon
1907: William R. Hungtington
1908: Henry Churchill King

Other Social Gospelers, such as Josiah Strong and Graham Taylor, addressed these same meetings. Walter Rauschenbusch, silent for so long on the race issue, ventured his first substantial comment on the race question at the annual meeting of 1913.

The involvement of Social Gospelers with the AMA, however catalytic, was mostly part-time. For a few leaders, however, the missionary education bridge meant full-time work in the South. Having examined the AMA as a kind of organizational case study, we will now find it useful to examine the odyssey of two young northern Methodist educators as individual case studies.

Joseph Crane Hartzell exhibited spirited leadership on the race question for more than a quarter of a century in the South. Hartzell was raised in Illinois and educated at Illinois Wesleyan and Garrett Biblical Institute. At age twenty-eight, in 1870, he became pastor of the Ames Chapel in New Orleans precisely because of his interest in what he called race adjustment. The chapel had been organized by northern Methodists, and a small number of blacks attended services. When a new chapel was built in 1868, blacks were restricted to the gallery. With Hartzell's arrival, all restrictions were lifted, although it appears that blacks usually sat in the gallery anyway. When Hartzell left the church, the restrictions were reimposed.[10]

Hartzell left Ames Chapel in 1873 to found the *Southwestern Christian Advocate.* In this post, he believed he could fulfill a more active role in promoting Methodist work among blacks. Hartzell financed the paper from his own funds and served without salary. The paper became an official journal of the church in 1876, although its egalitarian pronouncements rankled Methodists throughout the South. As editor, Hartzell was uncompromising in calling for the abolition of color lines within the Methodist church. He spoke against the segregating of blacks into separate districts within the church. He was for the election of black bishops but not to segregated constituencies.[11]

Joseph Hartzell's wife, Jane, shared her husband's commitment to the black people of New Orleans. She moved among the blacks of the city, discovering needs and marshaling resources. In 1877 she established a day school, Wesley Chapel. By 1879 she was supervising the activities of nine white and five black missionaries. By her appeals to the Methodist General Conference, she helped establish the Women's Home Missionary Society.[12]

After much controversy during his tenure with the newspaper, Joseph Crane Hartzell was moved over to the Methodist Freedmen's Aid Society in 1881, where he worked alongside Richard S. Rust. In 1888 he became the society's secretary. During these years, he was particularly critical of the New South mentality as it was being articulated by Henry W. Grady, editor of the *Atlanta Constitution.* Hartzell tells of a conversation with Grady in the editorial offices of the *Constitution* in which Grady outlined the assumptions of the leaders of the New South "toward the Negro."

1. The absolute supremacy of the white man at all hazards, because he is white and ordained by God to rule.
2. The relegation of the Negro to his God-appointed place as the best interest of society, in the judgment of the white man, may decide.
3. No interference from without.

In response to this blatant racism, Hartzell "remonstrated with him that his position was as un-American and barbarous as the deliverance of Alexander H. Stephens that slavery was to be the cornerstone of the Confederacy."[13]

In the 1890s, some twenty years after founding the *Southwestern Christian Advocate*, Hartzell's sense of urgency about racial reform was not diminished. While the South's own leaders were less vocal in the early nineties, Hartzell continued to speak his mind. In commenting on "a very able" letter sent to the Afro-American Council by Albion Winegar Tourgée in 1893, Hartzell underlined his own sentiments when he reported that Tourgée's "indictment against the American people for their treatment of the Negro was terrific."[14]

As Jim Crow laws were put in place in the 1890s, Hartzell became an outspoken foe. He was particularly upset at the lack of response by the churches to these laws. Speaking of the Jim Crow ordinances on the railroads, Hartzell complained that "not a single religious editor, so far as I know, has spoken a word against this law." After the Interstate Commerce Commission decreed that railroad accommodations must be equal for both races, Hartzell pointed to the heart of the issue as the "injustices of discrimination." Moving beyond the debatable issue as to whether railroad accommodations were equal, Hartzell declared that division of any kind "is un-American and un-Christian."[15]

As a transplanted northerner, what were Hartzell's attitudes about the northern treatment of blacks? He did not spare criticism of the North, but he did see two basic differences. The first concerned the legal basis of discrimination, which was growing in the South. The second concerned public opinion. Hartzell saw that Jim Crow could grow because it merely ratified public opinion, whereas he believed that discrimination in the North, although present, was a minority opinion. He saw the results of this discrimination in the South in the life of the churches when the southern Methodist church had written into the constitution of the Colored Methodist Church the proviso that only colored people could be members.[16]

Hartzell was concerned that "the reactionary wave on the Southern question is touching the Methodist Episcopal Church." He observed that for the northern Methodists there was no problem when "it was a question of sympathy and bread and clothing and a spelling book for the poor freedman just out of bondage." In other words, there was no lack of social concern. But the more fundamental issue in Hartzell's eyes was whether there could be a place for blacks within the church. The missionary education movement was producing men and women of culture and intellect, but the church seemed on the verge of reneging on its earlier promises. Hartzell knew why. "It is the old question of race and color. That is all. Questions of condition and office and recognition are merely excuses." He saw the irony and tragedy of the march of history whereby "now that the condition of the Negro is improved, the renewed efforts of the New South, abetted by the silent North to establish permanently the old law of tyrants as applied to inferiors is infinitely more absurd."[17]

These were courageous words, especially in the years they were spoken. Hartzell learned much about the shape of racism in his years in the South. But one more person was lost to the egalitarian cause in America when Hartzell was named missionary bishop for Africa. The exact reconstruction of the maneuvering that produced Hartzell's election is uncertain. Ironically, it may have been part of a series of moves to assuage black disappointments that year over the defeat of a candidate for bishop. In this context, Hartzell was elected for Africa, and M. C. B. Mason, a black man, was elected to succeed Hartzell as one of two secretaries of the Freedmen's Aid Society.[18]

Hartzell's story is included here, even though, unlike the others mentioned in this chapter, he did not participate in the unfolding story of racial reform in America in the next quarter century. He rendered distinguished service in Africa, but there were not many voices like his in America.

Wilbur Patterson Thirkield exemplified the best qualities of the younger missionary pastors and educators. Born and educated in Ohio, he completed his theological studies at Boston University in 1881. It could be said that Thirkield married racial reform early when he chose to be his bride, Mary Michelle (Mamie) Haven, the daughter of Gilbert Haven, Methodism's fiery abolitionist and racial egalitarian.[19] In 1883 Thirkield was called to Clark University in Atlanta, which Haven had helped to found. Once in Atlanta, Thirkield organized the Gammon School of Theology (now part of the Interdenominational Theological

Center) and served as its first dean. In 1889 Gammon became a separate institution with Thirkield as president.

Thirkield's years in Atlanta were both productive and stormy. Working as a northerner with southern blacks, he sometimes offended southern whites. For example, Thirkield wrote an article for the *New York Christian Advocate* in early 1890 that assayed the changes happening throughout the South. In words reminiscent of his father-in-law, Thirkield observed: "The condition of the races in the South is cause for serious thought, if not for alarm. No such strained relations have existed in twenty years. Since the days of reconstruction, there have not been so many clashings and warrings between the two races." What were the reasons for this crisis? Instead of blaming the North or southern blacks, Thirkield said that the reasons for renewed repression lay ultimately in the southern white understanding of the blacks.

> To the mass of the Southern people he is not yet regarded as a free man, but as a 'freed Negro,' and in every relation of life he is to be accorded, not the privileges of a man, but those of a Negro. They love the Negro, thousands of them with a tender regard, but they love him 'in his place'; and that place is a position of servility to the white man.[20]

This early observation of Thirkield, that "free" and "Negro" invoked contradictory rather than complimentary images for white southerners, became a recurring theme in later speeches and articles.

In approaching his vocation as an educator, the young Thirkield demonstrated more concern than most in the missionary campaign for undergirding the task with a sound theological foundation. Discouraged about the political maneuvering in the South, Thirkield believed that "the only hope left" resided in the church working through Christian schools and the Christian ministry to affect southern society. He argued that the task of the church was to draw the races together, but he quoted Albion Winegar Tourgée to show that this was not being done. To accomplish this action he suggested that theological categories needed to be broadened. The problem was that theology was often understood only in its vertical dimension—the solitary relation to God—but Thirkield believed that the newer theological thought could help energize the church in the horizontal dimension. "Let us remember that our church is here not only to redeem men out of sin, as understood in the strict theological sense, but to redeem them from the sin of caste and unchristian prejudice." The constructive basis for such a theology was "the recognition of the brotherhood of all men in Christ Jesus."[21]

Speaking within a culture that prided itself on its religious fervor, Thirkield's intention to make sin specific and advocate brotherhood made him a target for criticism. After a speech in Chicago on Negro education, informal conversations with reporters were turned into quotations by Thirkield, criticizing racism in the South. These remarks caused a furor in the southern press. Atticus G. Haygood threatened to resign from the board of Gammon and withdraw Slater Fund grants from other Methodist schools. Thirkield apologized privately to Haygood after complaining about misquotation.[22]

The Gammon president complained often about the crime of lynching. After denouncing the brutal lynching of Sam Hose in 1898, Thirkield spoke out in Atlanta, and his own life was threatened. The next year he led a protest against lynch law and was rebuked by more white Atlantans. The *Independent* and the *Outlook*, however, both took note of Thirkield's efforts and supported him.[23]

Thirkield served as president of the Congress on Africa, meetings held in Atlanta in 1895 under the auspices of the Stewart Missionary Foundation for Africa of Gammon Theological Seminary. The congress was divided into two parts, the first sessions focusing on the African continent and its peoples, and the latter sessions taking up the role of American blacks in Africa's "redemption." The meetings followed in the pattern of the Congress on Africa held at the World's Fair of 1893, and some of the same persons who were at Chicago were present in Atlanta as speakers. Black speakers included Alexander Crummel, Bishop Henry M. Turner, T. Thomas Fortune, and John Wesley Edward Bowen, Gammon's professor of historical theology.

Some who spoke accepted the partition of Africa by the European nations as steps in the direction of progress. Thirkield's assessment of the situation differed markedly. "While light is breaking in upon its darkness, the hand that blights and curses is not yet lifted." Assessing past and present dilemmas, he observed: "In other centuries the curse was the *Stealing of Africans from Africa*. Now, it is the game among European nations of 'shut your eyes and grab' in their efforts to *steal Africa from the Africans*."[24]

Thirkield resigned as president of Gammon in 1900. His experiences in Atlanta and throughout the South in these years would shape his future service to church and society.

The missionary education movement has been the subject of criticism from the perspective of the modern civil rights movement. There is indeed much to question and to criticize. In the 1880s and 1890s church missionary education societies retreated from egalitarian strategies begun in the decade after the Civil War. The best intentions were often mitigated by a paternalism that meant that white church leaders and educators knew best what was good for blacks. Leaders and schools that fell full sway under the philosophy and curriculum of industrial education prepared their graduates only to take up jobs in the lower socioeconomic stratum of society. The most fundamental flaw, however, from which everything else flowed, was the inability of a majority of the missionary educators to challenge the rebounding southern sentiments about race relations.

Accepting the validity of the criticism does not take away from the magnitude of the contributions of the churches toward black education. When both North and South were retreating rapidly from the hopes of Reconstruction, the churches did not lose hope that they could make a difference.

A perspective on the importance of Negro education in these years comes from graduates of these black colleges. George E. Haynes, a student and later faculty member at Fisk University, became both the director of National Urban League and the executive secretary of the Commission on Race Relations of the Federal Council of Churches. While at Fisk, Haynes said he was impressed by the "consecrated New England and Western white teachers who came to Fisk primarily through church missionary channels and gave the best of their thought and concern to Negro education in the South." Haynes said that these teachers were a model for his own later development.[25]

An even more well known graduate of Fisk University was W. E. B. Du Bois, who in 1896 became the first black to receive a Ph.D. from Harvard. Looking backward in 1903 on the missionary beginnings of black education, Du Bois called it "that finest thing in American history, and one of the few things untainted by sordid greed and cheap vainglory."[26]

I suggest in this chapter that the fruit of that missionary education is not to be seen alone in young black graduates. Fruit that was slower in ripening will be seen in white teachers and pastors who learned about black aspirations and frustrations through their involvement in black education. In the years before there was a significant migration of blacks from south to north, northern Social Gospel leaders gained their initial exposure to the race question through involvement in the structures and institutions of the various missionary education societies.

If education, then, was the vehicle for both black progress and northern white involvement, the story does not stay confined to the missionary education societies. The new century brought attempts to proclaim the gospel of education in new patterns and structures.

Part Two

DARKNESS OR DAWNING?
1898–1908

CHAPTER 6

The Gospel of Education

This movement has assumed that when philanthropy comes into the South with an exclusive interest in the Negro, it is likely to fail in its service both to the South and to the Negro. The South, under the irritations of such a policy, is tempted to leave the Negro wholly to the care of voluntary forces.

—EDGAR GARDNER MURPHY

The work of the North among the Negroes should be carried on in fellowship with the southern whites, not in antagonism to them; to attempt to force either political or social equality is to inflict incalculable injury on the Negro and on the nation. In a word, the northerner should recognize the fact that the southern white man now wishes to befriend the Negro; but the Negro should recognize the fact that he has to earn the southern white man's respect.

—LYMAN ABBOTT

Dr. Wallace Buttrick, executive officer of the General Education Board, an organization founded in 1902 to promote education in the South, liked to tell a story about having been invited to the White House by President Theodore Roosevelt. Asked to speak at Tuskegee Institute, Roosevelt sought Buttrick's counsel. The president said that in his speech, he would advocate industrial and agricultural education, "but I would stop there."

Buttrick replied that the teachers who were to instruct would require more advanced education.

"Yes, I grant that," said Roosevelt. "We must have normal schools to train teachers, but I'd stop there."

"How about the teachers in these normal schools?" asked Buttrick. "Who is going to train them?"

"Oh, I see," said Roosevelt slowly; "there is no place to stop."[1]

At the turn of the century, education was a central issue being discussed by friends and foes of blacks in the South. In these years, the gospel of education seemed to hold out its brightest promise. Yet at the same time, some questions persisted. Where do you start and where do you stop? In an earlier day, it was easier to sidestep questions about educational philosophies and the ability of blacks to learn, an ability that had never really been tested. The task was so vast that it was enough just to begin. But three decades and many institutions and pupils later, simple belief in education was complicated by questions, criticisms, and alternative philosophies.

Discussion among whites over the future of Negro education reached an important juncture in these years as a cluster of old and new organizations joined the debate. After a third of a century of leadership, the northern missionary societies, which had given birth to Negro education in the South, were reassessing their future role. At this same time, a new force emerged in the South that attempted to widen the scope of both black and white education on a scale much greater than anything attempted before.

The new southern education movement was ostensibly secular, but an assessment of its leadership reveals much of the impulse of a moderate social Christianity. The missionary education societies had fostered religious education. Could the southern education movement, born at a time of diminishing support for anything related to the welfare of blacks, succeed in propagating a gospel of education that would offer meaningful schooling for increased numbers of blacks? The story of its beginnings suggests an optimism about a bright new day that was dawning.

More than a generation after the commencement of Negro education in the South, a new beginning emerged from a small gathering of northern and southern leaders at Capon Springs, West Virginia, in the summer of 1898. "The First Capon Springs Conference for Christian Education in the South" developed from an initiative taken by Dr. Edward Abbott. Abbott was rector of St. James' Episcopal Church in Cambridge, Massachusetts, and the brother of Lyman Abbott. During an extensive tour of southern schools in 1897, Abbott stopped at the resort hotel in Capon Springs, operated by former Confederate captain William H. Sale. Abbott had attended the Mohonk conferences on Indian affairs and international arbitration in 1890, and convinced of their value and success, he envisaged a conference on education on the Lake Mohonk model to be held at Capon Springs. Sale agreed, and Abbott set about forming a committee to plan the agenda and invite the participants.[2]

Invitations were sent to nearly one hundred people. Thirty-six attended the following June, including fourteen ministers and nine presidents or representatives of colleges. After the singing of "Nearer, My God, to Thee" and prayer by Bishop Thomas Dudley of Kentucky, the conference began its regular sessions in the little chapel on the hotel grounds. Bishop Dudley was elected president. Jabez L. M. Curry, elderly agent of both the Peabody and Slater funds, was elected vice-president, even though not present at the conference. Hollis Burke Frissell, successor to Samuel Chapman Armstrong as principal of Hampton Institute, was elected chairman of the executive committee. In keeping with the general tone of the conference, each day was begun with a devotional service, and the final day, a Sunday, included public worship and an evangelistic service for the working people of Capon Springs.

Although the impetus emerging from Capon Springs quickly embraced white as well as black education, the focus of this first conference was definitely on Negro education. In such a case, Edward Abbott had felt compelled to say in his letter of invitation, "For reasons which I will not undertake here and now to explain, the persons to be invited will be restricted to members of the white race."[3]

In his letter, Abbott had asked for suggestions for topics. After sifting through the responses, he asked the conference to consider two major questions: How far can the public school system in the South be improved and made effective? and How far is it feasible to introduce industrial education? These questions would set the context for debate over the next fifteen years. As much as the churches had accomplished, with their own funds and with the aid of Peabody and Slater monies, the task of black education in the South was simply too great for church-related or private institutions. Could the lessons learned in more than thirty years of Negro education now be applied to public schools in the South?

The answers to both of Abbott's questions were optimistic in every address and comment. Amory Dwight Mayo, New England Unitarian minister, who since 1880 had worked for Negro education in the South, called for an end to the older distinctions between secular and religious education. "All American life is sacred, and there is no corner of it 'common or unclean' to the view of the Christian citizen."[4] If religious people, with their stake in and experience of education, came forward now in the adolescence of public education, they would have the great opportunity of shaping its present and future content.

In the midst of an enthusiastic willingness to import the lessons of industrial education to the public schools, President Wilbur P. Thirkield of Gammon Theological Seminary kept before the delegates the need for "higher education." Thirkield advocated higher education not as an alternative but as a complement to the adequate teaching of industrial education. He distinguished between the teaching of a race and the teaching of individuals. If industrial education was the primary present need of blacks, the leadership of the race was dependent on a select few individuals who must not be restrained but must be allowed to move up the educational ladder as far as their abilities could take them.[5]

As the meetings ended, conferees agreed upon a statement of purpose that articulated the religious and ideological basis of the deliberations. It began,

> The conference declares its deep and abiding interest in all efforts for the advancement of moral and religious education in the South along Christian lines, and especially that of the more needy of both races; and earnestly commends this noble work to the sympathy and support of all patriotic and Christian people, and, in particular, the southern people themselves.[6]

The first Capon Springs conference marked a watershed. A new kind of intersectionalism emerged in which the South, for the first time, gave promise of becoming an active partner in Negro education. Northern philanthropy would continue, but southern leaders and northerners more sympathetic to southern points of view would assume control of day-to-day direction of the educational enterprise.

As invitations went out for the 1899 Capon Springs conference, a hopeful future was forecast. Many new faces were present as the conference membership increased from thirty-six to seventy-five. Three northern philanthropists were among the most important additions. Robert Curtis Ogden, New York businessman, was elected vice-president and was elected president the following year. George Foster Peabody, a Wall Street banker born in Georgia, was a distant cousin of the founder of the Peabody Education Fund. William Henry Baldwin, Jr., had made his money at an early age after a brilliant career with several railroads. At thirty-one he took over the management of the Southern Railroad and now in 1899, at the age of thirty-six was president of the Long Island Railroad.

One reason for more than doubling the number of delegates was tied to Ogden's practice of bringing northerners to the South to introduce them to the campaign for Negro education. Among the leaders brought to Capon Springs in Ogden's private railroad car in 1899 was the Reverend Samuel D. McConnell, rector of Holy Trinity Church in Brooklyn and a spokesman for the Social Gospel within the Episcopal church.

In 1899 J. L. M. Curry was in attendance and was elected president of the proceedings. It was important to have this longtime friend of Negro education at the center of the new movement. An elder statesman in southern affairs, Curry was born in Georgia in 1825. After graduation from Harvard Law School in 1845, Curry served the South as a lawyer, legislator, teacher, college president, and minister. Curry had supported slavery, but within months after the close of the Civil War, he urged the Alabama Baptist State Convention, of which he was then president, to establish schools for the freedmen.[7] Ordained to the Baptist ministry in 1866, Curry never assumed a parish position, despite numerous invitations, but was continually active in the life of the Southern Baptist Convention. He had served the denomination as president of the Board of Foreign Missions.

Curry's involvement in the Negro question, however, generally found him working outside denominational structures. In 1881 Curry became general agent of the Peabody Education Fund, and in 1891 he succeeded Atticus Greene Haygood as general agent of the Slater Fund, holding both positions simultaneously. In Curry's efforts in behalf of the two funds, he spoke to every southern state legislature and to countless civic, business, and religious organizations. He told his audiences that education was the natural right of every individual, whether rich or poor, white or black. Since universal suffrage was an accomplished fact, illiteracy was a great danger to the functioning of the elective process. The prosperity of the region was also tied to the improvement of educational facilities for white and black. The separation of the races would continue to be the pattern in the future, but "Negro uplift" through education would enhance the well-being of the entire South.

Although the 1898 conference had embraced Christian education as a solution for the race problem, the 1899 gathering proved decisive in agreeing upon an altered strategy of arguing for Negro education within the larger context of the education of all needy people, both black and white. It was Curry who enunciated what eventually became future policy.

As the elder statesman surveyed in his address the history of education in the Southern states, he suggested a theme to be repeated in powerful centers in the North and the South. He told a story of "hope and courage amid the gloom of disappointment and poverty and despair." Curry detailed first what had been done for blacks and concluded, "Every southern man and woman is profoundly grateful for what northern people have done for the education of the Negroes; for making coequal citizenship of the two races in the same territory an endurable possibility." But Curry did not want to dwell on past achievements. Rather, he chose this keynote address to signal a new direction. "I shall not stultify myself by any fresh argument in favor of Negro education, but I must be pardoned for emphasizing the fact that there is greater need for the education of the other race."[8] Curry went on to make a persuasive appeal for universal education. The logic of the address, as far as blacks were concerned, was that the needs of blacks would be met in the long run by de-emphasizing separate, strictly black education and subsuming black education in a less visible way under universal education for all needy people.

Curry's address quickly became "the charter of the conference" and "furnished the basis of all the discussions in the conference for sixteen years."[9] This commitment to a universal strategy now became the basis for a renewed proclamation of a gospel of education.

The organizational turning point in the southern education movement came in 1901, when the conference, meeting in Winston-Salem, North Carolina, became a public forum. The word *Christian* was dropped from the title at this same time. Public, and ostensibly secular, the southern education movement has usually not been treated as part of the story of religion and reform in the South. It deserves to be. A check of the 1901 and later conference agendas reveals that noted religious leaders continued to be prominent in positions of leadership. At Winston-Salem the Ogden entourage from the North included Lyman Abbott, the Reverend Charles H. Parkhurst, minister of the Madison Square Presbyterian Church in New York, and Dr. Francis G. Peabody of Harvard, the first teacher of Christian social ethics in the United States. All three men, prominent Social Gospel leaders, addressed the conference.

Peabody expressed his appreciation for the progressive thrust of the meetings but admitted his relative ignorance of the question of education in the South, particularly as it applied to blacks. Peabody soon had the opportunity to learn more, as Ogden had him appointed to the board at Hampton.

Abbott, in addition to his address, put down his impressions in correspondence from Winston-Salem that was published in the *Outlook*. One paragraph from his report summarized the present state of his thinking.

The southerner has less prejudice against the Negro and more interest in his welfare than the northerner has; he desires the Negroes' education but believes that, whatever it may become in the future, it should now be industrial rather than literary; the South has spent on the Negroes' education between three and four times as much in school taxes as the North has spent in contributions; the work of the North among the Negroes should be carried on in fellowship with the southern whites, not in antagonism to them; to attempt to force either political or social equality is to inflict incalculable injury on the Negro and on the nation. In a word, the northerner should recognize the fact that the southern white man now wishes to befriend the Negro; but the Negro should recognize the fact that he has to earn the southern white man's respect.[10]

Parkhurst, best known as an anti-Tammany crusader, spoke from his New York pulpit a week later and told his congregation that one of the results of the conference was that "we learned to look upon matters more in the way in which the southern mind regards them." Parkhurst had been won over to the southern point of view that blacks could best earn long-term gains by being less vocal in the present. Not completely happy with all that he saw in the South, he concluded by putting the onus on the real attitudes in the North. "The southern white man dislikes the Negro and owns up to it. The white man in the North dislikes the Negro and lies about it."[11]

Ogden reported on the 1901 conference in a May speech to the Get Together Club in Brooklyn. His own strategy was that "the Negro problem must be solved by a triple alliance. It must be an alliance of the Northern white man and the Southern white man with the intelligent Negro."[12]

The missionary education bridge, this time traveled on by the railroad car, was bearing results, now and for the future. Peabody represented a leading northern educator, ignorant about the South, who was open to learning more. Abbott, already a supporter of both the missionary education societies and Booker T. Washington, later became an important publicist of the new southern education movement. Parkhurst, a newcomer like Peabody to Negro education, returned north from this experience to see with new eyes the racism that had always been there. Both Peabody and Parkhurst deepened their commitment to Negro education through their appointment to the board of trustees at Hampton. Many years later Peabody wrote the history of Hampton as a testament of love. Ogden, quiet and cautious, was a catalyst who continued year by year to expand the network of northern contacts.

As the delegates returned to their homes, the resolutions at the end of the conference had authorized the president, Ogden, to appoint an executive board and employ a secretary or agent. The goal was to conduct a campaign of education for free schools for all the people and a bureau of information and advice on legislation and school organization.[13] Later that year, around a luncheon table on the top floor of Wanamaker's store in New York, what finally came to be called the Southern Education Board was born. In fall meetings, when the question of finances was discussed, the first suggestion was made for a sister organization, the General Education Board. By 1902 both of these boards were in full-scale operation. The Southern Education Board acted to stimulate public opinion in the encouragement of education for whites and blacks. The General Education Board acted as a clearinghouse for philanthropic support of education, beginning with initial grants from John D. Rockefeller. The complementary nature of the two boards can be seen in the fact that eleven members of the Southern Education Board were also members of the General Education Board in the first decade of its existence. Baldwin and Ogden were the first two presidents of the General Education Board, and Peabody served both boards as treasurer.[14]

Of critical importance would be the secretary or agent assisting Ogden and actually carrying on the day-to-day operations of the board. Ogden knew right away whom he wanted for this strategic position: Edgar Gardner Murphy, a young Episcopal minister from Montgomery, Alabama.

Edgar Gardner Murphy's previous experience and outlook well qualified him for the task. Born in 1869 near Fort Smith, Arkansas, Murphy grew up in relative poverty, with the burden increased by the desertion of his father when he was six. The family moved at that time to San Antonio, where Edgar received his education through high school. The most formative association in these years was the parish life of St. Mark's Episcopal Church. Through the good offices of the St. Mark's pastor, Murphy received a scholarship to the University of the South in Sewanee, Tennessee. Graduating from Sewanee in 1889, he went to New York for a year's training at the General Theological Seminary. In New York, he served as a lay assistant to Dr. Arthur Brooks and also became acquainted with Brooks's more famous brother, Phillips, rector of Boston's Trinity Church. In 1890 Murphy returned to San Antonio to accept a position as lay assistant at St. Mark's.[15]

From 1893 to 1898 Murphy served parishes in Laredo, Texas, in Chillicothe, Ohio, and in Kingston, New York. His increasing involvement in social ministry and occasional lectures and articles brought him national attention. In 1898 he welcomed the opportunity to return to the South and accepted a call as rector of St. John's Parish in Montgomery, Alabama.

Murphy resigned from St. John's at the end of 1901 in order to accept the invitation to become executive secretary of the Southern Education Board. Murphy carried on the day-to-day operations of the board, working closely with Ogden. He saw this position as an opportunity to work for the whole South. At this time the South, with 25 percent of the nation's population, received only 3 percent of the contributions to education. He believed he could work well with northern philanthropists but was convinced also that wealthy southerners would rally behind the new movement. He was in full agreement that by emphasizing support for the lower-and middle-class whites, the support of black education would also be expanded.

By 1901, as we have observed, this "Christian education" movement for public education had become a public movement, but it is fascinating to look at its chief leaders and supporters. To a person, they exhibit the content and connections of a moderate social Christianity.

Wallace Buttrick, executive officer of the General Education Board, was called to that post in 1902 after twenty years in the Baptist ministry. He had just completed ten years' service as pastor of Emmanuel Baptist Church in Albany, New York. During these same years Buttrick also served as secretary of the Baptist Home Mission Society, which was entrusted with the oversight of Baptist schools for blacks in the South. After several visits to the South, Buttrick had proposed that the Baptists close their schools and start cooperating with the developing public educational movement in the South. This did not happen, but in 1902 he moved in that direction himself by agreeing to direct the General Education Board in its efforts to support the campaign for universal education.[16]

The three philanthropists most involved in the southern education movement were all active churchmen allied with Social Gospel leaders and causes. Robert C. Ogden, a Presbyterian, served as a Sunday school superintendent, initially at First Presbyterian Church in Brooklyn, and then for eighteen years at the Holland Memorial Chapel in Philadelphia. His Brooklyn pastor and lifelong friend Charles Cuthbert Hall, a leading Social Gospeler who was elected president of Union Theological Seminary in 1897, exercised a profound influence in encouraging Ogden's reform activities. Hall served as trustee at Atlanta University from 1890 until his death in 1908.[17]

George Foster Peabody, after moving from Georgia, attended the Reformed Church in Brooklyn Heights. In 1880 he became a member of the Episcopal church, serving as head of the vestry of Holy Trinity Parish in Brooklyn. Samuel D. McConnell, an advocate of a Social Gospel, was appointed rector in 1896. It was Peabody who suggested that McConnell come to Capon Springs in 1899. Peabody was also active in the national church, serving as a delegate to several general conventions. "One of the most prominent layman of his day in Episcopal Church affairs," Peabody was a prime mover in organizing the American Church Institute for Negroes in 1906. From modest beginnings, this Episcopal organization later aided eight centers of Negro education, generated by support from a budget that eventually reached $600,000 a year.[18]

William Henry Baldwin, Jr., son of abolitionists, was raised in a home espousing a tolerant Unitarianism. His father had left a successful business career to take over the day-to-day operations of the Christian Union in Boston. Baldwin, Jr., while differing in creed, supported the beginnings of YMCA chapters all over the country. He continually wrote and lectured on the role of ethics in business and lived out his ethics by his concern for the total welfare of the workers on his railroad.[19]

Encouraged by people with a record of support for church initiative in Negro education, the southern education movement wanted not to diminish the role of the church in education but to change its function. Entrusted with planning the Education in the South Conference in 1902, Murphy wrote to Mississippi Methodist bishop Charles B. Galloway, inviting him to speak at Athens, Georgia, on the topic "The Church and the Public Schools." Speaking of the underlying assumptions of the movement, Murphy told Galloway that the board was consciously building on the "heroic work that has been done by the denominational schools of the South." As for the present, "The realization of the church's duty to the public school will not only bring much of inspiration and encouragement into the schools of the people, but will serve, I believe, in spirit if not through formal method, to Christianize the education of the state."[20] To Christianize the social order was a dominant Social Gospel motif here employed by Murphy to galvanize the church's new opportunity in education. In the North the pressing Social Gospel agenda at this time was the cluster of reform issues related to industrialization and urbanization. In the South a primary reform agenda was education.

The focus on the public school was the means of implementing the strategy first articulated by Curry and now to be executed by Murphy with the backing of Ogden, Peabody, and Baldwin. The denominational schools were concerned with Negro education. If the southern education campaign was to succeed, the programs of the Southern Education Board and the funds of the General Education Board must be channeled into universal education. In addressing a convocation at Washington and Lee University in December, 1902, Murphy spelled out the reason.

> This movement has assumed that when philanthropy comes into the South with an exclusive interest in the Negro, it is likely to fail in its service both to the South and to the Negro. The South, under the irritations of such a policy, is tempted to leave the Negro wholly to the care of voluntary forces. If the South is not to draw the race line against one element of the population, the North should not draw that line against another. Racial favoritism makes for interracial hatred. The educational policy of genuine patriotism will include all the children of the underprivileged, white as well as black.[21]

This "Task of the South" address won much acclaim for Murphy and the southern education movement in both the North and the South. It is not difficult to see why. Murphy here exhibited in clear but concise prose the gifts of a publicist. Having lived both in the North and the South, his remarks revealed an understanding of the fears and hopes of both regions. The appeal to "genuine patriotism" became an underlying theme in many of Murphy's addresses. At the annual education conference at Richmond in 1903, Harvard's Francis Greenwood Peabody had high praise indeed: "The single address of Mr. Murphy on 'the task of the South' contains enough sound political economy and political ethics to satisfy an entire generation."[22]

But even in the beginning years of the campaign, there were critical voices. William Hayes Ward zeroed in on the southern education campaign philosophy of helping whites in order to help blacks. In a 1902 editorial in the *Independent* he wrote, "We should expect chief attention where schooling was least provided." Ward went on to ridicule the logic that we must educate whites to teach blacks to work, "who already do most of the work."[23]

Lyman Abbott early became a chief supporter of the movement. In 1900 he quarreled with Horace Bumstead, president of Atlanta University, who pointed out that of all blacks enrolled in "colleges" in the South, only 12 percent were actually doing college-level work. In response to Bumstead's call for more work that was actually college level, Abbott replied that he believed the emphasis should be on the lower

grades and industrial education. Abbott even went as far as to say that
two colleges would be sufficient for the present needs of the black population.[24]

After the 1903 conference at Richmond, Abbott spoke in his customary fashion about the bright prospects for blacks if only northern white
leaders would cooperate with the best people and thinking in the
South. These remarks were challenged from a surprising source. New-
ell Dwight Hillis, Abbott's successor at Plymouth Church, rebuked his
friend by observing, "Among the old leaders of the South, the ex-Pres-
ident [Grover Cleveland] and the editor are the most popular of all the
men in the North. Both the statesman and the editor have, for the hour,
lost faith in the republic, in the equality of the races, and in universal
suffrage."[25] No remark could more incisively point to Abbott's pilgrimage from reform to accommodation. One would have to say that Abbott
spoke for the majority opinion, but his point of view was not accepted
uncritically, even within his own circle.

The climax of the southern education movement came about 1907,
although it continued for another decade. By 1907 state educational
organizations were operating on their own momentum, and the Southern Education Board was branching out into specialized projects. There
were concrete accomplishments that to some supporters justified their
optimistic outlook. Most impressive was the expansion in public education in the years after 1900. In the eleven states where the Southern
Education Board operated, expenditures for schools increased by over
$14 million in the first five years of the board's operation. The General
Education Board granted millions of dollars to educational institutions.
People were taxing themselves for public education, and the Southern
Education Board could rightly take much of the credit.[26]

The failures of the movement were now becoming apparent also. In
1906 Washington wrote to Robert Ogden and complained that the
southern education campaign had meant "almost nothing so far as the
Negro schools are concerned." For his part, Ogden owned up to the
failures to implement the original Capon Springs goals for Negro education. A Washingtonian in outlook, he restrained his inclination to
speak, out of concern for southern partners in this intersectional alliance. Taking nothing away from the largely conservative attitudes of
the southern leaders associated with the board, the whole situation was
complicated by the fact that in many cases these leaders were officials
in public institutions. These institutions received their funding from
state legislatures, and thus their voices on Negro education, even when
inclined to speak courageously, could be easily and decisively muzzled.

The ultimate threat was always the provision that the only monies to be used for Negro education must come directly from black tax revenues. Ogden and Murphy became convinced that if this measure was ever put to the vote, the demagogues would carry the day.[27]

By 1907 Murphy was also discouraged. Sometimes apt to be more romantic than realistic, he expressed his dismay to Buttrick at the failure to help blacks. "There is not only no chance to help the situation of the Negro educationally, but it is steadily growing worse, and their schools, upon every sort of pretext, are being hampered and impoverished where they are not actually abandoned."[28]

What went wrong? The southern education campaign, despite its limited successes, failed in one decisive measure: the disparity between white and black education, in terms of per capita expenditures, was greater in 1910 than in 1900. In the end, the campaign was shackled by its own unrealistic premises. Early in the campaign reformers adopted the flawed strategy that blacks would benefit from a policy that publicly espoused white education first. This meant that the campaign for universal education saw blacks once again get the leftovers in public expenditures.

Lurking beneath the surface of education meetings and campaign strategies was a deep fear of actual southern sentiment. Wallace Buttrick, committed to the education of blacks through a lifetime of service, was nonetheless cautious in style, always afraid of pushing southern whites for fear of provoking a white backlash. Ogden and Murphy both feared the strategy of the militant segregationists, which was to demand that black education be supported only from black taxes.

The ultimate hope of the northern philanthropists and Buttrick and Murphy had been to interest the upper classes in the South as partners in the campaign. The appeal had always been that it was in their own self-interest as the conservatives of southern society. This approach was in line with the New South ideology of the period. But their appeal failed to southern leaders, whose bedrock New South belief was an unassailable commitment to white supremacy.

Even when black education was advanced, its northern and southern benefactors advocated a rather tightly circumscribed industrial education. Believing in the Tuskegee philosophy, utilizing Washington as a counselor, the southern education movement could not free itself from the assumptions and limitations of this approach.

Even though the southern education movement was in one way a larger undertaking than the individual efforts of the missionary societies, its focus, unlike that of the societies, was blunted almost from the beginning by the assumption that Negro education could only come alongside of white education. The emphasis on Negro education, which had been at the center of the first Capon Springs conference, had receded through the years. As the movement played itself out, what really happened was that Negro education came not alongside of, but on the heels of white education. Not all in the movement shared Murphy's commitment to black education.

Finally, the southern education movement shared with many contemporaries, black and white, religious and secular, an often naive, uncritical faith in the gospel of education. The education of whites, however, seemed to have little effect on the omnipresent white racism. The unrelenting facts were that educated blacks did not find open doors of employment waiting for them.

CHAPTER 7

Conservatives versus Radicals: Washington and Du Bois

I believe the past and present teach but one lesson—to the Negro's friends and to the Negro himself—that there is but one hope of solution: and that is for the Negro in every part of America to resolve from henceforth that he will throw aside every nonessential and cling only to essentials—that his pillar of fire by night and pillar of cloud by day shall be property, economy, education, and Christian character. To us just now these are the wheat, all else the chaff.

—BOOKER T. WASHINGTON

So far as Mr. Washington preaches Thrift, Patience, and Industrial Training for the masses, we must hold up his hands and strive with him, rejoicing in his honors and glorying in the strength of this Joshua called of God and of man to lead the headless host. But so far as Mr. Washington apologizes for injustices North or South, does not rightly value the privilege and duty of voting, belittles the emasculating effects of caste distinctions, and opposes the higher training and ambition of our brighter minds,—so far as he, the South, or the Nation does this,—we must unceasingly and firmly oppose them.

—W. E. B. DU BOIS

Kelly Miller, a prominent black leader at the turn of the century, began an article in the *Boston Evening Transcript* in September 1903 with a story.

When a distinguished Russian visiting this country was informed that some American Negroes were radical and some conservative, he could not restrain his laughter. The idea of conservative Negroes was more than the Cossack's risibilities could endure. "What on earth," he exclaimed with astonishment, "have they to conserve?"[1]

The ascendancy of Booker T. Washington was a mixed blessing for black Americans. Under his leadership blacks made strides in acquiring education and property but suffered losses in civil and political rights. Washington gained favor with presidents—he dined with President Theodore Roosevelt in a celebrated but controversial event in 1901— while southern governors took the lead in cementing discriminatory policies in state statutes. Washington was able to win financial backing from a coterie of northern philanthropists even as these same leaders pulled back from advocating policies that might offend business and civic leaders of the New South.

Even as Washington was being elevated to leadership, in part by whites who said he was the only one with whom they would deal, he was being challenged from within the black community. The primary challenge came from one who was at first sympathetic to Washington's goals and strategies. One of the congratulatory letters after the Atlanta exposition address came from a young W. E. B. Du Bois. "Let me congratulate you upon your phenomenal success at Atlanta—it was a word fitly spoken."[2] Within a decade Du Bois became the intellectual center of a challenge to Washington and "the Tuskegee machine."

The debate that developed between Washington and Du Bois was at the outset an intramural debate, a struggle for the soul of the black movement. The factions were sometimes called Bookerites and anti-Bookerites, or conservatives and radicals. Kelly Miller, in his article for the *Evening Transcript*, provided some definitions for his readers. "According to a strict construction of terms, a conservative is one who is satisfied with, and advocates the continuance of existing conditions; while a radical clamors for amelioration through change."[3]

But these black leaders had their white colleagues, allies, and sympathizers. I propose that this black intramural debate helped set the parameters and delineate the issues for whites who concerned themselves with racial reform in the first two decades of the twentieth century. It is not that many whites participated in the debate itself—but they responded to it. In time (and often there was a lag time involved), these whites were called upon to react to the changing positions and priorities of racial reform as articulated primarily by Washington and Du Bois. It is important to understand the various dimensions of the Washington–Du Bois debate as a barometer by which the changing mind of the Social Gospel can be measured.

The familiarity of white Americans with Washington was greatly enhanced with the publication of his autobiography, *Up from Slavery*, in March 1901. The success of this project was due in no small measure to Washington's friendship with Lyman Abbott. Apart from philanthropists, Abbott was becoming the leading supporter of Washington in the North. Washington's first article in the northern press appeared in Abbott's *Christian Union*, predecessor of the *Outlook*, and it was in the offices of the *Outlook* that *Up from Slavery* was edited. According to Louis Harlan, it was Abbott, rather than ghostwriter Max Bennett Thrasher, who "gave Washington needed advice on the organization and presentation of his past." Week by week Abbott reviewed the drafts and offered advice about organization, content, and style.[4]

Up from Slavery ran serially in the *Outlook* from November 3, 1900, to February 23, 1901. The *Outlook* had now passed the 100,000 mark in circulation. Periodicals and weekly newspapers occupied a quite different place in the culture of 1900 than they do today. It was quite common for *Up from Slavery* to be read aloud to the family or to neighbors. It was published in book form by Doubleday in March, 1901.

Reading *Up from Slavery* was a stirring experience. This was due in no small part to Abbott's continual encouraging of Washington to speak to the questions that were sure to be in the minds of the readers. Who would not be caught up in the story of a boy born in slavery who rose to become the leader of his race? A singular story, it was told in such a way as to convey the message of a way open for other blacks who would follow the path of "education," "hard work," "thrift," and "Christian character"—all favorite words in the Washington lexicon. Throughout, it was a story of hope for blacks. But it was also a story of conciliation with whites. Washington magnified the cooperation received from whites along the way and did not belabor the recent increases in discrimination.

On the last page of the autobiography, Washington acknowledged that there were others who read the signs of the times differently. But he turned this dilemma into an opportunity to reiterate to the reader his message of hope. "Despite superficial and temporary signs which might lead one to entertain a contrary opinion, there was never a time when I felt more hopeful for the race than I do at the present."[5]

Washington's hope was based in a carefully articulated strategy that he believed would lead to the eventual "uplift" of the race. He summed up this strategy in *The Future of the American Negro*, published in 1899.

> I believe the past and present teach but one lesson—to the Negro's friends and to the Negro himself—that there is but one hope of solution: and that is for the Negro in every part of America to resolve from henceforth that he will throw aside every nonessential and cling only to essentials—that his pillar of fire by night and pillar of cloud by day shall be property, economy, education, and Christian character. To us just now these are the wheat, all else the chaff.[6]

In a long review in the *Outlook*, this sentence was highlighted, accompanied by a comment from Abbott: "We believe that in this sentence is found the adequate and only solution to the race problem in the South."[7]

The issue in the intramural debate became: what is essential? Washington began by emphasizing property and economy because his reading of history told him that these were the keys to securing a place in society. Conversely, his sense for the tremendous influx of immigrants coming to this country was a warning that if blacks did not secure themselves within the economy, jobs would be taken by immigrants willing to start at the bottom. Implicit in this philosophy was Washington's faith in laissez-faire capitalism. He was a Republican who wanted to foster ties with business. He was, especially in his earlier years, distrustful of labor unions, which he viewed as dangerous to the economy and unfriendly to blacks. He wanted to position blacks as loyal workers who would not be susceptible to strikes or labor violence.

The way to achieve what was essential was "to start at the bottom." Washington's philosophy was pragmatic. He had developed at Tuskegee a curriculum based on industrial education because he believed it would be the best preparation for gaining an economic foothold in the South. He was not against higher education, as has sometimes been charged; rather, he believed that for the masses of blacks to seek higher education would not be farsighted but shortsighted. His concern was to prepare blacks to live in the real world of the South.

In this real world Washington adopted a strategy based on conciliation and accommodation. Washington believed that a minority race was better off winning rather than demanding their place in society. If he followed a policy of gradualism that seemed to eschew the more radical posture of the Reconstruction era, Washington never tired of citing statistics and telling human interest stories in asserting that indeed progress was being made. For example, when speaking of economic advancement, Washington cited statistics to show that blacks had now acquired in forty years land equal in area to the combined countries of Belgium and Holland.[8]

When speaking of strategy, we should remember that Washington was called the Wizard of Tuskegee by friend and foe alike—but never to his face. Harlan has aptly used this reference as the subtitle of the second volume of his study of Washington. The title suggested the skill and almost magical character of Washington's dealings with blacks and whites, friends and foes, conservatives and liberals. If Thomas A. Edison was the Wizard of Menlo Park, Tuskegee was the Oz, or the Emerald City blooming in the black belt of Alabama. From that unlikely base the so-called Tuskegee machine reached out to embrace white northern philanthropists and frustrate anti-Bookerite blacks.[9]

We now know more clearly that there were many levels to Washington's strategies. Washington did have hope that society would honor the hard work and Christian character of blacks and finally grant them a place in society. But he was also a pragmatist. On the few occasions when he publicly adopted a posture of protest, he believed the public outcry this produced in the South was counterproductive to his gradualist program of uplift.

Behind the public Washington was a private wizard who knew how to use his powerful allies to try to thwart increasing discrimination. His correspondence shows how he worked through his white allies to attempt to change the opinions of influential whites. In 1898, for example, Louisiana held a constitutional convention to discuss disfranchisement. J. L. M. Curry, an old friend of Washington, visited Tuskegee as part of a collaborative effort culminating in Curry's address to the convention arguing against a proposal to close black public schools. Washington worked hard on public letters to the Louisiana convention, and again to a similar Alabama convention. It was not revealed at the time that public statements were being accompanied by aggressive private maneuvers.[10]

Washington understood only too well the arithmetic of the South, and so he turned to the courts to try to stop the Jim Crow laws being passed in state after state. The grandfather clause, whereby illiterate whites were allowed to vote if their grandfathers were qualified, was particularly odious. Washington proposed to test the grandfather clause passed by the Louisiana convention of 1898. He undertook to raise money for the case. Washington contributed money to the Afro-American Council's legal bureau. He asked Richard Hallowell and Francis Garrison to raise money in Boston for legal fees. He helped recruit lawyers Albert E. Pillsbury, former attorney general of Massachusetts, and Arthur E. Birney, grandson of the Liberty party leader, James G. Birney, to help prepare the case. In all of the contacts and correspondence, it was always with the understanding that Washington's name not be used.[11]

Washington did speak up forcefully in public on a few occasions. At the close of the Spanish-American War a jubilee celebration was held in Chicago. Washington took the occasion to remind the audience of the loyalty of black Americans throughout the history of the republic. He contended that since blacks were willing to die for their country, they should surely be given every opportunity to live in the nation they loved. Toward the conclusion of the speech he summed up the record of victories in battles and then said, "There remains one other victory for Americans to win." America had won every conflict "except the effort to conquer ourselves in the blotting out of racial prejudice." In a prophetic utterance he told the more than sixteen thousand in attendance, "I make no empty statement when I say that we shall have a cancer gnawing at the heart of the republic that shall one day prove as dangerous as an attack with an army without or within." The speech was acclaimed across the country, but the southern press took strong exception to his remarks about racial prejudice. Because of the outcry he saw fit to write to the *Birmingham Age-Herald* explaining in a conciliatory tone his words so as to remove some of their force.[12]

W. E. B. Du Bois could not have had a more different origin or destiny. Du Bois and Washington were originally united in championing the advancement of their people, but the friendship they enjoyed for a few years dissipated in the midst of their contention over philosophy, strategy, and leadership.

Du Bois was born in Great Barrington, Massachusetts, in 1868. An excellent student, he wanted to attend Harvard, but this financial resources were not adequate. Because of his fine educational background he was admitted to Fisk College in Nashville, Tennessee, with sophomore standing in 1885. In choosing to attend Fisk, Du Bois entered a whole new world when he went south. A member of a New England black family that had been free since the American Revolution, Du Bois discovered a solidarity in the South with members of his own race who encountered discrimination daily. Graduating from Fisk in 1888, he was admitted to Harvard with junior standing and graduated in 1890. He was accepted into the Ph.D. program and, as part of his graduate program, studied for two years at the University of Berlin under a grant from the John F. Slater Fund.[13]

In 1894 he applied for a teaching position at Tuskegee, Wilberforce, in Ohio, and Lincoln, in Missouri. Within eight days he received a positive reply from all three, but as Wilberforce came first, he accepted it. He later mused about how different his life might have been if he had accepted the invitation from Tuskegee. In 1896 Du Bois received his Ph.D. from Harvard. His doctoral dissertation, *The Suppression of the African Slave Trade*, was published as the first volume of the new Harvard Historical Studies series. After two years in Ohio he accepted a fellowship at the University of Pennsylvania that enabled him to do the

research and writing for *The Philadelphia Negro,* a sociological study published in 1899 that brought him acclaim. In 1897 he accepted an appointment to Atlanta University, and he seemed firmly launched on an
academic career.

Du Bois came to Atlanta to supervise the sociology department but
became well known nationally for directing the annual Atlanta University conferences on urban Negro problems, begun in 1896 through the
initiative of President Horace Bumstead. Du Bois found, however, that
the study of "Negro problems" impelled him to do something about
the problems he was analyzing. Addressing the University of Atlanta
on the occasion of his seventieth birthday, Du Bois recalled how, at the
very time of the "widening success" of the conferences, "there cut
across this plan of science a red ray of emotion which could not be
ignored." In 1899 a poor black man in central Georgia, Sam Hose, had
killed his landlord in a dispute over wages. Hose could not be found,
and a report circulated that he had raped the landlord's wife. Du Bois
prepared a statement concerning the facts in the case and was headed
down to the *Atlanta Constitution* offices with a letter of introduction to
editor Joel Chandler Harris. He never got there. "On the way the news
met me: Sam Hose had been lynched, and they said his knuckles were
on exhibition at a grocery store on Mitchell Street." Du Bois was at a
crossroads. "I turned back to the university. I suddenly saw that complete scientific detachment in the midst of such a South was impossible."[14]

Du Bois continued at the university, but his involvement in practical
racial reform began to gain momentum. He decided that words could
be a form of action. In addition to his academic studies Du Bois contributed a variety of essays and articles in the next few years that challenged prevailing attitudes and laid the foundation for his own
philosophy and strategy. At the end of the 1890s his plan of action
focused on racial solidarity and economic development. There were
many similarities with the ideas of Washington. Although more outspoken than Washington about racial injustices, Du Bois was still willing
to be conciliatory.

Beginning in the new century, Du Bois placed more emphasis on
the priority of political and civil rights. As he developed his educational
views further, Du Bois became more forceful in his criticisms of industrial education. In the political arena, Du Bois was once willing to countenance southern restrictions to the franchise if applied equally to black
and white. But now he realized that restrictions would never be applied
fairly and that the full use of the ballot was imperative for meaningful

progress for black Americans. All these ideas were part of a personal odyssey taking Du Bois quickly along the road from accommodation to reform.

His various literary efforts culminated in 1903 with the publication of *The Souls of Black Folk*. This epochal work is without question the foundational document of the century in terms of race. A collection of essays, it received its coherence from Du Bois's oft-quoted assertion in the preface that "the problem of the Twentieth Century is the problem of the color line."[15]

Up to this point Du Bois had dealt with questions of philosophy and strategy, for the most part, without reference to personality. But in *The Souls of Black Folk*, a chapter entitled "Of Mr. Booker T. Washington and Others" challenged by name not only the philosophy and strategy but the personal leadership of Washington. Du Bois's assessment was that Washington "arose as essentially the leader not of one race but of two,—a compromiser between the South, the North, and the Negro." Washington had steered a course so that he could "gain the sympathy and cooperation of the various elements comprising the white South" as well as gain allies for his ideas in the North. The price of that compromise had been high. "Mr. Washington's programme practically accepts the alleged inferiority of the Negro races." In practical terms, Du Bois said that Washington was asking black people to give up—at least for the present period—three things: "political power, . . . insistence on civil rights," and the "higher education of Negro youth."[16]

Du Bois's appeal was broad-gauged. He was concerned especially about a group of black leaders who had hitherto said little publicly. He identified these persons as Francis Grimké, a Presbyterian minister, and his brother Archibald, a prominent lawyer; Kelly Miller, a professor at Howard; and J. W. E. Bowen, a professor at the northern Methodist church's Gammon Theological Seminary in Atlanta. These persons, so Du Bois said, recognized Washington's achievements and did not like dissension in the ranks, but Du Bois wondered out loud whether such leaders "can much longer be silent."

The Atlanta professor invited these leaders and others to join a new movement that will "ask of this nation three things:

1. The right to vote.
2. Civic equality.
3. The education of youth according to ability."

In announcing this program, Du Bois wanted his audience to know that blacks now had a duty "to oppose a part of the work of their greatest leader."[17] Bold words from a new leader.

In the concluding paragraph of the chapter, Du Bois described in vivid word pictures the issues that divided him and Washington.

> So far as Mr. Washington preaches Thrift, Patience, and Industrial Training for the masses, we must hold up his hands and strive with him, rejoicing in his honors and glorying in the strength of this Joshua called of God and of man to lead the headless host. But so far as Mr. Washington apologizes for injustices North or South, does not rightly value the privilege and duty of voting, belittles the emasculating effects of caste distinctions, and opposes the higher training and ambition of our brighter minds,—so far as he, the South, or the Nation does this,—we must unceasingly and firmly oppose them.[18]

The gauntlet had been thrown down. Notice the use of biblical imagery to draw the battle lines. Sales of the book skyrocketed, so that within two years it was in its sixth edition. As shall be seen, influential leaders who had supported Washington or remained silent with their criticisms were now drawn to Du Bois as the intellectual center of a new movement of protest. The debate was in full swing.

It is instructive to understand the role that religion played in the thought and action of Washington and Du Bois. Our chief interest in their personal religious pilgrimages is to comprehend better their ideas both about the church and about the relation of religion to reform. Even though their journeys were quite different, both Washington and Du Bois came to understand early the powerful role of the churches in American society.

As a boy in Malden, West Virginia, Washington was deeply involved in the Zion Baptist Church, which he found very meaningful at the time. Washington later remembered both the virtues and the shortcomings of the emotional services, led by an illiterate minister. Much more substance came into his life at Hampton, where Nathalie Lord, a favorite teacher, suggested that Washington spend the quarterhour between the end of classes and the noon meal reading the Bible. She read with him, and in that first year they worked their way through the Gospels, Acts, and the Epistles. Washington said later that this pattern so impressed itself upon him that he tried to read from the Bible daily during the rest of his life.[19]

Upon graduation from Hampton, Washington returned to Malden to teach at the Tinkersville School. In addition to these duties, on Sundays he taught at two Sunday schools, one at the Zion Baptist Church and the other at the Snow Hill salt furnace. He found time to serve also as clerk of the Mount Olivet Baptist Association.[20]

In 1878 Washington enrolled at Wayland Seminary, a Baptist institution in Washington, D.C. It is difficult to assess the Wayland experience because in later years Washington was reticent to discuss it. He
does not mention the seminary experience in *Up from Slavery* but says
only, "I decided to spend some months in study at Washington, D.C."
The records from the seminary are not available, having been destroyed
by fire. We know that in these years Washington was searching for a
career, but we do not know his motives for entering the seminary. We
also do not know his reasons for leaving.[21]

More than a decade later, as Washington ascended to his position
of power within the black community, he had deep suspicions of the
black church. His first publication in the northern press was a strong
critique of black ministers. Washington was invited to speak at the Fisk
commencement in 1890 and chose as his topic, "The Colored Ministry:
Its Defects and Needs." Published in August in Lyman Abbott's
Christian Union, the address was a harsh assessment of the state of the
ministry. There was an indictment for inadequate training. Good marks
were given to the minority of black clergy in the Congregational, Episcopal, and Presbyterian churches, but these ministers, he said, were
out of touch with the masses. As for the others, Washington was blunt:
"I have no hesitancy in asserting that three-fourths of the Baptist ministers and two-thirds of the Methodists are unfit, either mentally or
morally, or both, to preach the Gospel to any one or attempt to lead
any one."[22]

This address could not be gauged to win friends and influence
churches. Washington was met by a chorus of pained responses from
denominational leaders and the black press. Knowing Washington's
usual style of rhetoric, one finds these words all the more remarkable.
It seems that this early criticism by Washington is really the measure
both of his disappointment and yet his expectation for the black church.

At Tuskegee the goal of "Christian character" did receive a specific
place in the curriculum. Despite this emphasis, in the early years it was
said that Alabama black preachers would sometimes complain that Tuskegee "wasn't Methodist and wasn't Baptist, it wasn't Presbyterian or
'piscopalian, and it wasn't Christian!" This criticism probably suited
Washington fine because he was not interested in what he called sec-
tarianism. But every week students participated in preaching services
and prayer meetings and had the possibility of joining the Christian
Endeavor Society, the YMCA, and various missionary organizations.[23]

In *Up from Slavery*, Washington's tone about the churches changed.
"If no other considerations had convinced me of the value of the

Christian life, the Christlike work which the Church of all denominations in America has done during the last thirty-five years for the ele-
vation of the black man would have made me a Christian."[24] Given
Washington's earlier criticisms, we must ask what explains this change.
We have to keep in mind that the autobiographical Washington was
also the publicist who was proclaiming his Washingtonian philosophy
and strategy. It is possible to take Washington's comments as evidence
of a maturing and broadening understanding of the church. This evaluation is not inconsistent with sensing Washington's statement as part
of his now-developed strategy of courting rather than demeaning institutions important to the cause.

W. E. B. Du Bois's religious pilgrimage was complicated. In later
autobiographical statements Du Bois mentioned on several occasions
that his family on both sides for four generations was Episcopalian. His
actual religious training in Great Barrington, however, was received
primarily in the Congregational church. Characterizing the congregation as liberal, Du Bois said he listened once a week to a sermon by the
Reverend Evarts Scudder that was devoid of much theology but that
emphasized the practical tasks of "doing good."[25]
Through this Congregational church, in cooperation with three Congregational churches in Connecticut, money was raised enabling Du
Bois to attend Fisk in Nashville. At Fisk he joined the campus Congregational church. He wrote back to Pastor Scudder, asking for the prayers of the Sunday school to "help guide me in the path of Christian
duty." In the same letter he reported that during a recent revival there
were forty conversions.[26]
During the next three years at Fisk, Du Bois learned more to argue
than to believe. He quarreled with the orthodoxy taught in the classes
and rebelled against a perceived ethic of legalism exemplified when a
"hidebound old deacon inveighed against dancing." President Erastus
M. Cravath encouraged Du Bois to consider the ministry, but he was
already turning away from organized religion.[27]
In the following years at Harvard he still called himself a believer,
but during his studies in Germany he became what he called a freethinker. While teaching at Wilberforce, he was asked to lead in prayer at
the regular chapel services but at first refused to do so. At Atlanta
University, Du Bois said that an appointment to be head of a department was held up when he balked at leading in public prayer. When
told he could substitute the Episcopal Prayer Book, he acquiesced and
later even improvised some of his own prayers.[28]

The intersection of Du Bois's developing race consciousness and changing religious beliefs was articulated forcefully in what he called his Credo. Used in speeches in these years, it appeared in print for the first time in the *Independent* in October 1904. Next to *The Souls of Black Folk*, this became the best known of his writings. Widely reprinted, it was published in scroll form and could be seen hanging in black homes across the country. Because of its importance for our subject, it is printed here in its entirety.

> I believe in God who made of one blood all races that dwell on earth. I believe that all men, black and brown and white, are brothers, varying, through Time and Opportunity, in form and gift and feature, but differing in no essential particular, and alike in soul and in the possibility of infinite development.
>
> Especially do I believe in the Negro Race; in the beauty of its genius, the sweetness of its soul, and its strength in that meekness which shall inherit this turbulent earth.
>
> I believe in pride of race and lineage itself; in pride of self so deep as to scorn injustice to other selves; in pride of lineage so great as to despise no man's father; in pride of race so chivalrous as neither to offer bastardy to the weak nor beg wedlock of the strong, knowing that men may be brothers in Christ, even though they be no brothers-in-law.
>
> I believe in Service—humble reverent service, from the blackening of boots to the whitening of souls; for Work is Heaven, Idleness Hell, and Wages is the "Well done!" of the Master who summoned all them that labor and are heavy laden, making no distinction between the black sweating cotton-hands of Georgia and the First Families of Virginia, since all distinction not based on deed is devilish and not divine.
>
> I believe in the Devil and his angels, who wantonly work to narrow the opportunity of struggling human beings, especially if they be black; who spit in the faces of the fallen, strike them that cannot strike again, believe the worst and work to prove it, hating the image which their Maker stamped on a brother's soul.
>
> I believe in the Prince of Peace. I believe that War is Murder. I believe that armies and navies are at bottom the tinsel and braggadocio of oppression and wrong; and I believe that the wicked conquest of weaker and darker nations by white and stronger but fore-shadows the death of that strength.
>
> I believe in Liberty for all men; the space to stretch their arms and their souls; the right to breathe and the right to vote; the freedom to choose their friends, enjoy sunshine and ride on the railroads, uncursed by color; thinking, dreaming, working as they will in a kingdom of God and love.
>
> I believe in the training of children black even as white; the leading out of little souls into the green pastures and beside the still waters, not for self

truth; lest we forget, and the sons of the fathers, like Esau, for mere meat barter their birthright in a mighty nation.

Finally, I believe in Patience—patience with the weakness of the Weak and the strength of the Strong, the prejudice of the Ignorant and the ignorancy of the Blind; patience with the tardy triumph of Joy and the chastening of Sorrow—patience with God.[29]

The popularity of the Credo stemmed from Du Bois's ability to articulate the theme of race solidarity in powerful prose. What is striking is how much this self-styled freethinker undergirded his Credo with biblical allusions and metaphors. Used to reciting the creed in the Episcopal liturgy, the young Atlanta professor captured in high-liturgical form the common aspirations of blacks of varied educational and economic backgrounds. The opening affirmation, based on Acts 17:26, is the most common biblical text utilized in these years by black and white alike who addressed racial reform.

Du Bois is here announcing a black theology that anticipates by more than half a century some of the themes of contemporary black liberation theologies. There is a call for race pride. But there is also a call for service. The affirmation of peace, because of the Prince of Peace, is noteworthy in this era of jingoism following the Spanish-American War. For one who did not identify himself as a believer and was not related to the institutional church, this statement emerges from a deep belief in a God who is Creator if not Redeemer. But the task of redemption is now in the hands of men and women, who are to learn what it means to live as brothers and sisters.

In speaking about Du Bois's attitudes toward religion, we must distinguish between personal and public attitudes. Du Bois's personal religious odyssey was leading him away from historic Christian belief and institutional Christianity. But Du Bois the trained sociologist and increasingly the propagandist for reform approached religion publicly in terms of its function in society. Belief and function are two separate categories for the sociologist, which may or may not be joined in personal experience. To be sure the negative function of religion, its avoidance of racial reform, was responsible in part for Du Bois's odyssey leading him away from historic Christianity. At the same time, however, he understood the powerful role the churches, black and white, had played historically in society. There is not simply cold scientific detachment, however, for one senses a hope that the churches can yet play a decisive role in racial reform.

In any discussion of the young Du Bois, one must handle carefully the autobiographical material written so much later. His two autobiographies were published in 1940 and 1968. In later years his embrace of Marxism, leading finally to his taking up residence in Ghana, influenced significantly the way that he looked back upon the events of earlier years, especially his understanding of religion.

Du Bois's assessment of the black and white churches at the turn of the century was both astute and provocative. Already in 1900, in an article "The Religion of the American Negro," he connected his critique of black religion to his hopes for racial reform. He joined Douglass and Washington in a critique of black religion but went far beyond either in his analysis. Du Bois, who is often remembered for his stridency, began by expressing empathy for what he called "the peculiar ethical paradox" facing blacks in their religious life. Given the forces arrayed against black Americans, Du Bois saw that there was no single response but a number of responses. On the one hand, it was understandable how the black person, "conscious of his impotence," can become "bitter and vindictive," which meant that "religion, instead of a worship is a complaint and a curse, a wail rather than a hope, a sneer rather than a faith." On the other hand, there was another stream within black religion, "shrewder and keener," which saw in the strength of an antiblack movement an opportunity to be grasped. Forsaking ethical considerations and using a methodology that he likened to "Jesuistic casuistry," this group knew how to get next to the oppressor to win its own way.[30]

Du Bois saw dangers in both approaches: anarchy in the first and hypocrisy in the second. "The one type of Negro stands almost ready to curse God and die, and the other is too often found a traitor to right and a coward before force; the one is wedded to ideals remote, whimsical, perhaps impossible of realization; the other forgets that life is more than meat and the body more than raiment." Du Bois was here describing religious movements, but in outlining their characteristics, he was presaging the larger shape of radicals and conservatives arrayed for battle.[31]

CHAPTER 8

Shifting Allegiances

I do not believe in compromises, in surrendering, or acquiescing, even temporarily, in the deprivation of a single right, out of deference to an unrighteous public sentiment.

Yes

—FRANCIS J. GRIMKÉ

Any other class of the American people, under the strain of distress to which the Negro has been subjected, would imitate Job's distracted wife, and curse the white God and die. The Negro will neither curse nor die, but grin and live—albeit beneath that grin is a groaning of spirit too deep for utterance. The Negro says to his country, "Though you slay me, yet will I serve you."

—KELLY MILLER

W. E. B. Du Bois's *The Souls of Black Folk* created an immediate sensation when it was published in the spring of 1903. No chapter provoked more comment than chapter 3, "Of Mr. Booker T. Washington and Others." In this chapter Du Bois suggested that in the ongoing intramural debate within the black community, he looked forward to some shifting allegiances. As far as movement and change, Du Bois had some very specific "others" in mind. After observing that "the questions involved are so fundamental and serious" in the debate about the strategy to achieve racial justice, he named names. "It is difficult to see how men like the Grimkés, Kelly Miller, J. W. E. Bowen, and other representatives of this group, can much longer be silent."[1]

In these years of both darkness and dawning, many men and women changed their minds and shifted their allegiances. But these four men emerged as pivotal players in an ever-widening debate within the black community. Since all were advocates of the Social Gospel within the black church, their responses to the debate between Washington and Du Bois, between conservatives and radicals, are central to our story.

The brothers Grimké were born in South Carolina, the sons of Nancy Weston, a mulatto slave, and Henry Grimké, her white owner. Growing up in Charleston, they experienced the terror of an effort by a white half-brother to enslave them. After the Union victory they went north to pursue their education in Ashmun Institute, a preparatory school and college founded by Presbyterians in Chester County, Pennsylvania. The name was changed in 1866 to Lincoln University to honor the martyred president. In that same year the brothers, inseparable, began their studies in the preparatory school. Moving on to the regular college program, both boys distinguished themselves in the classroom. Frank graduated as valedictorian, and Archie ranked third in his class.

While at Lincoln, word of the academic achievement of Frank was published in the *National Anti-Slavery Standard*. Angelina Grimké Weld, of abolitionist fame, wife of Theodore Dwight Weld, read about the young Grimké. A letter of inquiry from her resulted in a joyous reunion at commencement week at Lincoln with the two boys, who, she discovered, were her nephews.[2]

After graduation Frank studied law at Lincoln, worked as a financial agent for the college, and then transferred to Howard University to continue his law studies. While in Washington, he attended the Fifteenth Street Presbyterian Church. When he decided to pursue the ministry, grateful for his Presbyterian heritage and training, Frank enrolled at Princeton Theological Seminary in the fall of 1875. He was one of three blacks enrolling that year. His best friend was a black student in his second year at the seminary, Matthew Anderson. Frank's three years at the seminary coincided with the last years of Professor Charles Hodge, architect for almost half a century of the Princeton theology. For the rest of his life Frank expressed his debt to Hodge. As Hodge's student, his own ministry was rooted in a biblical faith that could not be tilted by modern currents of biblical higher criticism or scientific Darwinism. Grimké was at home with the propositional approach to truth that was the hallmark of Reformed orthodoxy.

In 1878 Frank was invited to become the pastor of the Fifteenth Street Presbyterian Church in Washington, D.C. When Grimké came to Washington, blacks numbered almost one-third of the city's population. His church served the upper-middle-class to upper-class black community. The emphasis of his preaching was a personal commitment to Christ. He emphasized high moral conduct, saying again and again that Christians were to live not by impulse but by principle. The Fifteenth Street congregation soon renamed their pastor the "Black Puritan."[3]

The first national notoriety concerning Francis Grimké occurred in 1884. In 1880 he had been asked to join the Board of Trustees of Howard University. This association brought him into closer contact with fellow board member Frederick Douglass, who became the primary model for him of a strong black leader. In 1884 Douglass asked Grimké to be the officiating minister at his second marriage—to Helen M. Pitts, a white woman who had been his secretary. This action of Douglass offended both whites and blacks, and Grimké was caught up in the criticism.

Grimké knew the ground on which he stood: "It was nobody else's business." Forty years later Grimké said that intermarriage might not have been a wise thing to do, given the state of affairs in this country, but he would defend anyone's right to do so at all costs. "The right to marry . . . is inherent, God-given. No one may rightfully forbid it."[4]

The tremendous pace of Grimké's ministry took its toll in 1885. Near collapse, he decided to leave his beloved Fifteenth Street Church and seek a different, slower pastorate. He accepted a call to the Laura Street Presbyterian Church in Jacksonville, Florida.

In Florida he encountered again some of the same kinds of discrimination he had known as a youth in the South. Now he encountered the odious beginnings of Jim Crow segregation. He was especially incensed when he encountered it in the church. When evangelist Dwight L. Moody came to Jacksonville, he was encouraged by some to integrate his revival meetings. Moody, however, adopted the strategy of letting the local committee decide on arrangements. The result was separate meetings for blacks and whites. At other times and places Grimké praised Moody for "the tremendous work that he did, and the wonderful success which attended his efforts." But in Florida he confessed that "it is impossible to contemplate this man . . . without mingled feelings of pity and disgust." He denounced Moody's acquiescence to the standards of the world rather than the standards of the kingdom of God.[5]

From the beginning of his career Grimké was both a faithful and a provocative Presbyterian. He was elected moderator of the Presbytery of Washington City in 1880. But he was involved continually in what Louis B. Weeks has aptly called a lovers quarrel with the Presbyterian church over its racist policies.[6] In 1888 as the northern Presbyterian church gathered for its centennial celebrations in Philadelphia, talk of merger with the southern church was in the air. In this era of the retreat from Reconstruction, many northerners were more than willing to acquiesce to southern demands for segregated presbyteries and synods. Grimké came to Philadelphia and stayed with his seminary friend Matthew Anderson, founding pastor of the Berean Presbyterian Church. In an article that spring he had pleaded with the Presbyterian church "to stand by His inspired Word in its righteous opposition to all invidious distinctions." Asking the commissioners to consider the consequences of discrimination in its governing bodies, Grimké pleaded, "As I love the old Church, I pray God it may be saved the shame of such an act."[7]

Grimké returned to Fifteenth Street Church in 1889 and remained there until his retirement from active ministry in 1925. In 1893 he was reelected moderator of the Presbytery of Washington City. But as the years went on, Grimké was just as apt to boycott meetings as to be in attendance. Once, when the presbytery was scheduled to be at a "country meeting," in a town outside of Washington, Grimké wrote the presbytery in advance that he would not be present. He told the presbytery that "it has given a great deal of attention to the whites, but little or no attention to the colored people within its jurisdiction." Regarding the upcoming meeting, Grimké observed that "there doesn't seem to be Christianity enough in most of our white churches, especially in the southern section of our country, to make it possible to give decent entertainment to a colored gentleman." He made a declaration of where he stood in the most typical Social Gospel watchwords: "If there is any one thing that the religion of Jesus Christ stands for more than another, it is the fatherhood of God, and the brotherhood of man."[8]

On another occasion, as a member of presbytery known to be concerned about evangelism, Grimké was invited to meet with members of the General Assembly and synod committees on evangelism. He replied by saying that there would be no value for him in meeting with white committees operating under their present understanding of evangelism. He sent along a tract by Billy Sunday as an example of this kind of thinking. He went on to say, "Until evangelism clearly recognizes the evil of race prejudice, and includes it among the sins to be repented of in seeking to bring men into the church of God, it is a mockery, a mere sham, utterly unworthy of the Christian church." He quoted from the First Letter of John: "If a man say, I love God, and hateth his brother, he is a liar." There is no record of the committee's response.[9]

A divisive fight within the Presbyterian family occurred in 1904 over the merger of the northern Presbyterian church with the Cumberland Presbyterian church. The Cumberland church, centered in the South, was an all-white denomination. One of the issues became whether the governing bodies should be segregated or integrated. When the plan of merger made provision for all-white presbyteries and synods, Grimké took the lead in vigorous protest.[10]

The Presbytery of Washington City recognized Grimké's role in this issue and sent him as a commissioner to the General Assembly, meeting in Buffalo. In remarks on the floor of the assembly, Grimké challenged his fellow commissioners by asking them whether they wanted union at the price of "sanctioning the spirit of caste, or by putting the stamp of inferiority upon any class or race within the Church."

The reunion measure was adopted by the General Assembly and sent to the presbyteries for a yes-or-no vote. Grimké was a leader in the fight against reunion and campaigned vigorously in speeches and articles. On April 11 his own Presbytery of Washington City debated the issue. Grimké addressed the presbytery for an hour in his most brilliant and flaming oratorical style. When he was finished, his remarks were greeted with applause. Many whites wanted their opportunity to respond. One who did was Supreme Court Justice John Harlan. The man who had dissented in *Plessy v. Ferguson* now dissented again. Harlan was an elder in the New York Avenue Presbyterian church in Washington, D.C. He urged the presbytery, "Let us stand in the way of the fathers, and say to the world that as far as our church is concerned, we are race blind and color blind."[11] The most difficult blow of all occurred when Grimké's own Presbytery of Washington City voted for reunion.

Reunion was finally ratified by a large majority of the presbyteries. Through it all, Grimké earned a reputation among some as being bitter. But among blacks and some whites Grimké had stamped himself as a prophet within his church.[12]

In 1905 Archie moved into the Francis Grimké household in Washington. We should note here a contrast between the two brothers. Independently, and yet together, they had been shifting their allegiance from the Washingtonian philosophy to the program being advocated by Du Bois. But although the brothers were in agreement about philosophy and alike in their oratorical courage and skill, there was a significant difference. Francis believed that the minister's primary calling was first to his parish, then to the larger church, and, if time permitted, lastly to the larger community. Put another way, he believed his basic tasks were the preaching of the gospel and the pastoral care of his flock. At various times in his career it seems he could have accepted positions outside the parish, including the presidency of Howard University at a time of crisis in 1905–1906, but he was steadfast in the conviction that he had been called to the parish ministry.

He made quite sure that his sermons, which did deal with all manner of political, social, and economic issues, were published in pamphlet form and made available to a large mailing list. He wrote letters on occasion to public officials. But he went no further, however, in trying to extend his influence. He was quite content to let brother Archie and other black leaders use their influence in the NAACP or in lobbying

Congress or in whatever means or movements they chose. Henry J. Ferry notes the development of Social Gospel motifs in Grimké's ministry in the 1890s but observes that Grimké never abandoned his primary understanding of the locus of ministry as the parish.[13]

Grimké's self-understanding of ministry helps explain his role in the NAACP. After the Springfield riot in 1908 Grimké was one of six blacks who signed the call on Lincoln's birthday for a National Negro Conference to be held in May. But Grimké did not attend the conference, even though brother Archibald did. Many were critical of Grimké's absence, especially Oswald Garrison Villard, who had drafted the call.[14]

Francis was always supportive of the NAACP. He contributed financially and urged his congregation to do so. He commended the *Crisis* to his people. Any special program or drive of the NAACP would be mentioned from the pulpit. In these early days the NAACP was focusing much of its efforts through legal channels, and brother Archibald, living in the same house, was best equipped to discharge this part of the Grimké family stewardship.

Meanwhile Grimké was issuing his own call Sunday by Sunday at Fifteenth Street Presbyterian Church. His sermons were a remarkable blend of biblical exegesis and political commentary. Nowhere was he more cogent and persuasive than when he proclaimed his periodic messages on racial justice.[15]

The shift in Grimké's allegiance was announced in a sermon, "God and the Race Problem," preached on May 3, 1903, just weeks after the publication of *The Souls of Black Folk*. Grimké told his congregation that this new book "is one of the most remarkable contributions that has yet been made on the Negro question." Grimké praised the aspirations that Du Bois had set forth for blacks in such compelling prose. At the same time he derided the press for focusing on the words of the black leader, unnamed, "who does not want very much, who does not claim very much for his race; who thinks that an industrial education is quite sufficient; who thinks that the ballot is immaterial, that civil rights may be dispensed with."[16]

Grimké, sometimes viewed as bitter by whites, could be magnanimous toward those whites who joined the struggle for racial reform. In November and December 1898 he preached four sermons that analyzed the present crisis in race relations. In the third sermon, "Signs of a Brighter Future," he paid tribute to several white allies. First to be mentioned was William Hayes Ward, editor of the *Independent*. "I know of no man who appreciates more fully the nature of the fight that we are making, or who more deeply sympathizes with us than he does." Tribute was paid also to Albion W. Tourgée, "whose voice and pen have been used unsparing in our behalf," and George W. Cable, who mounted a consistent "protest against the barbarism of the South and in the interest of the oppressed."[17]

In 1903 Grimké delivered a sermon "God and the Race Problem." In this sermon he praised remarks made by Washington Gladden a few days earlier at the Atlanta University conference on the Negro church to the effect that if the black man was good enough to die for his country, he was good enough to share in the government of it.[18]

Grimké had the highest expectation when one of the Presbyterian church's own sons was elected to the chief office in the land. In November 1912 Grimké wrote to president-elect Woodrow Wilson. He confessed that black people had come to fear the triumph of the Democratic party, "lest their rights be interfered with." But Grimké had just read an address by Wilson entitled "The Importance of Bible Study" to a group of Sunday school teachers. He told Wilson that that single address "relieved my mind as to the treatment which the colored people are likely to receive from you and your administration." Grimké went on to say, "No American citizen, white or black, need have any reasonable grounds of fear from the Administration of a man who feels as he does, who believes as he does in the Word of God."[19] The letter was sent in a spirit of expectation and good will.

Ten months later Grimké wrote again to President Wilson. The new administration at Wilson's behest had put in place in federal office even more segregation than had existed before. To Grimké, Wilson had shown himself a southern Presbyterian who formulated his racial policies from a cultural rather than a Christian perspective. Because this second letter summarizes succinctly so much of Grimké's posture on race relations, it is here printed in its entirety.[20]

Washington, D.C., September 5, 1913

Dear Sir:

As an American citizen I desire to enter my earnest protest against the disposition, under your Administration, to segregate colored people in the various departments of the Government. To do so is undemocratic, is un-American, is un-Christian, is needlessly to offend the self-respect of the loyal black citizens of the Republic. We constitute one-tenth of the population, and, under the Constitution, have the same rights and are entitled to the same consideration as other citizens. We had every reason to hope, from your high Christian character, and from your avowal of lofty principles prior to your election, that your accession to power would act as a check upon the brutal and insane spirit of race hatred that characterizes certain portions

of the white people of this country. As American citizens we have a right to
expect the President of the United States to stand between us and those who
are bent on forcing us into a position of inferiority. Under the Constitution,
resting upon the broad foundation of democratic principles as embodied in
the Declaration of Independence, there are no superiors and inferiors. Before the law all citizens are equal, and are entitled to the same consideration.
May we not expect,—have we not the right to expect, that your personal
influence, as well as the great influence which comes from your commanding official position, will be thrown against what is clearly, is distinctly not
in accordance with the spirit of free institutions? All class distinctions
among citizens are un-American, and the sooner every vestige of it is
stamped out, the better it will be for the Republic.

Very truly,
Francis J. Grimké

This letter is remarkable in both its content and tone. Unlike the
congratulatory letter ten months previous, the content focuses upon
American democratic principles. The argument of this book is that Social Gospel leaders, both black and white, appealed to both the
Christian and civic Scriptures. The appeal here is to the Constitution
and the Declaration of Independence. It is also to the office of the president. The tone is strong—not in the public tradition of the Washing-
tonians—but not bitter. It appeals to hope, and that hope is rooted in
the "high Christian character" of the president.

Grimké's shift in allegiance, signaled by his sermon incorporating
The Souls of Black Folk in 1903, was complete by the time of the formation
of the Niagara Movement in 1905. At the same time, Grimké's thinking
about both Washington and Du Bois always showed an appreciation for
the strengths and weaknesses in each man and in the programs they
advocated. Grimké continued to affirm the Puritan values that first attracted him to Washington in his initial visit to Tuskegee. But with the
passing of years he saw Washington in a different light. As he came to
learn more about the Wizard of Tuskegee, he believed that power had
corrupted Washington. Washington continued to preach about values,
but in Grimké's estimation he was not practicing what he preached.
Word of Washington's dealings behind closed doors with northern cap-
italist backers undermined Grimké's confidence in him.

After the death of his wife, Charlotte, in 1913, Grimké began to keep
a journal. In his journal, undated, he confessed his concerns about both
Washington and Du Bois. In 1914 he wrote that in a speech in Burling-
ton, New Jersey, Washington told his black audience that "instead of

fighting segregation they had better give their attention to improving their homes, so that white people would not object to living near them." Grimké retorted that Washington knew well that this was not the issue at all. "The objection is not to living near the poorer and lower classes of colored people, but to living near any class at all. The more advanced the colored people are, the greater the objection." Grimké knew about this treatment firsthand from his own and his parishioners' experiences. The result of Washington's speeches, Grimké wrote, was that "the weight of his influence was thrown against the anti-segregation agitation."

Grimké concluded this entry with strong words that, uttered in the privacy of his journal, he did not repeat in public. In summarizing Washington's policies of accommodation, he said, "This is in line with what has been Mr. Washington's policy all along." There is nothing so bitter as when one feels that one has been taken in by initial words about morality and religion. Grimké went on to say, "It is because of this cowardly, hypocritical course on his part, that the enemies of the race, even the bitterest, have always been able to quote him in support of their low estimate of the race and of the treatment that ought to be accorded to it." In conclusion, in the admonition of a Puritan preacher, Grimké said, "Mr. Washington ought to be heartily ashamed of himself."[21]

Grimké also held ambivalent attitudes about Du Bois. He embraced Du Bois's philosophy and strategy as the best course to achieve racial justice. Privately, however, he had questions about Du Bois. In his journal he wrote, "Men, like DuBois, when they speak on economics, or on the civil and political rights of the Negro as an American citizen, speak with authority and may be safely followed." Du Bois had spoken recently at Howard University, and Grimké had heard that he had scoffed at religion. To this news Grimké wrote in his journal of Du Bois and others, "But when it comes to religion and morality, they are sadly in need of guidance themselves." He invoked words of Lincoln to the effect that we stand with people when they are right and part with them when they are wrong. Now he classed Du Bois with those who "are far, far out of the way as tested by the Word of God and the principles of Jesus Christ." Grimké, it should be noted, did not rebuke Du Bois publicly. But his hope, born of the vision of his teachers at Princeton Seminary, was that piety and learning belonged together.[22]

The lives of Archie and Frank were inextricably linked even in the period of their lives when they lived apart. While at Lincoln, both participated actively in the Ashmun Presbyterian Church, which Archie helped to organize. Archie was ordained an elder at age eighteen, unusual in the Presbyterian church for that time.

SP

After graduation Archibald enrolled at Harvard Law School. He became the first black graduate of the law school and stayed in in Boston to open a law office. It was difficult in those days for a black lawyer, and at first Grimké struggled financially. He supplemented his legal work by founding and editing *The Hub* in 1883, the first black newspaper in New England. After the newspaper ceased publication in 1886, he turned his interests to other writing projects, authoring two biographies, *William Lloyd Garrison: The Abolitionist* (1891), and *The Life of Charles Sumner: The Scholar in Politics* (1892).[23]

Archibald was a leader who always spoke his mind fearlessly. In 1885 he was elected president of the Massachusetts Suffrage League. In these years he became associated with a group known as the Boston radicals. Led by William Monroe Trotter, the group also included Clement Morgan, another lawyer. Trotter, the first black elected to Phi Beta Kappa at Harvard, was outspoken against all forms of discrimination. In 1901 he founded the *Boston Guardian* and become the most outspoken foe of Booker T. Washington.

In 1894 Archibald was appointed by President Grover Cleveland to be the consul at Santo Domingo in the Dominican Republic. He served in this post until 1898.

Du Bois did well to point up Archibald as a pivotal person in the Washington–Du Bois debate, for Grimké struggled in the years at the turn of the century with divided loyalties. Always known as an outspoken individual, he appreciated Trotter's willingness to take a stand in the tradition of abolitionist agitation. At the same time, his Presbyterian ethic convinced him that Washington was right in his insistence that blacks needed to learn the values of discipline and economic self-sufficiency if they were to move into the mainstream of American life.

After the publication of *The Souls of Black Folk* in the spring of 1903, Washington and his allies called a secret conference to be held at Carnegie Hall, New York, in January 1904. At the end of the conference Washington declared himself ready to work for "absolute civic, political and public equality." Du Bois, in response, said he was willing to work with Washington if Washington lived up to this promise. The confidential report of the conference drawn up by Kelly Miller did reveal a basis of agreement about future strategies.[24]

Emanating from the conference was a Committee of Twelve for the Advancements of the Interests of the Negro Race. The whole agreement between conservatives, moderates, and radicals began to collapse when most of the work and publications of the committee focused on the traditional Washingtonian themes of self-help, thrift, discipline, and so forth. One of the few exceptions to this tendency was Archibald Grimké's pamphlet *Why Discrimination Is Bad.*

In 1905 Archibald moved with his daughter, Angelina Weld Grimké, to Washington to live with Frank and his family. Reunited with his brother, Archibald appreciated the spiritual sustenance of the Fifteenth Street Presbyterian Church. Less vocal than his preacher brother about his faith, it nevertheless was a foundation for his active life. Reunited again, the brothers reinforced each other in their growing commitment to protest and agitation, even as that commitment took shape in different spheres.

Also in 1905 Archie became an early supporter of the Niagara Movement. Even with this move he was still not ready to break with Washington, for he considered part of the Washingtonian program essential for black progress.

The break finally came in 1906 over President Theodore Roosevelt's handling of the Brownsville incident, (discussed below in chapter 11) and over Washington's actions at the time. Angry at Washington, Archibald was silent in his criticism no longer.

As Niagara evolved into the NAACP, Archibald became a prominent leader. He was numbered among the committee of forty who prepared the way for the organization of the NAACP. In Washington he served as president of the NAACP branch. He could always be counted on to help with NAACP legislative or legal strategies in the nation's capital.

Always active in politics, Grimké was a constant monitor of presidential policies in relation to blacks. In 1899 he had condemned President William McKinley over his silence on growing racial oppression. Archibald and Francis had high hopes for Woodrow Wilson, a fellow Presbyterian. But it did not take long for Archibald to begin a steady stream of letters and articles opposing Wilson's policies. As Wilson increased segregationist policies in federal offices, Archibald joined with his brother and with Trotter, Du Bois, and others in protest.

A recognition of Archibald Grimké's contributions came in 1919 with the awarding of the Joel Spingarn gold medal by the NAACP. The award, given annually for "the highest and noblest achievement of an American Negro," was first presented in 1915. It was awarded to Grimké in recognition of his leadership in the Washington branch of the NAACP, his work with Congressional committees, and his continuing efforts against segregation in the federal government.[25]

A friend of the brothers Grimké was Washington resident Kelly Miller. A Congregationalist and a professor at Howard University, he was a mediating force in the debate between the conservatives and the radicals. At the same time, he was often attacked from both sides and accused of straddling the fence.

Kelly Miller was born in 1863 in Winnsboro, South Carolina. He graduated from Howard University in 1886. In 1887 he was the first black admitted to Johns Hopkins University, where he undertook graduate study in mathematics, physics, and astronomy. In 1890 he was invited to join the faculty at Howard. He taught mathematics at first, but his real interest became the development of the new discipline of sociology. He was a member of the faculty until 1934. He served as dean of the College of Arts and Sciences from 1907 to 1919. He was instrumental, with President Wilbur Thirkield, in guiding a dramatic expansion of Howard both in the natural and social sciences and in student enrollment.[26]

Early in his years at Howard, Miller achieved a national reputation through lecturing and writing. He forged his own role in the black intramural debate when in 1903 he wrote two anonymous articles for the *Boston Transcript* on radicals and conservatives. These articles helped popularize the names for the opposing sides of the debate. The articles were combined to become the opening chapter in his book *Race Adjustment*, published in 1906. No one in these years was better than Miller at placing the debate within perspective and at doing so with such deft—and sometimes devastating—prose.

Miller depicted Washington as "the storm-center about which the controversy rages." He positioned Washington as one who came upon the historical stage when the more aggressive policies of Frederick Douglass "had seemed to fail" during the retreat from Reconstruction. Miller insightfully compared Douglass and Washington. Although the article in one sense is a description of contending forces, in another sense it is a brief for Washington as the best hope of blacks at that moment in history. Miller was willing to admit some of Washington's shortcomings, but he found even more that was worrisome about his more radical opponents.[27]

He began the article by talking about the opponents, focusing more on William Monroe Trotter than on W. E. B. Du Bois. Affirming Trotter's brilliance and courage, Miller nevertheless believed he "lacks the moral sanity and pose of the great emancipator." He then launched into a devastating attack on Trotter as a leader of the radical forces. "Endowed with a narrow, intolerant intensity of spirit, he pursues his ends with a Jesuitical justification of untoward means." Miller, adding some material for his book in 1906 that did not appear in the original newspaper articles in 1903, believed that Trotter, not Du Bois, "is the real guiding power of the 'Niagara Movement.'"[28]

In treating Du Bois, Miller was more evenhanded but ultimately critical. Miller found it ironic that "the men who are now extolling him as the peerless leader of the radicals were a few years ago denouncing him bitterly for his restrained and reasoned conclusions." Miller extolled the literary genius evident in *The Philadelphia Negro* and *The Souls of Black Folk*. But the leap to the Niagara Movement manifesto authored by Du Bois required belief in what Miller called "mental and moral metamorphosis." Realizing that Du Bois was emerging as the leader of the radicals, Miller believed he was unsuited and should not accept the mantle. "Dr. Du Bois is passionately devoted to the welfare of his race, but he is allowing himself to be exploited in a function for which he is by nature unfit." Miller perhaps was thinking a bit of his own role when he answered the reader's question, Why is he unfit? "His highest service will consist in interpreting to the white people the needs and feelings of his race in terms of exact knowledge and nice language, rather than as an agitator or promoter of concrete achievement."[29]

In highlighting Washington's accomplishments, Miller chose to compare him neither to Trotter or Du Bois, who were both of somewhat dubious stature, but instead to Frederick Douglass. In this comparison Miller let us see his evaluation of Washington's strengths and weaknesses. This comparison, along with Du Bois's chapter in *The Souls of Black Folk*, was talked about throughout the black community. Miller put the comparison in a whole series of images.

> Douglass insisted upon rights; Washington insists upon duty. Douglass held up to public scorn the sins of the white man; Washington portrays the faults of his own race. Douglass spoke what he thought the world should hear; Washington speaks only what he feels it is disposed to listen to. Douglass's conduct was actuated by principle; Washington's by prudence. Douglass had no limited, copyrighted programme for his race, but appealed to the Decalogue, the Golden Rule, the Declaration of Independence, the Constitution of the United States; Washington, holding these great principles in the shadowy background, presents a practical expedient applicable to present needs. Douglass was a moralist, insisting upon the application of righteousness to public affairs; Washington is a practical opportunist, accepting the best terms which he thinks it is possible to secure.[30]

Miller's approach was to grant the best motives, if not always the best strategies, to Washington. He said that "Mr. Washington's bitterest opponents cannot gainsay his sincerity or doubt that the welfare of his race is the chief burden of his soul."[31] The focus of disagreement, however, was not motive but strategy. The complaint was that Washington was not willing to speak up to the vital issues of civic and political rights.

Miller's way with words was not simply the skill of a journalist. Trained as a mathematician, he early gravitated toward the new social science of sociology. The data he collected in a report for the United States Commissioner of Education, published in 1901, prepared him to be a knowledgeable participant, not just a commentator, in the debate between radicals and conservatives. "The Education of the Negro" was a long, detailed report filled with graphs and tables of information encompassing population, economics, employment, and per capita funding for education to which we shall return.[32]

Of the many persons involved in shifting allegiances, Miller is one of the most complex and thus most fascinating. August Meier identifies four "fairly distinct periods" in Miller's shifting relationship to Washington. Meier asserts that Miller at first opposed Washington's accommodationist philosophy, but from the late 1890s until about 1902, he supported Washington's calls for racial solidarity and economic self help. These attitudes grew out of Miller's belief that blacks could develop their own social, political, and religious institutions separate from white America. From the time Miller wrote "Conservatives and Radicals" in 1903, until the organization of the NAACP in 1909, Miller was a mediating presence. Accused by both sides of trying to straddle the fence, Miller defended his middle-of-the-road position by saying that "effective horsemanship is accomplished by straddling." Miller was one of the few black leaders who served on the boards of both the NAACP and the Urban League. Convinced that Washington's policies were not producing results, he moved towards the position of the NAACP after 1909.[33]

In 1903 Miller was invited by Du Bois to participate in the Atlanta conference on the Negro Church. Washington Gladden was impressed with Miller's paper, "Religion as a Solvent of the Race Problem," and promptly invited him to speak to the annual meeting of the American Missionary Association. Gladden also wrote to the *North American Review* encouraging their publication of Miller's address. This prompted an exchange of letters between these two Congregationalists.[34]

Miller's address was both an affirmation and a challenge. He is clear at the outset that he wished to approach religion as a sociologist. "Religion may be treated as a sociological phenomenon whose manifestation is as evident and whose effect is as easily measured as any other data with which the student of social subjects has to deal." Miller spent the first part of his essay affirming that "the conversion of the Negro to the Christian faith is as marvelous, and perhaps as momentous, as any event in the history of the church." He then spoke at some length about the varied dimensions of black religious history and experience.[35]

But affirmation leads to challenge. Miller's goal was to assess the role of religion in both the black and white communities. He began by asking whether or not the definition of religion was adequate for blacks at this transitional time. His answer was a Social Gospel answer. "The mission of Christianity is to bring about social salvation, as well as the salvation of souls." We have seen again and again that blacks and whites trained in sociology come to embrace a social understanding of Christianity. Without committing himself to a specific strategy of racial reform, Miller's point in this essay was that religion must play a vital role in racial reform. "The solution of the race question" would depend upon the "recognition of the fatherhood of God and the brotherhood of man."[36]

Whether it was religion or politics, Miller always seemed to be able to see both sides of an issue. Even though Meier suggests that Miller moved toward the Du Bois position after 1909, the Howard professor always retained a high regard for the practicality of Washington and a suspicion of the ability of Du Bois to translate words into deeds. Called "the Negro's chief intellectual protagonist" by Allain Locke, his Howard colleague, Miller offered a balanced perspective, which was sometimes in short supply in these years of confrontation and controversy.[37]

The fourth member of the "others" named by Du Bois was John Wesley Edward Bowen. Born in New Orleans in 1855, he graduated from New Orleans University in 1878. Feeling an early call to the ministry, he completed his theological studies at Boston University in 1885. He continued his studies at Boston University, and two years later he became the second black in America to earn a Ph.D. degree. From 1888 to 1892 he ministered to congregations in Newark, Baltimore, and Washington and at the same time taught at Morgan College in Baltimore and at Howard University. In 1893 he was offered the chair of historical theology at Gammon Theological Seminary in Atlanta. He remained at the seminary until 1932.

Du Bois predicted that Bowen would one day reject the Washingtonian philosophy. He never did. Although in his own mind an independent leader and thinker, his speeches and articles presented a fairly consistent intellectual version of Washington's program. Bowen did have some private misgivings, but in public he remained loyal to Washington.[38]

Bowen is an arresting figure because, as James M. Washington makes clear, he was a theological liberal who made conservative social pronouncements. More often in the black church one encounters a figure like Francis J. Grimké, who was a theological conservative making liberal social pronouncements.

Bowen's liberalism was nurtured in his studies at Boston University. The church history department was led during Bowen's student years by Henry C. Sheldon. Sheldon, a "transient Liberal Evangelical," authored *Unbelief in the Nineteenth Century*, in which he argued that the historian should aim to be an "objective" observer. The major influence on Bowen was Sheldon's teacher and friend Borden Parker Bowne. Bowne became a leading theologian in the wing of Methodism embracing a liberal theology. Later in his career Bowne was tried for heresy by the Methodist church. One of the five charges was that Bowne, in dealing with biblical authority and revelation, tended to harmonize biblical faith too much with currents of nineteenth-century liberalism. Bowne held that in the midst of the mystery of history is a God who is more immanent than transcendent. Bowne heralded a "progressive revelation," which meant that God's purposes for the world were still being revealed. A foundation of this revelation in all times was that this God is a Friend and Lover of all men and women.[39]

A bright, young J. W. E. Bowen adapted the main themes in Bowne's theology to the crisis of race relations in America. Bowen's dissertation has either been misplaced or lost, but he published a summary of it in the *Methodist Review* in 1891 under the title "A Psychological Principle in Revelation." Bowne had argued that many problems in history were the result of "human misapprehensions." The great possibility for humanity was that they could change their perceptions of reality. The fundamental changes would be in the mind rather than changes in human events. Bowen was excited about the prospect of being a teacher because of the possibility of changing the ideas in people's minds. Believing in "development" meant that new forms and new ideas could initiate new patterns of action.

In 1892 Bowen offered his opinion on the direction of "the Negro question" in *"What Shall the Harvest Be?" A National Sermon*, actually four sermons that were widely distributed. In what he called "A Series of Plain Talks to the Colored People of America on Their Problems," Bowen articulated his theology of history in popular language. The

whole tone was revealed in the opening words: "The times are ominous; ominous I believe not for evil, but for good." Bowen announced
himself as an "optimist of the purest type" concerning the future of
black Americans. How did he deal with the afflictions of slavery still so
close in memory? He believed that "the school of adversity is a necessary school to educate us." Bowen knew he was on difficult ground as
he tried to make sense of the immediate past. He said he would not
justify slavery or oppression. Bowen went deeper into the question of
how to understand the suffering of black Americans. He proclaimed, "I
am possessed of the opinion that God was in all of it." True to his
optimism, he announced that "under his hand some mighty results will
be brought out, which could not have come, had not this experience
been ours."[40]

In 1895 Bowen helped organize the Congress on Africa sponsored
by the Steward Missionary Foundation for Africa of the Gammon Theological Seminary. Bowen edited the addresses and delivered one of the
major speeches. In this speech, "The Comparative Status of the Negro
at the Close of the War and Today," Bowen was both apologetic and
upbeat. In summarizing the results of slavery, Bowen offered the opinion that blacks began their life in slavery with deficiencies in certain
areas: "self-reliance, self-control and self-command." But according to
Bowen these deficiencies were not simply part of the past, for "he [the
black] is still wanting in many of the fundamental virtues of a highly
civilized life." Included among these virtues for Bowen is the moral life.
"His moral sins in many cases are shockingly cruel."[41]

The question must be asked why Bowen would concede so much in
such an important address. It must be remembered that in these years
the proponents of black progress were in a dilemma. If they did not
point up persons and programs that added up to progress, detractors
of black advancement could say "I told you so." But if either whites or
blacks looked at black progress through rose-colored glasses, this would
only obscure the real tasks yet to be accomplished. One explanation for
this seemingly abasing attitude of Bowen was his concern for black
leaders, especially black ministers. As a theological educator he was
concerned about the status of the black ministry. As we saw in the
previous chapter, Washington, Du Bois, and others were often critical
of the black ministry. Bowen believed in a future ministry that would
be much better educated and thus prepared for changing American life.
But even in recognizing problems Bowen was remarkably upbeat about
the ministry in this address. "There are in Negro pulpits all over the
land and in the South some Negro preachers who, in intellectual ability,

in moral power and purity, and in spiritual insight and breadth of vision, are the equal of some of the best of the Anglo-Saxon race." It is precisely because of the problems, both educational and moral, that a well-prepared black ministry is so much needed.[42]

A second reason for Bowen's concessions in this speech are not immediately apparent in the speech itself. In the early 1890s Frederick Douglass had appealed for a revival of political activity in the spirit of Reconstruction radicalism. Bowen was opposed to this strategy. In 1894 he had congratulated black abolitionist William Still for refusing to go along with Douglass's call. In his letter to Still he said he regretted that in those days blacks had been "dragged from the plow to the legislature," and had become "drunken with the new wine of political power." Between the lines of the Congress on Africa address Bowen was asking blacks to look to their own resources, both educational and economic, and not to what he believed to be the "bankrupt" policies of political action.[43]

In the following two decades, Bowen stayed close to the Washington philosophy and strategy. In 1904 Bowen became the senior editor of the *Voice of the Negro*, a magazine established by Washington in that year to give voice to his program. His editorials praised the practical common sense of Washington and Tuskegee.

During the Atlanta riot of 1906, Bowen and members of his staff were lined up outside of Gammon Seminary and forced to submit to a search and to insults. The dignified Bowen was beaten over the head by a policeman with a rifle butt and badly injured.[44] Even this treatment in the city where Du Bois was arguing for a course of political action did not shake Bowen's commitment to Washington's program.

The battle between Du Bois and Washington, between radicals and conservatives, took place on many fronts and over diverse issues. It is not possible to touch on all issues, but the argument about industrial and higher education was central to the whole debate.

The debate has sometimes been falsely posed as a struggle between two opposing forms of education. Instead it was more a question of balance and proportion. It became commonplace to hear Washington and his supporters say that there was no debate; they supported both forms of education. In his biography of Washington, Harlan cautions against seeing higher education versus industrial education as "one of those polarizing differences" between Washington and Du Bois. Nevertheless, it is the argument in this chapter that there was a significant difference of opinion. If not polarizing, it is a difference that widened in this first decade of the new century. And this division always pointed to larger issues that divided conservatives and radicals.[45]

For white Social Gospelers, as has already been seen, initial involvement in racial reform was through involvement in black education. Whether through the church missionary societies' private institutions or through the southern education movement's advocacy of public education, industrial versus higher education was being debated continuously during these years. Washington is often credited with making industrial education prominent, but actually he was adapting a movement in effect for some decades. He had learned industrial education as a pupil and then a protégé of Samuel Chapman Armstrong at Hampton. Washington's leadership and entrepreneurial skills soon made Tuskegee the leader, even over Hampton, of black schools advocating industrial education.

It is worth remembering that the origins of industrial education had nothing to do with race. Johann Heinrich Pestalozzi, Phillip Emmanuel von Fellenberg, and others pioneered this approach in an educational reform movement in Europe in the early nineteenth century. They sought to relate education to the everyday lives of people and to emphasize learning-by-doing.

Even though industrial education was born out of reform instincts, it should not be forgotten that it took root originally in a class society. In such a society the presumption was that there would continue to be division based on history and heredity. In this kind of society there were limits to upward mobility and to social intercourse.

The South was a classist society. Du Bois, a light-skinned black intellectual from New England, struggled against classism as well as racism in his years in the South. In the focus on the evils of racism, to which our consciousness has been heightened because of the civil rights era, it would be easy to forget the lingering residue of classism in our midst.

An often-unappreciated part of Martin Luther King's social analysis was his attack on classism. As early as Montgomery and at the end in Memphis, he attempted to show that poor blacks and poor whites should have much in common. They were being kept apart by the machinations of people in the upper strata of society who had much to lose if the lower classes would ever unite.

Ideas about industrial education found congenial soil in reform movements in America before the Civil War. A new vehicle for this kind of education came into being with the proliferation of agricultural and mechanical colleges spawned by the Morrill Act of 1862. After the Civil

War black education participated in a generalized movement that encouraged industrial education.[46]

Support for this form of black education came directly from white philanthropic interests. From 1882 to 1903 the John F. Slater Fund, under the leadership of its agents Atticus G. Haygood and Jabez L. M. Curry, gave their stamp of approval by directing monies to schools fostering industrial education. When this preference became known, other black schools also began initiating industrial and agricultural departments.

Industrial education meant in practice a general range of offerings clustered around agricultural and building trades for boys and home economics and practical nursing for girls. Specific courses were available in many areas. Courses for boys included bricklaying, blacksmithing, carpentry, masonry, shoemaking, cabinetmaking, and animal husbandry. Among the courses offered for girls were sewing, knitting, and dressmaking. Printing was popular because of the opportunity for immediate financial return. Some of the better-endowed schools, such as Atlanta University, known primarily for the quality of its liberal arts offerings, secured heavy equipment to enable its students to do more with iron and wood. Programs for girls began to flourish in the 1890s in part because courses in home economics did not generally require such heavy equipment.[47]

The popular acclaim for this form of education came from all sides. The friendship of influential northern leaders opened the doors for broad intersectional support. William H. Baldwin, Jr., was probably Washington's closest white friend. Washington was indebted to Baldwin for helping put the operation of Tuskegee on a sound financial basis. Robert C. Ogden was an early supporter of General Armstrong and Hampton, and he likewise became a friend of Washington and Tuskegee. George F. Peabody assisted Washington with various fund-raising efforts.

The support these philanthropists offered for Hampton, Tuskegee, and their programs of industrial education was rooted in more than an obvious endorsement of an educational philosophy. Criticized by opponents as a materialistic philosophy of education, industrial education for these philanthropists was attractive because of its moral dimensions. Ogden, described in the fiftieth anniversary history of Hampton as a "spiritually minded man of the world," supported Hampton early because of its commitment to the building of Christian character. Industrial education was not simply the acquiring of skills, but, to use Hampton's motto, it was "education for life." Service remained a predominant motif in all the literature of Hampton and Tuskegee. Hampton separated from the American Missionary Association early on, and Tuskegee never did have this association, but both schools spoke of themselves as missionary enterprises. It was not the training of preachers for missionary duty in a foreign country but the training of workers who would take their places in the New South.

An issue that made industrial education a debatable subject was the assumption by its white advocates that such training was particularly appropriate for blacks. Embedded in their *noblesse oblige* posture was a racial theory of a backward or dependent race that was therefore best suited to this form of education. Also relevant here was a classist understanding of society. These northern philanthropists thought of themselves as realists who considered it foolhardy to challenge the white leadership of the South and their racial assumptions. Industrial education was a way to work within the system and at the same time aim for eventual uplift.

Different understandings of the shape of that uplift or advance was what transformed the discussion about industrial versus higher education into a sometimes seething debate. The discussion had been going on since the beginnings of black education after the Civil War. Higher education had been an original aim of the American Missionary Association. Missionary educators, raised in the common-school tradition of New England and trained in northern colleges, went south to raise up schools and colleges on a liberal arts model. The northern educators held no illusions about the quality of their institutions in their infancy. But they answered their critics by asserting that it was important to chart the right course—in this case a liberal arts curriculum—one that the students over time would come to appropriate.

The colleges of highest quality were probably Atlanta and Fisk, founded by the American Missionary Association, and Howard. The goal was to develop schools whose degrees would have equal value with a degree from a white college. Du Bois estimated that students at these schools were in fact about one year behind students at New England colleges. To reach this goal the curriculum, including languages, must be comparable. It became standard fare for those who derided higher education to tell the anecdote of the black student who asked her roommate, "Mandy, is yo' did yo' Greek yit?" But the advocates of higher education, in turn, often quoted John C. Calhoun's retort, "Show me a negro who knows Greek syntax, and I will then believe that he is a human being and should be treated like a man." Higher education was touted as the path that would win the day against all disbelievers.[48]

Until the 1890s this debate was largely among white educators and their churchly and philanthropic backers. In 1897 Du Bois went to Atlanta, and he and other black leaders began to challenge the dominant assumptions of industrial education. Just as Washington did not deny the importance of higher education, so Du Bois did not deny the necessity of industrial education. But this acknowledgment did not lessen the urgency with which Du Bois argued his case for higher education. Responding to the acclaim that industrial education was receiving from all quarters, Du Bois observed that "industrialism drunk with its vision of success" made the discussion of the issue so critical.[49]

Du Bois presented his case by arguing for a "talented tenth." This term was first used in 1896 by Henry L. Moorehouse, field secretary for the Baptist Home Mission Society. Du Bois adopted it as a rallying cry for his understanding of the priorities in education. Who made up the "talented tenth?" Usually the answer was doctors, lawyers, ministers, and teachers. In a 1903 essay Du Bois focused on the training of teachers. Where would black schools be without trained teachers? If northern white teachers came south after the Civil War, now it was time to train black teachers in the South. Du Bois was aware that the question had become whether to start at the bottom or the top. He answered the question directly: "Without *first* providing for the higher training of the very best teachers," the rapid multiplication of industrial training "is simply throwing your money to the winds."[50]

Of the many examples chosen to illustrate the case, he obviously delighted in focusing on the Tuskegee faculty itself. The credentials of the faculty were testimony of the importance of higher education. "Indeed some thirty of his chief teachers are college graduates, and instead of studying French grammars in the midst of weeds, or buying pianos for dirty cabins, they are at Mr. Washington's right hand helping him in a noble work." Du Bois's analysis often poked fun at Washington's anecdotes. But the Atlanta professor surely knew he was in a debate over strategy, for he complained that "the effects of Mr. Washington's propaganda have been to throw doubt upon the expediency of such training" for teachers who were part of the talented tenth.[51]

Some months before the publication of *The Souls of Black Folk*, many took notice of Du Bois for his article in the September 1902 issue of the *Atlantic Monthly*, an article that later became a chapter in *The Souls of Black Folk*. In "Of the Training of Black Men," Du Bois reviewed the four decades since the end of the Civil War, focusing especially on the various patterns of education. He paid tribute to the pioneers of the 1860s, especially the AMA, in remarks to be repeated in his forthcoming book.

He called the efforts of these New England missionary teachers "that finest thing in American history, and one of the few things untainted by sordid greed and cheap vainglory."[52]

This debate over industrial education can serve as a barometer of attitudes toward racial reform. Within the white Social Gospel movement Lyman Abbott, editor of the *Outlook,* continued to be a chief publicist for industrial education. He was a featured speaker at the Twenty-fifth anniversary celebration at Tuskegee in 1906 as recognition of his role supporting the Washingtonian philosophy of education.

By contrast, William Hayes Ward, editor of the *Independent,* was often a critic of industrial education. Ward was willing to give Washington his due, but his analysis of Washington's popularity probed its racist overtones. In an editorial in 1898, Ward described Washington supporters as people "who unconsciously sympathize with the idea that manual labor is as much as the Negro can properly aspire to." In 1902 Ward applauded efforts to raise funds for industrial education, but offered his own point of view on what should be the priorities in education.

> It must never be forgotten that the largest and most persuasive and controlling influence is always from the top and not the bottom. . . . The academy lifts the common school; the college lifts the academy; the university lifts the college, and never the reverse.[53]

Wilbur P. Thirkield, a corresponding secretary for the Freedman's Aid and Southern Education Society of the Methodist Episcopal Church, North, wrote to Du Bois congratulating him on his article "Of the Training of Black Men." Thanking Du Bois for his "epochal utterance," Thirkield told Du Bois of his own growing commitment to higher education. Thirkield indicated he hoped to use Du Bois's insights in his own work, saying "I have no hesitation in saying that this is the greatest deliverance, both in thought and expression, on this problem that I have ever read."[54]

Of those black leaders Du Bois was courting, Francis Grimké shifted away from Washington in part because of growing dissatisfaction with the results of industrial education. While serving a Presbyterian parish in Florida from 1885 to 1889 Grimké was able to visit Tuskegee Institute in Alabama. Grimké was impressed with Tuskegee's industrial education philosophy, its faculty, and the impressive buildings and fiscal management. But the thing that impressed him most was the commitment to "character-building." Grimké was drawn to the Tuskegee approach in these early days because he believed that at the heart of

Washington's industrial education philosophy was a commitment to spiritual values.[55]

In the spring 1903, when Grimké's shift of allegiance was being announced from his pulpit, he preached on "The Things of Paramount Importance in the Development of the Negro Race." One hears in this sermon Grimké's impatience with the Washingtonian philosophy. Now he critiques the values he once praised. Grimké said that the emphasis of industrial education was ultimately on "material things." He set the problem within the broader context of the direction of American culture. He quoted Bishop Henry C. Potter: "The cry now is, 'Great is the god of railroads and syndicates.'" Grimké's analysis was that "there is a movement already on foot, which has tended steadily to put the emphasis on material things, which is having its effect, and which will render it more and more difficult to give the proper direction to race development."[56] The antidote to this tendency was Grimké's call for old-fashioned moral character and a renewed emphasis on civil rights.

Kelly Miller was also concerned about moral values, but his extensive treatments of industrial and higher education were far-reaching. As with all other issues in the debate between conservatives and radicals, his speeches and essays were evenhanded. As an educator, sociologist, and churchman he saw the issue in its broadest dimensions. The report for the United States Commissioner of Education in 1901 was prepared just as Miller was reevaluating the whole issue of industrial education.

In a section called "The Higher Education of the Negro" Miller discussed the vexing question of the intellectual capacity of blacks. He did not try to answer the question scientifically, although hinting at new information in psychology, sociology, and anthropology. Rather he answered the question by marshalling a broad range of evidence of the achievement of blacks in a few short years. From blackbelt southern colleges, to Harvard and Dartmouth, came stories of black achievement.

In a section called "The Relative Claims of Industrial and Higher Education," Miller tried to put in perspective "the hue and cry" in favor of industrial education. Here, and elsewhere, he gently chided northern philanthropists who supported schools emphasizing industrial education. As a sociologist well acquainted with the discouraging story of opportunities for blacks in labor in northern cities, he asked "Who believes that the industrial disadvantages of the Negro . . . can be overcome or even materially altered by industrial education?" Miller painted a poignant picture: "To equip a considerable number of colored boys

. . . with the mechanical trades would be simply to furnish them with edged tools without anything to cut."[57]

Miller believed that the chief value of the industrial schools was not in the final analysis the trades but the values they taught. Miller would admit no inferiority on the part of blacks, but he would concede a backwardness borne out of a lack of experience in western culture. Miller sounded like Washington when he said that what was needed were the values of "thrift, economy, and decency." But Miller voiced Grimké's warning that the apology for industrial education must not plant the idea that the road to solving the race problem is for blacks to acquire money. "Those who argue thus show themselves ignorant of the law of moral reforms."[58]

Even though calling for balance, in the end Miller argued for the primacy of higher education. Using the same analogy as Du Bois and Ward, he said that "The educational impulse proceeds from above downward." The use of irony was part of Miller's oratorical style. In arguing for higher education he described a school "deservedly famous throughout the country." Everyone knew he was describing Tuskegee and its largely college-educated faculty as a fitting example of his top-down argument.[59]

What is noteworthy is that those shifting away from industrial education finally argue the issue in moral terms. This is precisely what Du Bois hoped would happen. Grimké did so in his jeremiads in a Presbyterian pulpit. In the less likely place of a report for the Commissioner of Education, Miller raises the level of debate also. "The Negro cries for justice and is offered a trade; he pleads for righteous laws, and is given an industrial school." It will be the cry for justice that will energize a new generation of black leaders.

It is not the whole story to say this was a black intramural debate. The debate was overheard by friends and foes within the white community. Insight into this debate—about ideas, strategies, and people—becomes a kind of litmus test in gauging the sensitivity of white advocates of the Social Gospel to the struggle for racial reform.

These responses were seen in a variety of white leaders in the following two decades. In the next chapter we will meet one of the most famous of the Social Gospel leaders, Washington Gladden—a man who met Du Bois and Miller and changed his mind about racial reform as he gained new experience and information emanating from this black debate.

CHAPTER 9

Washington Gladden:
A Northern Case Study

Does the Christian church believe that the Negro is a man? Does it
believe that Christ died for him? If the church responds affirmatively to
these questions, as it surely must, how does it move beyond mere verbal
or theological affirmation? It would seem that the great truth of the
Fatherhood of God and the Brotherhood of Man, which is shining forth
in these days with such compelling clearness, which is forcing men in
all lands to consider the cause of the poor and to do justly and love
mercy, must become the controlling influence in the church of Jesus
Christ everywhere.

—WASHINGTON GLADDEN

Washington Gladden has been called the Father of the Social Gospel.[1]
His wide-ranging ministry spanned six decades between the Civil War
and World War I. Historians of both the Social Gospel and race reform,
if they mention Gladden at all in connection with race, have nearly
always cited him as an example of the racism supposedly infecting the
whole movement.

But the story of the Social Gospel and race is a story of change.
Nowhere is this more true than in the pilgrimage of Washington Gladden. In the 1880s Gladden opposed efforts to protect black voting rights
in Ohio. But a series of experiences along the missionary education
bridge nearly two decades later led him into involvement in racial reform both at the local and national levels.

This chapter is a case study charting these changes in a prominent
northern Social Gospel leader. A number of questions need to be asked.
How did Gladden's views change? Why did he change? What were his
specific reform interests in relation to race? Did this practical reformer
offer any theological basis for those who would be involved in racial
reform?

Washington Gladden was born in 1836 in Pottsgrove, Pennsylvania.
Gladden's father was a New England schoolteacher who migrated west.

He died in 1841, and after an unsettling year, Gladden finally went to live on an uncle's farm near Owego, New York. Both Gladden's father and uncle were men of piety. Gladden's own religious faith was shaped in interaction with this area of western New York, often called the burned-over district because of the frequency with which the fires of revivalism had swept over the region in the early decades of the nineteenth century. As a young man Gladden was repelled by many of the excesses of local revival meetings. But he did embrace the evangelical Christianity of the day with its emphasis on personal salvation and the subsequent life of piety. Memorization of the Scriptures as well as the Westminster Shorter Catechism was the heart of the mild Calvinism of Gladden's early religious education.

The Christian faith as propagated in western New York was not simply personal to the exclusion of worldly problems. A concern for reform flowed from the ministry of evangelist Charles G. Finney and others. The swelling tide of antislavery sentiment was an important part of this religious reform and helped form the content of Gladden's earliest thinking. In 1850 forty-six members of the Presbyterian church in Owego withdrew to form their own Congregational church. The Presbyterian minister had been censured for praying for slaves. The desire to express their antislavery sentiments freely was a major reason for their action. Gladden had grown up attending the Presbyterian church, but in 1853 or 1854 he joined this splinter Congregational church. Reflecting upon this experience as the first opportunity to be part of a Christian community committed to confronting the issues of the hour, Gladden said in later years, "It was not an individualistic pietism that appealed to me; it was a religion that laid hold upon life with both hands, and proposed, first and foremost, to realize the Kingdom of God in this world."[2]

Gladden graduated from Williams College in 1859 and, following a short experience as a teacher in Owego, was ordained a Congregational minister at the outbreak of the Civil War. During the war years he was pastor of several churches in and around New York City. Proximity to New York afforded him the opportunity to attend lectures at Union Theological Seminary. Gladden never received formal theological training or a seminary degree, but he regularly pursued his own private theological study.

Two men influenced Gladden in decisive ways. Frederick W. Robertson, gifted Anglican preacher in Brighton in the south of England, lived just thirty-seven years. But after his death in 1853, his sermons and a thoughtful biography continued his influence on both sides of the Atlantic. If Robertson opened Gladden's eyes, Gladden was grateful to Horace Bushnell "for teaching me how to use them." Bushnell, pastor of the North Congregational Church in Hartford, Connecticut, was busy reshaping the New England theology coming down from Jonathan Edwards. Bushnell considered himself basically orthodox—his theology was often called Progressive Orthodoxy—but many at this time suspected him of heretical tendencies. From Bushnell, Gladden learned a new theory and use of language that liberated him from the scholasticism of a degenerate Calvinism. Even more important, Gladden built into his own preaching and ministry the reality that the gospel meant justice for the world as well as personal salvation. Many years later Gladden commented about Bushnell's theology that "his heresy was the unfaltering belief that God is just."[3]

In 1866 Gladden was called to serve the Congregational church in North Adams, Massachusetts, and he invited Bushnell to preach the installation sermon. In this western Massachusetts factory town, Gladden began to develop his understanding of the problems of labor and management.

The years 1871 through 1874 found him back in New York as religion editor of the *Independent*. Much of his energy went into exposing the corruption of the Tweed ring. The *Independent* was an influential moral force, but Gladden finally left the paper because he could not agree with a morality that disguised paid advertisements as editorials.

After three years Gladden was ready to return to the parish. He accepted a call to the North Congregational Church in Springfield, Massachusetts. In the introduction of this volume the story of his pivotal experience with the unemployed of Springfield is recounted. This story is a paradigm of Gladden's ministry, where experience triggered pastoral response, which became translated into preaching and which usually resulted in practical ministries.

In 1882 a larger opportunity beckoned. Gladden moved west to become pastor of the First Congregational Church of Columbus, Ohio. A growing city of just over fifty thousand people, Columbus was a center of special vitality and opportunity because of its place as state capital. The city was the home of an expanding state university and focal point for state institutions and reform societies. Believing when he went to Ohio that he might someday return to the East, Gladden actually spent the final thirty-six years of his life in the Midwest, although the influence of his ministry became increasingly national in scope.

Immediately after the Civil War, at the beginning of his pastoral ministry, Gladden became involved with the American Missionary Association. The AMA was primarily concerned with helping the newly emancipated freedmen, but it was interested in other races as well. In 1870 Gladden reported for a group that had been commissioned to study the conditions of the Chinese in California. This report helped lay the groundwork for beginning schools for the Chinese in Oakland, Stockton, Sacramento, and San Francisco.[4]

Although Gladden chaired the committee proposing Chinese education, he was more interested in the main effort of the AMA, which was black education. Writing on "The Southern Question" in the *Independent* in 1876, Gladden was realistic about the problems of the hour. He observed that blacks suffered "terrible violence and outrage" at the hands of southern whites, while whites suffered "corruption and extortion" from "Negro majorities and Negro office-holders." In this connection Gladden seemed ambivalent about the Fifteenth Amendment. On the one hand, the amendment gave the suffrage to many blacks who were not qualified, but on the other hand, "when we took the black man into the political household, we took him 'for better or for worse.'" Despite the difficulties, Gladden believed he saw an open door. What was happening below the Mason-Dixon Line "ought to make it plain to all good Christians that a work of immense importance is waiting to be done at the South."[5]

As political Reconstruction was ending in 1877, Gladden joined with others in regretting the excesses of the previous decade. At the same time, however, he gave what was reported as a stirring address on the changing role and the opportunities open to the AMA. He counseled teachers and missionaries in the South to be peacemakers, not as a way of avoiding attack on the sin of caste, but rather as a redemptive means of overcoming "the resentments of defeat and the prejudices of race."[6]

An opportunity to become involved in the race question closer to home presented itself when Gladden moved to Columbus in 1882. For a northern city, Columbus had a sizable black population, more than three thousand, or about 6 percent of the total population. The leader of the black community was the Reverend James Poindexter, pastor of the Second Baptist Church. Poindexter was also active in civic affairs, serving on both the city council and the board of education.

A barometer of Gladden's attitudes on racial reform in the 1880s can be gathered from two separate confrontations. The growing issue was whether it was more important to emphasize political rights or social and economic progress. During Gladden's first years in Columbus he quarreled with fellow pastor Poindexter, Gladden coming down on the side of amelioration of the race problem through economic and social progress rather than emphasizing political rights. In these same years,

General John Beatty, an Ohio Republican, instigated a campaign to protect black voting rights. Gladden disagreed with Beatty's campaign. The Columbus pastor said it was a mistake to put agitation for political rights ahead of programs to foster social and economic programs.[7]

Gladden continued to evidence concern and involvement in the race issue nationally through the AMA, but his reform instincts tended more toward ameliorism in the 1880s and early 1890s. Within a year after settling in Columbus, Gladden returned east to Brooklyn to read a paper to the AMA entitled "Christian Education in the South." Disputing a report recently released by the National Education Association, Gladden claimed that published illiteracy figures, although correct, had been wrongly interpreted. He pointed out that blacks were actually making greater strides, in terms of percentages in combating illiteracy, than were whites. In the same paper, Gladden commended the AMA teachers in the South for their witness to southern whites, "gently without censure or denunciation, by the silent witness of Christly lives." In these years Gladden eschewed any posture of militancy, but at the same time he believed it was the duty of the AMA to teach "that caste is un-Christian." He was forthright in criticizing a strategy of theoretically opening all schools to whites and blacks but at the same time saying that of course blacks would be happier and better off in their own churches and schools.[8]

At this same meeting Gladden was appointed to a committee whose purpose was to settle differences with another Congregational agency, the American Home Missionary Association. Both associations were working in the South, but the AHMA was fostering segregation by beginning all-white churches in areas where the AMA had established mixed congregations. The resulting agreement was a victory for the AMA in the sense that it was granted priority in the South, while the AHMA was given the West as its primary mission territory.[9]

At the annual meeting in 1895 Gladden's spoke on several occasions, and his remarks give evidence of a new awareness of obstacles to black progress. At a time when the AMA was being accused, both from within and without, of becoming less zealous about racial reform, Gladden spoke up more forcefully than formerly. As many were beginning to do, he denounced the rising madness of lynching as the number of black deaths due to lynching reached its peak in these years. But he encouraged the AMA to go beyond mere rhetoric and to work vigorously to inform and influence public opinion.[10]

In another address at the same meeting, Gladden stepped into the debate about whether or not to let the South establish its own pattern and timetable for race relations. Fifteen years earlier, convinced that Reconstruction had been an overreaction, Gladden had counseled patience. Now he countered the objection that the North should let the South alone. Retelling the parable of the Good Samaritan, he reminded his listeners that the Samaritan was traveling in a southern state when he met the wounded and needy traveler. The Samaritan could have said something to the effect that the people of this section will take care of the man's needs. Instead, the Samaritan said, "This poor man's needs are all the warrant I require." The nation and the AMA can and should intervene to meet the needs of black Americans.[11]

Gladden's faithful service to the AMA was recognized when in 1895 he was elected a vice-president. He served in this capacity until 1901, when he was elected president. The presidency at this time was still largely an honorary office, always signifying past contributions to the association but entitling the officeholder only to preside at the annual meetings. All this was changed in 1902, when the office of president was redefined to allow the officeholder to share in responsibility for policy. Gladden was reelected president, and the American Missionary commented, "Hereafter the office of President is to be one of real power as a member of the Executive Committee, and no man is more acceptable to the churches and constituents than is Dr. Gladden."[12]

In these years at the end of the century, Gladden was a man in transition on the race issue. Always concerned about race, he had been an advocate of accommodation in the almost two decades following the end of Reconstruction. In this posture he was willing to entrust the fate of southern blacks to southern whites. Any notable changes in black status in society would come as they proved themselves worthy. In 1895, the year in which he was elected a vice-president of the AMA, a new call for more determined action is evident in his remarks. A confirmation of his commitment to black education is signaled by his election as president of the AMA in 1901 and, more important, by his reelection in 1902 at the precise moment when the office for the first time involved the incumbent in policy-making.

The ideas and actions observable in the case study of Gladden do not remain as they were in 1902. His duties as president involved him in yet new experiences that further challenged his assumptions about race and reform. In 1903, as president of the AMA, Gladden received a series of invitations from Atlanta. He was asked to give the baccalaureate sermon at Atlanta University, address the university's eighth conference on Negro problems, and preach at the First Congregational Church, a black congregation.[13]

The annual conference "The Study of Negro Problems" had chosen the Negro church as its subject for that year. The conference organizer was W. E. B. Du Bois, at that time a young professor at Atlanta University, a school of AMA origin. Gladden had been asked earlier by Du Bois to offer summary remarks at the conclusions of the conference. Throughout the conference speakers had pointed to the barriers to full citizenship that were increasingly blocking the path of blacks. Gladden offered his own perspective in conclusion.

> People who are thoroughly fitted for good citizenship, and who show by their conduct that they have the disposition and the purpose to be good citizens, are not going to be permanently excluded in any part of this country from the responsibilities and duties of citizenship. That is as sure as tomorrow's sunrising. It cannot be that in the United States of America young men who are thoroughly intelligent, who know what citizenship means, who love their country, who are working to build up its prosperity and to secure its peace and who are ready to shed their blood in its defense, are going to be forbidden to take part in its government.

Gladden's remarks reflect his own positive experience of his encounters with blacks through the AMA in recent years. His comments might appear as banal or paternalistic, but evidently not to the conference organizing committee of Du Bois, Kelly Miller, and Mary Church Terrell, who chose to print them verbatim in the resolution that ended the conference.[14]

Between meetings Gladden toured Atlanta and the surrounding countryside. The poverty and squalor that was the daily environment of many black families disturbed and challenged his previous understanding of the black reality in the South. Having encountered the plight of the Chinese on the west coast, as well as that of European immigrants, Gladden now assayed the condition of the black population and concluded, "Deeper and more dire are their necessities than those of any other class."[15]

Individual leaders left their impressions also. Gladden talked afterward about the considerable time that he spent with Henry Hugh Proctor, pastor of the First Congregational Church. Proctor, a graduate of Fisk and Yale, was a friend of both Washington and Du Bois. First Congregational had been established under AMA auspices, but under Proctor's able leadership the congregation became self-supporting. Proctor was making a name for himself as a black Social Gospel pastor. Lyman Abbott called First Congregational "the best organized church in the South."[16] As Proctor showed Gladden around Atlanta, the northern Congregational pastor learned much firsthand information about the race problem in the South.

Gladden's appreciation of Proctor was evident the next year when Gladden was elected moderator of the National Council of Congregational Churches. He honored Proctor and the black community by declaring that the Atlanta minister was his choice to be assistant moderator. Proctor was nominated by Amory H. Bradford and elected.[17]

While attending the conference on the Negro church, Gladden was impressed with Kelly Miller and his paper "Religion as a Solvent of the Race Problem." A few months later, Miller, professor at Howard University and also a Congregational layman, wrote to Gladden thanking him for his efforts to encourage the *North American Review* to publish Miller's Atlanta paper. Miller was invited by Gladden to read a paper at the fall meeting of the AMA.[18]

But it was Du Bois, chairman of the conference, who made the most profound impression on Gladden. The Columbus pastor watched with increasing interest and respect as Du Bois led the conference. This was the first of the annual conferences that had focused exclusively on the Negro church, and Gladden was an attentive listener.

As Du Bois thanked Gladden for participating in the conference, he gave Gladden a copy of his newly published book, *The Souls of Black Folk.* On the train trip home its pages consumed his interest, so much so that it formed the basis of Gladden's sermon on Sunday in Columbus.

Gladden told his people that he had previously read a review of the book in the *Outlook,* "comparing it with Booker Washington's books, greatly to its disparagement." "I hope," the pastor said, "that none of you will accept that judgment until you have read *The Souls of Black Folk.*" Many people, including the *Outlook* editor, Lyman Abbott, had criticized Du Bois's spirit, calling it strident and overly critical. Gladden opened up a new window on the black experience for his people when he told them:

> It is easy to charge hypersensitiveness and morbidity upon the author, but I cannot bring myself to censure him. He is accused of being ashamed of his race. I do not think that this is true; but the fact that his race is in a position of inferiority, and that the prevailing sentiment of large portions of the country means to keep it there, is a fact which he cannot ignore.[19]

At this point, Gladden, whose understanding was being changed by experience, asked his congregation to enter into an experience that admittedly would require an effort of imagination. "Imagine yourself living in a civilization whose overwhelming sentiment puts you into a lower nature of being and means to keep you there; do you think that you could help making that sentiment a pretty large part of your consciousness?"[20]

Gladden had been struck by Du Bois's perception that black persons lived always with a double consciousness—their own and another defined for them by an alien culture. The preacher quoted at length from Du Bois so that his congregation might begin to glimpse what it meant to live with two ideals, two thoughts, two souls.

As the sermon continued, it was obvious that Gladden had not so much reached new firm conclusions but that his eyes and ears had been opened up to a new understanding of the black experience. This new perspective was challenging older attitudes held in common by whites enthralled with their own paternalistic rhetoric and the soothing words of Washington. The proof of a new perspective was when Gladden spoke of black disfranchisement in the South. Formerly he had said he would be willing to have qualifications for all men, but now he realized, as he did not before, that there was entrenched in southern politics one law for blacks and another for whites.

In this sermon one can overhear Gladden rethinking the whole subject of education for blacks. One has to keep in mind Gladden's deep involvement in the AMA and his basic allegiance to the philosophy of industrial education as espoused by Washington. But now the preacher tells his people, "The Negro man, no more than the white man, can live by bread alone." What about the weight given to economic self-help as the best path for blacks to follow? "Booker Washington puts much emphasis upon the development of economic efficiency among the Negroes. That is indeed a great need. But you will find, if you read the Du Bois book, that his political degradation has much to do with his economic inefficiency." And what if blacks do succeed economically? "Mr. Washington emphasizes the argument that if the Negro will but succeed in a material way all doors will be open to him. But that is not quite certain. The history of the Jews is evidence that industry and thrift do not disarm race prejudice."[21]

"The Race Problem," although never published, was a remarkable sermon. It was preached to help inform the First Congregational Parish in Columbus about the dimensions of the race problem. It is fascinating as a barometer of Gladden's changing views on race. Here he attempted to understand the admittedly strident voice of Du Bois at a time when many of Gladden's Social Gospel counterparts were critical if not hostile

to Du Bois. Although Gladden had long championed industrial education, which its adherents said would result in economic advancement,
he here indicated an apprehension that the economic plight of black
people was directly related to their political status. The telling conclusion in the sermon was the awareness that prejudice was such a primitive but complex phenomenon that it would be naive to think that
educational or economical advancement could easily overcome it.

Disturbed by what he had seen and read, Gladden was more than
ever convinced of the important role that the AMA had to play in the
South. Shortly before the annual meeting, Laforest A. Planving, a black
graduate of Straight University and founder of the AMA-sponsored
Point Coupee Industrial High School at Oscar, Louisiana, was mur-
dered. Gladden wrote a letter to the governor of Louisiana asking for
an investigation. With the specific event in mind, as well as all that had
grown out of his trip to Atlanta, there was a new urgency in Gladden's
presidential address in 1903. "For this Association, the way of duty is
very clear. It finds itself now, at the beginning of this century, with a
sacred charge to keep. It must stand here, as best it can, in Christ's
stead, bearing witness for Him on behalf of the neglected races of this
continent." Gladden spoke to the nadir of concern for blacks that Du
Bois had helped bring to consciousness. "If ever there was a time when
its voice might be silent or its energies relaxed, that time is now. If ever
there was need to hold up the standards of justice and to reaffirm the
fact of human brotherhood, that need is now upon us."[22]

This address, more than most, gives a clear theological basis undergirding Gladden's call to action. Alongside the "standards of justice"
and the reality of brotherhood, there was an appeal to the nature of the
kingdom of God. Gladden related the doctrine of the kingdom to the
immediate educational, economic, and evangelistic efforts before the
AMA. Gladden told the assembled delegates, "The Association was
born to bear witness, in a day when men's ears were stuffed with cotton, to the truth that black men are men; they are not only hands but
souls; that for them there must be not only bread but a kingdom—
hope, outlook, opportunity, a clear path to the heights of manhood."[23]

In this address, Gladden struggled with the contradiction between
the idea of full manhood for blacks and the prevalent notion that blacks
were somehow inferior. Not discussing inferiority as a biological phenomenon, Gladden found racial inferiority unacceptable in terms of
what it would mean both for a democratic republic and for Christianity.
Gladden had been saying for years that there were two poles around
which all else revolved in the Christian faith.

The one truth that we recognize as fundamental is the truth of the universal divine Fatherhood, with its corollary of the universal brotherhood. This truth is the sheet-anchor of our faith; everything that is significant or precious to us in the Christian religion springs from this truth and returns to it again.

Gladden now grounded his growing involvement in racial reform in these two truths. The doctrine of creation received its definition from an understanding of an equality among brothers and sisters. "Among brothers there is no distinction of superior and inferior." This truth had often been spiritualized, but Gladden would countenance none of this approach.[24]

In 1904, Gladden's last year as president of the AMA, he invited Du Bois to address the annual meeting in Des Moines. In this act Gladden was bringing his experience full circle. Gladden had gone to Atlanta, learned much from Du Bois, and shared the results with his people in Columbus. The AMA had been the educational vehicle—the "missionary bridge"—for Gladden's involvement in racial reform, and now he wanted Du Bois to help educate the missionary educators.

It was not unusual for blacks to address the AMA; they had done so since before the Civil War. Gladden had invited Kelly Miller to address the annual meeting in 1903. In inviting Du Bois, however, Gladden was bringing to Des Moines an already controversial figure. Du Bois's address was entitled "Higher and Advanced Education." Stepping into the midst of the debate about which kind of education would best benefit blacks, Du Bois encouraged the AMA to step away from the Tuskegee philosophy. He did so in a spirit of both challenge and affirmation. Paying tribute to the AMA, he observed: "It alone has from the first taken the most unwavering stand for a system of real education for the Negroes." Building on this foundation, Du Bois challenged the AMA to broaden its scope and set an agenda of full rights and privileges in all areas of society.[25]

At Des Moines, Gladden asked the AMA to accept his resignation as president in order that he might be free to accept election to the three-year office of moderator of the National Council of Congregational Churches. After a decade as vice-president and president, Gladden stepped aside from any official position with the AMA, but he continued his active interest in all its activities.

An address to the annual meeting of the AMA at Oberlin in 1906 reveals the extent of Gladden's movement from accommodation to reform. Shocked by the Atlanta race riots in September of that year, as well as by incidents in the North, Gladden delivered a hard-hitting

address. Deliberately setting his remarks within the context of emancipation, an act undertaken by the North, Gladden called for a perception of the race problem as a national problem. Deeply disturbed by the
actions of certain southern leaders (he named James K. Vardaman of
Mississippi and Hoke Smith of Georgia), he spoke out against the degradation of blacks taking place in the South by legal and illegal means.
Calling for the recognition for full humanity for blacks, Gladden said
of the prospect of whites and blacks living together amicably, "They
cannot live together unless both races have full opportunity to live a
complete human life." The *Congregationalist* called Gladden's address at
Oberlin "one of the strongest deliveries he ever made."[26]

Speaking in Cleveland several months later, Gladden told a church
gathering that the words at Oberlin had "produced no small stir
throughout the South." Gladden was less sanguine than a decade earlier. He outlined now what he believed were the two alternatives that
the country must face up to. "One . . . which seeks to recognize the
manhood of the Negro and to give him the right to become what God
meant him to be; the other . . . which proposes to reduce him to practical serfdom." Gladden lamented that the replies to his Oberlin address
had not been reassuring. "I have had some friendly and reasonable
letters; but the most of the utterances are bitter and violent, and sadly
lacking in logic. Almost unanimously they avow the purpose of depriv-
ing the Negro of political rights, and of keeping him in a position of
inferiority." As his own remarks became more forceful, he experienced
the full reality of racism expressing itself in bitter attacks against his
ministry.[27]

The AMA brought Gladden into contact with the race problem in
the South and the nation, but to test the hypothesis of the missionary
bridge it is important to examine his involvement in his home city of
Columbus, Ohio. The sizable black population in Columbus has already been mentioned. In the years that Gladden was a resident, the
city showed a steady increase in its black population, both numerically
and in percentage of the population, until World War I, when Columbus experienced the same marked increase in migration that was common to other northern cities (see table 4).

There were two sources of migration to Columbus: blacks moving
northward from southern Ohio, and blacks leaving their homes in
southern states, most notably North Carolina. As this migration began
to increase at the turn of the century, it created friction within Columbus. Resentment was focused upon the poorer, less educated blacks

coming from the South. This hostility was as evident in the older, more stable black community as it was among Columbus whites.[28]

The gradual change in Gladden's outlook was reflected in his ministry in Columbus. Pastor James Poindexter, who deserves mention in the ranks of black Social Gospelers, changed his mind about Gladden as Gladden's actions changed. The two became good friends. Gladden invited Poindexter into First Church on a number of occasions. In the later years of his ministry, Gladden invited a number of other black figures to speak to Columbus through First Church, including Booker T. Washington, Henry H. Proctor, Bishop Benjamin T. Tanner of the African Methodist Episcopal church, and the Fisk Jubilee Singers.[29]

An accurate estimation of Gladden's commitment to racial reform in Columbus was supplied by the black community there. In the aftermath of the Atlanta race riots of September 1906, over five hundred blacks gathered at the Shiloh Baptist Church to pay tribute to those who were standing with them. The Atlanta riots had raged on for four days, leaving 25 blacks and 1 white dead, and 152 persons seriously wounded. In the aftermath of the riots, blacks across the country had suffered physical and mental abuse. In this tense atmosphere, blacks in Columbus gathered to express their "heartfelt thanks" to five white men who had given "unswerving and loyal support to the end that justice and fair treatment of the Negro race may obtain in all portions of our beloved country." Gladden was one of the five men so honored, with special note made of his recent remarks at Oberlin.[30]

Throughout the nation Gladden preached a Social Gospel of practical action. Always a practical pastor and reformer, Gladden was not content with mere verbal or theological affirmations. He pressed for solutions whether he talked about the city or business monopolies or trade unions. Always in demand as a speaker, in the first decade of the century Gladden began to receive invitations to apply the Social Gospel

Table 4. The Black Population of Columbus, Ohio

Year	Black Population	% of Total Population
1880	3,010	5.8
1890	5,547	6.3
1900	8,201	6.5
1910	12,739	7.0
1920	22,181	9.4

Source: Richard Clyde Minor, "The Negro in Columbus, Ohio" (Ph.D. dissertation, Ohio State University, 1936), 11.

to the race problem as well. In 1906 Proctor invited Gladden to address the Second Convention of Congregational Workers among the Colored People, meeting at Memphis. In his address Gladden traced the scriptural basis and historical development of Congregational attitudes toward race problems. He spoke to the quandary that was in Congregational conversations across the country, to the effect that the church would be more successful if it frankly recognized the sociological realities of race and class. Commenting on the policies of Congregationalism in the South, Gladden said he "had no patience with a denominational propaganda in the South which sacrifices principles to success."[31]

Invitations came to speak at a number of the finest black colleges. In 1909 he was invited by President Wilbur P. Thirkield to speak at Howard University. At Howard, Gladden's celebrated hymn "O Master, Let Me Walk with Thee" had been adopted as the university hymn. He spoke at Founder's Day at Wilberforce in 1915. Gladden was invited by Atlanta University to preach the anniversary sermon at its fiftieth anniversary celebration in 1917. He also addressed a special conference on that occasion.[32]

Is it possible to discern any reoccurring theological themes undergirding Gladden's call for action on race? Rauschenbusch is best known for trumpeting a theology of the kingdom of God as the basis for a Social Gospel, and Gladden emphasized this theme also. In 1907 he was invited to speak on the topic "The Kingdom of God and the Race Problem" by President Charles Cuthbert Hall of Union Theological Seminary in New York.[33]

If there is one theological motif that Gladden utilized more than all others then it would be the fatherhood of God and the brotherhood of man. This theological motif has suffered from misunderstanding by later critics, who lampooned it as an example of liberal sentimentality. In recent years, commitment to nonsexist language has consigned the phrase to disuse. But to dismiss it for whatever reasons would be to miss a theological theme with special importance for racial reform.

For Gladden the fatherhood of God and the brotherhood of man signified a theological truth that needed to be central for modern ministry. This twin focus was a way of affirming the organic nature of reality. Deeply influenced by Horace Bushnell and the New Theology, Gladden decried the individualism rampant both in evangelicalism at the end of the nineteenth century and in much of American culture. The fatherhood of God was a way of saying that God was Creator of the whole universe. God was not the Creator spoken of by the deists of an earlier generation but a Father who cared for his children. Brotherhood (and we would add sisterhood) is a way of saying that in an organic universe we are all related to one another. We need each other; we belong to each other.

A central part of Gladden's growing criticism of evangelists such as Dwight L. Moody and Billy Sunday was that their so-called evangelical theology neglected the fatherhood of God and the brotherhood of man. An early supporter of Moody, Gladden changed his mind and was critical of Moody and especially Sunday, saying that after all was said and done, their ministries were irrelevant to the problems of society. They were silent about race and practiced segregation in their evangelistic meetings.

For Gladden, the practical reformer, it was often reform first and then theology. He was a man calling for action and solutions. His pilgrimage in racial reform is intriguing, however, in that as he became more practical and concrete, he also became more theological. The chief way he connected the theological and the practical concerns of racial reform was to lift up this motif of the fatherhood of God and the brotherhood of Man. This theme rings out in the best example of Gladden's mature writing on the race problem in these years. In "The Negro Crisis: Is the Separation of the Races to Become Necessary?" which appeared in the *American Magazine* in January 1907, Gladden interpreted the disfranchisement of blacks and other Jim Crow laws in the South as the first steps of a new kind of slavery. He challenged the church to stand up to racism by reaffirming its own beliefs. "Does the Christian church believe that the Negro is a man? Does it believe that Christ died for him? If the church responds affirmatively to these questions, as it surely must, how does it move beyond mere verbal or theological affirmation?" Gladden was certain that there was a theological mandate able to meet this contemporary challenge.

> It would seem that the great truth of the Fatherhood of God and the Brotherhood of Man, which is shining forth in these days with such compelling clearness, which is forcing men in all lands to consider the cause of the poor and to do justly and love mercy, must become the controlling influence in the church of Jesus Christ everywhere.[34]

In this article we get a clearer sense of what specific measures and organizations Gladden would criticize and support as he strove to become more specific in his call for practical action. In highlighting just why there was a present crisis, Gladden identified the real cause of the Atlanta riots as "the natural outcome of the exacerbation of feeling against the Negroes." He criticized the production of *The Clansman*, a play that depicted blacks in stereotypical racist ways. (The play later was made into the movie *The Birth of a Nation*.) Gladden confronted racism head on when he said that black sexual crimes had been greatly exaggerated as the cause of lynching, when the real cause of lynching was simply "race hatred."[35]

As Gladden analyzed the problems in the South, he pointed up the dichotomy between theoretical freedom and practical serfdom. Serfdom meant subjection. Gladden was aware of those who said they supported a partial diminution of rights because in the long run it would make for better relations between the races. He countered this argument by saying simply, "It does not seem to have been working that way, indeed, we might have known that it would not."[36]

Senator "Pitchfork" Tillman of South Carolina had predicted continuing racial strife, and Gladden wanted his readers to consider the prospect of a race war. Commenting that blacks had been "relatively quiet" as the political franchise had been taken from them, Gladden was sure that as it became evident that their intellectual and economic opportunities would soon dry up also, there would be the possibility of "serious trouble." Obviously Gladden did not want such a war or such a solution. He cited leaders in the South, including Edgar Gardner Murphy of the southern education movement, who were attempting to better present race relations. But if a race war began—one that Gladden said whites would not win as easily as they might think—he saw a final solution coming when the nation intervened after the cause of blacks had attracted worldwide attention and sympathy. The end result might have to be the separation of territory in a section of the country between whites and blacks; this would be the final separation hinted at in the title of the essay.[37]

But Gladden did not rest his complaint with the South alone. In this article he was intent on pointing up racism in the North. For the first time he went to some length to relate this racism to the central Social Gospel concern for labor. Citing a study by Mary White Ovington, Gladden pointed out that blacks had been systematically excluded from trade unions in the North. In New York City, for example, 102 different trade unions had no black members.[38]

Of the many responses to this article, one was preserved as especially heartening. A man whose father was "an old-time abolitionist," actually part of the group known as the Lane Seminary Rebels,[39] wrote to Gladden to say, "I am glad that there is at least one voice left that has something of the old ring."[40]

In 1909, at age seventy-three, Gladden published his *Recollections*. In a long chapter entitled "The Negro Problem," Gladden began by telling the history of the AMA and his own association with it. He then asked whether such an organization was still needed or whether black education could be left to the state public educational systems of the South. There was no question that there was still much left to be done, proof of which was the existence of the Southern Education Board. The real question continued to be the nature of that education. "The notion that education can be put up in air-tight, non-communicating compartments, and that the Negro's heart and hands can be adequately trained without developing his brain, deserves a place in the museum of psychological curiosities."[41]

Dominant in the *Recollections* was Gladden's understanding of the universe as based on morality and the kingdom of God as based on justice. Relationships between people, Gladden argued, are to placed within this context and cannot be based on altruism, which makes justice something to be dispensed by a beneficent individual or society rather than rooted in the moral fabric of society itself. This kind of analysis was the basis for Gladden's contention that the Social Gospel must move beyond charity to justice. Charity, which is too beholden to the good offices of the giver, does not address the root problems in a modern urban and industrial society.

Gladden pointed at the institution of slavery as a chief example of the problems in American society in the nineteenth century. "That is a slice of the retribution due for trying to build a civilization on prostrate manhood." But what Gladden saw in the present was "trying the same experiment over again in a slightly different form." But what if America persisted in that course? "We shall get it hammered into our heads one of these days that this is a moral universe; not that it is going to be, by and by, but that it is moral now, moral all through . . . and that no injustice fails to get its due recompense, now and here." The reality of the situation was that "the moral law admonishes us not to make our fellow man our tool, our tributary." This ringing jeremiad is the voice of a modern-day prophet awakened to the moral indignity of racism.[42]

The recognition of a new slavery "in a slightly different form" and the determination to do something about it was the posture of a man who had advanced a long way in his involvement in the race problem. Arriving in Columbus, Gladden was an accommodationist ready to support the Tuskegee industrial education philosophy and to criticize efforts to protect voting rights in Ohio. Through the "missionary bridge" of the American Missionary Association, Gladden made the slow pilgrimage to a more thoroughgoing reform position. Beginning in the middle 1890s and triggered by the Atlanta experiences of 1903, Gladden came to critique the separate but unequal realities of Jim Crow, south and north. W. E. B. Du Bois, especially his *Souls of Black Folk*, were the mentor and text who helped Gladden redefine the reality of the race problem. Gladden was a practical pastor and reformer, but more than many involved in racial reform, he undergirded his effort with theological substance, especially focusing on the fatherhood of God and the brotherhood of man.

At Gladden's death on July 2, 1919, the black community in Columbus remembered him as he had remembered them in life. Pastor Poindexter was a frequent caller during Gladden's last illness. Now large numbers of black men in their working jackets passed by the body as it lay in state.[43] Irving Maurer, Gladden's successor at First Church, recalled, "He was a friend of the Negro, and Columbus, always with a large Negro section, gave him abundant opportunity to practice the brotherhood he preached."[44]

CHAPTER 10

Edgar Gardner Murphy: A Southern Case Study

Our own sins, too, are real. We have faulted him for ignorance and then have left him ignorant; we have called him brutal and have treated him with violence; we have blamed him for indolence and then have at least denied him the great civic inspirations of labor—the inspirations of political responsibility, the quickening and steadying powers of a vote freely cast and fairly counted.

—EDGAR GARDNER MURPHY

In redrawing the map of the Social Gospel, this book has argued that we need to include the South. A closer look at the South will bring into sharper focus a number of significant reformers who owed their inspiration to the developing Social Gospel. Central to the myriad of concerns of these reformers was the struggle for racial justice. In the first rank of these reformers was Edgar Gardner Murphy.

In the story of the southern education movement in chapter 6 Edgar Gardner Murphy emerged as the most fascinating and complex figure. He emphasized education as a primary route of advancement for blacks, but he was concerned with many aspects of race relations. These other dimensions of racial reform need now to be reviewed and probed. Even though he lived less than half as long as Washington Gladden—his life was cut short at age thirty-nine—like Gladden's, Murphy's commitment to racial reform underwent growth and change. Although increasingly recognized as a reformer in the story of southern progressivism, Murphy has not been sufficiently appreciated for his connection with the story of the Social Gospel. Indeed, standard treatments of the Social Gospel ignore him completely. His career is investigated here as a southern case study.

Murphy's openness to the Social Gospel was awakened first by his university studies. Entering the University of the South at Sewanee, Tennessee, at age sixteen, Murphy was privileged to study under Wil-

liam Porcher DuBose. DuBose had come to Sewanee in 1872 and continued in this citadel of high-church Episcopalianism until 1908. DuBose
was the central figure in a southern theological tradition extending from
1830 to 1930. The irony was he was appreciated more abroad than at
home.[1] DuBose has enjoyed a renewed esteem in this country in recent
decades. W. Norman Pittinger observed that "William Porcher DuBose
was the only important creative theologian that the Episcopal Church
in the United States has produced."[2]

DuBose from the first exercised great influence on the young Murphy. They were teacher and apt student but became lifelong friends.
Murphy returned many times to visit DuBose at Sewanee, and DuBose
visited Murphy in Texas and New York. Murphy said of DuBose that
he was "one of the rare personalities of the world." Again Murphy
wrote, "I owe him almost all that I am in life."[3]

Murphy did owe to DuBose the basic orientation of his own theological thinking. It was not that DuBose was a teacher of the Social
Gospel, but rather that his mixture of theological modernism and Anglican orthodoxy prepared the way for Murphy's own translation of this
theological tradition into social reform. DuBose presented a Catholic
ecclesiology that emphasized unity over individuality. A continuing
question for both DuBose and Murphy and their constituencies was
whether the Episcopal church was Protestant or Catholic or both. Classic Anglicanism has perceived itself as the *via media* (middle way). Ad-
mitting a debt to the Reformers of the sixteenth century and to his own
evangelical experience of conversion, which utterly changed his life at
age eighteen, Dubose nonetheless was frightened by the individualism
too often encountered in both Calvinism and evangelicalism. He liked
to stress that the individual was always part of a larger whole. He or
she was linked with the saints of all ages and responsible to all persons
in the present.

DuBose's classical or conservative point of view was balanced by his
reception of some of the tenets of liberalism, or what came to be called
modernism. DuBose was open to both the emerging natural and social
sciences and to the results of modern biblical criticism. Especially important was his interpretation of salvation in terms of immanence. God
was to be found in the center of life, not above it. Emphasizing immanence over transcendence, DuBose portrayed Jesus as one who understood the human situation and came to minister in the midst of it. One
can see many of these themes articulated by the young Murphy.

From one perspective Murphy might be interpreted as a vivid example of what one person can do battling against personal illness and

social structures. He would seem to fit the American myth of the rugged individual. But he would not want to put this particular cast on his own life story. He said, in fact, "The struggle of the individual has been given an undignifying dignity." In countering the strains of contemporary life, Murphy argued for "the healthening force of the social impulse." Thus, in interpreting the message of the parable of the prodigal son, Murphy would have us "learn not Fatherhood alone, or sonship alone, but *Brotherhood* without which men shall never believe either in God or in themselves"[4]

This theme of brotherhood was central to Murphy's understanding of both society and the church. In a sermon entitled "The Social Prophecy of Jesus," Murphy proclaimed that individual souls always exist within the larger "mind-and-heart environment which we call Brotherhood." Given this context, "all the laws of Jesus are social laws." Finally, high-church ecclesiology and modern biblical scholarship undergirded Murphy's continual emphasis on the kingdom of God in his preaching and teaching. The gospel proclaimed by the church "is a gospel of the kingdom." Tutored by a theology of the kingdom that embraced both church and society, Murphy's faith pilgrimage brought him face-to-face on more than one occasion with the decision as to where best to serve— in the church or in society.[5]

Murphy's practical orientation to the Social Gospel developed through his parish experience. His first opportunity to lead his own parish came with his appointment in 1893 to Christ Church in Laredo, Texas. Although the young Episcopal priest had experienced the culture of Sewanee and New York, he looked forward to working in the midst of the poverty and ethnic tensions of a border town. Shortly after his arrival, these tensions broke into open frenzy when a four-year-old girl was brutally attacked and killed by a black man. The assailant was immediately lynched. The new pastor quickly called a meeting to protest the lynching. Murphy presented a resolution against lynching as a means of justice. It was passed by a voice vote, although only twenty-one men afterward signed the resolution. Murphy was opposed by some in his parish, but he would not be turned aside by religious or political pressure.[6]

Murphy became more deeply involved in the racial issue when he returned to the South in 1898. After serving parishes in Ohio and New York, he accepted a call as rector of St. John's Parish in Montgomery, Alabama. St. John's had a distinguished heritage and was attended by many of the "best" people of Montgomery. Under Murphy's guidance, the parish began to reach out in a new ministry of social concern.

Discovering that the Episcopal church in Montgomery had no ministry to half the city's people, the new rector invited all interested blacks to St. John's. Out of this invitation and effort grew a black parish, the Church of the Good Shepherd.[7]

But Murphy's vision reached beyond St. John's and Montgomery. And so in January 1990 he persuaded twenty-four of Montgomery's leading white citizens to join with him in organizing the Southern Society for the Promotion of the Study of Race Conditions and Problems in the South.

Within days after announcing plans for a conference in May, Murphy and others on the executive committee of the Southern Society were invited to attend the dedication of the Slater-Armstrong Memorial Center on the campus of Tuskegee Institute. To Murphy's surprise, Booker T. Washington asked him to share with the hundreds of guests and students plans for the upcoming race relations conference. His remarks, on the same program with such speakers as J. L. M. Curry, were punctuated by applause, and at the end the audience rose to cheer and wave their handkerchiefs, and the choir began the spiritual "Lay on Your Harps, Hallelu," and everyone joined in.[8]

That evening Murphy met with the Tuskegee Board of Trustees. William H. Baldwin, Jr., chairman of the trustees, and his fellow members Hollis Burke Frissell and Robert C. Ogden were tremendously impressed by the spirit and ideas of the young clergyman, who assured the trustees that the conference would be open to both races. Murphy invited Washington to participate as a speaker. The visit to Tuskegee marked the beginning of a long and close friendship with Washington.[9]

Even before the May conference, through his new friends Baldwin, Frissell, and Ogden, Murphy was invited to address a joint meeting in Philadelphia of the American Academy of Political and Social Science, the American Society for the Extension of University Teaching, and the Civic Club of Philadelphia. Speaking on the topic "The White Man and the Negro at the South," Murphy emphasized to this northern audience that the mind of the South was many minds. He commended the recent study by W. E. B. Du Bois, *The Philadelphia Negro,* which pointed up the complexities of the situation facing blacks in a northern city. Murphy was certain there was a national responsibility for the present situation, but it could best be exercised by aiding local responsibility. He expressed confidence that the better class of people in the South were working toward solutions of the race problem but emphasized several times that northern "intrusive" agitation would only hurt and delay good race relations. Much of the address was an explanation of the

present southern situation and a plea for understanding. In his conclusion, however, Murphy reached beyond the current rhetoric to speak of
some tragic realities in the relations of whites and blacks.

> Our own sins, too, are real. We have faulted him for ignorance and then
> have left him ignorant; we have called him brutal and then have treated him
> with violence; we have blamed him for indolence and then have at least
> denied him the great civic inspirations of labor—the inspirations of political
> responsibility, the quickening and steadying powers of a vote freely cast and
> fairly counted. But in justice to ourselves, we will at length be just to him,
> and in justice to himself, he will be true to us.[10]

With these words Murphy revealed an understanding of the depth
of the problem of race relations in the South. Not easily discouraged,
his organic vision for both society and the church led him to believe
that finally a sense of solidarity could bring forward a reconciling sense
of obligation to self, each other, and society.

Under Murphy's direction, the first annual conference of the Southern Society was held in Montgomery on May 8–10, 1900. The constitution of the organization stated:

> The object of this society shall be to furnish by means of correspondence,
> publication, and particularly through public conferences, an organ for the
> expression of the varied and even antagonistic convictions of representative
> southern men on the problems growing out of the race conditions obtaining
> in the South; and thus to secure a broader education of the public mind as
> to the facts of the situation and a better understanding of the remedies for
> existing evils.[11]

True to the stated objectives, and perhaps more than Murphy expected, the more than two thousand persons who attended each day's
proceedings heard "varied and even antagonistic convictions" from the
conference speakers. As at Lake Mohonk and Capon Springs, this variety did not include black leaders. In committee meetings, Murphy had
suggested that the program include one or two black participants. But
he acceded to the strong negative response to his suggestion in the
interest of saving what he believed was already a remarkable venture
for the South. Murphy continued to consult with Washington, "even
daring to invite him to his home in a move that breached the bounds
of southern race etiquette."[12] Even with blacks excluded as speakers,
Washington was hopeful about the conference.

Blacks were admitted to the meetings. In fact, as Murphy wrote to
Washington on Southern Society stationery, "From three to four
hundred colored people were occupying seats that were *wanted* by the

best *white* people of Montgomery." He told Washington that he agreed with the final decision not to include blacks as speakers. He said he did so for two reasons. Northern newspapers had called for such a move, but Murphy believed that the best way to ensure widespread positive response in the South was for the conference not to give any appearance of listening to northern counsel. In these years, he believed that vitriolic northern critics of the South were not helping blacks but only consolidating defensive support around the few representatives of southern white demagogic leadership. A second reason was Murphy's fear that in the midst of the bitter comments with which he found himself in strong disagreement, blacks would have been very hurt and might not have been able to restrain themselves. Murphy's sense of *noblesse oblige* is seen clearly when he told Washington, "I also see that it would be a great mistake to adopt a policy which would seem to make the Negro the chief advocate of the Negro's rights. . . . In other words, the cause of the Negro can be advocated more effectively by the white man, who is the Negro's friend, than by the Negro himself."[13] No statement strikes us as more conservative or paternalistic. It is also a statement that speaks of the climate of opinion of this period, accepted as much by Washington as by Murphy. Whether Murphy recognized it or not, this question of advocacy would be at the heart of efforts for racial reform. He was opting for the only strategy he thought possible in the South in the year 1900.

Murphy did not address the conference. Hilary A. Herbert, eight-term Montgomery congressman, opened the conference with a rambling speech in which he claimed that there was scientific evidence of black inferiority that was now manifesting itself in rising crime and idleness and missed educational opportunities. The next morning the conference heard from Alfred Moore Waddell, the mayor of Wilmington, North Carolina. Two years earlier the port city of Wilmington had been the scene of a race riot in which seven blacks were killed and thirteen injured. The Montgomery conference was weighted heavily toward moderates, but Mayor Waddell was not one of them. He told the assembly that blacks were "a menace to civilization and good government." On the other hand, an hour later the former governor of West Virginia, William A. MacCorkle, spoke forthrightly about granting blacks all of their constitutional rights, saying, "His privilege of franchise is as sacred as ours and should be sacredly guarded."[14]

The session on education was headlined by Frissell and Curry, who offered traditional comments on industrial education and the role of the stronger race in helping the weaker race. On the concluding morning, under the heading "The Negro in Relation to Religion," the provocative question was raised as to whether religious work among blacks could best be carried on through administration by whites or blacks. Both speakers, D. Clay Lilly, secretary of the Southern Presbyterian Board of Negro Evangelization, and W. A. Guerry, chaplain of the University of the South, used old arguments in favor of maintaining white control because they said it benefited blacks in the past and, because of their inferior abilities, would "in the providence of God" continue to be for their own good.[15]

The conference closed on a typically contradictory note. Murphy was outraged at a speech by Paul B. Barringer, chair of the faculty of the University of Virginia, who attempted to give irrefutable evidence for the decay of black life. Convinced that natural law would eventually eliminate the black race, Barringer said that philanthropy, even in the form of industrial education, was a waste. Former congressman W. Bourke Cockran of New York followed Barringer with a well-received address that ended the conference on an upbeat note of confidence and hope. A northerner who agreed with Murphy's conservative position on the franchise, Cockran did not have a progressive reputation on the race issue. But on this day, he observed that if outside coercion would cease and talk of black domination would be seen for what it was—a myth used by demagogues to keep themselves in power—progress could continue unabated. Affirming black advancement in but one generation since the war, Cockran held up Washington and Tuskegee as the pattern to follow: "Let there be a Tuskegee in every community, and I promise you that the next generation, instead of troubling about Negroes, will be celebrating a glorious success in settling a question graver than any presented to a nation in the history of the human race."[16]

After the conference Murphy spent the summer editing the proceedings for publication. He also tried in vain to launch a magazine *Race Problems: A Journal of Information and Discussion*. Filled with a vision of new possibilities in the South, he went ahead with plans for a Southern Society conference in 1901. No city offered to serve as host, however, and various persons offered the opinion that continued discussion might inevitably become too volatile because of the nature of the subject. It was better to quit while ahead.

But Murphy was only beginning. His acceptance of the position of executive secretary of the Southern Education Board involved a profound religious and vocational decision. Murphy presented his resignation to the St. John's vestry on November 27, 1901. Fifteen months later he resigned from the ordination of the Episcopal ministry. If we couple these two decisions with the decision of the southern education movement to drop the word *Christian* from its title and become a public movement, it is possible to interpret Murphy as a reformer who left behind his theological and ecclesiastical moorings. Many persons with reform instincts, then and now, who have felt shackled by the church's backward thinking and bureaucratic mind-set, have left the church behind. Often these people have not been counted when the story of religion and reform is chronicled. But is this what Murphy was doing? This whole episode needs closer scrutiny in order to appreciate Murphy's subsequent career.

The tone of Murphy's remarks to the church vestry at St. John's spoke of his deep commitment to ministry. It was not an easy thing to leave the parish duties at St. John's. He told the vestry that his decision was "my best response to God's will, and to the needs of our church and our country." His own thinking at this time was epitomized in the article "Reconstruction in Religion," published in the *Outlook*. Murphy affirmed the new social vision arising in the churches. "Think of the exciting and imperious challenge." He hoped the Christian community would respond to "the fine intolerant impatience of the new social ideal which the church is attempting to realize."[17]

It is important to understand just how much Murphy's own ministry had been increasingly characterized by the new social vision. Our immediate concern is the story of racial reform, but almost every one of these Social Gospel leaders was active in several reform efforts. As the ministry of St. John's extended to the west end of Montgomery, Murphy learned firsthand of the evils of child labor. In 1901 he led the way in founding the Alabama Child Labor Committee, the first such state committee in the nation. This committee and its aggressive strategy became a model for state committees across the country. Even after the assumption of his duties with the Southern Education Board, Murphy was active at the state and national level. In 1903 he delivered a speech entitled "Child Labor as a National Problem" before the annual meeting of the National Conference of Charities and Corrections. Fellow southern reformer Alexander J. McKelway called Murphy's speech "the greatest speech against child labor ever delivered in America."[18]

In a letter to his bishop, Murphy said he was taking the step away from ordination because of misunderstandings he had encountered stemming from society's ideas about the nature and role of the minister. He made it plain that his own sense of ministry would continue unabated. He spoke of his ministry in terms of concern for child labor (he was just then turning his attention to the formation of a National Child Labor Committee) and for improved education and race relations.

This new opportunity with the Southern Education Board was a logical extension of his own understanding of the missionary outreach of the church. Here was a possibility to relate his vision about the coming kingdom of God to education and at the same time exercise his considerable skills as a publicist and organizer.

To move from the sacred to the secular, from the parish to various reform interests, was not at all uncommon in this era of the Social Gospel. The whole point of the Social Gospel was to break down the artificial barriers between the sacred and the secular. Even before he made this move, Murphy expressed sentiments that foreshadowed his subsequent decision. While serving a northern parish, he sounded very much like his northern Social Gospel counterparts. He criticized any religion that would divide life into the sacred and the secular. "Jesus admits no such distinctions in His thought. Virtues to Jesus are not secular and religious, sacred and profane. All are sacred and religious."[19]

To be sure, then and now, many persons leave the parish ministry in disillusionment or bitterness, never caring to look back. This was not true for Murphy. He did shift his location, leaving the parish ministry, but he did not abandon his vocation—which he continued in his ministry as a reformer. His concern for both church and ministry continued to be attested both by Murphy and his friends.

With some sense for Murphy's reform activities in relation to race, it is important to ask about the ideas that undergirded his actions. Murphy was a thoughtful theologian even before social experiences challenged and ultimately reshaped his theology. As a reformer, one of his strengths was his skill as a publicist. The challenge was to communicate his ideas to a wide audience in a popular form.

Murphy lectured from time to time but expressed himself increasingly through his writing. Drawing on his broad experiences, he produced a full-length study, *Problems of the Present South*, in 1904. Only one of the eight chapter titles dealt specifically with the race problem, but actually every chapter touched upon this central southern issue. Murphy asserted that the last five years had seen new and acute dimensions of "the Negro question." Some of these problems were directly related to the fact of the advancement of blacks.[20] Murphy offered no easy solutions, but rather perspectives and alternatives. The white man in Africa was an African problem, and just so the African in America was an American problem. The problem would not go away, nor would it be solved by the appeal to time, as heard so often in this period. The problem was three-sided: moral, physical, and intellectual, and there was confusion within and between each part of the whole.

Murphy began with a double assumption: the inferiority of blacks and their improvability. The first assumption was held universally in the South. Hearing this assumption, we could dismiss Murphy as another racist conservative. A number of commentators have done so. But it was the content with which Murphy filled out the second assumption that distinguished him from his southern contemporaries.

Murphy said that black progress was readily observable in the fact that illiteracy had been reduced from 88 percent in 1870 to 52 percent in 1900. What was not so observable statistically was advancement on other fronts. Murphy pointed to the black family, church, and school, three institutions that were marked by impressive development in less than forty years.

In his analysis, Murphy anticipated the perplexing question of why other southern whites did not see progress also. The objective side of the answer was that "social cleavage" imposed its limitations upon the vision of the white community. The black loafer, even the worker at the lower rung of the industrial ladder, was quite visible to whites, but how many whites had ever been in a black home, school, or church? Given the present social barrier, Murphy argued that whites were not often able to evaluate properly the capacity of blacks to improve. But even when they could evaluate, masses of whites found their vision impaired by subjective factors. These masses Murphy referred to were lower-class and emerging middle-class whites. Over time they had defined themselves in southern society "upon the one ground of the unity of the race." A further distortion arose from the realities of economic competition. Many of these whites would not be favorably disposed to seeing blacks move up the ladder of advancement to rungs that they already occupied.[21]

How could such reluctance to recognize the gains that blacks had made be overcome? Murphy answered by appealing to the democratic idealism of the South. He argued that a democratic society could not long flourish with a dependent class. Furthermore, such a class could be permitted to continue only by disregarding the organic law of society. Disregard of blacks was not only unjust, therefore, but "in its reactive influence upon those who continue it, must result in a lowering of political standards and a vitiation of civic fibre." Harking back to his theological orientation of an organic understanding of society, Murphy argued that lack of concern for solving the race problem would in the long run prove "far more disastrous to the strong than to the weak."[22]

Murphy was concerned especially about the growing sentiment to spend white tax dollars only for white schools and black tax dollars for black schools. He was quick to point out that white wealth had always been bound to black labor. He opposed such plans because society was indivisible and because white and black ascendancy were inextricably tied together.

Finally, Murphy's appeal was to the old spirit of *noblesse oblige*, but in a new form. In the Old South, men and women of aristocratic birth had quite literally reached out to help the less privileged. In the New South, Murphy envisioned an alliance between whites of the middle class and older aristocratic families in order to work toward solutions of the race problem. The southern education movement focused on whites as well as blacks because only by means of education could whites be freed from fear and suspicion and forge a new spirit of helpfulness and cooperation.

Murphy was gratified at the general response to his book. But he confided to Washington his disappointment at not hearing from more blacks. He had wanted the publisher to send copies of his work to black newspapers, but this was not done.[23]

Even as illness confined him to his bed for weeks at a time, in 1908 Murphy was completing a new volume, *The Basis of Ascendancy*. In the early months of 1909, he sought in vain to find a publisher. Even though *Problems of the Present South* had received impressive reviews, it had not been a financial success. Now Murphy told Washington that neither Macmillan nor Doubleday would publish his new book and that he finally asked Longmans and Green to print it at his own expense.[24]

Murphy developed older arguments more fully in *The Basis of Ascendancy*, but there was also a shift of tone and emphasis. Murphy's growing impatience with white "racial aggression" in the South was now accompanied for the first time by a willingness to permit "gentle coercion" from outside the South.

The chapter entitled "The New Coercion" is the high point of Murphy's literary odyssey as a reformer. Murphy is at his best here, for he writes both as an erudite philosopher and as a popular propagandist. Always conscious of history, Murphy begins with the Civil War. An operative statement for his whole argument is a quotation from President Abraham Lincoln, who said that the outcome of the Civil War would be determined by "the preponderance of resources." Murphy argues powerfully that the resources were not military or political but something much greater. The South, tragically, was struggling against the wisdom of the whole world that a free labor system was the best basis for an industrial society.[25]

Taking time to blame the North for the evils of Reconstruction, Murphy argues that it is time now to put the race question into world perspective. If the South was provincial in its arguments before the war, it is running the same risk at the beginning of the twentieth century. Murphy grants that there continues to be unfair pressure on the South, which contributes to a spirit of disease in southern Society. "A challenge from without will be answered by a responsive challenge from within. Opposition will develop opposition—the return and recoil of our life upon itself." What can be the result? "The forces of rejection, of antagonism, of passionate segregation, will possess a profound and general power. An acute and exaggerated consciousness of section and of race will be inevitable."[26]

Taking pains to win the right to be heard by his fellow southerners, Murphy nonetheless invites the South to see beyond the overt coercion of an intruder to the gentle coercion of a world community. "Is not this very community of freedom into which the world invites us the source of our new coercion? Is not its hospitality—an intimate and universal invitation of its ideals, its democratic tendencies, its industrial and political assumptions—the real challenge to every provincial aspect of our development?"[27] Murphy speaks like a loving father when he says, "We may draw about ourselves the tense protections of our 'peculiarity,' the boundaries of our intellectual or political segregation." But to do so is to be doomed to provincialism. "The commerce of ideas, of intellectual and social influence, is impossible through erected barriers and unopening doors."[28]

How does this probing social analysis relate to the race problem? Murphy has laid a philosophical and historical foundation. "To talk, in an age like ours, of not educating any particular class of human beings or of deliberately holding any fraction or race of men at a permanently lower level of industrial or political opportunity is to talk a language as stale" as the words on an Egyptian mummy. What is the practical import in society? "A discrimination put into a law is a discriminatory law; a discriminating law, in a democratic society, is not a law, but a revision of the law at the command of the minority."[29]

Murphy issues a call for the South to move from "detachment and our isolation" into the mainstream of modern life. To reject the newer, freer impulses of the social awakening "is to deprive the South of that accumulated and collective energy" available to every modern state. The social forces at work in the world represent "not a propaganda, but an invitation." Murphy, ever the minister, is confident of the source of this new awakening. He invites the South to partake of "the blessings that are visitant whenever the thought of God has a practical reality and conscience a social significance."[30]

Aware that the education of blacks had not achieved all of its original promise, he asked his southern readers to think through the reasons why it did little good to teach a black man to read if the printed page contained nothing but deprecation and abuse. Murphy, the publicist, often couched his pleas for blacks in ways that would appeal to the self-interest of whites. He emphasized that the South, in its constant squabbling about blacks, was retarding its own growth and its own rightful partnership with the rest of the nation.[31]

The Basis of Ascendency was well received by many progressives, both black and white. Kelly Miller applauded it in the *Dial*. Robert R. Moton, eventual successor to Washington at Tuskegee, wrote from Hampton Institute to commend Murphy. "It is the fairest and most perfect statement from every viewpoint of the situation in general, and our American race problem in particular, that I have seen." The eminent economist Edward Atkinson was ebullient in his praise, calling it "the most important document yet issued and will do more to bring about true union of all the States" than anything since the Gettsyburg Address.[32]

The title caused some confusion. Against a background of personal misunderstanding, Oswald Garrison Villard reviewed the book in the *New York Evening Post*. He asserted that Murphy's idea of ascendancy was white over black. Murphy was taken aback by this critique. For "the gentle progressive," ascendancy was by definition related in Murphy's mind to his earlier ideas of *noblesse oblige* and the task of leadership. Ascendancy was a moral attribute applicable to a whole range of human associations. It was not an absolute status; rather, "the fact of deepest significance in reference to every human aggregate is the relative status of its development as compared with the former status or stages of its own advance." Ascendancy was a trajectory, and Murphy sought to interpret the concept so as to emphasize direction and progress.[33]

Murphy was optimistic about a third volume. He announced in the preface to *The Basis of Ascendancy* that *Issues, Southern and National* was "practically ready . . . for the press." This volume, Murphy promised, would offer "a more explicit statement of those principles of fundamental policy" undergirding a wide range of social issues.[34] This explicit statement would not be heard, for continued ill health prevented the publication of this study.

The southern education movement was at a crossroads in 1907, but its leader, Edgar Gardner Murphy, had little strength left to offer to the cause. Since 1893 he had suffered from a rheumatic heart condition. During these years as executive secretary, he was often prostrated for long periods of time, unable to work. By January of 1908, renewed illness convinced him that he was no longer able to continue his duties, and he communicated to Ogden his intention to resign. He somehow pressed on until May 1, but the Southern Education Board refused to consider his resignation until January 1909 so that his salary might continue.[35]

How does one take the measure of this man? Murphy does not fit neatly into the stereotypes that have been used to describe racial thought in this period. A southerner who had lived in the North, he understood both the northern and the southern perspectives on race. An idealist nurtured in a broad intellectual tradition, he was at one and the same time an intellectual and a publicist. Variously portrayed as a conservative or a moderate, as either reluctant or courageous, both the complexity and the development in Murphy admit to no simple generalizations.

Three features of his life can help us assess Murphy as a reformer. First, he understood himself to be a minister or priest. Even while leaving behind his Episcopal ordination, it is clear that he continued in his original calling.

Murphy's continuing fidelity to his ministerial calling is revealed in an episode at the end of his career. After the final session of the Conference for Education in the South in 1908, Episcopal bishop Thomas F. Gailor wrote to Murphy. Years before, Gailor had been chaplain at the University of the South when Murphy was a student. Now a bishop, Gailor wrote:

> I write this so that it may be in permanent form. I want you to know how glad I have been to see you again and to feel that the distinction you have earned has not changed the old simplicity of your Christian and church loyalty. The whole South realizes that your energy and earnestness and great efficiency have actualized what otherwise would have been only a dream for many years to come. I wish to assure you of our wide-spread conviction that you have done a noble work for your people and your Christ.[36]

Touched deeply by the letter, when health permitted, Murphy responded at length. In his reply, his first words were, "There was nothing in your letter for which I was so grateful as for your expression concerning the relations of my work to the church and to Christ."[37]

These words, coming at the conclusion of Murphy's service to the southern education movement, speak of the commitment that energized his entire career. We can see now that even when stepping outside the formal walls of the Episcopal church, Murphy conceived of his vocation as ministry. H. Shelton Smith sums up Murphy's career by observing, "In reality, Murphy was a preacher of what was then called the social gospel."[38] The fact that Murphy lived in the South and concentrated on education and race relations must become part of the redefinition of the meaning and geographical contours of the Social Gospel.

Second, he understood himself as a missionary from the South to the North. In one sense Murphy was an intersectional person. As executive secretary of the Southern Education Board, he was in regular contact with northern philanthropists and leaders. But he always thought of himself as a leader representing the best interests of the South.

Murphy's concern about his standing with the South can be seen in a private letter to Oswald Garrison Villard, the liberal editor of the *New York Evening Post*. Villard had become editor in 1903, and he worked hard to get southern moderates to stand up and be counted. At the same time, the *Post* was acquiring the reputation of being the "most bitter South-hating paper in the country." In this context Murphy wrote to Villard asking him to stop praising Murphy in public. The complexity of the situation is seen in Murphy's words to the editor: "Deeply as I value your approval, I would rather have you fight me than to have you praise me to the prejudice of my position among my people."[39] No words speak more clearly to the difficulty of Murphy's position, but also to his own sense of security as to the best way to advance the cause of racial reform.

An exchange with Booker T. Washington revealed further his sensitivities about southern opinion. Although toward the end becoming more outspoken, Murphy never wanted to be seen as a martyr or even as terribly unique. Writing to Washington, he said, "Whatever you may say of me—you will not call me '*brave*'—I am not brave: that is, not brave on the Negro question; and it irritates the South extremely to have a few of us who are really only voicing the feeling and faith of thousands singled out for 'moral approval.'"[40]

Both of these exchanges reveal much about Murphy's self-understanding. These comments exemplify Murphy's concern to be seen as a loyal southern son while at the same time moving the South forward in its posture vis-à-vis race relations.

Third, a closer examination of Murphy discloses a reformer on a journey. His life is not static but is changing and developing under the impetus of new experiences. A helpful way to characterize this journey is to see in Murphy a movement from idealism to realism.

Much about Murphy speaks to his idealism. Nowhere is it more visible than in his lifelong remarks about community. His ideas about community had been nurtured in Anglican theology and tempered through the southern patrician society into which he was adopted, not born. Murphy thought of community in large pictures and historical processes. Early on, he saw that the one who enslaves will suffer as much as the slave. He understood the need for universal education in the New South. His whole life was a response to the biblical teaching that to whom much is given, much will be required. For Murphy, the obligation to help those less fortunate than yourself was not a burden laid upon an individual but the definition of the reciprocal relationships in any viable community.

But idealists can become realists. It occurs again and again in our larger story when the irresistible force of racism bludgeons the ideals of reformers. Two recent books have included studies of Murphy. In each of these fine studies there is a tendency to view Murphy the reformer in static rather than dynamic terms. Thus Joel Williamson characterizes Murphy as "the ambassador of Conservative Southern White civilization to the intellectual North." Williamson recognizes Murphy as the one whose thoughtful arguments "shatter the racial sets of some leaders in Northern thought and make them rethink and adjust their pro-Negro biases in such a way as to favor the white South."[41] But in casting Murphy as the missionary to the North, we must not overlook his own self-understanding as a missionary to the South. In this latter role Murphy challenged southern conventions and worked behind the scenes to counteract white southern racism.

Ralph Luker, in *A Southern Tradition in Theology and Social Criticism, 1830–1930*, traces the contributions of James Warley Miles, William Porcher Dubose, and Murphy under the subheading "Religious Liberalism and Social Conservatism." In terms of race, Luker states that "theirs is an intellectual tradition which reflects a continuous attitude toward race relations through those decades of traumatic change." Perhaps more accurately, we could say that in encountering Murphy, we observe both continuity and change. Luker speaks of "the essentially racist character of Murphy's thought," but I believe rather that his thought changed under the influence of new experience and information.[42]

What is the evidence for this change and development? As Murphy encountered the entrenched opposition to racial change, he became more realistic. The opposition was there from the beginning, but at first he tended to explain it away because of his idealized vision of southern history and destiny. Thus his founding the Southern Society for the Promotion of the Study of Race Conditions and Problems in the South offered bright promise, but plans for an annual event and an accompanying journal never came to fruition. In Murphy's lectures and writings he marshaled the evidence for black progress in the black family, church, and school. But he was frustrated that this progress was not recognized. We have observed in chapter 6 Murphy's hopes for and gradual discouragement with universal education, which he had believed would be the best indirect route of advancing Negro education.

In all of his efforts Murphy believed in the democratic idealism of the South. Central to this idealism was a spirit of *noblesse oblige* that would characterize an emerging middle class. At first, when he was willing to admit obstacles, he posited the resistance in a few demagogic leaders who, he insisted, were not representative of general public opinion. Over time he was forced to admit more widespread opposition.

Faced with cumulating obstacles, Murphy became more realistic in his maturing understanding of racial reform. By 1906 Murphy exhibited increasing concern over white acts of oppression. In the past he had attributed such acts to an insignificant minority. Murphy admitted that he was deeply troubled by facts that showed that tens of thousands of duly qualified blacks were not permitted to vote. This was a turn of events he had said would not happen when he first proposed franchise amendments in 1900. A change of emphasis can be seen in his assertion in early 1907 that southern demagogues who were using the Negro question to gain political power were far more dangerous than northern critics.[43]

In his final book, *The Basis of Ascendancy,* Murphy was more sober than in his earlier writings. His acknowledgment of the problems led him to countenance "gentle coercion" as part of the solution. Each page reflects his understanding of the abilities and aspirations of black Americans.

A recognition of Murphy's understanding of the black experience was recorded by George E. Haynes more than a decade later. Haynes, the first director of the Urban League, wrote *The Trend of the Races* in his capacity as director of the Commission on the Church and Race Relations of the Federal Council of Churches. Haynes observed that "the Negro has a self and a soul, of the depth and mystery of which a white observer becomes aware only once in a great while."[44] A footnote to this observation refers the reader to Edgar Gardner Murphy and *The Basis of Ascendency.* Haynes, in the final analysis, offers the best succinct assessment of Murphy. He was that "once in a great while" person who spent a lifetime wanting to understand the "depth and mystery" of the souls of black folk.

When Murphy realized in 1908 that illness would force his resignation from the Southern Education Board, he was only thirty-eight years old. It is not improper for the historian to conjecture about what might have been, had Murphy been permitted to continue his work. Hugh C. Bailey, Murphy's biographer, believes that the evidence suggests a continuing liberal metamorphosis.[45]

I have argued that we must understand Edgar Gardner Murphy not in static but in developmental terms. Like Washington Gladden, Murphy changed his mind as new experiences and information intersected his life. From our vantage point there is much to criticize. Called a hero or brave by contemporaries, black and white, he may not appear courageous by the standards of the civil rights era. But we are obligated to understand reformers in their own context. To do so is to listen to the evaluations of their own contemporaries. He was brave to many blacks and an encouragement to other white reformers. Even in his hesitation and moderation, Murphy was the most consistent white southern spokesman for blacks in the first decade of the twentieth century. He is significant also as a leader in the beginnings of modern social Christianity in the South.

Part Three

NEW VENTURES
IN RACIAL REFORM,
1909–1925

CHAPTER 11

The NAACP and the Urban League

For it is fiery abolitionism as against the calm meliorism of Booker T. Washington, that this society [NAACP] preaches, and it is important that these two sides of the movement to alter the colored man's status should be clearly discerned.

—*CHICAGO EVENING POST*

Yet Jesus Christ was a laborer and black men are laborers; He was poor and we are poor; He was despised of his fellow men and we are despised; He was persecuted and crucified, and we are mobbed and lynched. If Jesus Christ came to America, He would associate with Negroes and Italians and working people.

—W. E. B. DU BOIS

The movement for racial reform in the Progressive Era culminated in the founding of the National Association for the Advancement of Colored People in 1909 and the National Urban League in 1910. Declaring itself against all forms of segregation, the NAACP abandoned amelioration to battle for equal political, legal, and social rights for black Americans. The National Urban League, on the other hand, concentrated its major efforts toward expanding employment opportunities and providing social services for the influx of blacks to the urban centers of the nation. Whereas in recent years the NAACP has been toward the right of the spectrum of civil rights organizations, in its early years it was often characterized, by its own members and others, as a militant organization. The NAACP became the major vehicle of protest and was opposed to accommodation. More accommodationist in its ideology, the Urban League adhered fairly closely to the Booker T. Washington schedule of priorities. Its persistent efforts helped open the economic marketplace to many blacks for the first time.

The NAACP and the Urban League have usually not been treated as part of the study of religion in this period. They were not chartered as

religious organizations. But the black church was present and accounted for at their birth, and some white Social Gospelers were early supporters of these new ventures in biracial reform.

In this chapter we investigate the role that religion played in the
origins of the NAACP and the Urban League. Who were the early leaders, black and white? What were their attitudes and actions? Specifically, what was the involvement in these new organizations of leaders,
both black and white, of the movement now coming to maturity—the
Social Gospel?

On August 14, 1908, a race riot erupted in Springfield, Illinois. Before it was over, 7 people died, 2 of them lynched, over 50 were wounded, and more than 3,600 militiamen were called in to restore order.
More than 2,000 blacks fled Springfield, and the local white citizenry
made it very plain that they wished these black residents would leave
for good.[1]

In the midst of complacency in Illinois and the nation, William
Hayes Ward, editor of the *Independent*, expressed shock at this riot in
the North in the home city of Lincoln.[2] Two weeks later, William English Walling, a settlement house worker and writer, published a six-
page article in the *Independent* that was the result of a personal investigation of the riot and its aftermath. As upset by the national apathy as
by the riot itself, Walling closed his article with a plea: "Who realizes
the seriousness of the situation? What large and powerful body of citizens is ready to come to aid?"[3]

Mary White Ovington, a young socialite turned New York social
worker, read the article and her response was immediate.

> I saw the article as soon as it came out. Its description of rioting and bru-
> tality was terrible, but I was familiar with that. What made me put down
> the magazine and write to Walling within the hour was the appeal to citizens
> to come to the Negro's aid. Du Bois was working with his own race. Here
> was a man who called upon both races in the spirit of the abolitionist to
> come forward and right the nation's wrongs.[4]

The institutional origins of the NAACP date from the first week of
1909 and a meeting at the New York apartment of William English
Walling. Also present were Mary White Ovington and Dr. Henry Mos-
kowitz, a social worker with New York's immigrant population. Mos-
kowitz was actually taking the place of Charles Edward Russell, a writer
and a close friend of Walling, who was unable to attend. At the meeting
it was decided to invite Oswald Garrison Villard, editor of the *New York*

Evening Post, to become the fifth member of the group. Shortly after that first meeting, the group was made biracial when Ovington suggested that two prominent black ministers, Bishop Alexander Walters of the African Methodist Episcopal Zion Church, and the Reverend William Henry Brooks, minister of St. Mark's Methodist Episcopal Church of New York, be asked to join the deliberations.[5]

Building on the impetus of Springfield, the group decided that February 12, 1909—the centennial of the Great Emancipator's birth—should mark the beginning of a national campaign on behalf of political and civil rights for black Americans. A call for a national conference was drafted, written largely by Villard. It was issued on Lincoln's birthday and contained the signatures of sixty people,—fifty-two whites and eight blacks. On May 31 and June 1, a National Negro Conference was held in New York City. William Hayes Ward acted as chairman, and speakers included Villard, Walling, Russell, Walters, as well as W. E. B. Du Bois and Mrs. Ida Wells-Barnett. Out of the conference came a Committee of Forty on Permanent Organization, and what became known as the NAACP was brought into being.[6]

Three organizations stood directly behind the National Urban League.[7] In 1906 Frances A. Kellor and some of her social work associates established the National League for the Protection of Colored Women. The NLPCW concerned itself with the housing, employment, and recreation of black women, many of whom were migrating to a hostile northern city from the South.

In the same year, William L. Bulkley, the first black principal in the New York school system, brought together sixty New York blacks and whites to organize the Committee for Improving the Industrial Conditions of Negroes in New York (CIICN). The primary goal of this organization was to expand the economic opportunities open to blacks.

In 1910 a third organization, the Committee on Urban Conditions, was formed. It was composed in part of people who had been active in both the NLPCW and the CIICN. The National Urban League actually was founded in 1911 as a consolidation of the three organizations, but it has always dated the beginning of its organizational life from 1910.

A patrician white family and a young black sociologist are representative of the diverse backgrounds of the leaders of the new Urban League. William Henry Baldwin, Jr., became acquainted with the race problem during his tenure as president of the Southern Railway in the 1890s. As has been noted in chapter 6, he was present at the second Capon Springs Conference for Christian Education in the South. He was elected both a trustee of the Southern Education Board and the first chairman of the General Education Board. He became a close friend and adviser to Booker T. Washington. Baldwin was a vigorous advocate of industrial education, not merely as a means of economic advancement for blacks but as the basis of interracial cooperation. Although he died in 1905, his ideas about economic cooperation and the power of good will by getting leaders together were echoed again and again in the first years of the Urban League.[8]

Ruth Standish Baldwin carried on the reform interests of her husband. A lifelong semi-invalid, she became more radical than her husband, joining the Socialist party and becoming a pacifist in World War I. Mrs. Baldwin served as the first chairman of the board of the Urban League. As candidate to direct the activities of the Urban League, she promoted a young sociologist, George Edmund Haynes.

Haynes was born in Pine Bluff, Arkansas, in 1880 and graduated from Fisk University in 1903. He received an M.A. from Yale in sociology in 1904 and then came to New York in 1908 to do graduate work at the New York School of Philanthropy (later the New York School of Social Work). In 1912 he became the first black to receive a Ph.D. from Columbia. When Haynes began his studies, the conventional wisdom was that blacks would continue to live in the rural areas, mostly in the South. Haynes's studies suggested to the contrary that blacks, like whites, were coming to the cities and that a great migration was about to take place.[9]

In the course of his studies of the conditions of blacks in New York, he was brought into contact with Mrs. Baldwin and other white reformers. Haynes, anticipating the problems that would accompany a great influx of blacks, was looking for ways to include blacks in existing social service organizations. Frustrated in these attempts, Haynes, Baldwin, and others founded a new organization to deal with the problems of urban blacks—the Urban League, of which Haynes became the first director. He helped to launch the league even while starting the sociology department at Fisk. Based in Nashville, Haynes traveled to New York on a regular basis.

The ideological origins of both of these organizations antedate the first decade of the twentieth century. Abolitionism was the ancestral spirit that energized a significant number of the white leaders of these two reform organizations, especially for the more militant NAACP. Of the fifty-two white signers of the NAACP call, James M. McPherson has concluded that at least fifteen were former abolitionists or the children or grandchildren of abolitionists. This list included William Lloyd Garrison, Jr., Fanny Garrison Villard, Edward Clement, Horace White, and William Hayes Ward.[10]

In *The Abolitionist Legacy: From Reconstruction to the NAACP*, McPherson traces the ideological roots of nearly three hundred abolitionists or the children or grandchildren of abolitionists. The abolitionist movement was made up of several contingents. Of the more than 88 percent who could be identified with a particular faction, 40.8 percent are identified as evangelical abolitionists. Of these evangelical, or Christian, abolitionists, as they were sometimes called, the major denominations represented were:

Congregational	45.1 percent
Methodist	23.0 percent
Baptist	10.6 percent
Presbyterian	10.6 percent
Quaker	8.8 percent

Another wing of the movement, the Garrisonian, makes up 27.8 percent of the total. It was not devoid of religious motivation, despite Garrison's criticism of the evangelicals. Among the Garrisonians the largest numbers came from among the Unitarians (34.3 percent) and the Quakers (25.7 percent). Of the 20.1 percent identified with the "Political" faction, 50 percent are Unitarian, followed by 15.8 percent who are Congregational.[11]

Among these children and grandchildren of abolitionists, those of evangelical lineage often came to these new ventures in racial reform via the missionary bridge of freedmen's education. In the NAACP, Horace Bumstead, who retired as president of Atlanta University in 1907, was active in the Boston branch. Wilbur P. Thirkield, founding dean of the Gammon School of Theology in Atlanta, served on an NAACP committee in the years he was president of Howard (1906–1912). James G. Merrill, former president of Fisk, and M. C. B. Mason, former secretary of the Methodist Freedmen's Aid Society, were active also.

On the Urban League side, Paul D. Cravath's father had been an official of the American Missionary Association and the first president of Fisk. A. S. Frissell's brother was the principal of Hampton.[12] George Edmund Haynes was on the faculty of Fisk.

For still others numbered among the abolitionist legacy, the religious orientation was present but more ambiguous. Mary White Ovington came from a New England abolitionist background. Her father left the Congregational church in a dispute over racial policy, and the family switched its allegiance to the Unitarian church. Oswald Garrison Villard was the grandson of William Lloyd Garrison. Garrison died in 1879, but abolitionism lived on in his descendants. Always interested in the race question, in 1902 Villard was invited by Robert Ogden to join the southern educational trip that culminated in the Conference on Education in the South annual meeting at Athens, Georgia. Exposed for the first time to all of the difficulties confronting blacks in the South, Villard later called that trip "the most important—and most educational—event in my life." Speaking of Villard's work in the North and the South, Mary White Ovington said, "Long before there was an NAACP, there was a Garrison in New York, setting forth in his larger *Liberator* the wrongs of the Negro race."[13]

For these early leaders, abolitionism was not simply a precedent, but a present reality and tactic. The new abolitionism, as it was called, was a self-conscious characterization of the NAACP, especially in the years through 1915. Sometimes "new abolition" was the heading over the opinion section in the NAACP periodical, the *Crisis*.[14] At the annual meeting in 1914, Joel E. Spingarn, a lawyer who had succeeded Villard as chairman of the board that year, sounded this theme in his keynote speech. The *Crisis* quoted approvingly an editorial comment in the *Chicago Evening Post* that said, "For it is fiery abolitionism as against the calm meliorism of Booker T. Washington, that this society preaches, and it is important that these two sides of the movement to alter the colored man's status should be clearly discerned."[15]

Despite the diverse ideology present among the new reformers, the rhetoric of the new abolitionism was reminiscent of the religious content of the past. If there was not so much talk of sin, the shadow of guilt was constant. The call itself was a listing of the wrongs of the country against the promise and hope that Lincoln inspired. The language of Villard's call and the talk of what Lincoln would find if he were to return were meant to evoke feelings of guilt among the readers.

Many of the early white leaders joined with black leaders in using imagery out of the Old Testament. Black Americans identified their plight with the people of Israel, who came out of bondage into the Promised Land. Mary White Ovington's autobiographical account of the NAACP is entitled *The Walls Came Tumbling Down*. The title page quotes the words from "Joshua fit de battle of Jericho." A summary issue of the *Crisis* in August 1919 epitomized the use of religious language as the medium of communication. The subheadings for a series of articles on page 1 began with the injunction "To Your Tents, O Israel!" by

W. E. B. Du Bois and concluded with "The Sword of the Spirit" by Oswald Garrison Villard.[16]

The most important black ideological precursor to the NAACP was the Niagara Movement.[17] W. E. B. Du Bois was the catalyst for the coming together of the more radical leaders of the "talented tenth" for three days of meetings at Fort Erie, Ontario, in July 1905. Black Social Gospel leaders J. Milton Waldron, Sutton E. Griggs, and Reverdy C. Ransom were leading members of the Niagara Movement. A speech by Ransom at the 1906 meeting (held at Harper's Ferry) was credited by Du Bois as being critical to the eventual founding of the NAACP.[18]

The first conference adopted an "Address to the Country," well described in its own words as a "statement, complaint, and prayer." Running counter to the posture of the Tuskegee movement, the Niagara platform placed the burden of the racial problem on the white community.

The Niagara Movement was a black organization, but it was not unmindful of its forebears, black and white. In November 1905 the Niagara Movement sponsored memorial services for three "Friends of Freedom." The services honored Frederick Douglass, William Lloyd Garrison, and Albion W. Tourgée.[19]

The response to the Niagara Movement among adherents of the Social Gospel was mixed. William Hayes Ward editorialized in the *Independent* that he did not wish to take sides in the growing intramural debate "for control of the public sentiment among the educated Negroes of this country." After this qualification, however, Ward endorsed "every word of the principles" formulated at the Harper's Ferry meetings. "They ask no compromise for all equal social rights," and the *Independent* was in full agreement with the demands.[20]

Lyman Abbott and the *Outlook* took quite a different position. Abbott offered the opinion that Du Bois and his cohorts would bring about more injury than benefit to blacks. Troubled by the "whine" of the Niagara leaders, Abbott concluded, "The real leaders of the American Negroes are not complaining; they are too busy inculcating habits of thrift, energy, and self-control among the people to whom they are proud to belong."[21]

After the Niagara meetings in 1906 the *Outlook* published the Niagara Platform, followed directly by the "Platform of the *Outlook*." Often Social Gospelers and the larger progressive community spoke in generalities about the race problem, but here is an opportunity for direct comparison of specific beliefs and goals. The Niagara Platform of 1906 included the following five points:

1. The right to vote.
2. Condemnation of all discrimination in public accommodations.
3. Freedom of social intercourse.
4. Equality in enforcement of laws.
5. A massive effort by the federal government to wipe out illiteracy in the South.

The *Outlook* responded point by point:

1. Manhood needed to come first, and then suffrage would follow. The ballot was not a natural right. However, the ballot "should be based on personal qualifications, not on race or color."
2. "It is better for both races that they have their separate schools and separate churches." Separate institutions were no more an injustice to blacks than whites, as long as the accommodations were equally good.
3. "Social fellowship cannot be restrained by law, neither can it be claimed as a right. In general, the way to secure social recognition is not to demand it."
4. The *Outlook* agreed with the demand for equality of law enforcement. Regarding the specific issue of congressional supervision of elections, this was totally unnecessary.
5. Agreeing with the desire to wipe out illiteracy, the *Outlook* attached a qualification that summed up its whole attitude toward education. "We also affirm as a truth of universal applicability that the end of all education should be to fit the pupil for the work which it is probable he will have to do, for the service which he will probably have to render."

In conclusion, the *Outlook* offered this advice to the Niagara leaders: "On the whole we think the Niagara Movement would be more useful if it demanded more of the negro race and put less emphasis on its demands for the negro race."[22] "Demand" was the issue as Lyman Abbott saw it between Du Bois and Niagara as opposed to his close friend Booker T. Washington.

Who could know in 1906 however, that Niagara was the precursor of a yet more demanding and comprehensive movement for racial reform?

The Niagara Movement continued to hold annual conferences through 1909 but before then had largely lost its energy and effectiveness. By 1909 most of its leaders were ready to join forces with the new NAACP. Having surveyed the origins of the NAACP and of the Urban League, we need to ask about the religious dimensions of these new organizations.

The religious affiliation of the whites who were in leadership roles was usually Protestant and most often Congregational, Episcopalian, or Presbyterian, with some Unitarians and Quakers. Jews were prominent also.[23]

The religious affiliation of blacks was balanced between African Methodist Episcopal, African Methodist Episcopal Zion, National Baptist, with lesser representation from predominantly white denominations (Congregational, Presbyterian, and Methodist).

Nancy J. Weiss has determined that of the board members during the NAACP's first decade, 12 percent of the whites and 38.1 percent of the blacks were ministers. For the Urban League, only 5.9 percent of the whites and 18.2 percent of the blacks were ministers.[24] Black advocates of the Social Gospel participated in both organizations in significant leadership positions. The NAACP attracted a significantly larger number of black ministers than did the Urban League. Better-educated ministers in northern urban centers were gravitating toward a strategy of protest and were moving away from the Washingtonian posture of accommodation.

With incorporation in 1911, the first elected officers of the NAACP included three black ministers among the four vice-presidents: Bishop Alexander Walters of New York, Bishop Benjamin E. Lee of Wilberforce, Ohio, and the Reverend Garnett R. Waller of Baltimore. By 1914 there were five vice-presidents, two of whom were ministers. Waller continued to serve. Elected with him was John Haynes Holmes, a young, white Unitarian from New York City.

A number of leading black Social Gospel ministers were elected to the board of directors of the NAACP in these foundational years. Included were three leading New York City ministers. Adam Clayton Powell, Sr., minister of the Abyssinian Baptist Church, served a congregation looked upon as a model church by blacks across the country. Hutchins C. Bishop, minister of the St. Philip's Episcopal Church, served as president of the organization that staged the famous "silent protest" parade down Fifth Avenue after the East St. Louis race riot of 1917. William Henry Brooks, minister of St. Mark's Methodist Episcopal

Church since 1897, was as a founding board member of both the NAACP and the Urban League.

Both the Grimké brothers, Archibald and Francis, were members of the original NAACP committee of forty. Archibald, a lawyer, served as president of the Washington, D.C., chapter. Francis was minister of the Fifteenth Street Presbyterian Church in Washington, D.C. A graduate of Princeton Theological Seminary, he was outspoken in his opposition to racist policies within the Presbyterian church and in his praise of the NAACP as a vehicle for change.[25] Richard R. Wright, Jr., editor of the AME journal the *Christian Recorder*, was active in the Philadelphia chapter of the NAACP.

Among the white leaders of the Social Gospel, a few were actively involved in the NAACP and the Urban League, and a larger number were supporters in the pulpit and the press. William Hayes Ward, editor of the *Independent*, chaired the National Negro Conference of 1909. He gave strong editorial support to the NAACP. Charles H. Parkhurst, pastor of the Madison Avenue Presbyterian Church, and Walter Laidlaw, executive secretary of the Federation of Churches and Christian Workers in New York City, signed the original call. Henry Churchill King, president of Oberlin College, served on the NAACP board in its first decade. Jane Addams and Florence Kelley, social settlement pioneers, served on the board also. Horace Bumstead and Wilbur Patterson Thirkield, both of whom have been mentioned already in speaking of the abolitionist connection, were active members of the Boston and Washington, D.C., chapters. Frank Mason North, chairman of the newly formed Commission on the Church and Social Service of the Federal Council of Churches, was outspoken in heralding the formation of the NAACP.[26]

In summary, a considerable number of Social Gospel leaders involved themselves at various levels in the NAACP and the Urban League. They are listed here in brief compass so as to be able to appreciate their numbers and contributions. But it is necessary also to focus more closely on several of these leaders in order to understand the connections between religious faith and social action in these new movements.

Alexander Walters was one of the two blacks invited to join the original organizing circle. Walters, a bishop of the African Methodist Episcopal Zion church, was already an enigmatic figure in the American black pantheon. In the years between 1898 and 1908, he served for seven years as president of the National Afro-American Council, the largest black organizational predecessor to the NAACP. The ambivalent attitudes toward Walters stemmed at first from criticism that he gave the National Afro-American Council over to the forces of Booker T. Washington.

In these same years he was one of the first blacks who counseled that it was in the interest of black Americans to forsake their historic alliance with the Republican party and vote Democratic in presidential politics. Walters pointed out that Republicans had moved a long way from the party of Lincoln. Theodore Roosevelt's actions in the infamous Brownsville incident highlighted for Walters this desertion of support for the aspirations of black Americans.

On the night of August 31, 1906, a band of men fired high-powered rifles in the town of Brownsville, Texas, killing one person and injuring others. Shortly before this incident the all-black Twenty-fifth United States Infantry Regiment had reported to Fort Brown, a regiment that had fought with distinction in Cuba and the Philippines. They had come from four years' duty in Nebraska and were unprepared for the racial segregation they encountered in Texas. Townspeople blamed the black soldiers for the incident, but the white commanders said that their men were innocent and that their guns had not been fired. The 167 men in the regiment were then asked to speak up against any who were guilty, but all remained silent. An investigation was completed, and Theodore Roosevelt announced his decision on election evening, November 6, 1906: all 167 men would be dismissed from the military "without honor," including five men who had won the Congressional Medal of Honor. Their dismissal meant the loss of all pensions.[27] Roosevelt rebuffed Booker T. Washington's private attempt to intervene. Walters conducted his own investigation through the National Afro-American Council, but with little impact.

The election of William Howard Taft in 1908 did nothing to change Roosevelt's policies. Walters campaigned for Woodrow Wilson in 1912 and told blacks that better days were coming. He was bitterly disappointed when Wilson backed away from support for black appointments. A counselor to presidents, Walters sought to influence Wilson's policies, but to no avail.[28]

Walters's commitment to racial reform was recognized by the invitation to give one of the addresses at the National Negro Conference in 1909, a pivotal event in the founding of the NAACP. Bishop Walters addressed the topic "The Civil and Political Status of the Negro" by reviewing the record of the federal government in the area of civil and political rights. He observed a lessening of commitment in protecting rights guaranteed under the Fourteenth and Fifteenth amendments.

Speaking to the problem of the hour, Walters said it was time to distinguish between "interest and concern" and action. Blacks "desired their full civil and political rights as guaranteed by the Constitution."[29]

A part of the original circle of the NAACP, Walters was elected to a three-year term as a vice-president of the new organization in 1912. But shortly he was involved in a controversy that led to his resignation from the NAACP. In the May 1912 *Crisis*, Du Bois presented a "church number" that focused on four black churches. Walters was upset when Du Bois reported publicly that the AME Zion church was the only denomination that did not turn in information for the issue. The editor went on to criticize the AME Zion church for financial mismanagement. Walters was devastated and reported his feelings to the board.[30]

The controversy over the AME Zion church and the criticism of Walters's support for Woodrow Wilson occurred in the same months. Ironically, Du Bois and Walters were leaders in advocating that blacks vote Democratic. But when Wilson reneged on promises that Walters had trumpeted in the black community, the bishop became the target of criticism within the inner circles of the NAACP. Oswald Garrison Villard, chairman of the NAACP Board of Directors, accused Walters of having prior knowledge of Wilson's intentions regarding systematic segregation in the federal government. Feeling betrayed by both Wilson and Villard and being criticized by Du Bois, Walters resigned from the board in November 1913.[31] In the storms of racial unrest there was sometimes as much fighting among friends as with enemies.

Two of the white reformers most actively involved in the NAACP were John Haynes Holmes and Rabbi Stephen Wise. They began their work in New York within weeks of each other in 1907, and their evolving friendship found them serving side by side in several reform causes. Holmes served on the boards of both the NAACP and the Urban League.

Holmes was the Unitarian minister of the Church of the Messiah, later renamed the Community Church. He had been influenced as a young man by the example of the abolitionist preacher Theodore Parker, who had known Holmes's grandfather. The young New York minister not only identified with the plight of blacks but also supported the equality of women and the rights of labor. Early in his ministry, encouraged by the words and actions of Lyman Abbott, Josiah Strong, and Washington Gladden, "he became more and more a disciple of the 'Social Gospel.'" Holmes had a special admiration for Walter Rauschenbusch and paid tribute to his great influence on his own understanding of the ministry and of "social service."[32]

Not simply an armchair member of the NAACP board, Holmes was active in the tactics of confrontation. A favorite approach was for Holmes and some white friends to pay for theater tickets several days in advance and then arrive at the entrance of the theater on the night of the performance with one or two blacks in their company. The blacks were told to say nothing, but the whites protested loudly when their tickets were not handed over. Timing their arrival to be almost at curtain time, a scene was created that usually brought on the police. Holmes and his friends withdrew in the face of force in order to have the whole matter turned over to the courts. Looking back on those early years, Holmes said, "My part in the founding of the NAACP, and in close affiliation with its work, constitutes one of the chief prides and joys of my life."[33]

Holmes was a trenchant social critic who saw that the problem of race went beyond cooperation or harmony. His city ministry taught him the complexities and problems of urbanization. Thus at the eleventh annual meeting of the NAACP, he declared that "the Negro question in this day is a problem of labor." Recognizing that blacks had been freed only theoretically, Holmes saw their biggest problems in the economic and political arenas. Convinced that economic oppression, even though of a differing kind, dogged white laborers, Holmes was hopeful that mutual oppression in the labor market might lead to mutual strategy for economic reform.[34]

No Jew was more influential as a reformer in these years than Rabbi Stephen Wise. Wise had rejected an offer to serve the prestigious Temple Emmanu-El and had instead founded the Free Synagogue in 1907. Holmes later said that Wise understood the misery of the Negro because he understood the misery of the Jew. Wise knew the abolitionist tradition well. He owned every volume of Theodore Parker, who was to Wise a superb example of the prophetic preacher. Imbued with the message of prophetic Judaism, Wise gave credit to the Social Gospel movement for helping to inform his ministry. He read the works of Josiah Strong and Lyman Abbott and admired Washington Gladden. At Gladden's death, Wise wrote to the editor of the *Ohio State Journal* at Columbus and praised "a nobly prophetic figure." Included in his tribute was an assessment that indicated Gladden's personal influence on Wise, a Jew. "Gladden was the bishop of men of all creeds and churches." As Wise's biographer has observed, "The language and thought used by Wise in the pulpit and on the platform were as much that of 'Social Gospel' Protestants as that of the Hebrew prophets."[35]

Holmes and Wise epitomized a prophetic ministry, utterly unafraid of opposition. Mary White Ovington recalled that from the first the NAACP sought to publicize the brutality of lynching. Stories on lynching were appearing on average every six days in the newspapers, usually pointing up the criminality of blacks and neglecting to note the criminality of white mobs. Ovington said that the NAACP tried to get ministers of established position in New York to speak at meetings held to protest against lynching. None accepted. Then two young men stepped forward—Holmes and Wise. "Our two young men have become great figures in New York, and have unswervingly followed the platform they set down for themselves that night."[36]

By 1919 the NAACP was sponsoring a national Anti-Lynching Conference in New York. Now more persons associated with the Social Gospel signed the original call, including John D. Hammond, Lily Hardy Hammond, Henry Churchill King, Charles S. Macfarland, John A. Ryan, Anna Howard Shaw, Albion W. Small, Graham Taylor, and Willis D. Weatherford.[37]

We have seen that many religious persons were officers of the NAACP and the Urban League, which is not the same thing as saying that there was a religious dimension to the ideologies and strategies of these organizations. In calculating religious influence, one usually categorizes allegedly religious people by their denominational affiliation. The history of religion has traditionally been the history of the clergy. Significant laypeople, men and women acting in the marketplace out of religious convictions, often have been overlooked. Religion itself is usually defined as a set of beliefs or a course of action held to by these religious people. The possibilities of religious influence, however, should not be confined by these categories. For instance, religion operates as a symbol system, capable of evoking deep responses. In this sense, religion can influence people directly whether or not they adhere to a set of beliefs or are ready to follow a course of action. The sociologist of religion has made us aware of the nontheological, nonideological aspects of religion that are fundamental, if often unexamined.

In this perspective, it is informative to examine the policy of the NAACP as it was disseminated by its chief publicity organ, the *Crisis*. By 1919 the NAACP boasted of over 50,000 members in local branches across the country, but in that same year for the first time, there were over 100,000 subscribers to the *Crisis*. That the *Crisis* did not always represent faithfully the majority views of the NAACP was one of the causes of the well-known internal struggles of these early years.

W. E. B. Du Bois, as editor, was at odds often with various officers over statements in the *Crisis*. He said that it was really impossible for an organization to speak with one voice. As it turned out, his own voice was certainly louder than all the rest.

In surveying the *Crisis* in its first decade in print, one is struck by the constant use of religion in issue after issue. Each year, for this entire period, there was an Easter and a Christmas issue, beginning with the cover or first page, and replete with poetry, songs, hymns, artwork, and editorial statements. Early on, Christian festivals became the vehicle for Du Bois's creative and pointed writing. In the December 1911 issue, after an editorial entitled simply "Christmas," there appeared a story "Jesus Christ in Georgia." It was written in the mode of Fyodor Dostoyevsky's "The Grand Inquisitor." The stranger, whom the faithful recognize as the Christ, returns not to Spain in the sixteenth century but to Georgia in the early twentieth century. Because the church has changed so much from its original charter, the returning Christ is not recognized. In the culmination of the story he is lynched. Because of their racial sin, Du Bois writes, white folks do not recognize the authentic Christ.

The strategy of comparing the origins of Christianity with the present beliefs and behavior of the church was used again and again. The December 1920 issue contained the story "Pontius Pilate." The biblical narrative and contemporary events were closely interwoven. In this instance Pontius Pilate was identified with the governor of Mississippi.[38]

To say that religion played a prominent part in the *Crisis* is not to confuse the NAACP periodical with religious publications of the day. Rather, it is to suggest that Du Bois, the sociologist and skillful propagandist, self-consciously utilized religion with his black and white readers.

In these years, Du Bois was arriving at a position regarding the churches that increasing numbers of black intellectuals in the decades ahead would hold. He believed he must criticize the church, black and white, for what it had done to stifle black progress. But whether Du Bois liked it or not, he recognized the black church to have been the germinal institution in the development of black people.[39] He therefore needed not only to goad and encourage the church as an institution but also to appeal to the religious convictions of his individual readers.

To ascribe these tactics to Du Bois is not to say that he was dishonest. Rather, he understood religion in a functional way. The truth claims of the religious ideology were not as important as the social role that religion played. The black church was the dominant institution in the present structure of the black community. When Du Bois spoke of the "talented tenth," he always included ministers, who represented the largest single occupational group on the NAACP board of directors.

Du Bois is often remembered for his criticism of the church, black and white, but he did not always criticize. Sometimes, as in an article in 1913, Du Bois called upon the church to discover the real Christ in the midst of the contemporary world. "Yet Jesus Christ was a laborer and black men are laborers; He was poor and we are poor; He was despised of his fellow men and we are despised; He was persecuted and crucified, and we are mobbed and lynched. If Jesus Christ came to America, He would associate with Negroes and Italians and working people." Here was a powerful proclamation that could be embraced by modern black liberation theology.[40]

A part of Du Bois's critical concern was the church's tendency toward divisiveness. The monthly church section in the *Crisis* was filled with reports of wrangling within various black denominations over matters of doctrine or between personalities. All of these internal struggles did not leave time for the church's real service to the community.

But Du Bois could encourage as well as excoriate. In 1916 he expressed a real measure of optimism as he called upon the church to be true to its own best self.

> Facing such problems what shall we do? The appeal is first of all to the mighty past. In slavery, in Reconstruction and in the days after, the Negro Church made the Negro race in America. Today it can remake it if it calls to the front its strong, honest men; if it puts aside petty sectarianism and creed, and if it works for social uplift and individual honor. Will the church do this? In the long run and after much travail of soul, we believe it will.[41]

Du Bois was aware of his white readers also. His concern with the white church went back to his leadership in the Niagara Movement. In commenting on the fifth demand of the Niagara Platform of 1905, "the recognition of the principles of human brotherhood as a practical creed," Elliot Rudwick observes, "Du Bois considered that the Niagara Movement's task was to interpret the real Christ to white 'Christians.'"[42]

It is illuminating to see the response of the *Crisis* to the variegated ideas and activities of white religion in America. An editorial entitled "The White Christ," in March 1915, indicted all the parties in World War I, which was depicted as a catastrophic example of the moral failure of white Christianity.[43]

The gyrations of evangelist Billy Sunday were held up as another example of white Christianity's irrelevance and moral degeneracy. Du

Bois stated that Sunday's campaign was devoid of any appeal to reason. He criticized Sunday's evangelistic preaching as neglecting any message about poverty, suffering, or racism. But still the white folks came forward, eager to hit the "sawdust trail."[44]

The editorial on Sunday provoked vigorous comments, pro and con, which were presented in the next edition. Later in the same year, the *Crisis* reprinted an article from the *Christian Recorder.* Richard R. Wright, Jr., editor of this AME publication, was active in the Philadelphia branch of the NAACP. In an editorial Wright criticized Sunday, and by implication much of conservative evangelicalism, for his failure to confront the race issue.

> The psychology of it is clear. "Billy" knew that on any of the other subjects, he had at the worst a half-approving audience. He knew that the public conscience has been sufficiently awakened to give approval, even though it does not give practical demonstration to his arguments about other wrongs. But for injustice for the black man there is no such public conscience. The nation will not apply its Bible to the Negro.[45]

The *Crisis* did not let this theme subside. Less than two years later it reported that black ministers in New York refused to cooperate with proposed Billy Sunday meetings. It was not that these black ministers were against evangelism or the campaigns of revivalism, but they were upset that they were ignored when the evangelistic campaign was planned.[46]

William R. Moody, son of the famous evangelist Dwight L. Moody, also came under attack. As president of the Mount Hermon School in Massachusetts, founded by his famous father, William Moody defended the fact that the school did not admit blacks by observing that these students could obtain a better education at "many richly endowed and well-equipped schools for the colored race throughout the South." W. E. B. Du Bois was at his best in his editorial reply: "This is true philanthropy and our hearts bleed at the spectacle of the poor white boy begging a chance while the idle and impudent Negro lads toast their heels in the munificence and wealth of Fisk, Hampton, and Atlanta."[47]

The *Crisis* was often critical of white religion—but not always. There was more a sigh of relief than a spirit of condemnation when the *Crisis* reported in 1914 that Walter Rauschenbusch had spoken out on the race question for the first time.[48] A bright young Baptist minister and social advocate, Harry Emerson Fosdick, was commended for a speech delivered at the International Convention of the YMCA. Fosdick was quoted in the *Crisis:* "Christ preached against racial prejudice. . . . The Bible talks good sociology when it says we are all made of one blood."[49]

Other persons associated with the Social Gospel received attention from the *Crisis*. One of the NAACP's earliest strategies was to strengthen the forces against lynching. In 1916 Philip G. Peabody of Boston offered the NAACP ten thousand dollars to further its antilynching program. The first step was to be the printing and distribution in the South of Willis D. Weatherford's forceful paper against lynching, prepared for the Southern Sociological Congress. Because of its activities in the South, the NAACP became aware of Weatherford, a young YMCA secretary who will be discussed in the next chapter. Board member Oswald Garrison Villard, in a letter to Jane Addams, described Weatherford as one of the "fine young Southerners of the radical kind."[50] The leaders of the NAACP were also cognizant of Weatherford's YMCA colleague Arcadius M. Trawick. Trawick's article "The Social Gospel and Racial Relationships," which will be discussed in the following chapter, was cited and commended to the readership of the *Crisis*. Weatherford and Trawick were applauded when they appealed for more field secretaries for the colored branch of the YMCA.[51]

The *Crisis* made its readers aware of efforts by the Federal Council of Churches to come to grips with race relations. Spurred by the American entrance into World War I, these efforts culminated in 1921 with the founding of an official ecumenical committee to coordinate an attack on racism. At the end of 1919 the *Crisis* reprinted with applause the "Constructive Program for Just Inter-Racial Relations" initiated by the Federal Council.[52] This story will be chronicled in chapter 15.

This chapter has traced the vital part that the maturing Social Gospel movement played in the foundational years of the NAACP and the Urban League. A host of individuals became involved in these organizations at the national and the local level. The lineage and language of abolitionism marked their background. Many of these persons learned firsthand of the race problem through their involvement in black education in the South. In a new missionary campaign religious language and symbols were employed skillfully in the cause of racial reform.

CHAPTER 12

The Student Christian Movement

White college men are showing rare courage in demanding of their
fellows that justice be shown the black man; black men are beginning
to see that all white men are not their enemies; and most important of
all, there has been cooperation between the men of both races on such
terms of mutual self-respect as would have been thought impossible
before this movement was started.

—EDITORIAL, *STUDENT WORLD*

Student activism arose as a pervasive phenomenon in the civil rights
movement in the 1960s. Students proved to be remarkably effective in
organizing, publicizing, and participating in the campaigns and march-
es that were a hallmark of those years. Leaders of various student
Christian organizations played an important role in a variegated movement. Larger church bodies and denominations were both courageous
and capitulating in their involvement in civil rights. But again and again
Christian students and student organizations were out in front of parent church bodies in their involvement in controversial issues. This has
not always been the case.

An arm of the churches as well as the child of the churches, what
became known as the Student Christian Movement did not occupy such
advanced positions on social issues in its early years. In the last decades
of the nineteenth century, the student movement lagged behind the
parent church bodies in social consciousness. Only in the early years of
this century was the student movement awakened to a social consciousness that profoundly altered the course it had been pursuing since its
birth as a national movement three decades earlier. This new social
concern was emerging at the same time that the student movement was
growing to maturity, ideologically and organizationally, and thus developing a distinctive and increasingly independent life of its own. Not
facing the same kinds of economic, social, and political pressures as

congregations and denominations, the Student Christian Movement was often more flexible and courageous in confronting social problems. Increasingly, it moved in advance of the churches on social issues. This profound change was due in large measure to an embracing of the Social Gospel by key leaders of the Student Christian Movement in the first two decades of the twentieth century. A commitment to racial reform played a central role in their appropriation of the Social Gospel.

Although student Christian societies go back to colonial times,[1] the modern Student Christian Movement is linked to the early years of the Young Men's Christian Association. Founded in London in 1844, the YMCA established its first chapters in North America in Montreal and Boston in 1851.[2] Originally operating in the centers of larger cities, student YMCAs were begun at the Universities of Virginia and Michigan in 1858. By 1875 there were over thirty student YMCAs flourishing in both denominational schools and state universities and colleges. At this time all of these groups were local in organization.

The student movement became national in vision and organization as an outgrowth of a dramatic spiritual awakening at Princeton in the winter of 1875–1876. Moved by a "College Mission," which included the first appearance on a college platform of evangelist Dwight L. Moody, delegations of Princeton students traveled to other campuses to share "the great things the Lord had done at Princeton." One Princeton student, Luther D. Wishard, initiated correspondence with two hundred colleges and universities to sound them out about forming an intercollegiate student Christian movement. Later he invited college leaders to meet with him at an 1877 meeting of the North American YMCA in Louisville. Out of that meeting the intercollegiate YMCA was born. Wishard became the organization's first student secretary or leader.[3]

Women students were active in many of the chapters of the YMCA from the outset. The student YMCA leaders saw no need for separate organizations. But by the early 1880s the city Ys were concerned about the increasing numbers of women active and in leadership roles. A movement developed for a separate women's organization, and the Young Women's Christian Association was founded in 1886.[4]

Almost from the beginning, the YMCA had a black constituency. The first colored men's YMCA was established in Washington, D.C., in 1853. The first student association at a black institution was organized at Howard University in Washington, D.C., in 1869. Twenty-one institutions were represented at Louisville in 1877 when the intercollegiate

YMCA was born, and three were black colleges—Fisk, Howard, and Walden. In 1888 the first black secretary, William Alpheus Hunton, was appointed to work with "colored" students. By 1900 there were sixty-one Negro student associations.[5]

From its beginnings on into the twentieth century, the work of the YMCA was segregated. There was a colored men's department for the parent YMCA, and there was separate work among Negro student associations. Indicative of the status of black students was their lack of participation in the important student conferences of these years. American black participation was almost nonexistent at the first eight gatherings of the World's Student Christian Federation. A black delegate participated at Williamstown, Massachusetts, in 1897; and Hunton attended the conference in Tokyo in 1907.

A powerful missionary interest was also developing in these early years. This interest became focused in 1886 at the first of the annual student summer conferences hosted by Dwight L. Moody at his newly constructed boys' school at Mount Hermon, across the river from Northfield, Massachusetts. Included among the delegates was Robert Wilder, who had been at the center of a group of Princeton students who had signed a pledge dedicating themselves to foreign missionary service. At Northfield, Wilder met daily with others who were interested in missions. By the closing day of the conference, the one hundredth "volunteer" had pledged his life to missionary service. From Mount Hermon, the appeal for missions swept the college campuses, and over 1,500 students signed the pledge in the 1886–1887 academic year. In 1888 the Student Volunteer Movement for Foreign Missions (SVM) was officially organized.

Emerging as the recognized leader of the student Christian movement was John R. Mott, a young recruit from Cornell. A leader in the Cornell YMCA and active at Mount Hermon, Mott became an associate national college secretary of the YMCA upon his graduation in 1888. His leadership abilities recognized by all, Mott assumed the position of secretary in 1890 and fulfilled those duties until 1915. He was also chairman of the executive committee of the Student Volunteer Movement from 1888 to 1920. With a world vision for Christianity, Mott was eager to establish ties between the student movements in various countries. Although he was a student secretary of the YMCA, Mott came to realize that it would be a mistake to bring together diverse student associations, not all with contacts with the YMCA, under one organization. Rather, Mott hoped for a federation of indigenous movements that would both preserve particularity and enhance understanding, missions, and the appreciation of the varied richness of the Christian faith. With Mott acting as the catalyst, the World's Student Christian Federation was born out of a meeting of student leaders in Vadstena, Sweden, in 1895. Although just thirty years old, Mott was elected general secretary of the WSCF, a post he held until 1920.[6]

For purposes of definition, prior to the early 1900s, when one spoke of the Student Christian Movement, it was understood to mean the intercollegiate YMCA and YWCA, the SVM, plus a few smaller, more specialized associations. As the Student Christian Movement in the United States, these groups were affiliated with the World's Student Christian Federation. After the early 1900s the scope of the Student Christian Movement sometimes included the newly developing denominational ministries on state university campuses.

As the movement for a social Christianity developed in the 1880s and 1890s, the YMCA often lagged behind the churches in social consciousness. At the YMCA Secretaries Conference in 1886, after considerable debate, the secretaries were "still of the opinion that it is unadvisable for the Association to engage in any organized effort for moral reform."[7] Why this point of view? The answer can be found in the fact that support for the program of the YMCA came from business classes, and with this support evolved a wedding to a conservative political and social posture. This relationship helps explain why the YMCA "was virtually oblivious to the rise of the labor movement as a social phenomenon." Then, too, the leadership of the local associations was largely a lay leadership and thus not as naturally conversant with the currents of thought stemming from the New Theology. In addition, there was an unwritten agreement that the YMCA, divided by the earlier abolitionist controversy, would henceforth try to avoid controversial issues.[8]

This all changed under Mott. The historian of the YMCA, C. Howard Hopkins, asserts that "the most significant new emphasis in the student work during Mott's secretaryship was his introduction of the social gospel years before the parent YMCAs became aware of it."[9] In 1895 Mott appended a bibliography on social Christianity prepared by Graham Taylor, professor of Christian sociology at Chicago Theological Seminary, to a student pamphlet on missions. For another decade, however, this emphasis on social Christianity remained latent as the Student Christian Movement focused on Bible study and mission study. These twin emphases were readily apparent in various student Christian publications and in the schedules of the growing number of summer conferences. A regular feature of these conferences was the seminars that were divided into two areas, Bible study and mission study. Until early in the twentieth century, mission study usually meant foreign missions.[10]

What was latent became highly visible in the first years of the new century. "Social service," the outgrowth of the developing Social Gospel, began to take its place alongside Bible study and foreign missions at the center of the student movement. Interest in the race question occupied a primary place in the expanding concern with social service. This interest was generated independently but simultaneously by various leaders in different sections of the country.

In April 1908 a remarkable meeting took place in Atlanta. At the initiative of Willis Duke Weatherford, YMCA secretary for the South and Southwest, three white men and four black men met together for six hours to discuss the racial situation in the South and how it might be improved. The black participants were John Hope, president of Atlanta Baptist College and later president of Atlanta University; Professor John Wesley Gilbert of Paine College, Augusta, Georgia; and two secretaries of the Colored Men's Department of the YMCA, William A. Hunton, and Jesse E. Moorland. The white participants were Weatherford, Walter R. Lambuth, missionary secretary of the Methodist Episcopal Church, South, and Dr. Stewart R. Roberts, a professor at the Atlanta School of Physicians and Surgeons.[11] All agreed that a major source of amelioration could be the young white college students populating the resurgent southern colleges and universities. Walter R. Lambuth suggested that a book be written that would inform and challenge the college generation about the present racial situation in the South. All were agreed that Weatherford should be the author.[12]

The fruit of Weatherford's research and personal experience appeared in 1910 as Negro Life in the South. By 1912 over ten thousand copies of the book had been studied by college men and women in the South, the number increasing to thirty thousand copies used by nearly fifty thousand students by 1916. The success of the venture was not simply in the printing of such a volume but in the way that it was discussed and applied according to a strategy carefully worked out by Weatherford. Weatherford had tried out the first draft of the book on a summer college conference in North Carolina in 1909. He was amazed to find that of the five seminars being offered, including seminars on the Bible and missions, over half the members of the conference signed up for the first attempt at talking about what was advertised as "the

Negro Problem."[13] At a similar conference in the Southwest, again over half the students enrolled in an identical seminar.[14]

All through 1911 reports poured in of the book's success. William L. Poteat, president of Wake Forest College, reported that 207 students were enrolled in study groups. The University of Virginia, the home of the first student association, communicated that more men were enrolled than ever before in a mission study. Similar encouraging reports came from the Universities of South Carolina, Alabama, and Oklahoma, as well as from Louisiana State University, Berea College, and Emory and Henry College.[15]

At Washington and Lee University in Virginia, a young man named Francis Pickens Miller was involved in the student YMCA when Weatherford's book was published. Miller one day succeeded John R. Mott as general secretary of the WSCF. In 1949 he made a courageous but losing bid for governor of Virginia, running on a platform that was remarkable for its progressive attitude toward blacks. In a published memoir, Miller tells what caused a change in his thinking.

> It was in one of these [YMCA] groups that I first began to take a serious interest in our race problem. I collected a number of students who were willing to discuss together a little book entitled *The Negro in the South* that had just been written by W. D. Weatherford, the student YMCA secretary for the Southern Region. What he said set in motion trains of thought and action which profoundly influenced my attitudes.[16]

The fact that the race question was so prominent in all of the student YMCA work in the South was due almost exclusively at first to the energy of Willis Duke Weatherford. Born in 1875 in rural west Texas, Weatherford studied at small Weatherford College in his hometown before completing his undergraduate education at Vanderbilt in Nashville. He continued on in graduate studies and earned a Ph.D. at Vanderbilt in 1902. During these years, he was elected president of the student YMCA, the first graduate student at Vanderbilt so honored. In March 1902, as Weatherford was completing his graduate work, a telegram arrived from John R. Mott asking him to do nothing about a future vocation until Mott could speak with him. Weatherford was subsequently offered the position of YMCA student secretary for fourteen states in the South and Southwest. He accepted.[17]

During the next six years, Weatherford talked and listened to both whites and blacks in his travels as a student secretary. He experienced both the public barriers and personal hurt of the race situation. Increasingly concerned about the plight of blacks, Weatherford came to see the challenge the race question posed for whites.

In this pioneer work, the first textbook in the field,[18] Weatherford was cognizant of the range of attitudes held by both whites and blacks. In the beginning of the study, he spoke a word in defense of the South's past conduct. The tone changed quickly, however, as he challenged the usual southern argument that whites in the South knew more about and could therefore better solve the race question. The plain fact that southerners did not really know blacks was the reason Weatherford was writing this book. Sounding somewhat like Edgar Gardner Murphy, Weatherford said that southern whites knew blacks only as workers, usually at menial tasks, but did not know their thought, religious life, or home life.

According to Weatherford, present race relations in the South were being exacerbated by three outspoken groups. First, there was a group of whites who were unable to see anything good in blacks. Tragically, some of these whites occupied high political office and used such shibboleths as "social equality" and "race amalgamation" to heighten fears and becloud issues. "We have had all too many of these political demagogues—these so-called 'defenders' of the white man's honor and the white woman's virtue."[19]

Weatherford was critical also of a second group, "the Radical Negro." In this classification he included W. E. B. Du Bois and William Monroe Trotter. In speaking of Du Bois's controversy with Booker T. Washington, Weatherford was most disturbed by the radical Negro's inability to recognize any whites in the South who were helping make progress in race relations. That his attitude toward Du Bois was not simply critical, however, was indicated in a later reference to an account by Du Bois of the death of his baby boy. At one point in the funeral process, someone inquired who it was that had died, and Du Bois heard the reply, "Just 'niggers.'" Weatherford asked his white readers, "Do you wonder that he is sometimes bitter?" In an appended bibliography, Weatherford had high praise for the book that was the source of this story, *The Souls of Black Folk*.[20]

Weatherford reserved but a paragraph for the third class, "the Northern enthusiast," who, he hoped, was dying out.

The bulk of *Negro Life in the South* was an able discussion of various facets of the present condition of blacks, including economic life, health and housing, education, and religion. After weeks and months of study and discussion, southern white students came to the final chapter, "What Can We Do?" In the midst of many specific suggestions, three themes emerged. First, whites were encouraged to see blacks as men and women, created in the image of God. Next, it was important to learn to know blacks in the specific conditions in which they found themselves. Although Weatherford repeated the southern dictum against social intermingling, at the same time he encouraged southern white students to go into black homes, churches, and schools. Finally, he urged whites to join with blacks, especially in education and religion, helping where they could.[21]

The style of the last chapter was quite practical, but from time to time Weatherford attempted to undergird practice with theology and theory. He characterized the present concern for blacks as part of a widespread social awakening. Three elements, he said, lay behind the awakening. First, there was the present philosophical principle of spiritual monism, manifesting itself in a spirit working toward unity in the world. Behind this tendency toward unity, manifest both in philosophy and the sciences, was a supreme force that Christians identified with God.

The second element was a corollary of the first—"the growing sacredness of the individual." This emphasis on the sacredness of the individual, a tenet of later nineteenth-century liberal theology, was tied in by the Social Gospel to the proclamation of the fatherhood of God and the brotherhood of man. Weatherford applied this teaching directly to the race question. In one of his more candid observations, however, he confessed, "I have sometimes felt that we really do not believe that the Negro is possessed of human personality."[22] Weatherford stressed again and again the sacredness of the Negro as a person.

The third element was the call to action predicated on a universal Father and common brothers and sisters. "If there is one supreme person—a Father God; if each individual is caught up into that Godhead and so becomes sacred; then, each man is brother to his neighbor just because they are both alike sons of God." Growing out of the recognition of God as the center of the universe and of the sacredness of the individual was the injunction for all persons to act with a sense of responsibility. Why? Because "every true brother must be interested in, and, so far as his power extends, responsible for, the welfare of every other brother in his universal household."[23]

Discussion did turn into action. There were reports from a number of institutions of cooperation between blacks and whites. At the University of South Carolina, white students organized a kind of chamber of commerce for black men in Columbia. At the University of North Carolina, a club room for black boys was set up near the campus.[24]

Weatherford longed for a better opportunity to talk about these issues. In 1912 the fulfillment of a personal vision occurred with the opening of the Blue Ridge Assembly near Black Mountain, North Carolina. In 1906 he had discovered over 1,500 acres of forested mountain land that he believed would be ideal for a conference center. In the next years much of his time went into planning a center that would attract students from all over the South. The heart of the summer conference at Blue Ridge became the elective seminars, always advertised under two headings, Bible study and mission study. These seminar topics continued the pattern in effect at Mount Hermon, Lake Geneva, Estes Park, and Pacific Grove. But what was distinctive about Blue Ridge was the regular pattern of seminars on blacks and race relations.[25] "The Negro Problem" seminar of 1909 and 1910 became the book *Negro Life in the South*, published in 1910. By 1912 Weatherford was offering two seminars, adding "Present Forces in Negro Progress," which developed also into a book published that same year.

By 1912 Weatherford was moving in new directions and was becoming more outspoken. In *Present Forces in Negro Progress* he was more direct in his evaluation of the record of the southern white churches.

> No Southern man of any pride can read the scant reports of our Southern churches in their efforts to uplift the Negro without hanging his head in shame. Of course, we have been poor. Of course, we do not forget the heartsickening scenes of reconstruction days. Of course, we have been misunderstood; but if we are men, we will forget the past in a mighty effort to redeem the present.[26]

At Blue Ridge, white students did not just study about blacks, they listened to them. As the years passed, such black leaders as George Washington Carver, James Weldon Johnson, and Robert Russa Moton came to the conference center.[27] White students talked also with black students, thanks to the establishment in 1912 of the first conference center for black students, at King's Mountain, North Carolina. Located a short distance apart, these two conference centers provided opportunity for dialogue. At the first King's Mountain conference, Weatherford was one of five whites who addressed the students.[28]

Exchanges with King's Mountain were not completely reciprocal. The exchanges reflected the possibilities but also the limitations in race relations and cooperation. When blacks came to Blue Ridge, they were welcomed but were segregated for meals and lodging. By contrast, at King's Mountain, whites were never segregated except at their own request. This fact is pointed up in Benjamin E. Mays's autobiography, *Born to Rebel*.[29] In amplifying his comments about Blue Ridge in a personal conversation with the author, Mays described Weatherford as being a "Jim Crow Liberal" in those years. That is, he was liberal in his day in his approach to race relations, but still he operated always within the social pattern of segregation. In further comments, however, Mays indicated that a white man in the South in those years really had no other option and that Weatherford was certainly courageous.

Weatherford could be paternalistic and segregating as well as courageous and outspoken. But his great capacity was to work with students for whom Blue Ridge was a ray of light in a previous existence totally bound by their middle-class southern white backgrounds. Even to ask southern students to work was something brand new to many of them. The story is told, and in varying terms was repeated many times, of the college girl who was asked to wait tables. As the noon meal began, Weatherford went to her section of the dining room only to find her tables unattended. Finding her in her room in tears, he was told that she could not wait tables because "that is what niggers do in my home." Aware of her background, Weatherford gently but firmly explained to her that any labor that benefited others was worth doing and that the word *Negro* was spelled with a capital *N* and did not have two *gg's* or an *i* in it.[30]

Weatherford turned his attention to white young men and women because he believed this was where the problem and the hope lay. He did not like speaking of "the Negro problem," as was the common parlance of the day. The most lasting impression of these years became the theme of *Negro Life in the South,* stated in italics on the last page. *"It is not the Negro that is on trial before the world, but it is we, we white men of the South."*[31]

Concern for the relations between the races was occurring in other wings of the burgeoning Student Christian Movement. A pamphlet entitled *The Negro Problem,* was published in 1908 as the outgrowth of a new kind of student ministry at the University of Wisconsin. The author, Richard Henry Edwards, whose title was Congregational university minister, was in the vanguard of the movement by denominations to set pastors free for full-time ministry among students and faculty. Edwards was, in fact, the first Congregational minister to bear this responsibility, having been appointed at Madison in 1906. Prior to the early 1900s, when one spoke of the Student Christian Movement, it was understood to mean the intercollegiate YMCA and YWCA and the Student Volunteer Movement, plus a few smaller, more specialized associations. As the Student Christian Movement in the United States, these groups were affiliated with the World's Student Christian Federation.

Prior to 1900, denominations had built halls to serve as meeting places for their students; at the University of Michigan, for example, both the Episcopalians and Presbyterians did so in 1887. But active ministry with students was left to the YMCA, YWCA, SVM, and the local churches. In the early 1900s, with great increases of students, especially at nondenominational institutions, all the major denominations moved to place their own representatives on campuses in full-time capacities. The first appointments were at the great state universities in the Midwest. The Methodists and Baptists each placed a person at the University of Michigan in 1904, followed by the Presbyterians in 1905 and the Episcopalians in 1907. By 1910, the Presbyterians had evolved a national plan of student ministry. Many of these university ministers were caught up in the rising social consciousness pervading the college campuses in the Progressive Era.[32]

Edwards came to the University of Wisconsin after two years as secretary of the YMCA student association at Yale and two years as assistant pastor of the First Presbyterian Church of New York City.[33] The pamphlet *The Negro Problem* developed out of a "Social Problems Group" begun by Edwards in 1906. As Edwards explained in an article in *Charities and the Commons*, it was essential to hear the best statement of the hard facts of various social problems. Visiting experts were brought in for this purpose. Next, various solutions were examined in discussion. Finally, "the question of the reality and extent of the contribution made by Jesus toward the solution of each problem was asked." Meeting on Sundays at the First Congregational Church in Madison, the group by 1908 was averaging over sixty persons in attendance and included, in addition to students and faculty, members of the Wisconsin State Legislature.[34]

Edwards published the pamphlet *The Negro Problem* as the second in a series of eight study guides. "The Negro problem" was still the way most Americans spoke about the race problem, but Edwards said on the first page that people should more properly talk about "the American Race Problem," indicating that the problem involved both blacks and whites. Moderate in his approach and tone, Edwards saw as rays of light in a difficult situation some evidence of economic advancement as well as of increasing opportunities in education. Agreeing that industrial education was the first essential, he emphasized that much more was presently needed, however, than the education of hands, and he went on to advocate higher education. Edwards did not hold out much "hope of the present advancement for the race in legislation or renewed agitation." The way forward was to be found in the common humanity that was at the heart of the Christian gospel.

> The more timely points of emphasis would seem to be—the realization of a common humanity and the mutual necessity for self-control; the right of every respectable man to be respected for his manhood; the larger recognition of mutual interdependence, and the cultivation, wherever possible, of mutual trust.[35]

An impressive feature of the pamphlet was the seventeen-page bibliography. Edwards credited W. E. B. Du Bois as being one of two persons who revised and approved it. Listed were materials representing all viewpoints, conservative to radical. The bibliography was certainly one of the most complete on the race question assembled during the Progressive Era.[36]

In 1908 and 1909 events occurred outside the United States that eventually influenced the student movement's social consciousness in general and its consciousness of race in particular. In preparation for the World's Student Christian Federation meetings at Oxford in 1909, the annual WSCF questionnaire of 1908 first asked the question, "Please indicate what your movement has done to promote the study of social problems, and also to enlist its members in Christian social service?" Once assembled in July 1909, the delegates, for the first time at the plenary sessions, heard a whole series of addresses devoted to social problems. The Oxford meetings made a deep impression on the American secretaries in attendance, as did a British conference on social problems convened afterward at Matlock.[37] A report of the Matlock conference was published in the American student periodical the *Intercollegian*, and subsequently a pamphlet from the conference, *Discipleship and the Social Problems*, was read widely and discussed by American student leaders.[38]

During these years, the WSCF had an uneven influence on the Student Christian Movement in the United States. Participation by Americans in world meetings was often limited by the great distances involved. In 1913, however, the WSCF meetings were to be held in the United States. As plans were being made, the WSCF, encouraged by some American leaders, made it clear that the meetings could be held only if the interracial principles of the federation were accepted, meaning that colored and white delegates would be treated on an equal basis. There was no problem with the hosts, for the meetings were to take place at Lake Mohonk, where, more than twenty years before, the Lake Mohonk conferences on the Negro question were held. Albert Keith Smiley, the first proprietor of the Lake Mohonk Mountain House, had died in 1912, but the inn remained in the hands of his Quaker descendants, who continued his policies. Whereas only two black delegates had attended previous WSCF meetings, at Lake Mohonk thirteen were present. The potential problems of eating together were solved by drawing lots before each meal to determine delegate seating. All went well, and Lake Mohonk was an important step toward interracial brotherhood. William A. Hunton, who had been the only black delegate in 1907, wrote of his experiences at Lake Mohonk, "One sensed most deeply the abiding spirit of brotherhood which ran like a golden thread through all the proceedings."[39]

In these same years the YMCA in the United States sought to strengthen its own involvement in the social arena. Influenced and encouraged by all these intersecting events and experiences, Mott moved to change the structure of the YMCA to reflect its growing concern for social "questions." In 1909 Edward C. Carter joined the staff as an associate to Mott, bringing to the position strong convictions about social reform. Carter's father, a Congregational minister, had been secretary of the Charity Organizations Society of Lawrence, Massachusetts. As secretary of the Harvard Christian Association, Edward Carter had encouraged students to become volunteer workers in social institutions in Cambridge, Boston, and New York. With Mott and Carter at the helm, in 1912 the YMCA decided to organize a new division in its student work—a department of social study and service. Indicative of the YMCA's wholehearted commitment was the fact that three secretaries were to work full-time in this area. They were Richard H. Edwards, who had broad responsibilities; Max J. Exner, responsible for sex education; and Arcadius McSwain Trawick, whose special concern was race relations.[40]

Edwards, Exner, and Trawick at the national level, and Weatherford and others at the regional level, began a more concerted effort to implement a social ministry that was now YMCA student association policy. In 1914 Edwards published a guidebook for volunteer service that set forth a purpose for social service that was clearly more than a hodgepodge of projects for "do-gooders." "The purpose of volunteer service as here set forth is the Christian purpose to advance the Kingdom of God on earth—the Christian Social Order." This purpose—to bring in the kingdom of God—was also clearly different from that espoused by many social justice progressives, although Edwards stated that the advancing of the Christian social order could include all lesser motives such as longings for humanitarian reform, economic justice, and social reconstruction. Like many of his Social Gospel contemporaries, Edwards did not abandon the evangelistic motive. He stressed again and again that social concern was an avenue for winning men to personal allegiance to Jesus Christ. In his own ministry, Edwards attempted to keep a balance: "The salvation of people and the betterment of conditions are two phases of one work—the achievement of the Kingdom of God."[41]

The culmination of the developing influence of the Social Gospel was evident at a special conference convened at Garden City, New York, in April 1914. This "Conference on Social Needs" was sponsored by the new Council of North American Student Movements, of which Mott was chairman. It was a picked gathering of Americans and Canadians, comprising twenty-five leaders of the Social Gospel and fifty secretaries of the YMCA, YWCA, and SVM. The secretaries listened to addresses by Walter Rauschenbusch, Graham Taylor, Harry F. Ward, Robert E. Speer, Charles R. Henderson, and Robert Woods.[42]

A report from the meetings, *Social Needs of the Colleges of North America*, spelled out the significance of the discussions.

> Perhaps the general opinion had been that the associations were so conservative that their spiritual message was entirely individual and not corporate. Now at least their leaders showed themselves open to new light, taking counsel with men and women of fearless thought and action in the social movement.[43]

This statement documents the changes we have been chronicling in the first years of the new century. The report was a manifesto for action on college campuses.

In the recommendations at the end of the report, four items were to be given the highest priority. One of the four was the eradication of "racial prejudice."[44] The Garden City conference did not talk a great deal about the race problem. C. Howard Hopkins suggests it was because this was not a problem facing both Canadians and Americans.[45] That the student movement was in advance of the churches was indicated by the fact that Mott was willing to translate the emphasis of the report into new national secretarial positions, including one whose exclusive focus was on race relations. This priority was higher than the importance it was given in these same years in the structure and strategy of the denominations.

Weatherford was present at Garden City and continued his work in the South. Edwards brought to his national staff position concern for race relations as well. But Mott's appointment of Trawick is a largely unknown but fascinating story of an able southern advocate of the Social Gospel working forcefully in the arena of race relations.

Arcadius McSwain Trawick was born in Tennessee in 1869. After completing work for his B.A. and B.D. at Vanderbilt, Trawick served as a Methodist pastor in Tennessee and Arkansas. In 1908 he was appointed a professor of sociology and psychology at the Methodist Training School (later Scarritt College for Christian Workers) in Nashville. In the same year he met Maude Wilder, a teacher at the Warriota Settlement, an inner-city youth center, who became his wife. He resigned from his position in 1911 in order to become a student secretary for the YMCA in the South.[46] An editorial in the Methodist student periodical *Epworth Era* described his new position as follows: "He has been engaged to work among the students in the South in the interest of the Negro specifically and of social betterment in general."[47] In 1912 he joined Edwards and Exner in the department of social study and service of the national staff.[48]

Trawick's orientation to ministry was energized by his experiences as a pastor, teacher, and YMCA worker. In his parish ministry he came to understand firsthand the problems of substandard housing and inadequate health care and the struggles of laboring people. As a teacher in Nashville he took his students from the classrooms of the Methodist Training School into the streets to learn about the social conditions in this southern city. Writing about housing conditions of the poor, Trawick called upon the church to "redeem the living conditions of the poor."[49]

In Nashville Trawick immersed himself in racial reform. He and his sister-in-law, Sarah Kate Trawick, were quite involved with Fisk University. Trawick took photographs showing the living conditions of blacks in Nashville. These pictures were published in the *Nashville Tennessean*. Their printing provoked an uproar from some whites that apparently prevented any further publication.

In all of his speeches and writings, Trawick paid close attention to what he called social conditions. Whether he was speaking of poor whites or blacks, Trawick was concerned to understand first of all the environment, or "social conditions," in which people found themselves.

An accurate understanding of the social conditions is the key to an appropriate solution. Trawick is a Social Gospeler in his rejection of charity and his call for justice. Called Pug by his friends because of his facial expressions, he was known as a man of both strength and empathy. In calling for social reform, Trawick said again and again that more than mere empathy is needed. In *The City Church and Its Social Mission*, published in 1913 as a study book for the YMCA, Trawick encouraged churches to become involved in housing regulation, education, and labor reform. In the same spirit as Washington Gladden, Josiah Strong, and Walter Rauschenbusch, this volume urged churches to go beyond acts of charity and deal with what we would call today the systemic problems of the city.[50]

Beginning in 1911, Trawick's primary assignment was race relations. He worked closely with W. D. Weatherford, his cousin and fellow Methodist minister. Upon joining the national staff of the YMCA in 1912, he began his work in a characteristically Trawick manner. He studied the social conditions that produced and provoked the race problem and then wrote a pamphlet, *Social Investigation, with Special Reference to the Race Question in the South*, published in the same year.[51]

Shortly after joining the national staff, Trawick became the catalyst for a major student event to be held in Atlanta in 1914. In 1913 a long-anticipated student volunteer quadrennial was held in Kansas City. More than three thousand students attended, including some black students. But Mott, Trawick, and Weatherford were not satisfied. It was decided to hold a large conference in the South that would be planned especially with black students in mind and that would also be interracial. It was suggested that the conference be held at Tuskegee or Hampton, but the black leaders vetoed this idea on the ground that the conference would be too identified with the philosophy of industrial education.[52]

Billed as the Negro Student Christian Conference, the event was held at Clark University and Gammon Theological Seminary in Atlanta. The conference brought together blacks and whites, students and leaders, under the theme "The New Voice in Race Adjustments." Altogether 661 were in attendance, 59 of whom were white church leaders and YMCA and YWCA secretaries. The 470 black students present represented eighty-eight institutions. The conference was interracial, but no white students attended.

The opening addresses were delivered by John R. Mott and Booker T. Washington. Mott, concluding a quarter century as chief secretary of the student department of the international YMCA, opened the conference by telling the assembled delegates that this was "one of the most significant gatherings held in this country." Mott, in typical fashion, spoke about the racial situation worldwide. His address barely touched upon the uniquely American scene. He declared that the problem between the races "was not a matter of external arrangements." The focus must be personal. "The disposition of men must be changed. Their motive-life must be influenced."[53]

Booker T. Washington spoke with optimism about the present moment. His message was much the same he had delivered hundreds of times. "We must teach our people everywhere that we are going to gain more through Christian service than by making demands." There was no direct reference to the intramural debate within the black community as to the best strategy for progress, but Washington was clear in his counsel to these students. "It does not help the race to have the feeling created that in proportion as the young men and women get education they become self-conceited, overbearing and carry a chip on their shoulder."[54]

In addition to Washington, black speakers included Major Robert Russa Moton, John Wesley Gilbert, Mrs. John Hope, and YMCA and YWCA secretaries. Other white speakers included Wilbur P. Thirkield, John D. Hammond, and James E. McCullough.

Many of the words were predictable and quite traditional. Yet some speakers accented themes important for the future instead of repeating past slogans. Thirkield, for example, spoke about a new day within the black community when the traditional role of black religion could not be presumed. He therefore called for both quality education and an increased social consciousness. John D. Hammond, president of Paine College in Augusta, Georgia, and secretary of the southern Methodist board of education, urged an increased emphasis on the liberal arts. "Industrial education is equally important for both races; but the education of any race, if confined to this sphere, will leave that race utilitarian in its morals and materialistic in its ideals." James E. McCullough, general secretary of the Southern Sociological Congress, called for "cooperation of white and Negro ministers for social service."[55]

A dynamic address was delivered by Maude Wilder Trawick. President of the Board of Directors of the YWCA, she gave a speech entitled "The Social Message of the Church." She took as her thesis words from Charles Stelzle, a Social Gospel pioneer who had just founded the Labor Temple in New York City, to the effect that the church was spiritually converted but not socially converted. She observed that "for generations the religious thought of the Church has been turned toward personal salvation." In the future the church must realize "the necessity of saving the community, State, and nation in order to reach the individual." How would this broader salvation take place? As a foundation, she called for doing away with the distinction between the sacred and the secular. Trawick then described the characteristics of social salvation. "The practice of social religion is clean living, social action, social justice." Maude Wilder Trawick and A. M. Trawick never tired of calling for "the gospel of social living." Although ready to use the term *Social Gospel* in their speeches, it was "social living" that was their trademark. Mrs. Trawick emphasized that "a clean life, expressed in social action, helps to bring in social justice."[56]

With the conference completed, it was time for an assessment. The *Student World* editorialized that "the most characteristic, and certainly the most difficult problems of our generation are the racial problems." If these difficult problems were highlighted by the conference, at the same time one has to agree with a correspondent in the same issue who observed that the conference was "notable in that all divisive questions, such as those of color, politics, and social segregation, were excluded."[57]

Will W. Alexander, a young Methodist pastor in Nashville (of the church that Willis D. Weatherford attended), who in a few short years would take the lead in a great movement of interracial cooperation across the South, sounded a note of both hope and warning in a report in the *North American Student.* "Cooperation was on the lips of everyone." But there was also warning. "The Negro, as a race, must come up, or both races must remain down."[58]

It is difficult to gauge the impact of such a conference. One learns not to equate words with action or effect. Mott's words were general and did not speak to the specific American situation. Nor did he hold up the Social Gospel watchwords of brotherhood and justice, as he did on other occasions. Others, such as Maude Wilder Trawick, spoke more forcefully at Atlanta.

But one has to be careful in assessing an event by simply reading the speeches delivered. As a case in point, biographer C. Howard Hopkins tells us that the Atlanta conference "had been a pivotal experience for Mott." Mott wrote to Mrs. T. B. Blackstone in Chicago, thanking her for her financial support for the conference and telling her that "the convention did more than any preceding event to create right relations between the Christian leaders of both races." Basil Matthews, with whom Mott collaborated closely on a biography published in 1934, said that as a result of this conference Mott acted decisively in 1915 to stop the showing of the celebrated Hollywood film *The Birth of a Nation* in YMCA facilities. The film was a gross caricature of blacks in America.[59]

Arcadius Trawick, in editing the addresses from the conference, summed up his own feelings about what had been accomplished. "There was need of such a convention in order to provide an expression of the religion which white men and women in the South profess to practice." Trawick expressed poignantly the problem that he had been encountering in his study of social conditions and racism: "It is at variance with Christian integrity to confess the brotherhood of man and continue to live in complacent indifference to its claims at our own doors." Trawick sounded a discordant note to the generally upbeat assessments of the conference when he observed that "the greatest of all evils growing out of contact of the two races on the Southern soil is the disregard of the claims of justice, kindness and brotherly love."[60]

A high point of Trawick's public remarks on the race problem occurred in 1916 in his article "The Social Gospel and Racial Relationships." This article suggests some of the ways Trawick's mind was changing and presents his viewpoint after five years of exclusive focus on the race issue. A continuing provocative issue in all of social reform was heredity versus environment. Trawick focused again and again on the environment as he described the social conditions that were the context of every reform issue. But when speaking of the race issue, many people of the period fastened on heredity to explain what they said was a black penchant for criminality, lack of discipline, and shiftlessness. Five years earlier Trawick had spoken of "superior and inferior races."[61] Now in 1916 Trawick said that the "attempt to classify races as superior and inferior is both unscientific and unchristian."[62] The answer lay not in heredity but in environment.

Taking issue with the usual white opinion that the "inferior" Negro had contributed nothing to society but his labor, Trawick detailed contributions by black pioneers, soldiers, inventors, pastors, and teachers. The "greatest and most enduring contribution" is the Negro church. Trawick, as did many defenders and advocates of blacks, underlined the positive side of religion and went to great lengths to reassure his white readers that religion was not a force for complaint or insurrection. But there was also in Trawick often a subtle, ironic, but unmistakable jab. In one place he said, "More prayers are uttered in Negro churches for white people than are uttered in white churches for Negroes."[63]

Trawick called for a Social Gospel that would result in joint social action between whites and blacks in such areas as health and housing for the poor, juvenile court work, community surveys, poor relief, social settlements, and the resolution of industrial disputes. Trawick was optimistic about the possibilities of such efforts. "Race cooperation conducted on such a fair and equitable basis as this will be a mighty agency in building up a nation in the fear of God and will furnish to all the world an object lesson in the eternal value of the gospel of social living."[64]

A year later Trawick summed up this approach in an article with the characteristic title "The Gospel of Social Living." Arguing that we could not afford the luxury of living in a divided society, Trawick called for a style of Christian living wherein "by the force of circumstances our thinking must be interracial."[65] Cooperation became the theme of Trawick and others who cut their eyeteeth early in their careers by working not only in parishes but with idealistic students across college campuses.

By 1916 the movement for improving race relations was gathering momentum, so much so that the student magazine of the WSCF reported:

> White college men are showing rare courage in demanding of their fellows that justice be shown the black man; black men are beginning to see that all white men are not their enemies; and most important of all, there has been cooperation between the men of both races on such terms of mutual self-respect as would have been thought impossible before this movement was started.[66]

Within a year, however, the energies of the prime movers behind the movement would be channeled in new directions. This change came about because of the entrance of the United States into World War I. Four days after the declaration of war against Germany, the YMCA established a War Work Council. John R. Mott, always the man equipped for the most difficult assignments, was named general secretary. By 1918 Edwards and Trawick had also shifted over into the War Work program.[67]

In 1919 Willis D. Weatherford left the YMCA student movement to establish the YMCA Graduate School in Nashville. In this new position he broke with southern tradition by taking white students to visit Fisk, across town in Nashville, and to Tuskegee, in Alabama.[68] The high point of his study of the Negro question was the publication in 1924 of *The Negro from Africa to America*. As late as 1965 George B. Tindall commented that this study "remains the best survey of Negro history by a white writer."[69]

Also in 1919 Richard H. Edwards was invited to take charge of the religious work at Cornell University. Arcadius M. Trawick soon returned to teaching, at Wofford College in South Carolina.

John R. Mott had resigned from leadership in the student department to become general secretary of the International Committee of the YMCA in 1915. By the 1920s, while still active as a consultant, he had moved on to give leadership in other ecumenical and missionary activities.

Almost at once, the leaders who had encouraged the Student Christian Movement to move forward in relating the Social Gospel to the race problem were now lending their considerable talents to new organizations and concerns. New leaders came to take their places, and the Student Christian Movement eventually moved even further in advance of the parent churches in their readiness to participate in the struggles for racial equality that lay ahead. But it was in the years immediately prior to World War I that the Student Christian Movement, energized by the Social Gospel, first embraced a new ministry of racial reform.

CHAPTER 13

The Changing Mind
of the Social Gospel

For years the problem of the races in the South has seemed to me so
tragic, so insoluble, that I have never yet ventured to discuss it in public.
—WALTER RAUSCHENBUSCH

For too long white Christians felt that individual kindness and justice
to individual Negroes was the full measure of Christian obligation. In
the great awakening now upon the South is seen and felt the birth of a
new consciousness and a new conscience—a sense of collective
responsibility for community conditions.
—LILY HARDY HAMMOND

A central theme in our story is that a whole coterie of Social Gospel
leaders changed their mind on the race issue during these years. Some,
like Lyman Abbott, retreated from earlier egalitarian strategies but still
devoted considerable energy to ameliorating racial conditions. Others,
such as Washington Gladden, moved from accommodation to reform,
embracing strategies that they once opposed. The mind of the Social
Gospel was divided on the race question. In this book we seek in particular to understand the thinking and action of those who gradually
became more engaged with the race issue.

In this chapter it is time to look again at the viewpoints of several
well-known Social Gospel leaders encountered earlier. It is important
also to meet a number of leaders who enter the story only in the first
and second decade of this century. Some of these forgotten reformers,
women and men, made important contributions to racial reform.

At the outset I acknowledge that my historical detective work has
been much influenced by the observation and understanding of the
notion of pilgrimage. I have watched what happens when college students and older adults become involved in immersion experiences in
Central America and South Africa. The same could be said for radically
new experiences within America. Their experiences call into question

previous assumptions about belief, culture, and specific social problems. They are opened up to new possibilities for faith and responsible social action and policy. These experiences usually trigger a return to the sources—biblical, historical, economic, political—with fresh eyes. A criticism always heard is, Why does someone have to go far away when similar problems are right around the corner? The answer is that the reality of experiences in another culture is often the most powerful way to see what is in one's own backyard. Thus an encounter with poverty in Central America or racism in South Africa opens one's eyes to the poverty and racism in one's own hometown.

These contemporary pilgrimages have been crucial in prompting the charting of the changes observed in the careers of a great many Social Gospel leaders. The question that kept emerging was how to understand the dynamics of these changes. I believe that the nature of the experience is critical. Experience is often more powerful than reading books, but it usually leads to reading books with new eyes. Washington Gladden's experiences in Atlanta helped prepare him to read *The Souls of Black Folk*, which in turn precipitated further changes in his thinking and action back home in Columbus.

Four primary figures will be encountered in this chapter. The experiences of two well-known Social Gospel leaders need to be updated as our book draws toward a close. Two new individuals are introduced whose pilgrimage is fascinating in itself but who also represent larger constituencies and movements.

It was not until the second decade of the century that the leading theologian of the Social Gospel, Walter Rauschenbusch, finally spoke out about the race issue. Speaking in October 1913 to the sixty-ninth annual meeting of the American Missionary Association, Rauschenbusch confessed, "For years the problem of the races in the South has seemed to me so tragic, so insoluble, that I have never yet ventured to discuss it in public."[1] In this address, "The Belated Races and the Social Problem," Rauschenbusch gave no further explanation for his silence, an aspect of his social consciousness that has puzzled many. His silence has been falsely generalized to include other Social Gospel leaders.

The remainder of the address was consistent with Rauschenbusch's more general statements on race in his other publications. He spoke of the Negro as a "belated" race, but did not do so from any strict Darwinian standpoint. In a publication of the same year, *Dare We Be Christians?* Rauschenbusch explicitly opposed Christianity to any "survival of the fittest" mentality. Christianity "does not call on the strong to climb to isolation across the backs of the weak, but challenges them to prove their strength by lifting the rest with them. It does not advise eliminating the unfit, but seeks to make them fit. It stands for the solidarity of the race."[2]

What was the solution to the race question? Rauschenbusch viewed the question as a southern problem but called for a national solution. "No solution by southern men can be permanent which does not satisfy the Christian consciousness of the whole nation." Crucial to the solution was the encouragement of the awakening of racial pride within blacks themselves. "No solution will satisfy the Christian spirit of our united nation which does not provide for the progressive awakening of hope and self-respect in the individual Negro and the awakening of race pride and race ambition in all Negro communities."[3]

In speaking out in 1913, Rauschenbusch attempted to relate his comments to the theology of the Social Gospel. Speaking of "a higher valuation of the human soul, a deeper respect for the dignity of human life," he told his audience, "I am thinking of the Negro in saying this." Although he touched upon areas where this dignity was to be achieved—labor and property rights, among others—he was not really specific. As for the posture that blacks should adopt in their struggle, Rauschenbusch spoke in a manner that evidenced some knowledge of the continuing debate over strategy and tactics. As for his own counsel, he acknowledged the criticism of Nietzsche that "Christianity has taught the virtues of servile patience and submissiveness." His own beliefs were "in gentleness and meekness, but not in servility. I have no faith in force methods, and even believe in nonresistance, but not in nonresistance of cowardice and silence."[4] In these latter remarks one senses the struggle within Rauschenbusch between the pacifism that became public in World War I and the call to social action.

These few brief comments should not be overvalued. Coming as they did from Walter Rauschenbusch, however, they were noted at the time. The *Crisis*, organ of the NAACP, commented that "Walter Rauschenbusch has for the first time spoken out on the Negro problem." Willis D. Weatherford invited Rauschenbusch to speak at a YMCA conference at Blue Ridge, North Carolina.[5]

Is there anything more to learn about Rauschenbusch's thoughts and actions on the racial question? In a new biography Paul M. Minus says simply, "More than most of his contemporaries, Rauschenbusch recognized the right of women and blacks to a share in the process, but he played no leadership role either locally or nationally in assuring their participation."[6] Minus affirms Rauschenbusch's concern for blacks, but we are given no new information.

It is worth remembering that the place where Rauschenbusch spent the last two decades of his life afforded little opportunity for daily contact with blacks. In the city of Rochester, out of a population of 162,608 in 1900, there were only 601 blacks.[7]

Because of the centrality of Rauschenbusch to the Social Gospel, it is important to ask why he did finally speak out in 1913. Earlier in the year Rauschenbusch had traveled to Nashville, Tennessee, for a speaking engagement. As was his habit, he decided to do some investigating on his own. He was interested in learning more about sharecroppers and schools. In his investigation he visited a section called black bottom, where "he saw Negro life at its worst." His friend Dores R. Sharpe believed this was the catalyst for his remarks to the American Missionary Association.[8]

The visit to "black bottom" was certainly not Rauschenbusch's only encounter with the race problems. In his papers is a folder labeled "Inter-Racial Relations." On a handwritten page headed "Christianity and Black Race" are some notes containing ideas voiced in his American Missionary Association address. On a trip to Cleveland in 1910, he visited the large black section of the city. In 1912, in a meeting set up by Graham Taylor, Rauschenbusch participated in a discussion period where there were a number of questions about the race question. Rauschenbusch's insight into the problem was revealed in a conversation in which he observed the way white society dealt with the problem. They preferred to help elevate a Booker T. Washington to a position of leadership and at the same time not deal with the masses of black people.[9]

As to the haunting question of Rauschenbusch's thoughts and feelings about the race issue in the last years of his life, I believe that the record may not yet be complete. From the time he spoke out publicly in 1913 until his death five years later, this pattern of reticence and virtual public silence appears to have continued unabated.

Josiah Strong was an activist in comparison with the scholarly Rauschenbusch. A pastor, home missionary, and author, Strong took the lead in attempting to marshal sociological data in the service of social reform. In 1898 he and William Howe Tolman founded the League for Social Service. The league undertook an ambitious program of popular education through establishing a bureau of information, publishing pamphlets, and sponsoring lecturers. Its group of sponsors included

Jane Addams, Hollis B. Frissell, Washington Gladden, Frederic Dan Huntington, William R. Huntington, Robert C. Ogden, and Henry C. Potter. In 1902 the league was reorganized as the American Institute of Social Service, and activities were expanded. An entrepreneurial reformer, Strong enlisted new sponsors Walter Rauschenbusch, Francis G. Peabody, George W. Coleman, Henry Churchill King, as well as Grover Cleveland and Woodrow Wilson.

The institute contributed to the daily nurture of the developing Social Gospel through a monthly publication, *The Gospel of the Kingdom*. Designed as a set of daily Sunday school lessons ("a course of study on living social problems in the light of the gospel of Jesus Christ"), these lessons had the widest circulation of any materials ever published in the interest of the Social Gospel. More than forty thousand readers in churches, YMCAs and YWCAs, colleges, universities, and seminaries followed these lessons from their inception in 1909 until 1916, the year of Strong's death. They consisted of Bible passages, topics for discussion, questions, and extensive bibliographies. In 1910 A section entitled "What to Do" was added to encourage readers further to translate words into actions. Many of the lessons were written by William Dwight Porter Bliss, but all were approved by the editor, Josiah Strong.[10]

The American Institute of Social Service dealt with the race issue as one of many problems within a broader concern. Strong received counsel on this issue from Augustus F. Beard, general secretary of the American Missionary Association, who was one of his closest friends.

In 1905 Strong wrote to Booker T. Washington to ask him to look over a bibliography that was about to be published. Washington approved the extensive bibliography, adding but one suggestion.[11]

It is possible to gauge Strong's changing thinking on the Negro question by following his speaking and writing from 1909 through his death in 1916. During the first year of *The Gospel of the Kingdom*, bibliographies were printed monthly. A bibliography on the Negro question was included in the August 1909 issue.[12] In the same issue Strong included an article of his own, "The Race Question." Here he attempted to present information about different aspects of the race question, such as population, industrial and economic status, education, and crime. Expounding the scriptural basis of the solution of the race problem, Strong called upon the churches to live out the "universal brotherhood of man, resting upon [the] universal fatherhood of God." He rejected what he considered two extreme approaches to the problem, namely to counsel immediate, wholesale change, or to wait for time to solve the problem. The church, Strong, argued, should "raise its protest against race prejudice and show the responsibility of brother for brother." What would be the best strategies in expressing this effort? It could do this most practically by helping black churches and black education. Strong told his readers that the race issue could not be cordoned off as a southern problem but that white churches had a special responsibility to help the increasing numbers of blacks in the North. Often aware of the dangers of paternalism in social concern, Strong counseled that the best way to be of help would be to guarantee fair treatment by the law.[13]

In 1910 Strong participated in a discussion of the race problem at the annual Sagamore Sociological Conference. He spoke first of the race problem as a world problem. As was his custom, he spoke optimistically of the tremendous resources available in the churches and in the nation. "Nowhere in the world are there such facilities for solving the race problem, which must be solved." But by now his optimism was tempered by a realization of the gravity of the problem. "Nowhere is the urgency so great as it is right here in the United States."[14]

A chastened Strong wrote "The New Race Problem" in *Our World* in 1913. He now admitted that "race antipathy . . . has not been outgrown by civilization, nor is it always overcome by the broadening influences of culture." Instead of disappearing, the race problem in Strong's view, "has become distinctly more complicated in recent times." Demonstrating more awareness of the crisis and eschewing optimistic solutions, Strong called for a constant vigilance against racism at home and abroad.[15]

Further development in Strong's thinking is evident in a lesson in *The Gospel of the Kingdom* in 1915. The Sunday school lessons for August focused on "The Race Problem." The lessons began by speaking of race as a world problem. In this context Strong still spoke of European immigrants as part of the race problem. In a marked departure from *Our Country* thirty years before, Strong was more sophisticated in his understanding of the concept of race. He quoted anthropologist Franz Boas, who, in *The Mind of Primitive Man* (1911), dealt a decisive blow to theories about superior and inferior races. Strong pointed out that color and pigmentation are due to environmental conditions. He believed that it was not possible any longer to speak of inherent mental inferiority.[16]

Strong spoke of the "amazing progress" blacks had made since the Civil War. He applauded especially their gains in literacy. He commended whites who had helped in this struggle, naming specifically Edgar Gardner Murphy. Strong asked his readers to consider what was still needed in the present and the future. His own answer was "civil and industrial equality."[17]

Strong's comments about race do reveal sentiments expressed elsewhere regarding other reform issues. He was not content with a call for compassion. In focusing on "civil and industrial equality," he recognized that the status of blacks ultimately depended not upon good will but upon good laws. A realist who was most content when he could marshal sociological data, Strong's study of the Negro question convinced him that as blacks moved North, there needed to be adequate societal structures in place. Liberty and justice would come when there was equal opportunity for all.

Within nine months Strong was dead. To set the record straight on his changing attitudes is not to argue that race relations became a major focus of his reforming efforts. It is to suggest that he was changing his mind in the last years of his life. He moved a long way from sentiments expressed in *Our Country* as in the last years of his life he addressed a number of the issues involved in racial reform.

A full four decades after the close of the Civil War, a young northern pastor emerged through the ranks of the American Missionary Association who was able to see more clearly than his contemporaries the present and future dimensions of race relations in the South. Harlan Paul Douglass combined the passion of his predecessors with the tools of the social sciences. Well known for his later work in community and ecumenical relations, Douglass has not received adequate recognition for his insights into the race issue. His book *Christian Reconstruction in the South* is a singular study of the race issue. Armed with sociological data, Douglass challenged then-current assumptions on the race question.

The Social Gospel was an integral part of Douglass's religious heritage and education. Born in Osage, Iowa, in 1871, he graduated from Iowa College (Grinnell) in 1891. One year of theological training was taken at Chicago and the final two at Andover. He was ordained a Congregational minister in 1894 and served as a pastor of Congregational churches in Ames, Iowa, and Springfield, Missouri. While in Springfield he also taught at Drury College. Douglass was appointed superintendent of education for the American Missionary Association in 1906, serving in that capacity until 1910 and as corresponding secretary until 1918. In his later years he became quite well known for his work in sociology and community analysis with the National Council of Churches and affiliated groups.[18]

The roots of Douglass's social consciousness can be seen in an unfinished graduate thesis in the general area of the ethics of the social questions. The specific focus was "The English Christian Socialist Movement of the Mid-Century." This thesis provides a clue not only to Douglass's foundations but to his understanding of the task of sociology as well. Douglass wrote that Frederick Denison Maurice and Charles Kingsley, English Christian socialist leaders, were not "sociological speculators, trying to find out by observation and logical processes the truth about society and social duty" but believed instead that the truth was already present in Christianity. "It was not a *theory* but a *message* which they announced in response to England's social need."[19] Douglass was himself an able theoretician, but it was the social message of Christianity that he sought to apply to the Negro question.

Douglass's message was presented in *Christian Reconstruction in the South*. Published in 1909, near the beginning of Douglass's work with the American Missionary Association, this volume was called by the author "a sociological perspective." At the outset he assessed the contemporary mood about the race problem. As a northerner, he described the "deliberately laudatory" mood that seemed to be the proper way for northerners to discuss the South. He contrasted this approach with the hard-hitting telling of the truth about the race issue coming from some courageous southerners. His own assessment was that there existed a continuing crisis in race relations. "The praise which has been lavished on the assimilated vigor of the American stock and on the triumph of their democratic institutions is justified only when one ignores the exceptional group—roughly one-eight of our mainland population."[20] Douglass invited his readers to explore with him the climate of opinion that masked the hard realities of the race issue.

Douglass early revealed his own point of view in a powerful anecdote. He told the story of old Aunt Dinah who died in Alabama. "She was a delightful example of the old-fashioned Negro type," many of which still survive. She accepted inferiority. "They only wanted to serve, to cling, to fulfill life on the level of subjection to some white master." He contrasted Aunt Dinah with the stereotypes held up continually by the white majority in the South—the picture of shiftless, irresponsible blacks. Granting this stereotype for the moment (Douglass challenged it later), Douglass argued that it was difficult to understand that old Aunt Dinah was actually less beautiful than "the too frequent representative of the new order—obnoxious in dress, in voice, in manners, an unsatisfactory worker and still less satisfactory enjoyer of the means of life, an irresponsible member of the state and a potential menace to it." Douglass was trying to make a case that slavery, even as Aunt Dinah was depicted through the lens of romantic racialism, was never to be preferred to freedom. "The most perfect slave is lower than the most imperfect freeman." What does it take for people to under-stand this reality? "Innate democratic passion."[21]

In the body of the book Douglass presented facts and figures about the life of black Americans in the South. He spoke about the efforts at black education and praised the efforts of the Conference for Education in the South. He was most critical of the white southern churches. "It is not to discredit its ardent piety to say that it has shown itself the least adaptive of the reconstructive factors of its section." Douglass was not optimistic about the next few years in the South. "The further cur-tailment of Negro political privileges in the South is to be expected." He foresaw this development because the Negro was now more "dan-gerous," having acquired education and property, a developing race consciousness, and competent leadership and organs of public opin-ion.[22]

This short-term outlook must not obscure the long-term prospect. The future was bright because of the increasing abilities of blacks them-selves, not simply as individuals, but as a social community. Douglass's response to the commonly held assertion that any progress blacks have made has been the result of the efforts of others was "Emphatically, No!" Describing the efforts of blacks to control their own destinies, Douglass praised the black church as historically "the chief institutional creation of the race and its success is a vast economic achievement." He was not so laudatory about the social consciousness of the contempo-rary black church, but he indicated that there were exceptions, such as Henry Hugh Proctor of Atlanta.[23]

Douglass was more sensitive than most whites in his knowledge of the forces then at work within the black community. He described in some detail the philosophies and strategies of Booker T. Washington and W. E. B. Du Bois. The young missionary administrator was pro-phetic in assessing the outcome of the intramural debate within the black community. "One may laugh if he will at the squabbles of the Negro on his side of the color-line." Douglass was not laughing and counseled his readers that it was time to listen. Through these debates "the race is beating into shape a disciplined and well-officered army, under experienced leadership." What will be the results? "It is forging weapons of group consciousness and control which will someday give its now voiceless power, wisdom, dignity, and weight in the counsels of the Republic."[24]

He was sympathetic to Washington but circumspect about complimenting his strategy. Douglass described Washington's regular trips to the North, coming each time with a different group of men who were meant to be examples of black progress. The difficulty with that strategy was that opponents could also marshal examples of failure. "It is not enough to enumerate; one must weigh the fact." The question was not whether black Americans have made progress, but how does that progress measure up, compared with the general progress that must be admitted for all Americans?[25]

In his argumentation Douglass made use of the work of Edward A. Ross, professor of sociology at the University of Wisconsin. Ross, raised as a Presbyterian, had become much more impressed with the social rather than the theological significance of religion. His 1907 book, *Sin and Society*, in some ways anticipated Reinhold Niebuhr's *Moral Man and Immoral Society* a quarter century later. Ross argued that good men and women are not enough to produce a good society. It is obvious that Douglass had listened to Ross's progressive counsel that meaningful reform strategy in modern society must pay attention to the aggregate of customs, laws, and social agencies. It was in the context of Ross's work that Douglass analyzed the so-called deficiencies of American blacks. He believed that certain deficiencies could not be denied at the present, but that was not the critical issue. The issue was whether these deficiencies were racial and whether they were inevitable. Douglass believed they were not and appealed to words from Ross. "The superiorities that, at a given time, one people may display over other peoples, are not necessarily racial." Challenging theories that trace differences to heredity, Douglass again quoted Ross. "To the scholars the attributing of the mental and moral traits of a population to heredity is a confession of defeat, not to be thought of until he has wrung from every factor of life its last drop of explanation."[26]

Douglass preferred to emphasize environment, from both sociological and theological perspectives. He pointed out that poverty and crime are neighbors. In many southern cities, the best black institutions were crowded into the same areas with the whites' worst institutions. The cruelest environmental factor consigning blacks to degradation was the thought patterns of whites. Every problem, every issue, every so-called deficiency was given a racial explanation.

As Douglass moved toward the conclusion of the book, he found hope in the new consciousness of world unity and the new Social Gospel. "Within this new world men have seen the social vision of the gospel which compels them to look beyond individual salvation to the

actual and active contacts of redeemed men in the kingdom of God."
Within the orbit of this social vision of the gospel, it will be "the passion
of brotherhood" that will ultimately triumph. The idea of brotherhood
can be supported now by the social sciences, so that sociology is written
for the first time without reference to race. In the end Douglass believed
that "it is still faith in the Gospel that is the final judgment." This gospel
is profoundly social. Douglass believed this Social Gospel alone provided the resources to encounter such a persistently social question as the
race issue. The young missionary educator ended his book with these
lines: "For not idly it is written, 'It is better for thee to enter into life
maimed, than having two hands to go into hell.' And what shall it profit
the Anglo-Saxon if he gain the whole world and lose his own soul?"[27]

This book was meant to be a charter for the ongoing work of the
American Missionary Association. Two years later, in 1911, Douglass
reported to the executive committee of the AMA his intentions to develop further the implications of the Social Gospel for the race issue.
He saw around him a changing understanding of Christian missions.
"The modern church cannot avoid increased emphasis on her social
ministries." The AMA should continue to focus on the church and the
school, "but church and school are both larger words meaning bigger
things than they used to." New ministries might include institutional
extension work in rural areas, new definitions of country churches, as
well as more broad-based work within cities. Douglass's message to the
committee was that "the missions of today cannot use the forms of
yesterday and remain the missions of Christ."[28]

The relatively brief career of Harlan Paul Douglass in the American
Missionary Association is quite remarkable. His work launched him
into a national ecumenical ministry where he was always probing for
the implications of the Christian faith for the larger structures and communities of the nation. But he always looked back to his early years
with the AMA with great affection and satisfaction. More than thirty
years later, at the end of World War II, Douglass reflected back on those
twelve years and called them the best period of his life.[29]

In Douglass it is possible to see the union of the older missionary
impulse with the newer Social Gospel. James M. McPherson, from his
studies of abolitionism, observes, "The individual who best personified
this fusion of evangelical abolitionism and the social gospel was Harlan
Paul Douglass."[30] Decades after the first traffic on the missionary
bridge, Douglass utilized both experience and data to urge new patterns of social ministry for an old organization. There is a sophistication
in *Christian Reconstruction in the South* that goes beyond mere moral

injunction, and yet there is a prophetic vigor that would have pleased the old abolitionists.

On a spring day in 1882, at the dedication of an industrial home for blacks, Atticus G. Haygood lamented the fact that southern white women had not yet seen fit to join in the mission of helping southern blacks. Comparing their absence with the presence of northern white women, Haygood observed, "Bear with their long delay. There are no better women in the world than the Christian women of the South."[31]

Haygood would have been pleased with the turn of events observable in the new century. Rising up within his own southern Methodist denomination were a band of women who pioneered in work with blacks in schools and settlement houses. These women moved beyond their male counterparts in their involvement with black education and related concerns. This was all the more remarkable in a southern society where women were put on pedestals and traditional mores restrained their entrance into politics or reform. The Social Gospel, north and south, was not always hospitable to women's aspirations and rights. It is all the more remarkable that toward the end of the story of the Social Gospel movement, a group of women joined its ranks as reformers with a special concern for race relations.

As early as 1894 the Woman's Parsonage and Home Mission Society of the Methodist Episcopal Church, South, prepared a reading list to educate its membership. Announcing this project, Lily H. Hammond said, "We want to know everything that is being done in all the world to uplift the fall, to better the condition of the poor, to bring classes together." The first books suggested were Josiah Strong's *Our Country* and Washington Gladden's *Applied Christianity.* Social Gospel authors, including Richard Ely, Shailer Mathews, Walter Rauschenbusch, and Charles Stelzle, were recommended frequently.[32]

In 1901 the Methodist Women's Board of Missions decided to add a girl's industrial training program at Paine Institute in Augusta, Georgia. To say "decided" may be to miss the import of this event. Belle H. Bennett had long wanted to start work with black girls. Born into wealth, Bennett experienced a conversion in her twenties and thereafter devoted herself to mission work. She became president of the Home Mission Society in 1896. According to Lily Hammond, Bennett wanted to start work with blacks but felt that prejudice must first be overcome. The decision to move forward was made at a famous prayer meeting in an upper room at St. John's Church in St. Louis. Shailer Mathews had just addressed the annual meeting of the Home Mission Society, and Bennett made a plea on behalf of Negro work. After a prolonged prayer meeting the decision was made to begin.[33]

Paine had been established by southern Methodists in 1882, with Haygood a vigorous advocate for its programs, but it had never received the full support of the denomination. The efforts at Paine were greatly enhanced with the arrival of John and Lily Hardy Hammond in 1910.

John Hammond was secretary of the southern Methodist Board of Education from 1898 to 1910. He accepted the presidency of Paine in 1911. Although committed to black education, he was not a good administrator and was encouraged to resign in 1916.

Lily, born of slaveholding parents, was more gifted and energetic than her husband. Some of her girlhood was spent in the North, but she lived most of her adult life in the South. Educator and organizer, she was at her best in publicizing her perspective on race relations to both southern and northern audiences.

In describing and analyzing Lily Hammond's thoughts on the race issue, one can see an admixture of paternalism, defensiveness, courage, and farsightedness. One reason for this combination is the changes in her outlook over the course of two decades. She changed her mind both in her understanding of the issues and in her strategy of communication.

In 1902 Hammond wrote an extended article for the *Outlook* entitled "A Southern View of the Negro." Her comments received the strong endorsement of editor Lyman Abbott. The author said she spoke for "a large and growing class of southern whites" who wished to befriend the Negro. In this article, friendship became the vehicle for defending the various actions of southern whites. She went on to express disapproval of many aspects of Negro education; to criticize the industry, cleanliness, and morals of blacks; and to defend the motives of many who wanted to disfranchise black voters. She echoed nearly all of her contemporaries in rejecting any possibility of social equality.[34]

The article had a hopeful side too. Hammond described the efforts at Paine. She spoke not only of the white faculty but of the young black faculty just being appointed. Her plea was for understanding, time, and financial help. She suggested, although she did not develop it in this article, that the fruits of education for blacks would be seen in increased emphasis on higher education.

Twelve years later Hammond wrote an important study on race that is quite different in substance and tone. *In Black and White: An Interpretation of Southern Life* is significant not only because of what it tells us about patterns of thinking in the South but because of its information about the evolution in Hammond's own thinking. It has been argued throughout this book that in almost every case concern for racial reform emerges out of a larger Social Gospel. Henry Warnock asserts that Hammond "embraced the social gospel."[35] This embrace is evident in her book.

Hammond described her own work as a teenager in a ministry to inner-city tenement dwellers. Looking back, she said that her only purpose then was "to save the souls of the tenement dwellers out of this world into another one." In describing the evolution in her thinking, she affirmed the influence of British writers Frederick D. Maurice and Charles Kingsley of an earlier generation and William T. Stead of the present generation in awakening her to the social dimensions of the Christian faith. From this perspective she analyzed the individualistic notions of her youth and commented that "nobody dissented from the doctrine that whatever was wrong in the general tenement-house environment was merely the outward and visible sign of the tenement dweller's inward and spiritual lack of grace." The remedy was simple: "If all their souls could only be saved, there would be nothing left wrong with the tenements." From her present vantage point she observed, "There was no sense of responsibility on landlords, on the health authorities, the employers of labor, or the public at large."[36] What was missing was any sense of the larger social dimensions of the problem.

Hammond was intent on bringing to bear a larger social consciousness to the issue of race. The first step, she said, was to "put away childish things—unreasoning prejudice and pride." This more mature thought included revising her view of creation so that she could see black women and men "made in the image of God as truly as we ourselves." This affirmation of creation did not mean that she renounced what she called separateness, even as she continued to expect that "social equality" would not be achieved in the foreseeable future. Rooting her argument in creation, she demonstrated a new tone when she suggested that whites should understand that blacks who wanted to buy property in desirable sections of the community did so not to display impudence but to live in an environment that would nourish the moral, educational, and spiritual life of their children.[37]

In advocating a strategy for change, a new emphasis is evident. She asked her southern audience to understand the sincere intentions of northern ventures toward southern blacks. As for the South, she criticized the fact that black pulpits spoke rarely about race relations, duty to black poor, and other interests of the kingdom of God. She did commend an emerging social consciousness among some southern leaders and spoke enthusiastically about the Southern Sociological Congress as "the first South-wide expression of this nascent conscience."[38]

The strategy Hammond called for reflected her own understanding of a Social Gospel heralding the largest dimensions of the kingdom of God. She identified the basis of race relations as justice. She spoke out against the unjust administration of criminal law in the courts. In lifting up the meaning of justice, she spoke to the solid southern opinion "against any attempt at regeneration by man-made law instead of by spiritual process." Her reply was that it was precisely social conditions that were a large part of the racial problem. The response to those social conditions must be social action on the part of the whole community. Hammond, writing in a style that could be both powerful and subtle, concluded by observing that "community action expressed in statutory law is more religious by far than any amount of prayer for the salvation of the poor offered by folk who go home to idleness." No northern Social Gospeler could have said it better. She pressed the indictment by asserting that "we have thrown on the poor, and on God's grace, responsibility for community conditions which defy the Bible law of human brotherhood."[39]

In 1917 she addressed an appeal to southern women in a pamphlet published by the John F. Slater Fund. She reviewed the work being done for racial adjustment by the denominations and such groups as the YWCA. She counseled that a continuing problem was the image or perception of what a "good" Negro should be. "Our ideal of a good free Negro has been too much like the one that fitted a good slave." Hammond argued that it was imperative that women change their perceptions of blacks as the precondition of racial reform.[40]

Hammond's concern for blacks was always part of her whole social reform interests. In 1918 she was asked to contribute to a volume focusing on labor that was part of a home mission study course. Her sympathies for labor were expressed in her judgment that laborers were the "poorest, most exploited world-class" of the day. Her advocacy of blacks focused now on the need for increased entrance into the labor market. More sympathetic than ever to the just grievances of blacks, she identified the basic issue as civil rights. "The lack of civil rights is increasingly a cause of bitterness among Negroes, and will cut deeper every year until those rights are granted." Hammond was hopeful that in the oppression felt among laborers, both black and white, there was the possibility of a common struggle for justice.[41]

Hammond believed that southern white attitudes would change when the progress of blacks was made known. In the following years she worked to bring to the attention of the public the increasing achievements of black men and women. To this end, she sponsored the Southern Publicity Committee, which, supported by the Phelps-Stokes Fund, worked to gather and disseminate news about achievements in all fields of endeavor. In 1917 she authored *In the Vanguard of a Race,* a volume in which she wrote about Booker T. Washington, Robert R. Moton, William N. DeBerry, Charles V. Roman, Nannie H. Burroughs, Harry T. Burleigh, and others. Her admonition to her white readers was that "how fast they climb will depend in large part on us, on our faithfulness to our common Lord, and on your obedience to His big, simple laws of justice and kindness to all."[42]

In seeking recruits to work with her in racial reform, Hammond spoke to the deepest instincts in women. In entreating women in 1917, she appealed to the reality of "womanhood as a thing deeper than race." She wanted white women to reach out to black women. She believed that women were a neglected army that could change the attitudes of a society about race.[43]

Although Hammond speaks to us today because of both her insights and her gifts with words, there were many other women, mostly forgotten, who deserve to be remembered. The first woman appointed specifically to work with blacks was Mary De Bardeleben. The daughter of an Alabama Methodist minister, she studied at the Methodist Training School at Vanderbilt (later Scarritt College). Intending to go into foreign missions, her encounters with the living conditions of blacks in Nashville led her to apply for full-time work home mission work among them. Discouraged by her parents and her bishop but supported by teachers at Scarritt, her application to the Woman's Home Mission Society was heard behind closed doors. After considerable discussion she was approved and began work in 1911 in Augusta, Georgia. Assigned to Paine Institute, with great energy she went quickly beyond her original mandate, organizing a number of new programs and activities. She formed the first settlement house for blacks in 1912. A community center was founded and named Galloway Hall in honor of Bishop Charles Betts Galloway. Mary De Bardeleben believed that the church must minister to the total life of the black community. In that spirit she organized a civic improvement league, a kindergarten, and a Sunday school.[44]

The stories of other church women, such as Lucinda and Mary Helm, Belle Bennett, and Carrie Parks Johnson, could be mentioned for their involvement in racial reform. I agree with Anne Firor Scott that the efforts of these Methodist women must receive major credit for bringing about a shift in the whole denominational reform effort. It is her judgment that "the directions in which these social concerns took Methodist women became fully apparent in 1916 when the Missionary Council adopted what amounted to a full-scale social gospel program."[45]

At the annual meeting of the Woman's Missionary Council in 1920, a motion was approved to establish a Commission on Race Relations. The women resolved "that as Christians and workers in God's Kingdom, we accept His challenge to show forth His power to settle racial differences." Carrie Parks Johnson of Georgia was elected to chair the new commission. Seeking assistance in formulating a plan of action, Johnson sought advice from Will Alexander, head of the newly formed Commission on Interracial Cooperation, who had come to Kansas City to address the council.[46] The CIC, formed by church people, set its sights on working inside but especially outside the churches to achieve the maximum impact in southern society. The results of that conversation form an important part of chapter 14.

In this chapter we have examined the changing mind of quite different Social Gospel leaders. It was important to hear the attitudes of two of the most prominent leaders, Walter Rauschenbusch and Josiah Strong, in the years around World War I, which were also the last years of their lives. Harlan Paul Douglass is another, much later example of the effect of the missionary education bridge. He also is important as a leader of the most important missionary education organization, the American Missionary Association. To speak of the changing mind of the Social Gospel is to consider not simply individuals but organizations. Finally, Lily Hardy Hammond is significant, as a woman and as a forgotten reformer. She also represents an upsurge of reform sentiment among church women in the South.

Both Douglass and Hammond really do typify the reality of bringing Social Gospel insights to bear on the race problem. From the outset the distinction has been made between social concern and Social Gospel. Admittedly this distinction is often difficult to discern. The argument has been that some of the individuals and organizations encountered in these latter years understand the problem far better than their predecessors, so that simple concern is no longer enough. No one said it better than Lily H. Hammond.

> For too long white Christians felt that individual kindness and justice to individual Negroes was the full measure of Christian obligation. In the great awakening now upon the South is seen and felt the birth of a new consciousness and a new conscience—a sense of collective responsibility for community conditions.[47]

Hammond would be the first to say that individual kindness was important. But her knowledge of the enormity of the problems meant that the present mandate was for collective responsibility.

In these years a number of organizations grew up that believed, with Hammond, in a corporate mandate. These organizations and movements believed that to fulfill that mandate they needed to move outside the churches.

CHAPTER 14

"The Church Outside the Churches"

I have had a new world opened to me, a world I had never conceived before, a world of which I had never dreamed. I saw these colored women, graduates of great institutions of learning. . . . I saw women of education, culture and refinement. I had lived in the South all my life, but I didn't know such as these lived in the land.

—CARRIE PARKS JOHNSON

As Christian workers in God's Kingdom, we accept His challenge to show forth His power to settle racial differences, thereby setting forth before the whole world an example of the power of Christianity to meet interracial crises everywhere.

—COMMISSION ON INTERRACIAL COOPERATION

In his influential study *Ministers of Reform: The Progressives' Achievement in American Civilization, 1889–1920*, Robert M. Crunden suggests that to understand the progressive ethos "is not all that complicated. Protestantism provided the chief thrust and defined the perimeters of discourse." According to Crunden, however, "The civil religion of American mission soon transcended its origins and became a complex of secular democratic values."[1]

How do we account for the rise of secular democratic values? Crunden asserts that as the ministry no longer was "intellectually respectable," a new generation of secular "ministers" grew up. These men and women became the leaders of the progressive movement, "urging reform on institutions as well as on individuals."[2] This observation of both kinds of ministers is true in part. By looking at the early lives of the progressive leaders, Crunden shows how many of them reacted against their strict Protestant upbringing but yet continued to use certain values from that heritage.

In this chapter, I suggest a different thesis to help explain the dynamic of progressivism: the status of the ministry remained high in this era, but that stature was measured in different ways. Social Gospel ministers of reform constituted an important part of the phalanx of progressivism. Monday newspapers still reported the content of Sunday sermons. Books of sermons continued to be in demand. But even if one argues that the adulation for the princes of the pulpits was starting to wane, ministers continued to be influential leaders because of a role that accompanied their embrace of the Social Gospel. They too became ministers of reform. Clerical and lay Social Gospel leaders occupied roles in society and in reform movements that seem long ago and far away to any observer of contemporary society. (The role of reformer is still acceptable in the black church, although on a reduced scale.) Washington Gladden was elected to the city council of Columbus, Ohio, without campaigning, defeating both a Republican and a Democrat. Charles Stelzle wrote a column for more than two hundred labor newspapers and was a regular speaker at the American Federation of Labor conventions. Richard T. Ely was a founder of the American Economics Association. Will W. Alexander became the director of the Commission on Interracial Cooperation. The listing could go on and on. Why were so many ministers active outside the churches?

The Church Outside the Churches, the title of a book authored by George W. Coleman in 1910, suggests an answer to this question. Active in city government, Coleman was a member of the Boston City Council from 1913 to 1915, serving as mayor in 1915. A Baptist layman, Coleman was publisher of *The Christian Endeavor World*. As one involved in reform activities in Boston, Coleman observed that "the social gospel is a prominent feature" in what he called peoples' gatherings starting up in the first years of the new century. From the Ford Hall Forum in Boston to the Southern Sociological Congress, persons motivated by a Social Gospel were organizing meetings where there was opportunity to deal with the difficult and often controversial issues confronting a changing America. Writing for the Northern Baptist Social Service Commission, Coleman encouraged his readers to discover the Social Gospel outside the walls of the churches in a whole host of these new organizations.[3]

The theological foundation for the vocation of ministers as reformers was grounded in the renewed emphasis on the kingdom of God. To be sure, ministers had always been reformers in America. But the vehicles for their reform had usually been the Christian voluntary societies or the denominational agencies. The fresh emphasis on the kingdom of God pointed to possibilities beyond the churches and voluntary societies. Walter Rauschenbusch expressed this truth in dynamic terms:

"The Kingdom of God breeds prophets; the Church breeds priests and theologians."[4] For many Social Gospel leaders the kingdom of God became the primary reality. The fact that this reality was not coextensive with the churches provided a linchpin for a new direction for their reforming efforts.

To think of this reality pictorially is to see two circles.

The kingdom of God is larger than the churches. Its content is defined by the ethics of Jesus. The gospel imperative is to help bring those ethics into being in the neediest places in society.

The trajectory of the kingdom of God set pastors and laity free to work with persons who did not start from Christian belief and with movements that might not be Christian by definition or charter. The ideological impulse of the kingdom prompted these leaders always toward ethics. As Rauschenbusch observed, "Only persons having the substance of the Kingdom ideal in their minds, seem to get relish out of the ethics of Jesus."[5] If the kingdom was larger than the churches, then there was warrant for advocating justice through organizations that were not church organizations. We have observed this impulse at work through those who joined the NAACP and the Urban League as an appropriate way to act out their Christian convictions. These two organizations were not Christian by definition, but many participants saw in them vehicles to work toward justice.

Taking our cue from George W. Coleman, we visit in this chapter a number of organizations in "the Church outside the Churches," seeking to understand their self-understanding as organizations or movements. Specifically we want to see if and how racial reform was addressed.

In the summer of 1906 a group of visitors was returning north after attending the twenty-fifth anniversary celebrations at Spelman Seminary, a school for black girls at Atlanta. The Reverend James A. Francis, pastor of the Clarendon Street Baptist Church in Boston, said to one of his deacons, George W. Coleman, "I wish there was a place where Christian ministers and layman could get correct information in regard to social and economic problems. Why not start a Christian Sociological Conference." "You have hit it exactly," Coleman replied. "That is just what we will have."[6]

Traveling the missionary bridge to the South, Coleman returned to the North to found the Sagamore Sociological Conference. The aim was to combine social Christianity and sociology in a conference that would meet annually at Sagamore Beach, Massachusetts. Coleman was a Baptist Sunday school teacher and served as president of the Boston Sunday School Teachers Union. The Northern Baptist Convention was organized in 1908, and in 1917 he was elected president. In 1907 the call for the first Sagamore Sociological Conference went out under Coleman's name, cosigned by Josiah Strong, Walter Rauschenbusch, Leighton Williams, Samuel B. Cooper, and Francis E. Clark. The signers declared that "the time is ripe for the establishment of a Conference of Sociology, which shall, in addition to a thorough consideration of the general topic, seek to emphasize and extend among Christian people, social standards and ideals."[7]

The first year's program included as leaders Josiah Strong, Leighton Williams, Charles Stelzle, Robert A. Woods, Edwin A. Mead, and Francis E. Clark. Clark was the founder of the youth movement "Christian Endeavor," with which Coleman was closely associated. More than 50 persons attended the conference for three days in June, which one visitor described as "Lake Mohonk on the seashore." The number rose to more than 100 in 1908, and by 1911 there were 250 in attendance. The list of speakers for the conferences reads like a Who's Who of the Social Gospel.

The original platform had stated the need for the establishment of practical common interests between people of different racial elements and forms of faith.[8] Attempts at carrying out this ideal were evident at many of the conferences. In 1909 Ray Stannard Baker, widely known muckraker who helped popularize progressive causes, was a featured speaker. In 1908 Baker had authored *Following the Color Line,* which had attracted much attention to the race issue. He addressed the Sagamore conference on the subject "The Negro in a Democracy." In 1910 George Sale, superintendent of education for the American Baptist Home Missionary Society, spoke on the topic "An Unsolved Problem of the American Democracy." Unlike some optimistic statements heard in the North in these years, Sale was much more sober. "In reference to the Negro in America, things have not worked out as was expected forty years ago. It is not too much to say that the general attitude of mind toward this problem is one of disillusionment and perplexity. In some respects it seems as if we are having to begin all over again."[9]

"Race Problems" was the theme of the entire conference for 1914. The topic referred to the Negro, the Asiatic, and the Jew, but the major emphasis was on blacks. More than six hundred people heard both white and black speakers. The conference was intent on bringing the best sociological data to bear on contemporary issues. In that spirit Daniel Evans, professor at Andover Theological Seminary, asked the question, "Is race antipathy rational?" He answered by saying that race antipathy was not rational, but rather "primarily instinctive, and secondarily acquired through experience."[10]

The highlight of the conference was the address by William N. DeBerry, minister of the St. John's Congregational Church in Springfield, Massachusetts. DeBerry was invited to speak because his congregation had become known nationally. A native of Tennessee who was a graduate of both Fisk and Oberlin, DeBerry had taken what was originally a temporary assignment at a small northern parish. He transformed it into an institutional church that was known as the embodiment of the black Social Gospel. Open seven days a week, St. John's provided a library, education and training classes, and clubs for hundreds of blacks in Springfield. In addition, the church owned homes and apartments to help meet the meets of people in an urban setting. The Inter-Church World Movement reported in a survey that DeBerry's church had "the most efficient system of organization and work of any church in the group surveyed, regardless of race or denomination."[11]

The title of his address, "What the Negro Wants," was taken from a story told by Frederick Douglass. When Douglass was asked, "Just what does the Negro want?" he replied, "He wants to be left alone." DeBerry observed that for that occasion the answer was both succinct and correct, but it was not correct for all times. DeBerry said that the question was being asked in a revised form today: "Just what does the educated Negro want?" The question was asked by the enemies of black education, who saw many blacks discontented with their lot in society. DeBerry then gave his own answer: "The educated Negro wants a man's chance; no more—and no less."[12]

But just as Douglass's answer was not finally sufficient, the same, DeBerry said, was true for his answer. It needed explanation. DeBerry broached the sensitive area of a social equality with a no and a yes. He said blacks had no desire to intrude into private circles of any kind where they were not wanted. But he pleaded for the freedom of whites to break bread with black friends without "being put under the ban of social proscription."[13]

DeBerry criticized the use of the fear of social equality in the South to curtail black "civil rights." In North and South DeBerry pleaded for a square deal in industry, for more and better schools. Appealing to ideals set forth in both the pledge of allegiance and Constitution, DeBerry said that blacks simply wanted the same opportunities being given to Greek, Italian, and Russian immigrants. "To withhold this is unjust, unfair, unworthy, and tyrannical."[14]

A week after the conference, Edmund F. Merriam, managing editor of the Baptist *Watchman-Examiner*, wrote, "It is the only occasion of which I know when the subject [of the race problem] was discussed with frankness, fairness, and from every point of view."[15]

Within a year after beginning the Sagamore Conference, George W. Coleman launched another educational venture that eventually influenced thousands from all walks of life instead of the more select hundreds who gathered at Sagamore Beach. Daniel Sharpe Ford, owner of *The Youth's Companion*, had left the Boston Baptist Social Union more than a third of a million dollars for a building that would be "for the spiritual and temporal benefit of workingmen and their families."[16] After a visit to the Cooper Union in New York, Coleman, then president of the Baptist Social Union, was convinced that the new Ford Hall could be well used. The plan was to begin a series of Sunday night meetings that could appeal to people outside the churches, especially working people, but with a definite Christian emphasis.

The first program of the Ford Hall Forum was presented in February 1908. For the first year or two the future of the venture was uncertain. Working people and immigrants did not respond in large numbers, both groups being outside the orbit of normal Baptist circles. The tide turned in November, when four ministers representing four different denominations spoke on socialism, and 1,500 people had to be turned away.

Now there was a more serious problem. This kind of meeting only increased the suspicions already harbored by many Baptists about the content of the Ford Hall meetings. Through this difficult period Coleman received strong support from Walter Rauschenbusch and the influential Baptist periodical the *Watchman-Examiner*. At this time there were suggestions that Ford Hall go it alone, apart from church auspices. To have followed this suggestion, however, would have been to abandon Coleman's basic premise in beginning the project. As Coleman said in

1915, "The Open Forum idea as developed at Ford Hall has come out of the heart of the church." Reflecting on the value of the meetings, he stated, "It is my conviction now that whatever service we have rendered to the people who have gathered there Sunday nights for eight seasons, our chief contribution has come from the reaction of our work on the life of the churches." Coleman was underscoring his desire that there be two-way traffic. He wanted church support, but he hoped that the ideas generated at the forum programs could be fed back into the life and ministry of the churches.[17]

Coleman believed deeply in the centrality of the church, but he wished to expand its definition and role. He was certain he knew why the church was experiencing difficulties in urban areas.

> A too-narrow interpretation of the simple gospel to the neglect of a more ample unfolding of the whole gospel may be responsible in large part for the increase of the flock that is outside the fold. It is certainly emphatically true that thousands who are unwilling to listen to a gospel of the future life embedded in terms of sectarianism, are hungering and thirsting mightily for a gospel of righteousness for this present life.[18]

A gospel of justice and righteousness was central to the programming of the Ford Hall Forum. Approximately one-half of the speakers during the first eight seasons were ministers, the large majority of them advocates of a Social Gospel. The usual program included a prayer and hymns, as well as popular and patriotic music. The speaker was given one hour for his presentation, and one hour was reserved for discussion.

The subject of race, especially "the Negro question," was the subject of many forums. In 1911 W. E. B. Du Bois addressed a meeting on the subject "The World Problem of the Colored Line," and everyone who wanted to attend could not be accommodated. He spoke again in 1920 to another overflow audience. Mary Church Terrell, the first president of the National Association of Colored Women, spoke on "Uncle Sam and the Sons of Ham" in 1914. Divergent points of view were presented by such white speakers as John Haynes Holmes, Rabbi Stephen S. Wise, Stanton Coit, a pioneer in social settlement work, and Samuel S. Mitchell, a southern moderate who was president of the University of South Carolina.[19]

A statistic emerges in summarizing the programming for the first years of the Ford Hall Forum. A cataloguing of the various topics presented during the first eight seasons shows that the comprehensive heading "Race Problems" was treated more often (19 percent) than any other topic, with the exception of the more general topic "Religion and the Church."[20]

The phenomenon of reform-minded people working outside of the churches to achieve specific reform agendas was also occurring in the South. The Southern Sociological Congress was called into being in 1912 by Governor Ben W. Hooper of Tennessee at the urging of Kate Bernard, the progressive commissioner of charities and corrections of Oklahoma.[21] Modeled after the National Conference of Charities and Corrections, the first executive committee was made up of social workers in Nashville. The organizers conceived of the Southern Sociological Congress's task as "to bring together the representative people from the entire South interested in social welfare for the purpose of studying and improving the social, civic, and economic conditions of the South."[22]

The first congress met in Nashville in May 1912. Over one thousand delegates from twenty-eight states attended the four days of addresses and discussions on such topics as child welfare, courts and prisons, public health, education, social work, and the church and social service. One of the planks of the "Social Program of the Congress" adopted at Nashville stated that the SSC stood for "the solving of the race question in a spirit of helpfulness to the Negro, and of equal justice to both races."[23]

From the outset, the section of the congress dealing with race problems attracted the greatest number of delegates.[24] James H. Dillard, director of the Jeanes and Slater funds and past president of Tulane University, was chairman of the standing committee on "Negro Problems." Other members of the committee included John D. Hammond, Bishop Wilbur P. Thirkield, Hollis B. Frissell, Bishop Walter R. Lambuth, George A. Gates, and Willis D. Weatherford.

Eleven addresses were delivered in the section meetings, six by whites and five by blacks. Between 250 and 400 people attended the sessions, about half of them black. Black visitors sat on the same floor with whites, but in separate sections.

Where race is concerned, actions are ultimately of more importance than words. A dramatic incident in 1914 put to the test the words of the first two congresses. Willis D. Weatherford, as chairman of the Committee on Organization, became embroiled in a controversy involving black delegates and visitors to the annual meeting in Memphis. The National Conference of Charities and Corrections was meeting in Memphis at the same time. On the first evening of joint meetings at the

Orpheum Theater, blacks were not segregated in the usual manner but sat on the main floor with the white delegates. The next morning a group of Memphis businessmen protested against this arrangement to the owner of the theater and to the two organizations. At the next night's meetings, at the direction of the National Conference of Charities and Corrections, blacks were strictly segregated and as a consequence walked out. The following morning, Weatherford stated that blacks would not be segregated at the evening meeting. The local committee and the owner of the theatre, however, would not agree to this arrangement. Weatherford thereupon moved the evening session to the First Methodist Church. The meeting was subsequently attended by the largest gathering of the congress. This action won for Weatherford new friends in the black community.[25]

The congress had no direct connection to the churches, but church people were much in evidence at congress sessions. As Weatherford said at Houston in 1915, "The members of the Southern Sociological Congress are members of the churches, and it is mainly through the churches that they have received their social impulse and training."[26] James E. McCullough, the general secretary of the SSC, was a Methodist minister who had been involved in student work. For a time he was president of the Methodist Training School in Nashville and was currently general secretary of the American Interchurch College for Religious and Social Workers. In regard to social issues, he had a reputation for being one of the most liberal southern Methodist leaders.[27] McCullough had been frustrated by the church's inability to move more vigorously in the area of reform, and so "he began to move outside the organization in order to accomplish his objectives." McCullough was one of those responsible for inviting northern Social Gospel leaders to address this southern forum. These speakers included Walter Rauschenbusch, Samuel Zane Batten, Charles S. Macfarland, Florence Kelley, Charles R. Henderson, and Graham Taylor. A religious tone was so prominent at these meetings that some of the delegates complained that the congress was "too damned pious." There was, to be sure, an official congress "Battle Hymn," sung to the tune of "Tipperary."[28]

Southern white speakers at the annual sections on race included Methodist leaders Lily H. Hammond and John L. Hammond, YMCA leaders Weatherford and Arcadius M. Trawick, Episcopal bishop Theodore D. Bratton of Mississippi, as well as William L. Poteat, president of Wake Forest College. Poteat was one of the few progressive leaders in the Southern Baptist Convention. In 1913 he was elected the first chairman of the newly organized Social Service Commission of the convention.[29]

The SSC consistently included blacks within its program to a degree unprecedented in the South. In 1915 McCullough stated that there were 220 black members.[30] Black speakers included George E. Haynes, Richard R. Wright, Booker T. Washington, and Robert R. Moton.

For its leadership on racial reform the Southern Sociological Congress received the commendation of Ray Stannard Baker. Writing an article in 1916 entitled "Gathering Clouds along the Color Line," Baker outlined why "discontent and unrest" among blacks had been growing in the last two years. He noted that Uncle Sam "no longer appears as a friend"—a not too veiled reference to the black disappointment with the Wilson administration. Baker also criticized increasing segregation, discrimination in education, and the lack of criticism of the movie *Birth of a Nation*. All of such examples added up to an "unwillingness to do justice to the Negro." The major bright spot for this northern journalist was a new generation in the South. He singled out Weatherford and the Southern Sociological Congress for particular praise. Commenting on the Southern Sociological Congress in Atlanta, he said that these meetings were "the most impressive discussion of the Negro question ever held in the South."[31]

Baker was right in his assessment. Isolation is a perennial problem confronting reformers, especially in a task such as racial reform, which challenges the basic attitudes and structures of society. In the civil rights years, organizations such as the Southern Christian Leadership Conference acted as clearinghouse, information center, and command post, thus counteracting forces that continually wanted to isolate and defeat the civil rights movement. The annual meeting of the Southern Sociological Congress was much more than a place to hear addresses. It was a place to exchange information and to plan new strategies. New organizations emerged from the congress meetings. The first was the Commission of Southern Universities on the Race Question. This commission, under the leadership of James H. Dillard, with members drawn from eleven southern state universities, sought to effect a more enlightened attitude to race relations among white college students.[32] The SSC thus became the major rallying center in the South for racial reform. E. Charles Chatfield is correct in his assessment: "Through the Congress the social gospel was propagated in the South [and] interest was stimulated in social problems and racial relations."[33]

After 1915 the SSC embarked on a public health crusade. Blacks were included within this concern, but this limited focus was detrimental to discussion and action on so many other timely aspects of the race question. In 1916 the headquarters of the SSC was moved to Washington, D.C., in an effort to make the organization more truly national. In

1919 a new sectional Southwestern Sociological Congress was formed but never really got off the ground. By 1920 the SSC was no longer an important vehicle for whites and blacks interested in race problems. A major reason for this was the formation in 1919 of a new, more thoroughly progressive organization, focusing solely on race relations.

World War I proved to be a liberating experience for many young American black soldiers. In Europe they found themselves entertained in white homes. Conversing with whites in this setting was a whole new experience. They had been sent by their country "to make the world safe for democracy," but on both sides of the Atlantic they began to wonder out loud about the democracy they were experiencing back home. At home a violent race riot erupted in the first war summer in 1917 in East St. Louis, Illinois, just two days before the fourth of July. The casualties included at least thirty-nine blacks and nine whites. In response, the NAACP, under the leadership of Hutchins C. Bishop, minister of the St. Philip's Episcopal Church, staged a "silent protest" parade down Fifth Avenue in New York City. Some of the signs asked, "Mr. President, why not make America safe for democracy?"[34] On the other side of the Atlantic, the enthusiastic patriotism of blacks had met segregation in the armed forces at every turn. This experience only made their reception by some white Europeans all the more eye-opening. The question in their conversations was, How could blacks continue to accept second-class citizenship in the land that proudly pledged "liberty and justice for all"?

This same question was being asked by Willis D. Weatherford. During the First World War, while still a YMCA student secretary, Weatherford aided in the program of the War Work Council of the YMCA. As part of his efforts, he initiated a school at the Blue Ridge conference center in North Carolina to help train secretaries for work among the armed forces. The eighth session of the school was concluding when the armistice was signed in 1918. On the day after the armistice, Weatherford spoke with one of the faculty members, L. William Messer, a YMCA leader from Chicago, about the difficulties that blacks would encounter upon returning home from Europe. Weatherford knew from his contacts with blacks that they were being welcomed by whites in Europe. He knew their aspirations and understood that they would not be content with the racial patterns existing in the American democracy.[35] Weatherford invited Will W. Alexander, a young Methodist minister who had joined the War Work Council Staff in 1917, to join the conversations.

The outgrowth of the discussion was that Weatherford and Alexander gathered a small group of whites together at the Georgian Terrace Hotel in Atlanta in January 1919. The group included Wallace Buttrick of the General Education Board; James H. Dillard, director of the Slater and Jeanes funds; John J. Eagan, an Atlanta industrialist; M. Ashby Jones, a Baptist minister in Atlanta; and Richard H. King, who served on the War Work Council also.[36] The idea that emerged from the meeting was to put together quickly a staff of two men—one white and one black—for each state in the South. These leaders would bring people together in cities and towns, in churches and schools, to discuss ways to improve race relations at the local level. The money to finance this initial program came from a $75,000 grant from the War Work Council and from funds provided by Eagen. Anticipating an urgent situation, working within the machinery of the YMCA, the Commission on Interracial Cooperation was born.[37] Over the next twenty years, it became a leading force for change in the South. In the 1940s it evolved into the Southern Regional Council, broadening its base and its concerns.

A Methodist minister and a Presbyterian layman led the way for the Commission on Interracial Cooperation. Will W. Alexander became the director of the CIC and remained at this post for the life of the organization. For Alexander the CIC was the way to live out ministry in the marketplace. By family influence, his life had always seemed to be directed toward the Methodist ministry. Born and raised in rural Missouri, after theological studies at Vanderbilt he accepted a call to become the pastor of the Belmont Methodist Church in Nashville.[38]

The Belmont Church was a white-collar congregation, but Alexander soon made friends in the working-class section of Nashville, In the winter of 1914 a recession hit the South, triggered by the collapse of the cotton market. Unemployment rolls lengthened. In this particularly cold winter, a printer had opened his back room to some of the unemployed. Alexander found himself stopping every afternoon to talk with them. When it came time for the annual Christmas sermon at the Belmont Church, instead of talking exclusively about Bethlehem in the first century, he talked about these men with no place to go in the twentieth century. As he told the congregation about these urgent human needs, a very unusual thing happened. Someone in the congregation called out in the midst of the sermon, "What do you want us to do about it?" After a moment's hesitation, Alexander told his people about a loan fund that John Wesley had used to help the needy. Before he left the church that day, Alexander received over $1,500. The man who spoke out was Willis D. Weatherford.[39]

By the end of the week, Alexander was in the midst of a community-wide appeal that increased the fund to over $30,000. As Alexander dispensed these monies from the headquarters near the working-class neighborhoods, blacks as well as whites came to receive aid. Southern custom should have dictated setting up a separate entrance or line for blacks, but Alexander treated each race equally. "I didn't know any better than to do by the Negroes just as I did by the whites."[40]

In 1916, as part of the regular reassignment of Methodist ministers, Alexander moved to Murfreesboro to the First Methodist Church. As in Nashville, his concern for blacks—their homes, playgrounds, schools, and position before the courts—often aroused opposition in his own congregation. In 1917 Alexander accepted an invitation from John R. Mott and Weatherford to join the War Work Council. He did so, however, with a sense of discouragement over these experiences with race in his parish work. "They wanted me to love the Lord, but they didn't want me to love any Negro children."[41]

Under Alexander's direction, the work of the Commission on Interracial Cooperation proceeded quickly. By July 1919 it was reported that meetings had been held in 452 counties in the South. Of these conferences, 106 had included whites and blacks sitting down together to share information and concerns.

To aid in training leaders, Weatherford conducted schools for whites at Blue Ridge, and Alexander held schools for blacks at Gammon Theological Seminary in Atlanta. More than eight hundred whites and five hundred blacks were reached through these training sessions. These meetings served both to gather information about racial conditions in the South and to discuss the immediate problem of working with returning black soldiers.

A strength, and later a weakness, of the Commission on Interracial Cooperation was that it had no ordered strategy. Blacks and whites did not have to say yes or no to a program. They were encouraged simply to talk together. This first step, however, was a big one in 1919. As Alexander said, "We had no philosophy about the ultimate solution of the race problem, but we discovered that here was a method of getting from here on a little further and it would work."[42]

Within the first year of its organizational life, the CIC struggled with the question of black representation on what was in effect the executive committee. In July 1919 a consultation was held with Robert Russa Moton, Booker T. Washington's successor at Tuskegee, and Robert Elijah Jones, Methodist minister and editor of the *Southwestern Christian Advocate*. Both were invited to become permanent members. Moton and

Jones weighed the merits of the invitation for several weeks, in part a reflection of the present feelings between blacks and whites in the South, before deciding to accept. Moton had never forgotten Weatherford's courageous action in challenging segregation at the Southern Sociological Congress meeting in Memphis. At meetings in June 1920 at least twenty-one blacks were present, even though most were not members of the executive committee.[43]

In the first year as director of the Commission on Interracial Cooperation, Alexander was still on salary from the YMCA. In these early years, Alexander continually looked for inspiration and help from John R. Mott and various associates in the YMCA. Of the other early leaders, all were either ministers or associated with religious work. Richard H. King, a YMCA secretary, had been the principal of the YMCA summer school at Blue Ridge in 1919. He was the first director of the CIC but quickly gave way to Alexander, remaining a vice-president and serving for many years as chairman of the executive committee. M. Ashby Jones was pastor of the Ponce de Leon Avenue Baptist Church in Atlanta. Within the Southern Baptist orbit, he was known for his social concern and has been described as "a recognized and outspoken exponent of applied Christianity." John J. Eagen, the first chairman of the Commission on Interracial Cooperation, had been a member of both the executive and finance committees of the War Work Council. He was a member of the International Committee of the YMCA. A loyal Presbyterian, he was an "ardent supporter financially and otherwise" of the Federal Council of Churches and was committed to an ecumenical approach to both church and society.[44]

The career of Eagen, so important to the early success of the CIC, is an especially powerful model of the Social Gospel. His life story transcends many stereotypes and is the story of the transformation of a southern layman who was a powerful industrialist. At the beginning of the CIC, Eagen contributed much of the funds to start up the organization. In his business he personified Social Gospel ideals. He tried to live out the ethics of the kingdom of God in employer-employee relations. He introduced profit sharing into the American Cast Iron Pipe Company in Birmingham. He went as far as to ask employees to help set company policy.

A methodological question that has been present throughout this study, heightened perhaps by reference to a layperson, is how is it possible to claim a Social Gospel orientation as a rationale for a specific agenda for reform. In Eagen's case, the evidence is multiple and clear. Will Alexander tells of walking home with Eagen one afternoon when

the conversation turned to a specific social issue. Alexander says that
the mild-mannered Eagen expressed "an opinion that was so radical in
terms of the conventional atmosphere in which he had grown up" that
Alexander asked him where he got his present ideas. Eagen responded
by telling of a visit of Josiah Strong to Atlanta. Strong stayed in the
Eagen home and made a tremendous impression on the young man.
"He interpreted Christianity in terms that I had never heard, emphasizing the social implications as the central thing in the Christian ethics."
The friendship of Strong and Eagen grew through the years.[45] Strong
sent his Atlanta friend many books on the Social Gospel.

Eagen tried to put these ideas to work in all his ventures. He practiced them in his church, Central Presbyterian in Atlanta, where he
served as a deacon, elder, and, from 1900 to 1920, superintendent of
the Sunday school. Under his leadership, the Sunday school grew from
250 to a membership of 1,500. Eagen continually urged the members
take the lessons of the Bible and the Christian education classes into
fields of social service. His own social service endeavors found him as
one of the organizers of the Christian Council of Atlanta, founding
president of the Prison Association of Georgia, and chairman of the
board of the Berry Schools, established for underprivileged children in
the back country near Rome, Georgia. He led an attack to transform the
red-light district in Atlanta, a campaign characterized by compassion
and rehabilitation for those caught in the network of prostitution and
crime.[46]

Throughout his life Eagen had been a friend of blacks, and in the
last years of his life the organization of the Commission on Interracial
Cooperation consumed much of his energies. His involvement in the
CIC heightened his awareness of the racism practiced by whites in the
South. Dr. Isaac Fisher of Fisk University tells of a conversation in
which Eagen asked him, "Why don't all of you hate us?" On the other
hand, after an early meeting of the CIC in Ashville, moved by a strong
speech of a black woman appealing for a Christian attack on the race
issue, Eagen said to a friend, "We have in this thing an instrument for
remaking race relations in the South and for bringing the Kingdom of
God." After surveying "the real desires of the Negro," Eagen listed the
goals of the Commission on Interracial Cooperation as follows:

1. Justice before the law, to include prevention of lynching and other denials of legal justice to the Negro.
2. Adequate educational facilities.
3. Sanitary housing and living conditions.

4. Recreational facilities.
5. Economic justice.
6. Equality of traveling facilities.[47]

The Commission on Interracial Cooperation, committed to changing public opinion and in some instances public policy, decided to make its primary target the church members of the South. Morton Sosna, in his study *In Search of the Silent South: Southern Liberals and the Race Issue*, is struck by the use of the words *Christ* and *Christian* ten times in a first CIC declaration of principle of but a few hundred words.[48] The directorate was composed of church leaders, and the CIC directed much of its initial appeal to church people of the South. To catch the direction of this appeal, it is worth hearing this resolution from early 1920 in its entirety.

> We, the members of the Inter-racial Committee, firmly convinced that the promotion of the best interests of the Negro race and the improvement of race relationships are fundamentally and primarily a religious task and that every phase of the situation must be met in a spirit of justice, righteousness and brotherly love, definitely commit ourselves to the policy and plan of enlisting the cooperation of all religious organizations and while, therefore, we seek the cooperation of all agencies and organizations—business, social, education—we especially appeal to all pastors of all denominations to interpret to their congregations the religious aspects of this question, and to all church boards and assemblies to have in mind always what may be done to promote better relationships between the races.[49]

This resolution, which became the basis of an appeal, says a great deal about both the ideas of the organizers and their understanding of the role of the churches. For several decades white southerners had been saying privately and publicly that they were tired of talking about the race issue. Now along comes the CIC with a plan to get people talking at every level of society.

To give organizational muscle to the appeal, a "Christian Leaders Conference on Inter-Racial Cooperation" was convened at Blue Ridge in August 1920. Seventy persons from twelve states and representing fifteen denominations attended. Although primarily a southern venture, these leaders came from both sides of the Mason-Dixon Line. The official *Minutes* of the CIC recorded in optimistic tones the import of the conference. "For the first time in their history, representatives from Southern and Northern denominations sat face to face in the presentation of this great home mission task."[50] Alexander, Weatherford, Jones, and Bishop Theodore D. Bratton, Episcopal bishop of Mississippi, were among the representatives of the CIC. Out of this conference came "An Appeal to the Christian People of the South." At the outset, the signers reaffirmed their fidelity to "the best traditions and the convictions of the south, and especially to the principle of racial integrity." (All appeals in the South needed to begin with a word of reassurance.) The appeal went on, however, to delineate areas that needed to be discussed by local organizations: lynching, justice in the courts (including the formation of legal aid societies), traveling facilities (no issue was taken with separate facilities), housing, and education. In addition, there were four specific suggestions aimed at religious organizations:

1. Encouragement for ministers to teach on interracial issues.
2. Support for CIC policies.
3. Formation of local committees.
4. Initiation of studies by denominations.[51]

The CIC leaders realized that there was a long way to go in enrolling church leaders in a new venture in race relations. But representatives within the churches, especially the southern Methodist and Presbyterian churches, indicated a desire to cooperate.[52] The cooperation included financial commitment to the new movement. It is worth noting the extent to which the early funding of the CIC came from both the YMCA and the churches. In 1919 and 1920 the YMCA, working through the War Work Council, gave the CIC $445,000. In 1921 the figure was $150,000. The Methodist Episcopal Church, South (to which Alexander and Weatherford belonged), made the most significant contribution among the churches, but sizable gifts were made also by the American Missionary Association, the Presbyterian Church, U.S.A., and the Council of Women for Home Missions.[53]

The efforts of church women to work alongside the Commission on Interracial Cooperation is a remarkable episode in the first years of the organization. Although the CIC had discussed the need for the involvement of women, it was a group of Methodist women who took the initiative in setting in motion actions that would lead to a women's division within the CIC. The momentum from nearly two decades of concern for racial reform was evident in the annual meeting of the Women's Missionary Council of the Southern Methodist Church meeting in April 1920 in Kansas City. Belle H. Bennett, president of the council, spoke of the "tense situation" that had developed between the races and challenged the assembled women to work in church and community to bring some amelioration to the situation. Will Alexander had been invited to the meetings, and he encouraged the women to set up a standing committee to study the "New Negro." One result of these meetings was a series of resolutions, the first of which stated that "as Christian workers in God's Kingdom, we accept His challenge to show forth His power to settle racial differences, thereby setting forth before the whole world an example of the power of Christianity to meet inter-racial crises everywhere."[54] Another resolution authorized the setting up of a Commission on Racial Relationships mandated both to study the dimensions of racial relationships and to suggest avenues for co-operation for the purpose of bringing about better conditions.

This new commission was invited by Alexander to send represen-tatives to the next meeting of the executive committee of the CIC. Lily H. Hammond and Carrie Parks Johnson were two of three women in attendance. At this June meeting, plans were laid for a conference of white church women in the South. Funded by the CIC but planned by the Methodist women under the leadership of Johnson, this conference took place on October 6 and 7 in Memphis. Nearly one hundred women were in attendance, representing all of the major denominations as well as the YWCA. Highlighting the program were addresses by four black women—Margaret Murray Washington (Mrs. Booker T. Washington), Elizabeth Ross Haynes (Mrs. George E. Haynes), Jennie Dee Moton (Mrs. Robert R. Moton), and Charlotte Hawkins Brown. Will Alexander was present, and he later described the electric feeling when the black women first entered the room. One white woman rose, followed by the others, someone began to sing "Bless Be the Tie That Binds," and tears where shed by almost everyone.[55]

These southern white Methodist women took the initiative, with Alexander offering counsel along the way. He knew from his own ex-perience what happens when blacks and whites begin talking with each other. Following up on his suggestions, two members of the newly formed Methodist Women's Commission attended the biennial session of the National Association of Colored Women's Clubs. Johnson summed up her impressions: "I have had a new world opened to me, a world I had never conceived before, a world of which I had never dreamed." She added, "I saw these colored women, graduates of great institutions of learning. . . . I saw women of education, culture and refinement. I had lived in the South all my life, but I didn't know such as these lived in the land."[56]

The long-term result of various conversations and conferences was that women, both white and black, became a part of the CIC. In 1921

Johnson joined the staff as the first director of women's work and continued in that capacity until 1924. She was succeeded by Mrs. Jessie Daniel Ames.

"The Church Outside the Churches" moved back and forth freely from church to secular structures. Men and women within the churches often gravitated to secular reform organizations because they experienced greater freedom to pursue their goals. Less often, the lessons learned in these organizations were plowed back into more traditional church structures.

Many lessons were learned in the early years of the southern experiment called the Commission on Interracial Cooperation. These lessons bore fruit in an even larger, ecumenical commitment to race relations. This fascinating story brings us to the Federal Council of Churches.

CHAPTER 15

Ecumenical Race Relations

A close observation of opinion among all classes of Negroes discloses a
slowly increasing spirit of resistance to injustice and mistreatment.
—GEORGE E. HAYNES

Most of us are ready to condemn race prejudice in the abstract.
However, more energy has been spent in the condemnation of race
prejudice in the abstract than finding ways by which race prejudice can
be supplanted by racial appreciation and goodwill.
—WILL ALEXANDER

The culmination of the institutional acceptance of the Social Gospel
within the mainstream of American Protestantism occurred with the
organization of the Federal Council of Churches of Christ in America
in 1908. The Federal Council was the climax of many unitive forces in
the nineteenth century. But it was also the culmination of the crescendo
of the Social Gospel's pervasive influence. The historian of the Federal
Council of Churches spoke of the birth of the council thus: "On the one
hand it established church federation on a recognized and national basis
and on the other hand it gave official ecclesiastical form to the Social
Gospel."[1]

Standing immediately behind the Federal Council was The Open
and Institutional Church League, organized by various leaders within
social Christianity in 1894, and the National Federation of Churches
and Christian workers, founded in 1900. The latter organization viewed
itself as the forerunner of a federation of churches. At an Inter-Church
Conference on Federation held in 1905, plans were drawn up for what
became the Federal Council of Churches.[2]

The Federal Council of Churches did not distinguish itself in its first
years by its concern for blacks or for race relations. Black churches were
admitted into membership in the Federal Council from the beginning,
but black leaders did not play a prominent role in its organization. At
the Inter-Church Conference on Federation of 1905, no blacks served
on an executive committee of fourteen. Four addresses were delivered

on the topic "A United Church and the Social Order," but none of these touched upon the race question. W. B. Derrick, a bishop in the African Methodist Episcopal Church, spoke on "The Work of Evangelization among Negroes." Derrick, an advocate of a Social Gospel, reminded his listeners of a vocal minority within the black community who were highly critical of the churches because of the failure to be more courageous in the pursuit of civil rights. But the burden of his remarks on this occasion was to assert that blacks would continue to support the church as the primary institution in their life together.[3]

When the Federal Council was organized at Philadelphia in 1908, the same pattern of limited participation by blacks persisted. Every denomination was allotted a certain number of delegates according to the denomination's size, but individual blacks were not given major leadership roles. At Philadelphia, a Commission on the Church and Social Service was organized. Its membership included most of the leading Social Gospelers—Walter Rauschenbusch, Josiah Strong, Graham Taylor, Samuel Zane Batten, and Shailer Mathews. Frank Mason North, executive secretary of the Methodist New York City Extension and Missionary Society, was elected chairman. Charles Stelzle, secretary of the Presbyterian department of church and labor, supervised the daily work of the commission as a voluntary secretary. Congregationalist Charles S. Macfarland was named secretary on a full-time basis in 1911. Also in that year Washington Gladden and William Hayes Ward were added to the commission. It was not until 1912 that Bishop Alexander Walters became the first black member.

One of the most lasting accomplishments of the Commission on the Church and Social Service was the hammering out of the "Social Creed of the Churches." Revised and broadened from an original creed formulated by Frank Mason North and the Methodist church, the Social Creed of the Churches was adopted at the Federal Council quadrennial session of 1912 and continued unmodified until 1932. Ten of the sixteen points dealt with conditions affecting the well-being of laboring men and women. Several points emphasized justice for all persons, but there was no specific mention of the race question.[4]

The Federal Council's serious involvement in the race question followed the organization of the Committee on the Work of the Negro Churches in 1916. A white man, missionary educator and bishop Wilbur P. Thirkield, served as the first chairman. Three prominent blacks, all identified with the Social Gospel—Bishop Alexander Walters, Henry H. Proctor, and Richard R. Wright, Jr.—served on the committee of seven.[5] The first report of the committee, delivered at the St. Louis quadrennial in 1916, precipitated a heated discussion. In speaking about lynching, a white delegate mentioned the provocation of black attacks on white women. A black delegate quickly responded, raising the problem of the safety of Negro women from white assault. After angry words the blacks withdrew to caucus, and order was restored only after considerable effort.[6]

It was the new situation created by the American entrance into the First World War that drew the Federal Council into the midst of race relations. More than 350,000 blacks served in the armed forces, but their service was in accord with the patterns of segregation so deeply ingrained in American society. In September 1917 the War-Time Commission of the Federal Council asked the Committee on Negro Churches to study the needs of these Negro troops. The committee responded with recommendations that included the urgency of recruiting black chaplains for black troops as well as a series of other proposals to promote the general welfare of black personnel. The War-Time Commission adopted the proposals and appointed a special Committee on the Welfare of Negro Troops. By early 1918 the Committee on Negro Churches and the Committee on the Welfare of Negro Troops were in effect merged.[7]

The new enlarged Committee on the Welfare of the Negro Troops included among its members black leaders John Hope, Thomas Jesse Jones, and Robert R. Moton. White leaders included James H. Dillard, M. Ashby Jones, George Foster Peabody, and Robert E. Speer. In February 1918 the committee appointed Charles Williams, physical director at Hampton Institute, as field secretary. During the spring and summer months, Williams and Thirkield visited the camps and adjacent communities where black troops were stationed. Williams's reports were forwarded not only to the Federal Council committee but to the War Department.[8]

In August the committee met to hear the Williams report. Williams detailed the consistent degrading presence of segregation that dogged the black soldier wherever he went. The physical facilities for black troops were almost always inferior to those enjoyed by white troops. Recreational facilities in the South were segregated or nonexistent for black troops. Prostitution was allowed to flourish in black sections of adjacent communities. Of the more than 350,000 blacks serving in the armed forces, almost half of them were in noncombat units, most of them serving as stevedores. These men thus received no military training. Engaged in every conceivable kind of labor, these men made a valuable contribution to the war effort that was seldom recognized. The churches, black and white, did little to help the situation, and within the military there was a continued scarcity of black chaplains.[9]

A good portion of the report covered matters over which the Federal Council exercised little control. The committee therefore asked the War-Time Commission to arrange a meeting with the War Department. In late September the committee's recommendations were presented to the assistant secretary of the War Department, Frederick P. Keppel. The presentation was made by M. Ashby Jones, white Baptist minister from Atlanta. The conference was cordial, but the report was a strong protest against discriminatory practices against black troops. Keppel did not directly oppose any of the recommendations but offered in explanation for the present situation a defense of segregation heard so often: These problems "could be solved in time, but in the meantime it is necessary to organize an army rapidly."[10]

In less than two months the war was over. The committee continued to work in behalf of black troops into 1919. To its credit, the Committee on the Welfare of Negro Troops carried its concern for blacks to the federal government as well as to numerous camps and communities. Even more important, this special wartime committee helped to pave the way for a permanent Commission on the Church and Race Relations within the Federal Council of Churches.

In June 1921 the Federal Council of Churches organized the Commission on the Church and Race Relations. Coming into being thirteen years after the founding of the Federal Council itself, the time lag reflected both the problem of earlier indifference and a growing consciousness about racism in the churches in the aftermath of World War I. Race riots erupted across the nation in the summer of 1919. The worst occurred in Chicago, but riots also broke out in Washington, D.C.; Longview, Texas; Omaha, Nebraska; and Knoxville, Tennessee. The rioting was more widespread than in 1917, sending a shock wave through the nation.[11] Many churches, sensitized to the race question through their participation in the Federal Council's efforts to assist black personnel serving in World War I, were alerted to a clear and present danger that all was not well on the home front.

More than one hundred white and black church leaders were appointed to assist in the work of the new commission. In announcing the creation of the commission, the Federal Council stated, "'There is no force so great,' said Victor Hugo, 'as that of an idea whose hour has come.' The idea that friendly and effective cooperation between the white and colored races is really practicable is one whose hour has clearly come."[12]

The first meeting of the Commission on Negro Churches and Race Relations was called to order in Washington, D.C., on July 12, 1921, by Robert E. Speer, president of the Federal Council. Speer characterized the problem of race relations as "the most difficult of mankind and as presenting the most searching test of our Christian ideals and principles." Speer, a layman who was president of the Board of Foreign Missions of the northern Presbyterian church, was much interested in the race question both in the United States and around the world. He told the assembled gathering that in approaching the theory of race relations it was important to start from the twin foundations of "God as the common Father of all" and "humanity as an organ." Each of these foundations was an encouragement to "think of ourselves as all bound together in one bundle of life." Speer has often been remembered as an evangelical missionary statesman, claimed by those on the conservative side of the theological spectrum. But he really was an evangelical Social Gospeler who represented a determination to proclaim a gospel that was both individual and social. He was just now working on a book on race relations that would be a milestone in this transitional period.[13]

The Federal Council, Speer suggested, had a crucial role to play in dealing with the national problem of race relations. Representing the life of the churches, both black and white, the Federal Council "ought to afford a central meeting place for all the agencies dealing with various phases of race relations." Speer's vision was carried through in the future direction of the commission. In reading through minutes and reports, one is struck by the intention to cooperate with the Commission on Interracial Cooperation, the NAACP, the Urban League, the YMCA, the YWCA, and other organizations.[14]

In attempting to understand the impetus for the Federal Council's program for race relations, we must remember that back of the Commission on Race Relations stood the Commission on Interracial Cooperation. The example of the Atlanta-based CIC, chronicled in the last chapter, is a critical linkage in comprehending the goals and direction of the new commission. Fully one-third of those invited to the initial meeting of the Commission on Race Relations were also members of the Commission on Interracial Cooperation.

When Speer concluded his opening remarks, he introduced the person chosen to be the first chairman of the commission, John J. Eagen. This southern Presbyterian layman was currently chairman of the Commission on Interracial Cooperation. Eagen chaired the Federal Council

Commission until his untimely death in the spring of 1924. The minutes of the council are filled in its first years with words of appreciation and respect for this industrialist who epitomized the Social Gospel in business and labor.

Eagen introduced Will W. Alexander, the director of the Commission on Interracial Cooperation, who spoke to the new commission on the work of the CIC. M. Ashby Jones, one of the original inner circle of the CIC, also became deeply involved in the Federal Council commission. As chairman of both commissions, Eagen reported to a board meeting of the CIC that the Federal Council was "so impressed by our meeting here last March that they have organized a Commission."[15]

In two reports to the Federal Council in 1921, the newly created Commission on the Church and Race Relations leaned heavily upon the experience of the CIC. The first meeting of the commission was held in July. One of the nine purposes agreed upon was "to make more widely known in the Churches the work and principles of the Commission on Inter-Racial Cooperation." Meeting again in November, the commission consolidated these nine purposes into three main tasks. First, there was to be concerted efforts to bring the leaders of the churches of both races together in conferences that could lead to cooperation in local communities. Second, a publicity campaign was to be mounted concerning "the Christian ideal in race relations," experience in racial cooperation, the achievements of blacks, prevention of mob violence, and so forth. Finally, there would be the effort to make the churches more effective advocates of better race relations, with specific attention to "equitable provision" for health, housing, and other aspects of community welfare.[16]

The commission planned to operate with one white and one black secretary, "objectifying as clearly as possible the ideal of racial cooperation." The white secretary elected was Will Alexander, southern Methodist minister and director of the CIC. He served in this capacity without salary until 1931. It was understood from the beginning that Alexander's primary responsibility would continue to be with the CIC. The black secretary elected was George E. Haynes, Congregational layman and a founder and director of the Urban League. Haynes was the day-by-day director of the commission. The major initiatives of the commission in future years would be under Haynes's leadership. In 1934 he became executive secretary, a position he held until his retirement in 1947.[17]

George E. Haynes was the heart, soul, and mind of the commission. He had been uniquely prepared for this position in which he served for a quarter of a century. When Haynes graduated from Fisk in 1903, he was qualified to be part of Du Bois's "talented tenth." Already a poised and intellectual young man in his bearing, Haynes never forgot his rural roots in post-Reconstruction Arkansas.[18]

In 1903 Haynes entered Yale University to pursue a master's degree. Yale was not a particularly open-handed place for blacks in those years. But Haynes found a hospitable teacher in William Graham Sumner. Through Sumner's classes and conversations in the professor's home, Haynes experienced a "conversion" to the relatively new discipline of sociology (Sumner referred to it as societology). Haynes later credited Sumner with teaching him a "method of dispassionate analysis, classification, comparison and inductive conclusions in the field of human affairs."[19] This social science method was working its way into the ministries of many Social Gospel reformers. None learned it better than Haynes.

One idea taught by Sumner proved important to Haynes in his later work in interracial cooperation. Sumner believed that social groups respond to both pleasurable and unpleasurable experiences. The experiences of one group or generation can "become habitual and regulated and take on the nature of a social force for other groups and succeeding generations."[20] Haynes understood far more than his teacher the possibilities of pleasurable experiences in the arena of race relations. What was crucial was creating possibilities for interracial cooperation that could hold the promise of becoming a social force that in turn would become habitual in the life of a people.

Haynes received his M.A. from Yale in June 1904. Some of Haynes's teachers and friends encouraged him to become a minister. During his year at Yale Haynes was active in the Dixwell Avenue Congregational Church in New Haven. Not certain of the direction to take, he decided to explore the ministry by enrolling in Yale Divinity School.

His studies were interrupted in February 1905, when fire consumed a section of Hot Springs, Arkansas, including his family home. He hurried home to find his mother living in a tent. At his mother's urging he returned to Yale to finish his studies for the year. But now his younger sister Byrdie needed financial help to be able to enter Fisk's preparatory school. He felt he needed to give up school for gainful employment.

Right at this time Haynes was offered a job with the Colored Men's Division of the YMCA. After a summer pastorate at a mission Congregational church at Haverhill, Massachusetts, he reported to the Colored Men's Division headquarters in Atlanta on September 1. He joined the senior secretary, William A. Hunton, and his associate, Jesse E. Moorland, at a time of great growth in the YMCA.

Haynes credited his association with his two colleagues as critical in developing his sense of Christian ministry and in affirming his skills in interracial cooperation. Hunton, a graduate of Wilberforce Institute of Ontario, began his service with the YMCA in 1888 and became secretary of the Colored Men's Department in 1890. He served in that capacity until his death in 1914.[21] Moorland, valedictorian of his class at Howard University, joined the YMCA staff in 1901 and served as secretary of the International Committee for the Colored Men's Department from 1902 until 1924. He consigned to Howard University his private library on slavery and the Negro in Africa, known today as the Moorland Collection.[22]

Haynes's task for the YMCA was to be the liaison between the college and city associations and the division office. He endured the Jim Crow regulations in his constant travel. Despite many problems Haynes testified that he "found evidence of the Holy Spirit in the enlarged vision and greater efficiency of my work, and as a beginner in Christ's work for the world I could not have hoped for better companionship and guidance."[23]

Shortly after Haynes began work with Hunton and Moorland, the three were invited by Willis D. Weatherford, the white YMCA secretary working with college students in the South, to meet together to consider "what might be done to improve the feeling and thinking in the direction of race relations in the South." After several meetings the group encouraged Weatherford to write a study guide, which was eventually published in 1910 as *Negro Life in the South*. Haynes was enthusiastic about the project and commented a quarter century later that "this initial effort in interracial understanding helped to produce a number of liberal leaders of thought in the white South today."[24]

Haynes left the YMCA in 1908 to enroll in the graduate school of Columbia University. Grateful for his experiences with the YMCA, he was resolute in his determination to pursue studies in sociology. In his work Haynes was influenced from several directions. He acknowledged the groundbreaking work of W. E. B. Du Bois's study *The Philadelphia Negro*. His own efforts focused on the economic aspects of the problems of black migration, especially employment. His concern for interracial cooperation was uppermost on his mind, for he believed that the coming employment crisis would be "fundamental to the relations of whites and Negroes in America."[25]

While at Columbia Haynes did some of his work at the New York School of Philanthropy. In the years at the turn of the century, philanthropy was changing its focus from individuals to social systems. As urban and industrial problems exploded in exponential growth, the older social-service model of working with individuals was proving inadequate. In line with the new sociology, philanthropy was seeking to discover underlying causes for social problems. Haynes was an apt learner was was influenced as much by his work at the School of Philanthropy as by his studies at Columbia.

While still in the midst of his graduate work, Haynes became the first director of the Urban League in 1910. Concurrently he pursued his career as a sociologist by founding the department of sociology at Fisk. This period in his life was chronicled briefly in the earlier chapter on the Urban League. It is of interest to add that Haynes was always moving out of the classroom as a reformer. Thus at Fisk he persuaded the Woman's Missionary Council of the Methodist Episcopal Church, South, to fund a social center in a nearby black neighborhood. Bethlehem House became Haynes's laboratory where he could train black social workers. Always with an eye on the changing character of urban, industrial America, Haynes was convinced that both black colleges and the Urban League ought to be training black social workers for the new situation that was beckoning. Although there were scattered courses in sociology offered, Haynes wanted Fisk to be the leader in the training of a cadre of social workers.[26]

At this time Haynes's vision exceeded Fisk's vision. President George Gates was not sure what to make of his young entrepreneurial assistant professor. Haynes was advised to consult with the American Missionary Association, which still was the largest source of Fisk's funding. As it turned out, the AMA official Haynes consulted was Harlan Paul Douglass. Douglass, sympathetic by his own training to Haynes's goals, was impressed by Haynes's "unusual preparation." Douglass counseled the Fisk president to follow Haynes's suggestions.[27]

The black migration that Haynes predicted and the outbreak of World War I soon created another job opportunity for the Fisk sociologist. In 1900 only about 10 percent of blacks lived in the North. Between 1900 and 1910 almost 200,000 blacks migrated from the South. As America prepared to enter the Great War, migration surged into the hundreds of thousands annually. This wave of migration suddenly caught the attention of various officials in Washington.

Secretary of Labor William B. Wilson was concerned about the labor force in the new wartime effort. As a part of his concern he created the position of director of Negro economics. On May 1, 1918, Haynes was sworn in as director. Haynes was soon off on a tour of cities to discover firsthand the problems of black workers. In July Haynes spoke and listened at a special session of the Southern Sociological Congress attended by seventy-five blacks and two hundred whites. After his first six months in office, there were in place almost 225 Negro Workers' Advisory Committees in eleven states.[28]

Much of the impetus for the program was fueled by wartime concerns. With the war over and budget trimming setting in, Haynes's department became expendable. It continued through the Wilson presidency, but with the inauguration of the Republican Warren G. Harding as the twenty-ninth president in 1921, Haynes was soon out of a job.

As it turned out, the political termination that came with a change of party in the White House opened a much larger door for Haynes. Some time has been taken to tell the story of his varied experiences in graduate school, at the Urban League, at Fisk, and at the Labor Department, because no one could have been better prepared to lead the new Commission on Race Relations just being formed by the Federal Council of Churches.

If the Federal Council was slow to act on the race question, when action finally came, it was prodded by persons long active on many fronts in the struggle for racial reform. In September 1919 the Home Missions Council convened a special committee of blacks and whites that drafted a report to the Federal Council. Chaired by Bishop Wilbur Thirkield and consisting of Haynes, Dr. James Dillard of the Jeanes-Slater Fund, Dr. Robert Jones, editor of the *Southern Christian Advocate*, Professor Kelly Miller, and philanthropist George Foster Peabody, the report was part confession. "We must confess that the Church and its Ministry as related to the welfare of the Negro has been too little inspired by the fundamental principles and ideals of Jesus Christ."[29]

Haynes was invited to speak about the report at the biennial meeting of the Federal Council in Boston in 1920. In a pronouncement entitled "A Crisis in Democracy," the Federal Council placed the race issue within the context of the mandate of the Christian faith for brotherhood. At the same meeting the president of the Federal Council, Robert E. Speer, called a meeting of leading white and black church leaders to meet in Washington, D.C., in July 1921. A Commission on the Church and Race Relations was finally to be organized.

In Haynes's first months as director he launched a whirlwind of activities and projects. All of his previous training came into play. With the Commission on Interracial Cooperation taking responsibility for most of the work in the South, Haynes turned much of his attention to the Midwest. It was to the cities of the upper Midwest that blacks from the South were coming in staggering numbers. A few examples tell the story (see table 5).

Haynes visited various midwestern cities and returned with systematic reports on conditions affecting blacks and black-white reactions. After a trip to Minneapolis he filed a typical report. Working with local colleagues, Haynes listed four sources of his study.[30]

1. Visits to 173 businesses.
2. Home-to-home visits to 150 families. In the visits to the families Haynes wanted to ascertain:
   A. Composition of family
   B. Housing conditions
   C. Connections with agencies and organizations of the city
3. Tabulation of information about 150 families under the care of Family Welfare Association
4. A study of population figures, including:

	Total Population	Black Population
1890	166,092	1,354
1900	252,718	1,584
1910	298,672	2,592
1920	376,665	3,927

All through these years Haynes kept informing the commission of the latest figures on black migration from the South. At one board meeting he reminded them that migration figures from 1910 to 1920 averaged 35,000 per year, whereas from October 1922 through September 1923, the estimate was between 200,000 and 300,000.

At the same time that studies of local conditions were being initiated, the commission's basic strategy was to begin local interracial com-

Table 5. Black Population of Some Midwestern Cities

City	Black Population in 1910	Black Population in 1920	% Increase
Chicago	44,103	109,894	149.5
Cincinnati	19,639	29,636	50.9
Detroit	5,741	41,532	623.4
Gary, Ind.	383	5,299	1283.6

Source: Samuel Kelton Roberts, "Crucible for a Vision: The Work of George Edmund Haynes and the Commission on Race Relations, 1922–1947" (Ph.D. dissertation, Columbia University, 1974), Appendix A, 263.

mittees. Sometimes such a committees came into existence as a response to a local crisis. Whether it was Chicago or Johnstown, Pennsylvania, the Federal Council offered its resources in getting whites and blacks to start talking with each other. As the idea of the interracial committees caught on, communities started them without being precipitated by overt conflict or crisis. Often a conference on race relations would be held, sometimes sponsored by the local council of churches, and out of that forum would develop an interracial committee.

In all of this rush of activity, Haynes was not simply a bureaucratic organizer. His own ideas about interracial cooperation were energizing the activities of the commission. While serving briefly with the Interchurch World Movement in 1919, Haynes had been commissioned to conduct a survey of black churches and their involvement in interracial affairs. When the Interchurch World Movement collapsed, the Council of Women for Home Missions and the Missionary Education Movement of the United States and Canada asked Haynes to expand his survey into a book that could be used by study groups. He thus authored *The Trend of the Races*, which was published originally in 1920. The book sold over 60,000 copies within the first year. But now that Haynes was the director of the commission, the sales and use of the book rapidly expanded. In 1922 sales totaled almost 600,000 copies.[31]

Haynes's commitment to interracial cooperation is the thesis of the book. He traced the foundation of interracial cooperation, paying tribute especially to two southern organizations, the Southern Sociological Congress and the Commission on Interracial Cooperation.

In a chapter entitled "We Face the Future," Haynes surveyed three schools of Negro thought. He began with the left wing, wherein he talked about socialism and the Marcus Garvey movement. He described the persons of the center movement as the spiritual descendants of the abolitionists. They believed in protest and agitation. The prime example here was the NAACP. The examples he used for the right wing were Tuskegee and Hampton.[32] Even though Booker T. Washington had died in 1915, the right wing was epitomized by the continuing Washingtonian philosophy.

Haynes declared that the objectives of the center and the right did not differ. Both sought full justice, manhood rights, and equal opportunities. The difference was in strategy. The right wing was too ready to settle for amelioration. Because of this strategy Haynes said that the right wing was having difficulty maintaining its influence. It was being pressured from the other two wings. This pressure was exacerbated by the response of the white majority. "The tardy response of the

white world in removing some of the outstanding ills and allowing Negroes to share in those advantages which make the name of America
a synonym for opportunity." Haynes gave voice to a question
many were asking: What is the mood of blacks at the present moment?
His answer: "A close observation of opinion among all classes of Negroes discloses a slowly increasing spirit of resistance to injustice
and mistreatment."[33]

From his office in New York Haynes initiated many programs to
combat the rising spiral of racism. The most well known was Race Relations Sunday. Begun as an experiment on the Sunday nearest Lincoln's birthday in February 1923, Race Relations Sunday became an
annual event that epitomized much of Haynes's sociology and strategy.
The underlying assumption of his work was that "racial attitudes have
their basis in painful or pleasurable experiences arising through the
contact of individuals" and groups.[34] In diverse cities across America—
Chattanooga, Chicago, Little Rock, Los Angeles, Muskegon (Michigan),
and New Orleans—the pattern for the first observance of Race Relations
Sunday was basically the same. Black and white pastors exchanged
pulpits. "Pleasurable contacts" were initiated. The responses from pastors and congregations were overwhelmingly positive.[35]

In preparation for Race Relations Sunday in 1924, materials were
mailed to churches from the New York offices that in this second year
gave more direction and content. Suggestions were made for sermons
and special addresses. Examples included "The Application of the Ideal
of Christian Brotherhood in Race Relations" and "The Opportunity of
the Church for Promoting Better Race Relations in America." A poem
by the young Joseph R. Cotter, Jr., appeared in many bulletins that
year and in succeeding years.

> Brother, come!
> And let us go unto our God.
> And when we stand before Him
> I shall say—
> "Lord, I do not hate,
> I am hated.
> I scourge no one,
> I am scourged.
> I covet no lands,
> My lands are coveted.
> I mock no peoples,
> My people are mocked."
> And, brother, what shall you say?[36]

It is within the scope of our story to look only at the first five years of Haynes's twenty-five-year career with the Commission on the Church and Race Relations. Both an intellectual and an organizer, Haynes and his career must not be too easily depicted. It is worthwhile asking where Haynes would put himself in his description of the three wings of black thought.

We know that he did not think of himself as part of the left wing. But on one occasion at a board meeting of the commission he defended Marcus Garvey in the face of what he deemed to be unfair criticism. Haynes, who knew both rural and urban blacks, understood well the frustrations that propelled the left-wing movements.

Haynes has often been grouped with the right wing of Washington-ians. He sometimes spoke out against an overzealous militancy of the left wing. Haynes had a deep respect for Booker T. Washington, whom he wanted on the board of the Urban League. Washington was finally elected, but only months before his death in 1915. But Haynes became increasingly disenchanted with Washington's "passive acceptance of in-justice and caste distinction." Furthermore, he did not believe Washing-ton's philosophy was suited to the situation of urban blacks.[37]

Haynes saw himself as part of the broad center party. He believed the center could embrace both the NAACP and the Urban League. He saw himself as a moderate, not a militant. He struggled with the tem-perament and strategies of W. E. B. Du Bois. An intellectual like Du Bois, Haynes was a gentle man who worked hard at listening to the other person's point of view. He almost always took an optimistic atti-tude toward life and its problems. Bothered by Du Bois's intellectual arrogance, he gave him his due as a leader of the race. Appreciative of the NAACP's strategy of agitation through the legislative and judicial processes, Haynes's direction first of the Urban League and then of the Commission on Race Relations attempted to work through conciliation and persuasion.

Haynes always took a long-term view of race relations, which some-times left him open to criticism from more militant blacks. For example, in 1924 the Federal Council held its quadrennial meeting for the first time in the South. John J. Eagen was in part responsible for the invita-tion to Atlanta. He assured the council that at the downtown Presby-terian church where he served as an elder the meetings would not be segregated. Eagen delivered on his promise. But for large public wor-ship service on Sunday, a larger space was needed, and the city audi-torium was secured. Despite vigorous negotiations, the city would not relent in its public policy, and this meeting was segregated. Nearly all of the local black religious and civic leaders boycotted the service, but Haynes attended. It was his policy to work from within, but in this instance he chose a path different than that followed by his local black colleagues.[38]

At the same time, Haynes referred to himself on numerous occasions as a spiritual descendent of the abolitionists. As a representative of all the churches, he saw himself in a different position than if he were simply a leader of movement for racial reform. He believed it was his responsibility to listen. He saw himself as a mediator between differing theologies and strategies.

His sociological approach, with its attention to systems as well as individuals, puts him "within the Social Gospel movement." In writing to Moorland some years after he left the YMCA, Haynes wanted his old friend to be assured "that the Bible and prayer are still a part of my routine." But in commenting on "my religious development," Haynes said that he was now inclined "less toward discussion and more toward a burning desire to act." He summed up his present focus by saying, "In a word, the doing of Christ's will and the bringing of His Kingdom are becoming more and more a practical everyday matter."[39]

Haynes's major strategy for bringing in the kingdom in his calling was interracial cooperation. The highlight of the effort of the early years of the Commission on the Church and Race Relations was the first National Interracial Conference, held in Cincinnati in March 1925. The conference was the culmination of all of the work to establish local and state committees. A total of 114 black and 102 white delegates gathered, representing local and regional interracial committees and such organizations as the YMCA, YWCA, Urban League, and various social and mission agencies of the churches. Under the umbrella of race relations there were sessions on education, housing, health, the press, social agencies, judicial processes, and the church.

Will Alexander addressed the conference and reminded the delegates: "Most of us are ready to condemn race prejudice in the abstract. However, more energy has been spent in the condemnation of race prejudice in the abstract than finding ways by which race prejudice can be supplanted by racial appreciation and goodwill."[40]

Sherwood Eddy, missionary evangelist of the YMCA, spoke to the race issue from the perspective of his twenty-nine years abroad. Eddy, who had been converted to the Social Gospel in the early 1920s, had become its leading advocate within YMCA circles.[41] He told the delegates, "America leads the world in race prejudice." He used lynching as an example, observing that "we are the only country that descends to this disgraceful, this pathetic barbarism." Eddy's counsel was to go beyond mere ameliorism. "I believe in full equality of race treatment; I believe in one unbroken brotherhood."[42]

If many of the remarks were hortatory, it was left to Haynes to put the whole interracial movement into historical perspective. He began with an overview of the trajectory of segregation. He pinpointed 1890 as the beginning of segregation and reminded his listeners that in that year housing was not segregated in Memphis, Nashville, Atlanta, or Louisville. He focused on the experiences of World War I as that time when "we awoke to some of the possibilities of this segregation, some of its sad tragedies."[43]

But the conference was not just recitation of the past. It was meant to be an affirmation of what is possible in the tried and true method of blacks and whites sitting down to listen and to talk with each other. The culmination of Haynes's remarks was a story he told often. It concerned the early days of the Commission on Interracial Cooperation in Atlanta. A group of white men asked a group of black men to come and meet with them. The blacks came, "rather suspicious, not knowing what the white men wanted." When they discovered that they simply wanted to meet and talk about the racial situation in the community, the black men arose, with tears running down their cheeks. "Gentlemen, you have already done the greatest thing that you could do in helping the situation. You have come to confer with us as men and ask us to join hands with you in meeting it."[44]

This first national interracial conference ended in a spirit of celebration. There was little dissension among the delegates. From the historian's perspective the observation must be made that for many of those assembled the act of talking together was an end in itself. Later leaders looked back and asked if that end was enough or if it could have been the platform for more vigorous action. It should not be minimized, however, that there was now in place a structure to deal with race relations at the national level. Building on the model of the Commission on Interracial Cooperation, networked in numerous local and regional committees, the commission became both a national forum and organization. In both the Federal Council of Churches as well as its successor, the National Council of Churches, the Commission on the Church and Race Relations became a prophetic catalyst in keeping the race issue before the churches in the decades before the rise of the modern civil rights movement.

Epilogue

A young, Baptist student enrolled in Crozer Theological Seminary in the fall of 1948. Only nineteen, the son of a black Baptist minister, he was a graduate of Morehouse College in Atlanta. Now he came north for his seminary training. At this Baptist seminary in Chester, Pennsylvania, the seminarian recorded an experience at the beginning of his theological education. "I came early to Walter Rauschenbusch's *Christianity and the Social Crisis*, which left an indelible imprint on my thinking by giving me a theological basis for the social concern which had already grown up in me as a result of my early experiences."[1] Within seven years Martin Luther King, Jr., would become the leader of a civil rights movement that captured the attention of the whole world. Known to many today mainly as a reformer, King saw himself as the son of a black Baptist minister who walked self-consciously in the tradition of the Social Gospel.

Less than two years later, on April 4, 1950, Justice Robert H. Jackson was pondering the segregation cases then pending before the Supreme Court. He wrote to friends in Jamestown, New York, about his wonder at encountering the name of Albion W. Tourgée, once a resident of nearby Mayville. Jackson had gone over Tourgée's old brief in the *Plessy* v. *Ferguson* case, decided by the court in 1896. Jackson was struck again by Tourgée's oft-repeated metaphor: "Justice is pictured blind, and her daughter, the Law, ought at least to be color-blind." With the segregation cases soon to be argued in the Supreme Court, Jackson mused, "Tourgée's brief was filed April 6, 1896, and now, just fifty-four years after, the question is again being argued whether his position will be adopted and what was a defeat for him in '96 be a post-mortem victory."[2]

Within four years Jackson's question would be answered. In *Brown* v. *Board of Education of Topeka*, the Supreme Court struck down the "separate but equal" holding of *Plessy* v. *Ferguson*. In that historic moment a lawyer for the winning side was Charles Sheldon Scott. His father, Elisha, was the most famous alumnus of the school in Tennesseetown founded by Charles M. Sheldon. Sheldon took a particular interest in Elisha Scott, who named his son after the author of *In His Steps*. Elisha Scott became a leading attorney in Topeka, as did his sons, John Scott and Charles Sheldon Scott. The Scott family persists in arguing civil rights cases today.[3]

One of the ironies of American life is that as a people we often suffer from historical amnesia. We do not remember the past. In preparing this book, I have been told again and again that our culture does not believe in precedent. The precedents of Rauschenbusch, Tourgée, and Sheldon could be multiplied, but in an epilogue these examples can only be suggestive. This book has been offered in the conviction that in continuing to confront the central American dilemma of race, we need desperately to know the past as we attempt to chart the future.

By the early 1920s the momentum of the Social Gospel was slowing. The voices of its foremost leaders—Washington Gladden, Walter Rauschenbusch, Lyman Abbott, and Josiah Strong—were all stilled between 1916 and 1922. The climate of opinion in the country was changing. The political achievements of the progressive movement under Theodore Roosevelt and Woodrow Wilson now seemed in disarray, to be supplanted by the politics of "normalcy" of Warren G. Harding and Calvin Coolidge. The wave of nationalism that crested in World War I now engulfed the nation in a tide of negative crusades—the Ku Klux Klan, the Red Scare, and anti-immigration legislation—all of which meant a far-reaching attack on civil liberties.

In the days of its maturity, the Social Gospel brought to bear on a whole cluster of problems in American society the belief that men and women were by God's design brothers and sisters and should move toward living out their relationships with each other in love and justice. This book has tried to make clear that for many leaders of the Social Gospel, racial reform was a serious part of this social justice crusade. While for many it was never the central focus of their attention, nonetheless it was a significant issue to which they devoted time and energy. This was true for such well-known leaders as Lyman Abbott, Washington Gladden, Henry C. Potter, Reverdy D. Ransom, Charles M. Sheldon, and Alexander Walters. In addition to the major figures, there was an even larger number not heretofore included in the histories of the Social Gospel for whom racial reform was a major concern. This list

includes Will Alexander, Harlan Paul Douglass, John J. Eagen, Francis
J. Grimké, Lily H. Hammond, George E. Haynes, John Haynes Holmes,
Edgar Gardner Murphy, Henry Hugh Proctor, Wilbur P. Thirkield,
Albion Winegar Tourgée, Arcadius M. Trawick, William Hayes Ward,
and Willis D. Weatherford.

The above list includes white and black, pastors and laypersons, all
working for racial reform. A large number of these leaders were southern born and based. A significant contingent were laypersons. Many of
the most vocal black leaders, such as a Francis J. Grimké, were leaders
in predominantly white denominations. The pervasiveness of racism
meant that these particular black ministers usually adopted a prophetic
stance on race early in their careers. Women played a larger and larger
role as the movement for racial reform gathered momentum in the early
twentieth century.

Many advocates of the Social Gospel worked as reformers outside
of denominational structures. Frustrated by the lack of action in their
respective churches, ministers participated in all manner of organizations in the Progressive Era. Because the persons who advocated a Social Gospel believed that the kingdom of God was taking shape in every
corner of the world, they were free to affirm the struggle for racial
justice wherever they found it taking place. The opportunity to work
for improvements in race relations came through such organizations as
the Commission on Interracial Cooperation, the NAACP, the Southern
Sociological Congress, and the Urban League.

A central discovery in this story has been what I have called the
missionary education bridge. In charting the pilgrimage of northern
leaders, again and again the road led south. Traveling south to teach,
pastor, or serve as trustees at black colleges, they were taught in the
schoolhouse of race. When the surge of migration began to bring blacks
north in the second decade of this century, the Social Gospel leaders
most ready to respond were those who had learned valuable lessons
via the missionary bridge.

The leaders of the Social Gospel were divided among themselves
about solutions to the race problem. This considerable division should
not obscure the more important reality that the issue was discussed and
debated. Lyman Abbott, by the first years of the twentieth century, had
retreated from earlier, more egalitarian beliefs. He utilized the pages of
the *Outlook* to support Booker T. Washington, publish his own platform
on the Negro question, and criticize W. E. B. Du Bois and the Niagara
Movement. His good friend Washington Gladden, on the other hand,

moved from accommodation to reform. After meeting W. E. B. Du Bois and reading *The Souls of Black Folk,* Gladden changed his mind about Washington and the priorities for racial reform.

A major reason for deciding to tell the story in largely narrative form was to capture the sense of how many persons related to the Social Gospel changed their minds in these years. The misreading of the Social Gospel on race has been due to historians' casting these leaders in the concrete of their own words at a particular moment and letting them stay there. Many of the addresses or sermons on racial reform either were never published or were given insufficient recognition, either in their own Progressive Era or by the first generation of historians of the Social Gospel. The prevailing climate of opinion usually dictates what is deemed important.

Until recently the neglect of the black Social Gospel has obscured from our vision important leaders, addresses, and strategies. Much work still needs to be done in this area. This oversight is being redressed, but there is still neglect of the role of black women.[4]

It is possible to criticize the Social Gospel from many vantage points. Martin Luther King, Jr., critiqued Rauschenbusch for his "superficial optimism concerning man's nature."[5] A young Reinhold Niebuhr, after a visit to Europe in 1923, came home disillusioned with the results of the Versailles Peace Treaty. Commenting about Woodrow Wilson, the son of a Presbyterian minister, he observed tartly that Wilson "trusted too much in words."[6] Niebuhr's critique can be applied to the ministers of the Social Gospel in their struggle for "liberty and justice for all." Not only did they trust in the words of sermons and addresses, they trusted in the whole gospel of education. The enterprise of education is based on the presupposition that ideas and words can change actions. The "Christian realism" of Reinhold Niebuhr and others, suspicious of liberalism's faith in reason, would argue for a more tough-minded approach to social change.

But it is hard to be too critical of the Social Gospel for not realizing that racism is a cancer in the very soul of American society. Racism changes its name from slavery to caste to Jim Crow to segregation, but still it persists. The Social Gospel, through bitter experience, moved inexorably toward strategies of agitation that focused in organizations such as the NAACP. Even as the Social Gospel led an advance in social strategy from charity to social action, just so its leaders came to emphasize change through the legislative and judicial processes in order to alter the structures that sanctioned racism.

It is daunting to recognize that race is such a timeless issue in America. It admits to no easy solution. We still struggle to come to terms with the centrality of race for the meaning of our civic and Christian creeds and constitutions. But in another sense it is a timely issue. At the beginning of this half century of the story, it was almost always spoken of as "the Negro question." We now see the issue, we may hope, in much larger perspective. Some in our story foreshadowed a different vantage point. Albion Winegar Tourgée thundered at Lake Mohonk, "So far as the peaceful and Christian solution of the race problem is concerned, indeed, I am inclined to think that the only education required is that of the *white* race."[7] The education required is about a race problem that is now seen to be white and black.

And what of the future? In the spring of 1963, Martin Luther King, Jr., was in the midst of the battle for Birmingham. Surveying all that had happened across the South he wrote of his encouragement that black ministers, "with a growing awareness that the true witness of a Christian life is the projection of a social gospel," were joining the struggle for racial justice. In April 1963, in the face of determined opposition, King attempted to rally both blacks and whites to the cause of racial reform. As only he could he plunged into a speaking campaign to business, labor, religious, and social groups of all kinds. In a crucial meeting he addressed two hundred ministers. King, recounting this and similar meetings, said he always began at the same place: "I stressed the need for a social gospel."[8]

Concern for individuals is important, but the pioneers of the Social Gospel discovered that even compassion is not enough in a rapidly changing and complex American society. Love and justice must march hand in hand if we shall overcome. In conclusion there is the appeal to learn from individuals, and movements, and organizations that deserve to be known as part of the lineage of the civil rights movement that needs to be continued in our time. However the future story of racial reform will unfold there will be a continuing need for a Social Gospel.

Appendix

Persons Related to the Social Gospel, 1877–1925

Name	Birth/Death	Denomination	Reform Work	Primary Places of Service
Abbott, Lyman	1835–1922	Congregational	Pastor, Editor, Black Education, Trustee	New York City, Brooklyn
Addams, Jane	1860–1935	Presbyterian	Settlement House	Chicago
Alexander, Will W.	1884–1956	Methodist, N.	Pastor, CIC	Nashville, Atlanta
Ames, Jessie Daniel	1883–1972	Methodist, S.	Women's Suffrage, CIC	Texas, Atlanta
Anderson, Matthew	1848–1928	Presbyterian	Pastor, Institutional Church, Urban League Philanthropist	Philadelphia
Baldwin, Ruth S.	1865–1934		Urban League	New York City
Baldwin, William H., Jr.	1827–1911	Unitarian	Philanthropist, Urban League	New York City, South
Behrends, A. J. F.	1839–1900	Congregational	Pastor, AMA	Providence, Brooklyn
Bennett, Belle H.	1852–1922	Methodist, S.	Methodist Women's Missionary Council	Kentucky, Tennessee
Bishop, Hutchins C.	1858–19 ?	Episcopal	Pastor, NAACP	New York City

AMA = American Missionary Association
CIC = Commission on Interracial Cooperation
Commission on Race Relations was a part of the Federal Council of Churches.
Trustee = a member of the Board of Trustees of a Black College
WSCF = World's Student Christian Federation

Persons Related to the Social Gospel, 1877–1925 *(Continued)*

Name	Birth/Death	Denomination	Reform Work	Primary Places of Service
Bishop, Samuel H.	1864–1914	Episcopal	Black Education Urban League	New York City, South
Bowen, John W. E.	1855–1933	Methodist, N.	Seminary Professor, Pastor	Atlanta
Bradford, Amory H.	1846–1911	Congregational	Pastor, AMA, Trustee	Montclair, NJ
Bratton, Theodore D.	1862–19 ?	Episcopal	Pastor, Bishop, Black Education	North Carolina, South Carolina, Mississippi
Brooks, William H.	1859–1923	Episcopal	Pastor, Urban League, YMCA	New York City
Buttrick, Wallace	1853–1926	Baptist, N.	Black Education, General Education Board	New York City
Cable, George W.	1844–1925	Presbyterian, Congregational	Author	New Orleans, Northampton
Coleman, George W.	1867–19 ?	Baptist, N.	Ford Hall Forum, Sagamore Sociological Conference	Boston
Crummel, Alexander	1819–1898	Episcopal	Missionary Educator,	Africa, Washington, D.C.
Curry, Jabez L. M.	1825–1903	Baptist, S.	Black Education	Virginia, Alabama
DeBerry, William N.	1870–1948	Congregational	Pastor, Institutional Church, Trustee, AMA	Springfield, Mass.

Persons Related to the Social Gospel, 1877–1925 *(Continued)*

Name	Birth/Death	Denomination	Reform Work	Primary Places of Service
Derrick, William B.	1843–1913	AME	Bishop, Federal Council of Churches	New York City
Dole, Charles F.	1845–1927	Unitarian	Pastor, Trustee	Boston
Douglass, Harlan P.	1871–1953	Congregational	AMA Executive, Trustee	South
Du Bois, W. E. B.	1868–1963	Congregational Episcopal	Professor, Editor, NAACP	Atlanta, New York
Dudley, Thomas U.	1837–1904	Episcopal	Bishop, Black Education	Kentucky
Eagen, John J.	1870–1924	Presbyterian	Industrialist, CIC, Federal Council on Race Relations	Atlanta
Edwards, Richard H.	1877–1954	Congregational	Campus Ministry	Univ. of Wisconsin
Fosdick, Harry M.	1878–1969	Baptist, N.	Pastor	New Jersey, New York City
Galloway, Charles B.	1849–1909	Methodist, S.	Bishop, Black Education	Mississippi
Gladden, Washington	1836–1918	Congregational	Pastor, AMA	Columbus, Ohio
Grimké, Archibald	1849–1930	Presbyterian	Lawyer, NAACP	Boston, Washington, D.C.
Grimké, Francis J.	1850–1937	Presbyterian	Pastor, NAACP, Trustee	Washington, D.C.
Hall, Charles C.	1852–1909	Presbyterian	Pastor, Seminary President, Trustee	Brooklyn, New York City

Persons Related to the Social Gospel, 1877–1925 (Continued)

Name	Birth/Death	Denomination	Reform Work	Primary Places of Service
Hammond, John D.	1850–19 ?	Methodist, S.	Black Education	Georgia, the South
Hammond, Lily H.	1859–1925	Methodist, S.	Black Education	Georgia, the South
Hartzell, Joseph C.	1842–1928	Methodist, N.	Black Education, Missionary, Pastor, Editor	New Orleans, Africa
Haygood, Atticus G.	1834–1896	Methodist, S.	Educator, Bishop, Black Education	Georgia
Haynes, George E.	1880–1960	Congregational	Sociologist, Urban League, Federal Council Race Relations	Nashville, New York City
Holmes, John Haynes	1879–1964	Unitarian	Pastor, NAACP, Urban League	New York City
Hunton, William A.	1863–1916		YMCA	Atlanta
Johnson, Carrie P.	1866–1929	Methodist, S.	Methodist Women's Missionary Council, CIC, Federal Council	Georgia
Jones, M. Ashby	1868–1947	Baptist, S.	CIC, Federal Council Race Relations, Trustee	Atlanta
King, Henry C.	1858–1934	Congregational	College President, NAACP	Oberlin, Ohio
Mayo, Amory Dwight	1823–1907	Unitarian	Black Education	Boston, the South

Persons Related to the Social Gospel, 1877–1925 (Continued)

Name	Birth/Death	Denomination	Reform Work	Primary Places of Service
McConnell, Samuel D.	1846–1939	Episcopal	Bishop, Pastor,	Philadelphia, Brooklyn
McCullough, James E.	1823–1907	Methodist, S.	Pastor, Educator, Southern Sociological Congress	Nashville
Miller, Kelly	1863–1939	Congregational	Professor, Sociologist, Author	Washington, D.C.
Moorland, Jesse E.	1863–1940	Congregational	YMCA, Trustee	Atlanta, Washington, D.C.
Moton, Robert R.	1867–1940	Baptist	Educator, Trustee	Virginia, Alabama
Mott, John R.	1865–1955	Methodist, N.	YMCA, WSCF	New York City
Moxom, Philip S.	1848–1923	Congregational	Pastor, AMA	Boston, Springfield, Mass.
Murphy, Edgar G.	1869–1913	Episcopal	Pastor, Black Education, Southern Education Board	Montgomery, New York City
North, Frank M.	1850–1935	Methodist, N.	Pastor, Hymn writer, NAACP	New York City
Ogden, Robert C.	1836–1913	Presbyterian	Philanthropist, Black Education, Trustee	Philadelphia, New York
Ovington, Mary W.	1865–1951	Unitarian	Social Work, NAACP	Brooklyn
Parkhurst, Charles H.	1845–1921	Presbyterian	Pastor, Trustee	New York City

Persons Related to the Social Gospel, 1877–1925 (Continued)

Name	Birth/Death	Denomination	Reform Work	Primary Places of Service
Peabody, George F.	1852–1938	Episcopal	Philanthropist, Black Education, Trustee	New York City
Peabody, Francis G.	1847–1936	Unitarian	Professor, Sociologist, Trustee	Cambridge, Mass.
Poindexter, James	1819–1907	Baptist	Pastor	Columbus, Ohio
Potter, Henry C.	1835–1908	Episcopal	Pastor, Bishop, American Colonization Society	New York City
Powell, Adam C., Sr.	1865–1953	Baptist	Pastor, Institutional Church, NAACP	New York City
Proctor, Henry H.	1868–1933	Congregational	Pastor, Institutional Church	Atlanta, Brooklyn
Ransom, Reverdy C.	1861–1959	AME	Pastor, Social Settlement, Editor	Chicago, Boston, New York
Rauschenbusch, Walter	1861–1918	Baptist, N.	Pastor, Seminary Professor, Theologian	New York City, Rochester
Sheldon, Charles M.	1857–1946	Congregational	Pastor, Author	Topeka, Kansas
Smiley, Albert K.	1828–1912	Quaker	Lake Mohonk Conferences, Trustee	New York

Persons Related to the Social Gospel, 1877–1925 (Continued)

Name	Birth/Death	Denomination	Reform Work	Primary Places of Service
Speer, Robert E.	1867–1947	Presbyterian	Missionary Secretary, Federal Council of Churches	Philadelphia
Strong, Josiah	1847–1916	Congregational	Pastor, American Institute of Social Service	New York City
Terrell, Mary Church	1863–1954		National Association of Colored Women, Women's Suffrage, NAACP	Washington, D.C.
Thirkield, Wilbur P.	1854–1936	Methodist, N.	Seminary & College President, Black Education, Bishop, Trustee	Atlanta, Nashville, Washington, D.C.
Tobias, Channing H.	1882–1961	Methodist, N.	YMCA	Georgia, Washington, D.C.
Tourgée, Albion W.	1838–1905	Methodist, N.	Author, National Citizens Rights Association, Lawyer	Greensboro, N.C., New York, Chicago
Trawick, Arcadius M.	1869–1958	Methodist, S.	Pastor, YWCA	Nashville, the South
Trawick, Maude Wilder	1875–1963	Methodist, S.	YWCA, Trustee	Nashville, the South

Persons Related to the Social Gospel, 1877–1925 (*Continued*)

Name	Birth/Death	Denomination	Reform Work	Primary Places of Service
Walters, Alexander	1858–1917	AME Zion	Pastor, Bishop, Afro-American Council, NAACP, Trustee	
Wells-Barnett, Ida B.	1862–1931	Presbyterian	Afro-American Council, Anti-Lynching League, NAACP	New York City, Chicago
Ward, William Hayes	1835–1916	Congregational	Editor, AMA	New York City
Washington, Booker T.	1856–1915	Baptist	Tuskegee President, Black Education	Alabama, Nation
Weatherford, W.D.	1875–1970	Methodist, S.	YMCA, Trustee	Nashville, the South
Wise, Stephen	1874–1949	Reform Judaism	NAACP	New York City
Wright, Richard R., Jr.	1878–1967	AME	Editor, NAACP, Trustee	Philadelphia, Chicago

Notes

Preface

1. Eric Foner, *Reconstruction: America's Unfinished Revolution, 1863–1877* (New York, 1988), 1.
2. C. Howard Hopkins, *The Rise of the Social Gospel in American Protestantism, 1865–1915* (New Haven, Conn., 1940), 3.
3. David M. Reimers, *White Protestantism and the Negro* (New York, 1965), 53.
4. George M. Fredrickson, *The Black Image in the White Mind: The Debate on Afro-American Character and Destiny, 1817–1914* (New York, 1971), 302.
5. Thomas F. Gossett, *Race: The History of an Idea in America* (New York, 1965), 197.
6. Preston M. Williams, "The Social Gospel and Race Relations: A Case Study of a Social Movement," in *Toward a Discipline of Social Ethics: Essays in Honor of Walter George Muelder,* ed. Paul Deats, Jr. (Boston, 1972), 237.
7. Robert Moats Miller, *American Protestantism and Social Issues, 1919–1939* (Chapel Hill, N.C., 1958), 9.

Introduction

1. For the standard history of the Social Gospel, see Hopkins, *Rise of the Social Gospel.* See also Henry F. May, *Protestant Churches and Industrial America* (New York, 1949); Aaron I. Abell, *The Urban Impact on American Protestantism* (Cambridge, Mass., 1943); Robert T. Handy, ed., *The Social Gospel in America* (New York, 1966); and Ronald C. White, Jr., and C. Howard Hopkins, *The Social Gospel: Religion and Reform in Changing America* (Philadelphia, 1976).
2. Carl Degler, *Out of Our Past: The Forces That Shaped Modern America* (New York, 1950), 347.
3. Shailer Mathews, "Social Gospel," in *A Dictionary of Religion and Ethics,* ed. Shailer Mathews and Gerald Birney Smith (New York, 1921), 416.
4. The indigenous character of the Social Gospel has been challenged by William R. Hutchison, "The Americanness of the Social Gospel: An Inquiry in Comparative History," *Church History* 44 (Sept. 1975): 367–81.
5. Dores Robinson Sharpe, Rauschenbusch's secretary and official biographer, says that "Beneath the Glitter" was published first in the "daily press." It was subsequently published as part of some weekly Sunday school lessons for the *Christian Inquirer,* 1887 (Sharpe does not list volume or pages); Sharpe, *Walter Rauschenbusch* (New York, 1942), 80 n. 2.

6. Reverdy C. Ransom, *The Pilgrimage of Harriet Ransom's Son* (Nashville, 1952), 49.
7. Paul Minus, *Walter Rauschenbusch: American Reformer* (New York, 1988), does an excellent job of tracing the evolution of Rauschenbusch's theology of the Social Gospel. The words from the *Baptist Congress* (New York, 1889), 55–56, are quoted on p. 68.
8. Theodore T. Munger, *The Freedom of Faith* (Boston, 1883), 25.
9. Kenneth Cauthen, *The Impact of American Religious Liberalism* (New York, 1962), 27–30.
10. Hopkins, *Rise of the Social Gospel*, 195–97; White and Hopkins, *Social Gospel*, 151–52, 167 n. 13.
11. The distinction between social concern and the Social Gospel is pointed up by William R. Hutchison, *The Modernist Impulse in American Protestantism* (Cambridge, Mass., 1976), 165 n. 36.
12. Donald K. Gorrell, *The Age of Social Responsibility: The Social Gospel in the Progressive Era, 1900–1920* (Macon, Ga., 1988), makes an impressive contribution by focusing on the institutionalization of the Social Gospel in the years 1900–1920.
13. Richard Hofstadter, *The Age of Reform* (New York, 1955), 152.

1. "The Negro Question"

1. For an excellent study of Reconstruction, See Eric Foner, *Reconstruction, America's Unfinished Revolution 1863–1877* (New York, 1988).
2. Isabel C. Barrows, ed., *First Mohonk Conference on the Negro Questiony* (Boston, 1890), 7.
3. Benjamin F. Trueblood, "Mohonk and Its Conferences," *New England Magazine* 16 (June 1897): 454, 464.
4. Larry E. Burgess, *Alfred, Albert, and Daniel Smiley: A Biography* (Redlands, Calif. 1969), 1–2.
5. Barrows, *First Mohonk Conference*, 9.
6. Philip Butcher, "George W. Cable and Booker T. Washington," *Journal of Negro Education* 17 (Fall 1948): 465–66.
7. William Hayes Ward, "A Negro Conference," *Independent* 42 (June 12, 1890): 7.
8. *Christian Union* 41 (June 12, 1890): 830.
9. Smiley to Rutherford B. Hayes, Nov. 26, 1889; Atticus G. Haygood to Hayes, May 12, 1890, Rutherford B. Hayes Papers, Hayes Memorial Library, Fremont, Ohio.
10. Barrows, *First Mohonk Conference*, 103. See also *New York Christian Advocate* 65 (May 29, 1890).
11. Barrows, *First Mohonk Conference*, 7.
12. Ibid., 25, 82.
13. Ibid., 84. Some of these same points were restated a week later in two articles in the *Christian Union* 41 (June 12, 1890): "Where Is Thy Brother?" (Editorial), 829; and "The Lake Mohonk Conference on the Negro Question," 830–32.
14. Barrows, *First Mohonk Conference*, 97.
15. Albert K. Smiley to Albion W. Tourgée, Mar. 13, 1890. Albion W. Tourgée Papers, Chautauqua County Historical Museum, Westfield, New York.
16. Otto H. Olsen, *Carpetbagger's Crusade: The Life of Albion Winegar Tourgée* (Baltimore, 1965), 307.
17. May, *Protestant Churches and Industrial America*, 207. See also Hopkins, *Rise of the Social Gospel*, 140–48.
18. As did Harriet Beecher Stowe, Tourgée published a sequel detailing specific events that stood behind the novel. His "Invisible Empire" first appeared as part 2 of *A Fool's Errand* in 1880.

19. Albion W. Tourgée, *A Fool's Errand* (New York, 1879); see also the introduction in the edition edited by John Hope Franklin (Cambridge, Mass., 1961).
20. Quoted by Tourgée in "A Bystander's Notes," *Chicago Daily Inter Ocean*, May 10, 1890.
21. Rutherford B. Hayes, Diary, June 6, 1890, Hayes Papers.
22. Barrows, *First Mohonk Conference*, 104.
23. Ibid., 106.
24. Ibid., 108, 110.
25. Ibid., 111.

2. Reappraisal in the North

1. The classic statement that the phenomenon known as Jim Crow occurred relatively late, in the 1890s and early 1900s and not earlier as many had assumed, was first set forth by C. Vann Woodward in *The Strange Career of Jim Crow* (New York, 1955).
2. The 95.5 percent for the thirty-year period 1889–1918 compares with the percentage of the black population in the South as follows: in 1890, 90.3 percent of blacks lived in the South; in 1900, 89.7 percent; in 1910, 89.0 percent; and in 1920, 85.1 percent *(Negro Population, 1790–1915)* [Washington, D.C., 1918; reprint, New York, 1968], 33; *Fourteenth Census of the United States, 1920*, vol. 2 (Washington, D.C., 1921) percentage calculated from the table on p. 19).
3. Daniel W. Crofts, "The Blair Bill and the Elections Bill: The Congressional Aftermath to Reconstruction" (Ph.D. diss., Yale University, 1968); see also Crofts, "The Black Response to the Blair Education Bill," *Journal of Southern History* 37 (Feb. 1971): 41–65. In addition, see Allen J. Going, "The South and the Blair Education Bill," *Mississippi Valley Historical Review* 44 (Sept. 1957): 267–90.
4. John A. Garraty, *Henry Cabot Lodge: A Biography* (New York, 1953), 117–25. and Rayford W. Logan, *The Betrayal of the Negro: From Rutherford B. Hayes to Woodrow Wilson* (New York, 1965), 70–75 (formerly published as *The Negro in American Life and Thought: The Nadir, 1877–1901*).
5. Louis R. Harlan, *Booker T. Washington: The Wizard of Tuskegee, 1901–1915* (New York, 1983), vii. See also Harlan, *Booker T. Washington: The Making of a Black Leader, 1856–1901* (New York, 1972).
6. Booker T. Washington, "Chapters from My Experience," *World's Work* 21 (Nov. 1910).
7. Booker T. Washington, *The Negro and the Atlanta Exposition* (Baltimore, 1896), 12.
8. Ibid., 13.
9. Ibid.
10. Ibid., 13–14.
11. Ibid., 14.
12. Quoted in Booker T. Washington, *Up from Slavery* (New York, 1901), 160.
13. *Outlook* 52 (Sept. 28, 1895); 53 (Jan. 11, 1896); *New York Christian Advocate* 70 (Sept. 26, 1895): 617; *Interior* 26 (Sept. 26., 1895): 1284.
14. *Christian Recorder*, Sept. 26, Nov. 28, 1895, cited in August Meier, *Negro Thought in America, 1880–1915* (Ann Arbor, Mich., 1963), 171, 302; *Independent* 47 (Oct. 3, 1895).
15. Walter Rauschenbusch, "Limits of Immigration," *Seventh Annual Session of the Baptist Congress* (New York, 1988), 86–87, cited in Walter Rauschenbusch, *The Righteousness of the Kingdom*, ed., Max L. Stackhouse, 33 n. 26.
16. An excellent biography is Minus's *Walter Rauschenbusch*. See also the earlier biography by Rauschenbusch's secretary, Sharpe, *Walter Rauschenbusch*.
17. See Max Stackhouse's Introduction, Walter Rauschenbusch, *The Righteousness of the Kingdom*, 14–20.
18. Ibid., 102–3.

19. Ibid., 110.

20. Unfortunately there is no published biography of Strong. After his death in 1916, Strong's daughters, Elsie and Margery, worked for decades on a biography that was never published. Various manuscripts of the biography are in the Josiah Strong Papers, the Burke Library, Union Theological Seminary, New York.

21. Josiah Strong, *Our Country* (New York, 1885), 179.

22. Ibid., 178.

23. Dorothea R. Muller, "Josiah Strong and American Nationalism: A Re-Evaluation," *Journal of American History* 53 (Dec. 1966): 487–503, discusses the stereotypical image of Strong in American history textbooks and attempts to correct these distortions.

24. For biographical information on Crummel, see Wilson Jeremiah Moses, *Alexander Crummel, A Study of Civilization and Discontent* (New York, 1989), and Henry J. Young, *Major Black Religious Leaders, 1755–1940* (Nashville, 1977), chap. 9, 110–26.

25. Josiah Strong, "Brothers and a Story," *American Missionary* 49 (Dec. 1895): 423; *Congregationalist* 80 (Oct. 31, 1895): 661.

26. Strong, "Brothers and a Story," 423–24.

27. Edwin S. Redkey, *Black Exodus: Black Nationalism and Back-to-Africa Movements, 1890–1910* (New Haven, Conn., 1969). The only histories of the American Colonization Society unfortunately stop at the Civil War or shortly thereafter. See Philip H. Staudenraus, *The African Colonization Movement, 1816–1865* (New York, 1961); and Willis D. Boyd, "Negro Colonization in the National Crisis" (Ph.D. diss., UCLA, 1953).

28. Henry Cadmon Potter, "The Laborer Not a Commodity," in *Christian Thought*, 4th ser. (New York, 1886), 289–91.

29. Hopkins, *Rise of the Social Gospel*, 150.

30. Biographies of Potter include George Hodges, *Henry Codman Potter* (New York, 1915); Harriet Keyser, *Bishop Potter: The Peoples' Friend* (New York, 1910); and James Sheering, *Henry Codman Potter* (New York, 1933). In *A Memorial to Henry Codman Potter* (New York, 1909), Booker T. Washington eulogized Potter in terms of his contributions to the welfare of blacks. A study by Curtis R. Grant, "The Social Gospel and Race" (Ph.D. diss., Stanford University, 1968), recognizes Potter as one of five central Social Gospel figures. But Grant's study is confined to Potter's published writings, and there is no mention of Potter's involvement in the American Colonization Society.

31. Redkey, *Black Exodus*, treats Turner in chaps. 2 and 8–10. Turner was known within white Protestantism but had few close ties with the major leaders of social Christianity.

32. Ibid., 99–216; *New York Christian Advocate* 67 (Mar. 3, 1892).

33. Redkey, *Black Exodus*, 217–28.

34. Henry Codman Potter, "Address" *Liberia Bulletin* 2 (Feb. 1893): 17.

35. "Future Policy of the Society," *Liberia Bulletin* 2 (Feb. 1893): 6.

36. Henry Sloane Coffin, quoted in Ira V. Brown, *Lyman Abbott: Christian Evolutionist* (Cambridge, Mass., 1953), vii. This sentiment was echoed by William Warren Sweet, who said, "No religious leader in modern American has exercised a more abiding influence than has Lyman Abbott" (*Makers of Christianity* [New York, 1937], 320).

37. Brown, *Lyman Abbott*, 100.

38. Lyman Abbott, *Reminiscences* (New York, 1915), 95–112; Brown, *Lyman Abbott*, 18–20.

39. Lyman Abbott, "The Issues and Duty of the Hour" (Sermon), *Terre Haute Weekly Express*, Sept. 17, 1862, Abbott Memorial Collection, Bowdoin College, Brunswick, Maine.

40. Ira V. Brown, "Lyman Abbott and Freedmen's Aid, 1865–1869," *Journal of Southern History* 90 (Feb. 1949): 22–38.

41. Lyman Abbott, *The Results of Emancipation in the United States* (New York, 1867), 17, 30, 33.

42. Lyman Abbott, "Equal Rights," *American Freedman* 1 (Apr. 1866): 2–3.

43. Lyman Abbott, "Southern Evangelization," *New Englander* 89 (Oct. 1864): 701.

44. *Christian Union* 41 (June 12, 1890): 829.

45. Lyman Abbott, *The Rights of Man* (New York, 1901), 224–25.

46. *Christian Union* 34 (Dec. 30, 1886): 26.

47. Ibid., 42 (July 3, 1890): 3. See also July 10, 35–36; July 31, 131; and Aug. 7, 163.

3. Beyond Accommodation to Reform

1. *Independent* 48 (Mar. 5, 1896): 315–16; James M. McPherson, "The Anti-Slavery Legacy: From Reconstruction to the NAACP," in *Towards a New Past*, ed. Barton J. Bernstein (New York, 1968), 135; *Independent* 88 (Sept. 11, 1916): 363–64.

2. William Hayes Ward, "A Negro Conference," *Independent* 42 (June 12, 1890): 814–15.

3. *Independent* 42 (June 26, 1890): 880; (July 10): 959. See also July 3, 919–20; July 17, 992. Richard E. Welch, Jr., "The Federal Elections Bill of 1890: Postscripts and Prelude," *Journal of American History* 52 (Dec. 1965): 511–26, utilizing correspondence of the bill's Senate floor leader, Senator George F. Hoar of Massachusetts, argues persuasively that the bill was more a debate on the issue of black personhood than it was an organized strategy to undermine conservative white control of politics in the South, although the latter was certainly one factor in the contest. According to Welch, the defeat of the bill "more clearly marked the acceptance of Negro subjugation than the culmination of sectional reconciliation" (p. 511) This point was made at the time in the *Independent* 42 (Sept. 4, 1890).

4. *Independent* 40 (Dec. 20, 1888).

5. Ibid. 38 (Mar. 18, 1886).

6. Ibid. 41 (May 30, 1889).

7. Ibid. 56 (May 5, 1904).

8. Ibid. 45 (Sept. 28, 1893); 48 (Oct. 8, 1896).

9. Ibid. 44 (May 19, 1892).

10. Materials about Sheldon's life and ministry are to be found in the Sheldon Memorial Room, Central Congregational Church, Topeka, Kansas. For general biographical information, see Charles M. Sheldon, *Charles M. Sheldon: His Life Story* (New York, 1925), an autobiography that is helpful in its general story line but not always accurate in specific details; and Timothy Miller, *Following In His Steps: A Biography of Charles M. Sheldon* (Knoxville, Tenn., 1987).

11. See Charles Yrigoyen, Jr., "Charles M. Sheldon: Christian Social Novelist," *Bulletin of the Congregational Library* 33 (Winter 1982): 4–16. I am grateful to the Congregational Library of the American Congregational Association for allowing me to use a version of Yrigoyen's article longer than the published one; reference is made to p. 9 of the longer version.

12. Local historian John W. Ripley has offered the best treatments of the story surrounding *In His Steps*. See "'In His Steps' on Stage and Screen," *Shawnee County Historical Society* 43 (Dec. 1966): 66–69; "Last Rites for a Few Myths," *Shawnee Country Historical Society* 44 (Autumn 1968): 1–25; and, Miller, *American Protestantism and Social Issues*, 66–102.

13. Eric F. Goldman, "Books That Changed America," *Saturday Review*, July 4, 1953, 9.

14. Wayne Elzey, "'What Would Jesus Do?': *In His Steps* and the Moral Codes of the Middle Class," *Soundings*, Winter 1975, 58.

15. Sheldon, *Charles M. Sheldon*, 82–88.

16. Ibid., 82.

17. Knowledge of Tennessetown comes from papers, programs, and pictures in the Sheldon Memorial Room. Some pictures from Tennesseetown are on display in Sheldon's backyard study, which is now in Gage Park in Topeka. See also Sheldon,

Charles M. Sheldon, 91–95; an article by Sheldon in the *Topeka Daily Capital*, Mar. 19, 1944; and Miller, *American Protestantism and Social Issues*, 46–65.

18. See Thomas C. Cox, *Blacks in Topeka, Kansas, 1865–1915* (Baton Rouge, La., 1982).

19. Charles M. Sheldon, "A Local Negro Problem," *Kingdom* vol. No. 852 (Apr. 10, 1896): 828; Editorial note, *Independent* 48 (May 1896): 655.

20. *Independent* 48 (May 1896): 655.

21. A good summary of the work is contained in Leroy A. Halbert, *Across the Way: A History of the Work of Central Church, Topeka, Kansas, in Tennesseetown* (privately printed, 1900), in Charles M. Sheldon Room, Central Congregational Church, Topeka, Kansas.

22. Halbert, *Across the Way*, 3–6.

23. Charles M. Sheldon, *The Redemption of Freetown* (Boston, 1898), 5, 22.

24. Charles M. Sheldon, *In His Steps* (Chicago, 1897); Sheldon, *Redemption of Freetown*, (Chicago, 1899) 22.

25. Sheldon, *In His Steps*,

26. Ibid., Sheldon, *Redemption of Freetown*, 37.

27. Daniel Day Williams, *The Andover Liberals* (New York, 1941); *Redemption of Freetown*, 5.

28. Charles M. Sheldon, "A Local Negro Problem," 28; Thomas C. Cox, *Blacks in Topeka*, 151.

29. *Independent* 48 (May 1896): 665.

30. Harrison Kelley to Albion W. Tourgée, Jan. 7, 1890; Joseph D. Taylor to Tourgée, Feb. 6, 1890; Feb. (n.d.) 1890, Tourgée Papers.

31. Olsen, *Carpetbagger's Crusade*, 304.

32. J. H. Jenkins to Albion W. Tourgée, Jan. 3, 1892, Tourgée Papers. Some of these letters appear in Otto H. Olsen, "Albion W. Tourgée and Negro Militants of the 1890s: A Documentary Selection," *Science and Society* 28 (Spring 1964): 183–208.

33. T. Thomas Fortune, *Black and White: Land, Labor, and Politics in the South* (New York, 1884), 83–84.

34. The Afro-American League, later called the Afro-American Council, had a very uneven existence and influence from 1887 to 1908. See Emma Lou Thornbrough, "The National Afro-American League, 1887–1908," *Journal of Southern History* 27 (Nov. 1961): 494–512. At its organizational meeting in Chicago in 1890, whites were excluded, but Tourgée sent his greetings (p. 498).

35. Ibid., 498.

36. Albion W. Tourgée to Henry M. Turner, Nov. 7, 1893, Tourgée Papers.

37. Albion W. Tourgée, "The Bystander," *Chicago Daily Inter Ocean*, Oct. 22, 1892.

38. Ida B. Wells to Albion W. Tourgée, July 2, 1892, Tourgée Papers; Ida B. Wells, *Crusade for Justice: The Autobiography of Ida B. Wells*, ed. Alfreda M. Duster (Chicago, 1970), 193.

39. Francis H. Rowley to Albion W. Tourgée, July 18, 1893, Tourgée Papers.

40. Albion W. Tourgée to Francis H. Rowley, Sept. 1893; Tourgée to R. E. Hull, n.d. [1890], Tourgée Papers.

41. Wells, *Crusade for Justice*, 120–21.

42. Albion W. Tourgée, "The Bystander," *Chicago Daily Inter Ocean*, Oct. 27, 1894.

43. Louis A. Martinet to Albion W. Tourgée, Oct. 5, 1891; Nov. 16, 1891, Tourgée Papers.

44. For a remarkable study of *Plessy v. Ferguson*, see Charles A. Lofgren, *The Plessy Case: A Legal-Historical Interpretation* (New York, 1987).

45. Ibid., 3.

46. Sidney Kaplan, "Albion W. Tourgée: Attorney for the Segregated," *Journal of Negro History* 49 (Apr. 1964): 131–32.

47. Tourgée planned to attend but was prevented by illness. Albert K. Smiley to Albion W. Tourgée, May 18, 1891, Tourgée Papers.

48. Trueblood, "Mohonk and Its Conferences," 462. Albert K. Smiley wrote to Rutherford B. Hayes on Nov. 20, 1891, informing Hayes that it was best to "omit" the

Negro conference for the next year, but he didn't say why (the letter was written by a secretary while Smiley was at his winter home in Redlands, California). Two decades later it was suggested that several other considerations were behind the decision not to reconvene after 1891: Lake Mohonk was too far for southerners to come; the conference setting was removed from the problem; and, blacks should work out their own solutions. Isabel C. Barrows, "A Moral Citadel," *Outlook*, XCVII, Mar. 25, 1911, 667–79.

4. Dissenting Voices in the South

1. Arthur S. Link, "The Progressive Movement in the South, 1870–1915," *North Carolina Historical Review* 23 (Apr. 1946): 172–95. See also C. Vann Woodward, *Origins of the New South, 1877–1913* (Baton Rouge, La., 1951), 350–455; Herbert J. Doherty, Jr., "Voices of Protest from the New South, 1875–1910," *Mississippi Valley Historical Review* 42 (June 1955): 45–66; Ann Firor Scott, "Progressive Wind from the South, 1906–1913," *Journal of Southern History* 29 (Feb. 1963): 57–70; and Jack Temple Kirby, *Darkness at the Dawning: Race and Reform in the Progressive South* (Philadelphia, 1972).

2. Woodward, *Strange Career of Jim Crow*, 91.

3. Hopkins, *Rise of the Social Gospel*; May, *Protestant Churches and Industrial America*; and Abell, *Urban Impact on American Protestants*, do not treat the South, although Hopkins does note the work of the Southern Sociological Congress. Paul A. Carter, *The Decline and Revival of the Social Gospel: Social and Political Liberalism in American Protestant Churches, 1920–1940* (Ithaca, N.Y., 1956); Miller, *American Protestants and Social Issues*; and Donald M. Meyer, *The Protestant Search for Political Realism, 1919–1941* (Berkeley, Calif., 1960), study the two decades after World War I, but even for this period there is scant attention directed toward the South.

4. John Lee Eighmy, "Religious Liberalism in the South during the Progressive Era," *Church History* 38 (Sept. 1969): 360.

5. Dewey W. Grantham, *Southern Progressivism: The Reconciliation of Progress and Tradition* (Knoxville, Tenn., 1983), 23. Grantham discusses the Social Gospel also in chap. 7, entitled "Social Justice."

6. Wayne Flint, "Dissent in Zion: Alabama Baptists and Social Issues, 1900–1915," *Journal of Southern History* 35 (Nov. 1969): 523–42; John Lee Eighmy, *Churches in Cultural Captivity: A History of the Social Attitudes of Southern Baptists* (Knoxville, Tenn., 1972); John Patrick McDowell, *The Social Gospel in the South: The Woman's Home Mission Movement in the Methodist Episcopal Church, South, 1886–1939* (Baton Rouge, La., 1982); J. Wayne Flint, "Feeding the Hungry and Ministering to the Broken Hearted: The Presbyterian Church in the United States and the Social Gospel, 1900–1920." in *Religion in the South*, ed. Charles R. Wilson (Jackson, Miss., 1985), 83–137.

7. *Proceedings of the Southern Baptist Convention, 1892* (Atlanta, 1892), Appendix A. iv.

8. *Proceedings of the Southern Baptist Convention, 1891* (Atlanta, 1891), Appendix B, xxxvi.

9. It is difficult to corroborate actions recorded at the Southern Baptist Convention or to use Baptist periodical literature to arrive at official or even representative positions. The nature of the denomination emphasized autonomy. There was no periodical of comparable standing to the Methodist *Nashville Christian Advocate*. To sort through the variety of periodicals, reliance is placed upon the research of Rufus B. Spain, *At Ease in Zion: A Social History of the Southern Baptists, 1865–1900* (Nashville, 1966). The *Religious Herald* of Richmond was sympathetic to a more active social consciousness and represented the more liberal thinking of the Upper South.

10. *Proceedings of the Southern Baptist Convention, 1895* (Atlanta, 1895), 14–16; Spain, *At Ease in Zion*, 28–29, 66; Robert Andrew Baker, *Relations between Northern and Southern Baptists* (Fort Worth, 1948), 189–90.

11. Spain, *At Ease in Zion*, 64.

12. For a superb study of a complicated story see James Melvin Washington, *Frustrated Fellowships, The Black Baptist Quest for Social Power* (Macon, Ga., 1986), 159, 179, 183.

13. H. Shelton Smith, *In His Image, But . . .* (Durham, N.C., 1972) 231, 279.

14. *Nashville Christian Advocate* 51 (Sept. 13, 1890); 53 (May 26, 1892); 56 (Aug. 15, 1895). A biography of Hoss by Isaac Patten Martin, *Elijah Embree Hoss, Ecumenical Methodist* (Nashville, 1942), like so many southern biographies written before the late fifties, includes nothing about Hoss's attitudes toward blacks, even though he commented on the race question frequently as editor of the *Nashville Christian Advocate.*

15. Elijah Embree Hoss, "Why the Difference?" *Nashville Christian Advocate* 59 (Dec. 1, 1898).

16. H. C. Reed, "The Southern Presbyterian Church and the Freedmen," *Southern Presbyterian Review* 36 (Jan. 1885): 83–108.

17. Andrew E. Murray, *Presbyterians and the Negro: A History* (Philadelphia, 1966), 150.

18. Harold W. Mann, *Atticus Greene Haygood* (Athens, Ga., 1965), 116–34.

19. Atticus Greene Haygood, *The New South: Gratitude, Amendment, Hope* (Oxford, Ga., 1880), 13; Atticus Greene Haygood Papers, Emory University, Atlanta. Haygood may have borrowed the phrase "The New South" from Grady, but Grady is reported to have said, "I lighted my torch at Haygood's flame" (Elam F. Depsy, *Atticus Greene Haygood* [Nashville, 1940], 6, quoted without citation).

20. Atticus Greene Haygood, *The New South,* ed. and with an introduction by Judson C. Ward (Atlanta, 1950), v. In addition the sermon was published in the *New York Christian Advocate* and the *Macon* (Ga.) *Wesleyan Christian Advocate.*

21. Atticus G. Haygood to Eugene R. Hendrix, Jan. 26, 1881, reprinted in Dempsy, *Atticus Greene Haygood,* 329.

22. Atticus Greene Haygood, *Our Brother in Black* (New York, 1881), 163.

23. Ibid., 12. Fredrickson, *Black Image in White Mind,* has an illuminating discussion of romantic racialism in chap. 4.

24. Haygood, *Our Brother in Black,* 144.

25. Dempsy, *Atticus Greene Haygood,* 150.

26. Atticus G. Haygood, *Sermons and Speeches* (Nashville, 1883), 352–53; John E. Fisher, "Atticus Haygood and National Unity," *Georgia Historical Quarterly* 50 (June 1966): 113–25.

27. Atticus G. Haygood, "The South and the School Problem," *Harpers New Monthly Magazine* 89 (July 1889): 229; *Proceedings of the Trustees of the John F. Slater Fund for the Education of the Freedmen, 1891* (Baltimore, 1891), 34–39.

28. Atticus G. Haygood, "The Education of the Negro," in *Pleas for Progress* (Nashville, 1889), 21.

29. Smith, *In His Image But . . . ,* 279, citing *Nashville Christian Advocate* 43 (Aug. 18, 1883).

30. *Nashville Christian Advocate* 43 (Sept. 8, 1883). Responses continued in the issues for Sept. 22, 29; Oct. 6, 13, 20.

31. Haygood, *Our Brother in Black,* 262.

32. Mann, *Atticus Greene Haygood,* 158.

33. Ibid., 160.

34. Hopkins, *Rise of the Social Gospel,* 113–14.

35. Joel Williamson, *The Crucible of Race: Black-White Relations in the American South since Emancipation* (New York, 1984), 88–93.

36. Paul M. Gaston, *The New South Creed: A Study in Southern Mythmaking* (New York, 1970), 134–35.

37. Ibid., 134.

38. Mann, *Atticus Greene Haygood,* 183.

39. George W. Cable, "My Politics," in *The Negro Question: A Selection of Writings on Civil Rights in the South,* ed. Arlin Turner (Garden City, N.Y., 1958), 2; Arlin Turner, *George Washington Cable* (Durham, N.C., 1956), 157.

40. George Washington Cable, "The Good Samaritan," in *The Negro Question*, ed. Arlin Turner (Garden City, N.Y., 1958), 36.

41. George Washington Cable, "The Freedman's Case in Equity," *Century Magazine*, 30 (Jan. 1885): 413.

42. Ibid., 414.

43. Henry W. Grady, "In Plain Black and White," *Century Magazine* 30 (Sept. 1885): 674–91.

44. Thomas U. Dudley, "How Shall We Help the Negro?" *Century Magazine* 30 (June 1885): 279.

45. George W. Cable, *The Silent South* (New York, 1885), 52, 54.

46. Lucy L. Cable Bikle, *George W. Cable: His Life and Letters* (New York, 1928), 194–202.

47. Lyman Abbott, "Mr. Cable and His Church Work," *Christian Union* 36 (Oct. 27, 1887): 428–29.

48. George Washington Cable, "Congregational Unity in Georgia," *Congregationalist* 74 (Sept. 26, 1889): 317. See also *Minutes of the National Council of the Congregational Churches of the United States, 1889* (Boston, 1890), 27, 278–81.

49. *Minutes of the National Council of the Congregational Churches of the United States, 1892* (Boston, 1893), 21, 25–26, 34.

50. W. E. B. Du Bois to George Washington Cable, Feb. 23, 1890, in *The Correspondence of W. E. B. Du Bois*, vol. 1, ed. Herbert Aptheker (Amherst, Mass., 1973), 7.

51. This letter is reprinted in Philip Butcher, "George W. Cable and Booker T. Washington," *Journal of Negro Education* 17 (Fall 1948): 465–66.

52. Lawrence J. Friedman provides a suggestive analysis of Cable's probings as reflected in his literary creations. See *The White Savage: Racial Fantasies in the Postbellum South* (Englewood Cliffs, N.J., 1970), 106–8.

53. George W. Cable, "Address," *American Missionary* 45 (Jan. 1891): 12.

54. Turner, *George Washington Cable*, 258–59.

55. Wherever Cable's involement in racial reform is discussed, his roots in and concern for the church have usually been overlooked. Joel Williamson, however, does take some note of Cable's religious roots. But Williamson then sets up an artificial distinction wherein Haygood is the apostle to the church and Cable is the emissary to the secular world, 93.

56. Cable, "Address," 13.

57. Albion W. Tourgée to D. Augustus Straker, Feb. 27, 1890, Tourgée Papers.

58. *Nashville Christian Advocate* 57 (Jan. 23, 1896): 8; *Macon Wesleyan Christian Advocate* 60 (Jan. 22, 1896): 57; these and other clippings in the Haygood Papers; H. H. Proctor, "A Memorial to Bishop Haygood," *Independent* 48 (Mar. 5, 1896): 320C.

59. Olsen, *Carpetbagger's Crusade*, 339.

60. Albion W. Tourgée to President William McKinley, Nov. 23, 1898, William McKinley Papers, Library of Congress, cited in Olsen, *Carpetbagger's Crusade*, 346.

61. Olsen, *Carpetbagger's Crusade*, 347.

5. A Missionary Education Bridge

1. I am indebted to James M. McPherson for information and insights in this chapter. See his *Abolitionist Legacy: From Reconstruction to the NAACP* (Princeton, N.J., 1975), 143–48.

2. Ibid., 143–44.

3. See Richard Bryant Drake, "The American Missionary Association and the Southern Negro, 1861–1888" (Ph.D. diss., Emory University, 1957).

4. See James D. Tyms, *The Rise of Religious Education among Negro Baptists* (New York, 1965).

5. See Ralph E. Morrow, *Northern Methodism and Reconstruction* (East Lansing, Mich., 1956).

6. Murray, *Presbyterians and the Negro*, 180.

7. H. Peers Brewer, "The Protestant Episcopal Freedmen's Commission, 1865–1878," *Historical Magazine of the Protestant Episcopal Church* (Dec. 1957), 381.

8. Francis G. Peabody, *Education for Life: The Story of Hampton Institute* (New York, 1918), 315.

9. Ibid., 314.

10. Biographical information is contained in the Joseph Crane Hartzell Papers, Drew University. See also Barbara Myers Swartz, "The Lord's Carpetbagger: A Biography of Joseph Crane Hartzell" (Ph.D. diss., State University of New York at Stony Brook, 1972).

11. See a typewritten history of the *Southwestern Christian Advocate* in the Hartzell Papers.

12. Mason Crum, *The Negro in the Methodist Church* (New York, 1951), 80–81.

13. Joseph Crane Hartzell, *Methodism and the Negro in the United States* (New York, 1894), typed copy in Hartzell Papers, 4.

14. Joseph C. Hartzell, "The Negro National Council," Dec. 6, 1893, unspecified clipping in Hartzell Papers.

15. *Southwestern Christian Advocate*, Jan. 28, 1892; Hartzell, *Methodism and the Negro*, 2.

16. Hartzell, *Methodism and the Negro*, 4–5.

17. Ibid., 7–8.

18. McPherson, *Abolitionist Legacy*, 267.

19. Gilbert Haven died in 1880, and thus his career ended at the point where this book begins. For an able study of Haven, see William B. Gravely, *Gilbert Haven, Methodist Abolitionist* (Nashville, 1973).

20. Wilbur Patterson Thirkield, "The Race Crisis and the Methodist Episcopal Church in the South," *New York Christian Advocate* 65 (Feb. 20, 1890): 67.

21. Ibid., 68.

22. McPherson, *Abolitionist Legacy*, 179.

23. *Independent* 51 (June 15, 1899); *Outlook* 61 (Apr. 1, 1899).

24. J. W. E. Bowen, ed., *Africa and the American Negro: Address and Proceedings of the Congress on Africa* (Atlanta, 1896; reprint, Miami, Fla., 1969), 13. See also *New York Christian Advocate* 81 (Jan. 2, 1896): 10.

25. Quotation from Haynes *Memoirs* (no page cited), cited by Daniel Perlman, "Stirring the White Conscience: The Life of George Edmund Haynes" (Ph.D. diss., New York University, 1972), 32.

26. W. E. B. Du Bois, *The Souls of Black Folk* (Chicago, 1903), 82.

6. The Gospel of Education

1. Raymond B. Fosdick, *Adventure in Giving* (New York, 1962), 188; Fred L. Brownlee, *New Day Ascending* (Boston, 1946), 167.

2. *Boston Transcript*, Sept. [n.d.], 1898; *Cambridge Chronicle*, Aug. 17, 1898; Edward Abbott Scrapbooks, Abbott Memorial Collection, Bowdoin College; Charles William Dabney, *Universal Education in the South*, vol. 2 (Chapel Hill, N.C., 1936), 3–5.

3. Edward Abbott to the Reverend A. B. Hunter, Jan. 12, 1898, Southern Education Board Papers, Southern Historical Collection, University of North Carolina, Chapel Hill.

4. Amory Dwight Mayo, "The New Education—the Christian Education," in *Proceedings of the First Capon Springs Conference for Christian Education in the South, 1898* (Washington, D.C., n.d.), 16.

5. Wilbur P. Thirkield, "How Far Shall the Higher Education Be Attempted?" in *Proceedings of the First Capon Springs Conference* (Washington, D.C., n.d.), 17–20.
6. *Minute Book, First Capon Springs Conference for Christian Education in the South, 1898,* 6, Southern Education Board Papers.
7. Jessie Pearl Rice, *J. L. M. Curry: Southerner, Statesman, and Educator* (New York, 1948), 55, 193–94.
8. J. L. M. Curry, "Education in the Southern States," in *Proceedings of the Second Capon Springs Conference for Christian Education in the South, 1899* (Washington, D.C., n.d.), 26, 28.
9. Dabney, *Universal Education in the South,* 8.
10. Lyman Abbott, "Some Southern Impressions," *Outlook* 67 (Apr. 27, 1901): 947–48.
11. *New York World,* Apr. 29, 1901, Scrapbook, Southern Education Board Papers.
12. *Brooklyn Standard Union,* May 24, 1901, Scrapbook, Southern Education Board Papers.
13. *Proceedings of the Fourth Conference for Education in the South, 1901* (published by the Committee, 1901), 12.
14. Louis R. Harlan, *Separate and Unequal* (Chapel Hill, N.C., 1958), 85–86; see also *The General Education Board* (New York, 1915), 3–14, and Fosdick, *Adventure in Giving,* 1–24.
15. For biographical information on Murphy, see Hugh C. Bailey, *Edgar Gardner Murphy: Gentle Progressive* (Coral Gables, Fla., 1968); and Maud King Murphy, *Edgar Gardner Murphy, from Records and Memories* (New York, 1943).
16. Dabney, *Universal Education in the South,* 154–55; Fosdick, *Adventure in Giving,* 14.
17. Philip Whitewell Wilson, *An Unofficial Statesman: Robert C. Ogden* (Garden City, N.Y., 1924), 112–23, 152–64, 177–92; "Service in Honor of Life and Work of Robert Curtis Ogden," Dec. 19, 1915, Holland Memorial Presbyterian Church, Presbyterian Historical Society, Philadelphia; Basil Douglas Hall, *The Life of Charles Cuthbert Hall* (New York, 1965), 149, 143–44; for a sketch of Hall as president of Union, see Robert T. Handy, *A History of Union Theological Seminary* (New York, 1987), 102–17.
18. Louise Ware, *George Foster Peabody* (Athens, Ga., 1951), 13, 16, 118–20, 131; James Thayer Addison, *The Episcopal Church in the United States* (New York, 1951), 344–45. See also Robert W. Patton, *An Inspiring Record in Negro Education: Historical Summary of the Work of the American Church Institute for Negroes* (New York, 1940).
19. John Graham Brooks, *An American Citizen: The Life of William Henry Baldwin, Jr.* (New York, 1910), 19–20, 22, 92–93, 101–24.
20. Edgar Gardner Murphy to Charles B. Galloway, Feb. 5, 1902, Letterbook, 15, Southern Education Board Papers.
21. Edgar Gardner Murphy, *The Task of the South* (Montgomery, Ala., 1902), 5.
22. Francis G. Peabody, "Knowledge and Service," in *Proceedings of the Conference for Education in the South, Sixth Session* (New York, 1903), 127.
23. *Independent* 54 (Apr. 24, 1902).
24. *Outlook* 64 (Jan. 13, 1900): 97–98.
25. *New York Tribune,* June 1, 1903.
26. Bailey, *Edgar Gardner Murphy,* 174.
27. Booker T. Washington to Robert C. Ogden, July 18, 1906 (copies to Wallace Buttrick, Hollis B. Frissell, and George F. Peabody), Booker T. Washington Papers, Library of Congress.
28. Edgar Gardner Murphy to Wallace Buttrick, Nov. 4, 1907, Southern Education Board Papers.

7. Conservatives versus Radicals: Washington and Du Bois

1. Kelly Miller, "Washington's Policy," Boston *Evening Transcript,* Sept. 18, 1903.
2. W. E. B. Du Bois to Booker T. Washington, Sept. 24, 1895, in *Correspondence of Du Bois.*

3. Kelly Miller, "Washington's Policy," 49.

4. Lyman Abbott to Booker T. Washington, Oct. 1, 1900; Washington to Abbott, Oct. 8, 1900; Abbott to Washington, Jan. 8, 1901, Washington Papers; Harlan, *Booker T. Washington, 1856–1901*, 247–48.

5. Washington, *Up from Slavery*, 226.

6. Booker T. Washington, *The Future of the American Negro* (New York, 1899), 132.

7. *Outlook* 64 (Jan. 6, 1900).

8. Booker T. Washington, "The Economic Development of the Negro Race since Emancipation," in *The Negro in the South* (Philadelphia, 1907), 72–73.

9. Harlan, *Booker T. Washington, 1901–1915*, viii.

10. Booker T. Washington, *The Story of My Life and Work* (Toronto, 1900), 248–58; Harlan, *Booker T. Washington, 1856–1901*, 290–91.

11. Harlan, *Booker T. Washington, 1856–1901*, 297–98; McPherson, *Abolitionist Legacy*, 363–64.

12. Washington, *Story of My Life*, 260–77.

13. For autobiographical information, see W. E. B. Du Bois, *Dusk of Dawn: An Essay toward an Autobiography of a Race Concept* (New York, 1940); and *The Autobiography of W. E. B. Du Bois: A Soliloquy on Viewing My Life from the Last Decade of Its First Century* (New York, 1968). Biographies include Francis L. Broderick, *W. E. B. Du Bois: Negro Leader in a Time of Crisis* (Stanford, Calif., 1959); Manning Marable, *W. E. B. Du Bois: Black Radical Democrat* (Boston: 1986). Elliott M. Rudwick, *W. E. B. Du Bois: A Study in Minority Group Leadership* (Philadelphia, 1960).

14. W. E. B. Du Bois, "A Pageant in Seven Decades, 1868–1938," in *W. E. B. Du Bois Speaks*, ed. Philip S. Foner (New York, 1970), 38–39.

15. Du Bois, *Souls of Black Folk*, i.

16. Ibid., 43, 37–48.

17. Ibid., 50–51.

18. Ibid., 53–54.

19. Washington, *Story of My Life*, 47–48, 63; Harlan, *Booker T. Washington, 1856–1901*, 49, 67–68.

20. Harlan, *Booker T. Washington, 1856–1901*, 82–85.

21. Washington, *Up from Slavery*, 61; Harlan, *Booker T. Washington, 1856–1901*, 96–98.

22. See Booker T. Washington, "The Colored Ministry: Its Defects and Needs," *Christian Union* 42 (Aug. 14, 1890).

23. Basil Mathews, *Booker T. Washington: Educator and Inter-Racial Interpreter* (Cambridge, Mass., 1948), 125–26.

24. Washington, *Up from Slavery*, 136.

25. Du Bois, "Autobiography", 88–90, 285.

26. W. E. B. Du Bois to Pastor Scudder, Feb. 3, 1886, in *Correspondence of Du Bois*, 5; Du Bois, *Autobiography*, 285; Du Bois, *Dusk of Dawn*, 33.

27. Du Bois, *Autobiography*, 285; Du Bois, *Dusk of Dawn*, 33; Broderick, *W. E. B. Du Bois*, 14.

28. Du Bois, *Dusk of Dawn*, 56, 63.

29. "Credo," *Independent* 57 (Oct. 6, 1904).

30. W. E. B. Du Bois, "The Religion of the American Negro," *New World* 9 (Dec. 1900): 622.

31. Ibid., 622, 623.

8. Shifting Allegiances

1. Du Bois, *Souls of Black Folk*, 50.

2. Much of the following biographical material is in Henry Justin Ferry, "Francis James Grimké: Portrait of a Black Puritan" (Ph.D. diss., Yale University, 1970). For pub-

lished materials, see Louis B. Weeks III, "Racism, World War I, and the Christian Life: Francis J. Grimké in the Nation's Capital," *Journal of Presbyterian History*, 51 (1973): 471–87; and Clifton E. Olmstead, "Francis James Grimké: Christian Moralist and Civil Rights," in *Sons of the Prophets* (Princeton, 1963). Unfortunately Olmstead's essay fails to appreciate Grimké's biblical and prophetic ministry and portrays his jeremiads against the Presbyterian church, Booker T. Washington, and Woodrow Wilson only in a negative light.

3. Ferry, "Francis James Grimké," Ibid., 136–41.

4. Francis James Grimké, "The Second Marriage of Frederick Douglass," *Journal of Negro History* 19 (July 1934): 325.

5. *The Works of Francis J. Grimké*, ed. Carter G. Woodson (Washington, D.C., 1942), 3:420 (hereinafter cited as *Works*); Francis J. Grimké, "Mr. Moody and the Color Question in the South," in *Life and Writings of the Grimké Family*, ed. Anna J. Cooper (Washington, D.C., 1951), 58, cited in Ferry, "Francis James Grimké," 169.

6. Louis B. Weeks III, "Francis J. Grimké: Racism, World War I, and the Christian Life," in *Black Apostles: Afro-American Clergy Confront the Twentieth Century* (Boston, 1978), 60.

7. Francis J. Grimké, "It Is Drawing the Color Line," in *Life and Writings of the Grimké Family*, ed. Anna J. Cooper (Washington, D.C., 1951), 52–53; Henry B. Ferry, "Racism and Reunion: A Black Protest by Francis James Grimké," *Journal of Presbyterian History* 50 (1972): 78–82.

8. Francis J. Grimké to the Presbytery of Washington City, Oct. 4, 1908, *Works* 4:115.

9. George G. Mahy to Francis J. Grimké, Oct. 1, 1918; Grimké to Mahy, Oct. 4, 1918, *Works* 4:225–26.

10. Ferry, "Racism and Reunion," 77–88; see also Murray, *Presbyterians and the Negro*, 199–201.

11. Ferry, "Francis James Grimké," 264.

12. Ferry, "Racism and Reunion," 82–88.

13. Ferry, "Francis James Grimké," 188.

14. Ibid., 188–89.

15. The author read many of Grimké's sermons in pamphlet form in the collection at the Robert E. Speer Library at Princeton Theological Seminary. For the convenience of the reader the citation, where possible, is from *Works*. Please note that the date in the text and the date in the *Works* are sometimes at variance, the editor often printing a later version of the sermon.

16. Francis J. Grimké, "God and the Race Problem," *Works* 1:367–68.

17. Francis J. Grimké "Signs of a Brighter Future," *Works* 1:271–72.

18. Ferry, "Francis James Grimké," 244.

19. Francis J. Grimké to Woodrow Wilson, Nov. 20, 1912, *Works* 4:129–30.

20. Francis J. Grimké to Woodrow Wilson, Sept. 5, 1913, *Works* 4:133–34.

21. Francis J. Grimké, *Works* 3:7.

22. Ibid., 465.

23. Unfortunately there exists no full-length biographical study of Archibald Grimké. See the article by Clarence G. Contee, Sr., in *Dictionary of American Negro Biography*, ed. Rayford W. Logan and Michael R. Winston (New York, 1982), 271–73.

24. Meier, *Negro Thought in America*, 176–77.

25. Charles Flint Kellogg, *NAACP: A History of the National Association for the Advancement of Colored People*, vol. 1, *1909–1920* (Baltimore, 1967), 140–41.

26. There is no full-length biographical study of Miller. See the essay by Michael R. Winston in *Dictionary of Negro Biography*, ed. Rayford W. Logan and Michael R. Winston (New York, 1982), 435–39.

27. Kelly Miller, *Race Adjustment* (New York, 1906), 12,18.

28. Ibid., 13,15

29. Ibid., 15.

30. Ibid., 18.

31. Ibid., 19.

32. Kelly Miller, "The Education of the Negro," *Report of the Commissioner of Education for the Year 1900-1901*, Vol. 1 (Washington, D.C., 1902), 731–859.

33. August Meier, "The Racial and Educational Philosophy of Kelly Miller, 1895–1915," *Journal of Negro Education* (Spring, 1960), 121–27; Kelly Miller, "Come Let Us Reason Together," *Voice of the Negro*, 3 (1906), 67.

34. Kelly Miller to Washington Gladden, Sept. 26, 1903, Gladden Papers.

35. Kelly Miller, "Religion as a Solvent of the Race Problem," in *Race Adjustment*, 133.

36. Ibid., 146.

37. Allain L. Locke, Introduction, in Kelly Miller, *The Everlasting Stain* (Washington, D.C., 1924), xiii. Even though Miller became more critical of Washington towards the end of Washington's life, five years after his death he praised him for being "a pragmatist of the first water." See "Booker T. Washington Five Years After," in Kelly Miller, *The Everlasting Stain*, 253–70.

38. Bowen is another figure in need of a full-length study. For much of the information in this section, I am indebted to James M. Washington, Union Theological Seminary (New York) and his unpublished paper "John Wesley Bowen: Atlanta's Forgotten Black Historical Theologian."

39. Ibid., 4–5.

40. J. W. E. Bowen, *"What Shall the Harvest Be?" A National Sermon.* (Washington, D.C., 1892), 16, 26, 39, 41.

41. J. W. E. Bowen, "The Comparative Status of the Negro at the Close of the War and Today," *Addresses and Proceedings of the Congress on Africa*, ed. by J. W. E. Bowen (Atlanta, 1896), 168.

42. Ibid, 173.

43. J. W. E. Bowen to William Still,———12, 1894, cited in August Meier, *Negro Thought in America, 1880-1915* (Ann Arbor, MI., 1966), 36–37, 286, n. 25; Washington, *John Wesley Edward Bowen*, 32.

44. Joel Williamson, *The Crucible of Race*, 40.

45. Harlan, *Booker T. Washington, 1901–1915*, 174–75.

46. August Meier, "The Beginning of Industrial Education in Negro Schools," *Midwest Journal* 7 (1955): 21–44; McPherson, *Abolitionist Legacy*, 110–12.

47. Meier, *Negro Thought in America*, 90–91; McPherson, *Abolitionist Legacy*, 212–14.

48. McPherson, *Abolitionist Legacy*, 203–5.

49. W. E. B. Du Bois, "The Talented Tenth," in *The Negro Problem* (New York, 1903; reprint, Miami, 1969), 61.

50. Ibid., 58–59; Henry L. Moorehouse, "The Talented Tenth," *Independent*, Apr. 23, 1896, cited in McPherson, *Abolitionist Legacy*, 222.

51. W. E. B. Du Bois, "Of the Training of Black Men," *Atlantic Monthly* 90 (Sept. 1902): 291.

52. Du Bois, *The Souls of Black Folk*, 82.

53. William Hayes Ward, Editorial, *Independent*, 50 (December 8, 1898): 1708-9; "The Top and the Bottom," 54 (March 13, 1902), 646-48.

54. Wilbur P. Thirkield to W. E. B. Du Bois, Oct. 14, 1902, xx-xx

55. Ferry, 161-62.

56. Francis G. Grimké, "The Things of Paramount Importance in the Development of the Negro Race," *Works*, Vol. I, 383-84.

57. Miller, "The Education of the Negro," 822.

58. Ibid., 820, 821.

59. Ibid., 821.

9. Washington Gladden: A Northern Case Study

1. Hopkins, *Rise of the Social Gospel*, 25–26. Henry F. May, assessing Gladden's total contribution to religion and reform, concluded that Gladden was "probably the most

influential of the Social Gospel leaders" (*Protestant Churches and Industrial America*, 171).

2. Washington Gladden, *Recollections* (New York, 1909), 63. For biographical information, see Jacob H. Dorn, *Washington Gladden: Prophet of the Social Gospel* (Columbus, Ohio, 1968). Handy, *Social Gospel in America*, 19–32; and Kenneth Lee Brown, "Washington Gladden: Exponent of Social Christianity" (Ph.D. diss. Duke University, 1964).

3. Gladden, *Recollections*, 119.

4. Brownlee, *New Day Ascending*, 56; *American Missionary* 14 (Dec. 1970): 271.

5. Washington Gladden, "The Southern Question," *Independent* 28 (Sept. 7, 1876).

6. *American Missionary* 21 (Dec. 1877): 1–2.

7. J. S. Himes, Jr., "Forty Years of Negro Life in Columbus, Ohio," *Journal of Negro History* 27 (Apr. 1942): 136, 139, 148; Dorn, *Washington Gladden*, 396–97.

8. Washington Gladden, "Christian Education in the South," *American Missionary* 37 (Dec. 1883): 385–91.

9. *American Missionary* 37 (Dec. 1883): 354; 38 (Jan. 1884): 2–3.

10. Washington Gladden, "Address on Lynching," *American Missionary* 49 (Dec. 1895): 406–8; *Congregationalist* 80 (Oct. 31, 1895): 661.

11. *American Missionary* 49 (Dec. 1895): 392.

12. Ibid. 56 (Nov. 1902): 449.

13. Horace Bumstead to Washington Gladden, Jan. 22, 1903; W. E. B. Du Bois to Gladden, Jan. 24, 1903; Henry H. Proctor to Gladden, Apr. 14, 1903, Washington Gladden Papers, Ohio State Historical Society, Columbus, Ohio.

14. Washington Gladden, "Remarks," in *The Negro Church*, ed. W. E. Burghardt Du Bois (Atlanta, 1903), 204–7; and Mary Church Terrell, Kelly Miller, and W. E. B. Du Bois, "Resolutions," ibid., 208.

15. Washington Gladden, "The Race Problem," Sermon, May 31, 1903, 3–4, Gladden Papers.

16. Henry Hugh Proctor, *Between Black and White, Autobiographical Sketches* (New York, 1925), 109.

17. Ibid., 13, 17; Henry H. Proctor, "Our Colored Moderator's Southern Mission," *Congregationalist*, 100 Oct. 14, 1915, 551.

18. Kelly Miller to Washington Gladden, Sept. 26, 1903, Gladden Papers; *American Missionary* 57 (Dec. 1903): 318.

19. Gladden, "Race Problem," 23.

20. Ibid., 24.

21. Ibid., 26–30.

22. Washington Gladden, "Presidential Address," *American Missionary* 57 (Dec. 1903): 324–25.

23. Ibid., 325.

24. Ibid., 323.

25. *Congregationalist* 89 (Oct. 29, 1904): 620; *American Missionary* 58 (Dec. 1904): 334.

26. Washington Gladden, "The American Missionary Association and the Problem of Emancipation," *American Missionary* 60 (Dec. 1906): 314–15; *Congregationalist* 91 (Nov. 3, 1906): 567.

27. Washington Gladden, Sermon (untitled), Pilgrim Church, Cleveland, Feb. 13, 1907, 34, 36, Gladden Papers.

28. Himes, "Forty Years of Negro Life," 134–36, 141.

29. Henry H. Proctor to Gladden, Aug. 29, 1907, Gladden Papers.

30. *Ohio State Journal*, Oct. 27, 1906; Dorn, *Washington Gladden*, 301. The Atlanta riots were the worst of the decade. See Charles Crowe, "Racial Violence and Social Reform: Origins of the Atlanta Riot of 1906," *Journal of Negro History* 53 (July 1968): 234–56; and Crowe, "Racial Massacre in Atlanta, September 22, 1906," ibid. 54 (Apr. 1969): 150–73.

31. *Congregationalist* 91 (Oct. 6, 1906): 449; *American Missionary* 60 (Dec. 1906): 306.

32. Wilbur P. Thirkield to Gladden, Oct. 1, 1909; W. S. Scarborough to Gladden, Feb. 24, 1915, Gladden Papers.
33. Charles Cuthbert Hall to Gladden, Nov. 12, 1907, Gladden Papers.
34. Washington Gladden, "The Negro Crisis: Is the Separation of the Two Races to Become Necessary?" *American Magazine* 63 (Jan. 1907): 300–301.
35. Ibid., 297–98.
36. Ibid., 299.
37. Ibid., 299–301.
38. Ibid., 296.
39. The Lane Theological Seminary was a Presbyterian seminary in Cincinnati. In 1834, Theodore Dwight Weld, a convert of the Finney Revivals, brought an anti-slavery gospel to the seminary. At Weld's urging, a group of students denounced the American Colonization Society for its racial position. The trustees responded by disciplining the students. As a result, a vocal minority, known henceforth as the Lane Seminary Rebels, left for Oberlin.
40. Edward S. Steele to Gladden, Dec. 28, 1907, Gladden Papers.
41. Gladden, *Recollections*, 370–71. Much that is in this volume reproduces the published and unpublished sermons, addresses, and articles of the preceding years.
42. Gladden, *Recollections*, 371.
43. Unsigned letter to Miss Ruth A. Polley, Nov. 30, 1931, Washington Gladden Papers, First Congregational Church Archives, Columbus, Ohio.
44. Irving Maurer, "Glimpses of Washington Gladden," Address, Minnesota Congregational Club, St. Paul, Dec. 1, 1930, Washington Gladden Papers, First Congregational Church Archives.

10. Edgar Gardner Murphy: A Southern Case Study

1. See Ralph E. Luker, "Liberal Theology and Social Conservatism: A Southern Tradition, 1840–1920," *Church History* 50 (June 1981): 193–204; Luker, *A Southern Tradition in Theology and Social Criticism, 1830–1930* (New York, 1984).
2. W. Norman Pittenger, "The Significance of DuBose's Theology," in William Porcher DuBose, *Unity in Faith*, ed. by W. Norman Pittinger (Greenwich, Conn., 1957), 21.
3. Quoted in Bailey, *Edgar Gardner Murphy*, 3–4.
4. Edgar Gardner Murphy, *The Larger Life* (New York, 1897), 24–25, 45; *Proceedings of the Twenty-fourth Episcopal Church Congress, 1898* (New York, 1898), 1120.
5. Murphy, *Larger Life*, 158.
6. A copy of the resolution and a clipping from the *Laredo News* are in the Edgar Gardner Murphy Papers, Southern Historical Collection, University of North Carolina, Chapel Hill. Years later, in a letter to Booker T. Washington, Murphy recalled the lynching (Murphy to Washington, Jan. 1, 1902, Booker T. Washington Papers).
7. A pamphlet entitled "An Episcopal Church for the Negroes of Montgomery, Alabama" is included in the Murphy Papers.
8. Edgar Gardner Murphy, "An Address at Tuskegee of Edgar Gardner Murphy," Murphy Papers.
9. Bailey, *Edgar Gardner Murphy*, 32–36; M. K. Murphy, *Edgar Gardner Murphy*, 26–27; Harlan, *Separate and Unequal*, 292.
10. Edgar Gardner Murphy, *The White Man and the Negro at the South* (n.p., n.d.), 39; M. K. Murphy, *Edgar Gardner Murphy*, 28.
11. *Race Problems of the South: Report of the Proceedings of the First Annual Conference Held under the Auspices of the Southern Society for the Promotion of the Study of Race Conditions and Problems in the South* (Richmond, 1900; reprint, New York, 1969), 9.
12. Harlan, *Booker T. Washington, 1856–1901*, 293.

13. Edgar Gardner Murphy to Booker T. Washington, Feb. 7, 13, 1900; May 30, 1900, Washington Papers.
14. *Race Problems of the South,* 23–38, 42, 63.
15. Ibid., 83–97, 105–34.
16. Ibid., 178–94, 216–17; *Outlook* 65 (May 19, 1900): 160–62.
17. *Montgomery Advertiser,* Nov. 28, 1901; Edgar Gardner Murphy, "Reconstruction in Religion," *Outlook* 67 (Mar. 23, 1901).
18. Elizabeth H. Davidson, *Child Labor Legislation in the Southern Textile States* (Chapel Hill, N.C., 1939), 121–34; White and Hopkins, *Social Gospel,* 87–92.
19. Murphy, *Larger Life,* 153.
20. Edgar Gardner Murphy, *Problems of the Present South* (New York, 1904), 162–63.
21. Ibid., 162–71.
22. Ibid., 188.
23. Edgar Gardner Murphy to Booker T. Washington, Aug. 20, 1904, Washington Papers.
24. Edgar Gardner Murphy to Booker T. Washington, Mar. 8, 1909, Washington Papers.
25. Edgar Gardner Murphy, *The Basis of Ascendancy* (New York, 1909), 176.
26. Ibid., 193–94.
27. Ibid., 192.
28. Ibid., 196, 195.
29. Ibid., 197.
30. Ibid., 201, 195–96.
31. Ibid., 25, 126–27, 138–39, 195–96, 238–39, 242.
32. Robert R. Moton to Edgar Gardner Murphy, Sept. 22, 1909, Murphy Papers; these testimonials are in the final pages of Murphy, *Basis of Ascendancy,* 251, 253.
33. Murphy, *Basis of Ascendancy,* 209–10.
34. Ibid., xi.
35. Bailey, *Edgar Gardner Murphy,* 179–81.
36. M. K. Murphy, *Edgar Gardner Murphy,* 98.
37. Ibid.
38. H. Shelton Smith, *In His Image, but: Racism in Southern Religion, 1780–1910* (Durham, N.C., 1972), 285.
39. Edgar Gardner Murphy to the Editor, *New York Evening Post,* Mar. 12, 1909, cited in McPherson, *Abolitionist Legacy,* 376.
40. Edgar Gardner Murphy to Booker T. Washington, July 27, 1909, Booker T. Washington Papers.
41. Williamson, *Crucible of Race,* 331–32.
42. Luker, *Southern Tradition,* 11, 357.
43. Edgar Gardner Murphy, "The Task of the Leader," *Sewanee Review* 15 (Jan. 1907): 25–27.
44. George E. Haynes, *The Trend of the Races* (New York, 1922), 97.
45. Bailey, *Edgar Gardner Murphy,* 192.

11. The NAACP and the Urban League

1. James L. Crouthamel, "The Springfield Race Riot of 1908," *Journal of Negro History* 45 (July 1960): 164–81.
2. *Independent* 65 (Aug. 20, 1908): 399–400. There were follow-up comments in the editorial section the next week (Aug. 27, 1908, 442–43).
3. William English Walling, "The Race War in the North," *Independent* 65 (Sept. 3, 1908): 532–33.
4. Mary White Ovington, *The Walls Came Tumbling Down* (New York, 1947), 102.
5. Kellogg, *NAACP,* 12.

6. *National Negro Conference, Proceedings* (New York, 1909); Elliott M. Rudwick, "The National Negro Committee Conference of 1909," *Phylon* 18 (4th Quarter 1958): 413–19; Jack Abramowitz, "Origins of the NAACP," *Social Education* 15 (Jan. 1951): 21–23.

7. See Nancy J. Weiss, *The National Urban League, 1910–1940* (New York, 1974). For an account by one of the founders, see L. Hollingsworth Wood, "The Urban League Movement," *Journal of Negro History* 9 (April 1924): 117–26.

8. Weiss, *National Urban League*, 34–39.

9. Ibid., 30–31.

10. McPherson, "Antislavery Legacy," 149–50.

11. McPherson, *Abolitionist Legacy*, Appendix A, 406–8.

12. Weiss, *National Urban League*, 51–52.

13. Mary White Ovington, *Crisis* 32 (June 1926): 76.

14. *Crisis* 7 (Mar. 1914): 227; see also 8 (Apr. 1914): 289; 9 (Apr. 1915): 280.

15. Ibid. 7 (Mar. 1914): 227.

16. Ibid. 18 (Aug. 1919): 182.

17. Elliott M. Rudwick, "The Niagara Movement," *Journal of Negro History* 42 (July 1957): 177–200. The other important precursor was the National Afro-American League, in existence off and on from 1887 through 1908. See Thornbrough, "National Afro-American League," 494–512.

18. W. E. B. Du Bois, "A Word," in *The Negro: The Hope or the Despair of Christianity*, ed. Reverdy C. Ransom, (Boston, 1935), 127.

19. Olsen, *Carpetbagger's Crusade*, 352.

20. *Independent* 61 (Aug. 23, 1906): 472.

21. *Outlook* 80 (July 29, 1905): 796.

22. Ibid. 84 (Sept. 1, 1906): 3–4. A specific comparison with "Booker Washington's Platform" is offered the following week (Sept. 8, 1906, 54–55).

23. Weiss, *National Urban League*, 52–53; Kellogg, *NAACP*, 125.

24. Weiss, *National Urban League*, Table V, 377.

25. *Crisis* 9 (Mar. 1915): 229.

26. This information is from national and local records of NAACP in the Library of Congress. For North's involvement in NAACP, see Walter Muelder, *Methodism and Society in the Twentieth Century* (Nashville, 1961), 60.

27. Williamson, *Crucible of Race*, 354–55; George M. Miller, "'A This Worldly Mission': The Life and Career of Alexander Walters (1858–1917)" (Ph.D. diss., State University of New York at Stony Brook, 1984), 262–66. Miller (pp. 291–94) provides a detailed chronology of the Brownsville incident up to the present. In 1972 the 167 victims of racial injustice were finally granted honorable discharges, although two of the 167 could be found. In an emotional ceremony in 1973, Dorsie Willis, one of the two, received his discharge and a public apology on his eighty-seventh birthday.

28. Miller, "A This Worldly Mission," argues that Walters was not an accommodationist but rather should be seen as a vigorous advocate of protest for full civil and political rights for blacks. Miller believes that the National Afro-American Council deserves to be seen as a precursor of the NAACP, as is evidenced by the invitation to Walters to join the NAACP. Miller argues further that Walters criticized Roosevelt and backed away from his support for Wilson.

29. Ibid., 325, citing words from Walter's address to the National Negro Conference.

30. Ibid., 331–33.

31. Ibid., 368–89.

32. Carl Hermann Voss, *Rabbi and Minister: The Friendship of Stephen S. Wise and John Haynes Holmes* (Cleveland, 1964), 65–66, 72–73; John Haynes Holmes, *I Speak for Myself* (New York, 1959), 80–81.

33. Holmes, *I Speak for Myself*, 200.

34. *Crisis* 19 (Feb. 1920).

35. Voss, *Rabbi and Minister*, 38–39; Stephen Wise to Editor, *Ohio State Journal*, July 3, 1918, Washington Gladden Papers, First Congregational Church Archives.

36. Ovington, *Walls Came Tumbling Down*, 113.
37. *Crisis* 18 (May 1919).
38. Ibid. 3 (Dec. 1911): 70–74; 21 (Dec. 1920). In Du Bois's first attempt at autobiography, *Darkwater: Voices from within the Veil* (New York, 1920), he develops the same theme as the 1911 article in a chapter entitled "Jesus Christ in Texas," 123–33.
39. S. R. Fullinwider, *The Mind and Mood of Black America: Twentieth Century Thought* (Homewood, Ill., 1969), 58.
40. *Crisis* 6 (Oct. 1913): 291. I agree with a recent biographer who observes, "One critical component of Du Bois' thought frequently ignored was his profound sense of morality and his black prophetic Christianity" (Manning Marable, *W. E. B. Du Bois, Black Radical Democrat* [Boston, 1986], ix).
41. *Crisis* 11 (Apr. 1916): 270.
42. Rudwick, "Niagara Movement," 179.
43. *Crisis* 9 (Mar. 1915): 238.
44. Ibid.
45. Quoted in *Crisis* 10 (Sept. 1915): 224.
46. *Crisis* 14 (May 1917): 90.
47. Ibid. 21 (Feb. 1921).
48. Ibid. 7 (Mar. 1914).
49. Ibid. 25 (Jan. 1923).
50. NAACP Board Minutes, Apr. 10, May 8, 1916; Oswald Garrison Villard to Jane Addams, Jan. 11, 1913, NAACP Papers, Library of Congress.
51. *Crisis* 14 (May 1917); 25 (Jan. 1923).
52. Ibid. 19 (Nov.–Dec. 1919).

12. The Student Christian Movement

1. Clarence P. Shedd, *Two Centuries of Student Christian Movements* (New York, 1934).
2. C. Howard Hopkins, *History of the YMCA in North America* (New York, 1951).
3. Luther D. Wishard, "The Beginning of the Students' Era in Christian History" (typescript, 1917), YMCA Historical Library, New York; Charles K. Ober, "The Beginnings of the American Student Movement," *Student World* 6 (Jan. 1913): 10–18. See also Ruth Rouse. *The World's Student Christian Federation: A History of the First Thirty Years* (London, 1948), 23–29; Shedd *Two Centuries*, 91–170; and Hopkins, *History of the YMCA*, 271–308.
4. See Anna V. Rice, *History of the World's YWCA* (New York, 1947); Elizabeth Wilson, *Fifty Years of Association Work among Young Women, 1866–1916* (New York, 1916); and Mary S. Sims, *The Natural History of a Social Institution: The Young Women's Christian Association* (New York, 1936).
5. Shedd, *Two Centuries* 238–76; Rouse *World's Student Christian Federation*, 92–98.
6. For an excellent biography of Mott, see C. Howard Hopkins, *John R. Mott, 1865–1955* (Grand Rapids, Mich., 1979); Rouse, *World's Student Christian Federation*, 174.
7. Hopkins, *History of the YMCA*, 401.
8. Ibid., 391–402.
9. Ibid., 635.
10. An informative collection of pamphlets and brochures of conferences from all over the country is preserved at the YMCA Historical Library.
11. Willis D. Weatherford, *Negro Life in the South* (New York, 1910), v.
12. Wilma Dykeman, *Prophet of Plenty: The First Ninety Years of W. D. Weatherford* (Knoxville, Tenn., 1966). Much of the information that follows can be found in Willis D. Weatherford, "History of the Student Young Men's Christian Association in the

South" (typescript, 1949); and Weatherford, "Colored Young Men's Christian Association" (typescript, 1951), both in the YMCA Historical Library.

13. Weatherford, "Colored Young Men's Christian Association," 18.

14. Willis D. Weatherford, "The First Stages in Solving the Race Problem," *Southern Workman* 39 (Nov. 1910): 590.

15. *Intercollegian* 33 (May 1910): 196–97.

16. Francis Pickens Miller, *Man from the Valley* (Chapel Hill, N.C., 1971), 18–19.

17. Dykeman, *Prophet of Plenty,* 41. Dykeman's is the only biography of Weatherford. As Dykeman says in chapter 1, however, her account "is neither definitive biography nor formal scholarship."

18. George B. Tindall, "Southern Negroes since Reconstruction: Dissolving the Static Image," in *Writing Southern History: Essays in Historiography in Honor of Fletcher M. Green,* ed. Arthur S. Link and Rembert W. Patrick (Baton Rouge, La., 1965), 341.

19. Weatherford, *Negro Life in the South,* 12.

20. Ibid., 153, 178.

21. Ibid., 149–76.

22. Ibid., 152.

23. Ibid., 150–51.

24. Weatherford, "Colored Young Men's Christian Association," 22.

25. This new pattern is observable in the brochures of student conferences in the YMCA Historical Library.

26. Willis D. Weatherford, *Present Forces in Negro Progress* (New York, 1912), 164.

27. Dykeman, *Prophet of Plenty,* 95–96.

28. *Student World* 5 (Apr. 12, 1912): 76.

29. Benjamin E. Mays, *Born to Rebel* (New York, 1971), 126.

30. Dykeman, *Prophet of Plenty,* 87.

31. Weatherford, *Negro Life in the South,* 176.

32. Clarence Prouty Shedd, *The Church Follows Its Students* (New Haven, Conn., 1938), 12–28.

33. Ibid., 18.

34. Richard Henry Edwards, "The Social Problems Group: A Method for the Popular Study of Social Conditions," *Charities and the Commons* 21 (Oct. 17, 1908): 103–7.

35. Richard Henry Edwards, *Studies in American Social Conditions,* vol. 2, *The Negro Problem* (Madison, Wis., 1908), 13.

36. Ibid., 15–32.

37. Harry Melvin Philpott, "A History of the Student Young Men's Christian Association, 1900–1941" (Ph. D. diss., Yale University, 1947), 97–98; William H. Morgan, *Student Religion during Fifty Years* (New York, 1935), 98.

38. *Intercollegian* 32 (Oct. 1909): 20.

39. Rouse, *World's Student Christian Foundation,* 175; Weatherford, "History," 27–28.

40. Philpott, "History," 87–88. 95; Hopkins, *History of the YMCA,* 636.

41. Richard Henry Edwards, *Volunteer Social Service by College Men* (New York, 1914), 10–11.

42. Hopkins, *John R. Mott,* 418–19; an appreciative article by Walter Rauschenbusch appeared in *North American Student* 2 (June 1914): 439–40.

43. *Social Needs of the Colleges of North America* (New York, 1914), 5.

44. Philpott, "History," 110.

45. Hopkins, *John R. Mott,* 419.

46. Arcadius McSwain Trawick, Employment Record, YMCA Headquarters, New York.

47. *Epworth Era* 17 (July 27, 1911): 1.

48. I am indebted to Oakley H. Coburn, librarian at the Sandor Teszler Library at Wofford College, Spartanburg, South Carolina, for information about Trawick.

49. Arcadius M. Trawick, "Housing Conditions of the Poor in Nashville," *Missionary Voice* 1, (May, 1911): 17.

50. Arcadius M. Trawick, *The City Church and Its Social Mission* (New York, 1913).
51. Morgan, *Student Religion during Fifty Years* 92. This pamphlet could not be found in the YMCA Historical Library.
52. Weatherford, "Colored Young Men's Christian Association," 27–30.
53. A. M. Trawick, ed., *The New Voice in Race Adjustments* (Nashville, 1914), vii; John R. Mott, "Fostering Right Race Relations" (Atlanta, 1914), in *Addresses and Papers of John R. Mott* (New York, 1947), 332.
54. Booker T. Washington, "The Basis of Race Progress in the South" (Atlanta, 1914), in *Addresses and Papers of John R. Mott* (New York, 1947), 336.
55. Trawick, *New Voice in Race Adjustments*, 100–107, 58, 188–94.
56. Ibid., 63–64.
57. Editorial, *Student World* 7 (July 1914): 115; Harlan P. Beach, ibid., 111.
58. Will W. Alexander, *North American Student* 3 (Oct. 1914): 35–36.
59. Hopkins, *John R. Mott*, 550; Basil Matthews, *John R. Mott, World Citizen* (New York, 1934), 303–5.
60. Trawick, *New Voice in Race Adjustments*, 9.
61. Arcadius M. Trawick, "The Student Conference at Montreat," *Epworth Era* 17 (July 27, 1911): 2.
62. Arcadius M. Trawick, "The Social Gospel and Racial Relationships," *Epworth Era* 23 (Nov. 1916): 108.
63. Ibid., 110–11.
64. Ibid, 113.
65. Arcadius M. Trawick, "The Gospel of Social Living," *Methodist Review* 66 (Apr. 1917).
66. *Student World* 9 (July 1916): 115.
67. For a discussion of the War Work Council, see Hopkins, *History of the YMCA*, 486–504.
68. Dykeman, *Prophet of Plenty*, 151–52.
69. Tindall, "Southern Negroes since Reconstruction," 341.

13. The Changing Mind of the Social Gospel

1. Walter Rauschenbusch, *The Belated Races and the Social Problems* (New York, 1914), 11. This American Missionary Association pamphlet was also published as "Belated Races and the Social Problems," *Methodist Review Quarterly* (South) 63 (Apr., 1914): 252–59. The specific paragraphs on "the Negro question" were printed under Rauschenbusch's name as "The Problem of the Black Man," *American Missionary* 68 (Mar. 1914): 732–33.
2. Walter Rauschenbusch, *Dare We Be Christians?* (Boston, 1914), 57–58.
3. Rauschenbusch, "Problem of the Black Man," 732–33.
4. Rauschenbusch, *Belated Races*, 10.
5. *Crisis* 7 (Mar. 1914): 232–33. Willis D. Weatherford to Walter Rauschenbusch, 1914, Walter Rauschenbusch papers in possession of Dores R. Sharpe. I have examined Rauschenbusch papers at the American Baptist Historical Association and papers when they were still in the possession of Dores R. Sharpe, Rauschenbusch's private secretary and biographer. Sharpe was reluctant to turn over papers to the American Baptist Historical Society. He did so finally, but I will indicate materials that came from his home in Pasadena, California.
6. Minus, *Walter Rauschenbusch*, 121.
7. "Report of the YMCA Committee to Investigate Social Conditions of Men and Boys in Rochester," *Rochester Union and Advertiser*, May 30, 1904. This clipping is found in Rauschenbusch Scrapbook, part 1, Rauschenbusch Papers, American Baptist Historical Society.

8. Sharpe, *Walter Rauschenbusch*, 165–66. Some of this information was related to me by Sharpe in a visit to his home in Pasadena in 1971 and 1973.
9. This information was garnered from conversations with Sharpe and from a search of papers in his possession.
10. Hopkins, *Rise of the Social Gospel*, 262–63.
11. Elsie Strong, and Margery Strong, "Memorial Biography of Josiah Strong," typescript, 409, Josiah Strong Papers; Josiah Strong to Booker To Washington, Nov. 15, 1905; Washington to Strong, Nov. 18, 1905, Washington Papers.
12. *Gospel of the Kingdom* 1 (Aug. 1909): 83.
13. Ibid., 83–87.
14. Josiah Strong, *Sagamore Sociological Conference* (Boston, 1910), 50–51.
15. Josiah Strong, *Our World* (New York, 1913), 107.
16. *Gospel of the Kingdom* 7 (Aug. 1915): 113–19.
17. Ibid., 121–23.
18. Biographical materials can be found in the Harlan Paul Douglass papers at the Amistad Research Center, Tulane University, New Orleans.
19. Harlan Paul Douglass, "The English Christian Socialist Movement of the Mid-Century" (typed thesis, n.d.), 62, Douglass Papers.
20. Harlan Paul Douglass, *Christian Reconstruction in the South* (Boston, 1909), v–viii, 28.
21. Ibid., 34–35.
22. Ibid., 47, 58, 64–65, 122.
23. Ibid., 148, 157, 163.
24. Ibid., 165.
25. Ibid., 167.
26. Edward A. Ross, *Foundations of Sociology* (New York, 1905), 353, quoted by Douglass, *Christian Reconstruction in the South*, 170. See also Julius Weinberg, *Edward Alsworth Ross and the Sociology of Progressivism* (Madison, Wisc., 1972); Edward A. Ross, *Sin and Society* (Boston, 1907).
27. Douglass, *Christian Reconstruction in the South*, 368, 392.
28. Harlan Paul Douglass, Brief of Secretarial Report to Executive Committee of the American Missionary Association, Feb. 14, 1911, 5, Douglass Papers.
29. *Chicago Advance*, 1945, 10.
30. McPherson, *Abolitionist Legacy*, 197, 346–47.
31. Atticus G. Haygood, *Sermons and Speeches*, 378.
32. McDowell, *Social Gospel in the South*, 15.
33. Henry Y. Warnock, "Moderate Racial Thought and Attitudes of Southern Baptists and Methodists, 1900–1921" (Ph.D. diss., Northwestern University, 1963), 47–48; McDowell, *Social Gospel in the South*, 26.
34. Lily Hardy Hammond, "A Southern View of the Negro," *Outlook* 72 (Mar. 14, 1902).
35. Warnock, "Moderate Racial Thought," 73.
36. Lily H. Hammond, *In Black and White: An Interpretation of Southern Life* (New York, 1914), 25–26, 28, 37.
37. Ibid., 87–88, 124.
38. Ibid., 182–83, 210–12; the Southern Sociological Congress will be discussed in chapter 14.
39. Ibid., 134–35.
40. Lily H. Hammond, *Southern Women and Racial Adjustment* (Baltimore, 1917), 5.
41. Lily H. Hammond, "Among Negro Laborers," in *The Path of Labor* (New York, 1918), 112, 121.
42. Lily H. Hammond, *In the Vanguard of a Race* (New York, 1917), 15.
43. Hammond, *Southern Women and Racial Adjustment*, 5.
44. Crum, *Negro in the Methodist Church*, 84–85; Noreen D. Tatum, *A Crown of Service: A Story of Woman's Work in the Methodist Episcopal Church, South, from 1878 to 1940* (Nash-

ville, 1960), 249–50; Ann F. Scott, *The Southern Lady: From Pedestal to Politics, 1830–1930* (Chicago, 1970), 142–43; McDowell, *Social Gospel in the South*, 85–86.

45. Scott, *Southern Lady*, 143.
46. McDowell, *Social Gospel in the South*, 88.
47. Hammond, *Vanguard of a Race*, 175.

14. "The Church Outside the Churches"

1. Robert M. Crunden, *Ministers of Reform: The Progressives' Achievement in American Civilization, 1889–1920* (New York, 1982), x.
2. Ibid., ix.
3. George W. Coleman, *The Church Outside the Church* (Philadelphia, 1910), 5–6.
4. Walter Rauschenbusch, *A Theology for the Social Gospel* (New York, 1917), 137.
5. Ibid., 134.
6. This story was found among miscellaneous items on the 1914 Sagamore Sociological Conference on "Race Problems," part of four volumes of reports, newspaper accounts, and correspondence about the Sagamore Sociological Conferences at the American Baptist Historical Society, Rochester, New York (hereinafter cited as the Sagamore Sociological Conference Papers).
7. A copy of the original letter is in the Sagamore Sociological Conference Papers.
8. Statement in Sagamore Sociological Conference Papers.
9. *Boston Traveler*, June 29, 1910.
10. *Eighth Year of the Sagamore Sociological Conference* (Boston, 1914), 10.
11. Cited in Hammond, *Vanguard of a Race*, 77.
12. William N. DeBerry, "What the Negro Wants," in *Eighth Year of the Sagamore Sociological Conference* (Boston, 1914), 10.
13. Ibid., 11.
14. Ibid., 13–16.
15. *Watchman-Examiner* 96 (July 9, 1914): 908.
16. George W. Coleman, ed., *Democracy in the Making: Ford Hall Forum and the Open Forum Movement* (Boston, 1915), 16; see also Reuben L. Lurie, *The Challenge of the Forum: The Story of Ford Hall Forum and the Open Forum Movement* (Boston, 1930), 26–31.
17. Coleman, *Democracy in the Making*, ix, xi.
18. Coleman, *Churches outside the Church*, 28.
19. Scrapbooks containing programs, reports, newspaper accounts, and correspondence relating to the Ford Hall Forum are at the American Baptist Historical Society, Rochester, New York.
20. Coleman, *Democracy in the Making*, 39.
21. For the origins of the Southern Sociological Congress, see two articles by E. Charles Chatfield: "The Southern Sociological Congress: Organization of Uplift," *Tennessee Historical Quarterly* 19 (Dec. 1960): 328–47; and "The Southern Sociological Congress: Rationale of Uplift," ibid. (Mar. 1961): 51–64. See also John Joel Culley, "Muted Trumpets: Four Efforts to Better Southern Race Relations, 1900–1919" (Ph.D. diss., University of Virginia, 1967), 114–23.
22. James McCulloch, ed., *The Call of the New South* (Nashville, 1912), 7.
23. Ibid., 9.
24. Chatfield, "Organization of Uplift," 336.
25. Dykeman, *Prophet of Plenty*, 75–77; Culley, "Muted Trumpets," 126–29. Dykeman states that Weatherford acted to desegregate the seating arrangements completely. Citing local newspapers, Culley says that blacks still sat separately, but at the same level as whites and in sections heretofore reserved for whites.
26. James E. McCulloch, ed., *The New Chivalry: Health* (Nashville, 1915), 13.

27. John Olen Fish, "Southern Methodism in the Progressive Era: A Social History" (Ph.D. diss., University of Georgia, 1969), 39, 206.
28. Kirby, *Darkness at the Dawning*, 51.
29. For information on Poteat, see Eighmy, *Churches in Cultural Captivity*, 84-85.
30. James E. McCullough to Emmet J. Scott, June 10, 1915, Washington Papers.
31. Ray Stannard Baker, "Gathering Clouds along the Color Line," *World's Work* 32 (June 1916): 232–36.
32. Cullley, "Muted Trumpets," 125, 169–204.
33. Chatfield, "Organization of Uplift," 328.
34. Elliott M. Rudwick, *Race Riot at East St. Louis, July 2, 1917* (Carbondale, Ill., 1964).
35. Weatherford, "Colored Young Men's Christian Association."
36. Will Alexander, Oral History Project, 1952, Columbia University, New York, 169–77.
37. Much of the information that follows was found in minutes, pamphlets, and newspaper clippings in the Commission on Interracial Cooperation Papers, Negro Collection, Atlanta University (hereinafter cited as CIC Papers).
38. For biographical information on Alexander, see Wilma Dykeman and James Stokely, *Seeds of Southern Change: The Life of Will Alexander* (Chicago, 1962).
39. Will Alexander, Oral History Project, 108–12.
40. Ibid., 119.
41. Ibid., 169.
42. Ibid., 182; "Minutes of the Inter-Racial Conference," July 17, 1919, CIC Papers; Edward F. Burrows, "The Commission on Interracial Cooperation, 1919–1944" (Ph.D. diss., University of Wisconsin, 1954), 47, 50.
43. Burrows, "Commission on Interracial Cooperation," 54–56.
44. Ibid., 112, 114; Robert E. Speer, *John J. Eagen: A Memoir of an Adventurer for the Kingdom of God on Earth* (Birmingham, Ala., 1939).
45. Speer, John J. Eagen, 10, 109.
46. Ibid., 40–41, 51–55.
47. Ibid., 200, 106.
48. Morton Sosna, *In Search of the Silent South: Southern Liberals and the Race Issue* (New York, 1977), 23.
49. *Minutes*, Mar. 23, 1920, 10–11, CIC Papers.
50. *Minutes*, Nov. 17, 1920, CIC Papers.
51. "An Appeal to the Christian People of the South," 6–9, CIC Papers.
52. *Study of the Origins and Organizations of the Commission on Interracial Cooperation*, Exhibit N [possibly an application to a foundation for funding], 1–2, CIC Papers.
53. Burrows, "Commission on Interracial Cooperation," 146–49, 151.
54. Mrs. J. W. Perry and Miss Estelle Haskin, "Report of the Commission on Race Relations," CIC Papers, as cited in ibid., 59.
55. Burrows, "Commission on Interracial Cooperation," 63.
56. Mrs. Luke Johnson (Carrie Parks Johnson), "Minutes of Interracial Commission," Nov. 17, 1920, 29–30, as cited in "Background," an unsigned report of women's work within the CIC; Mrs. Luke Johnson, "The Business of Peace" (Address), as cited in "Background," 11a; both quotations from Burrows, "Commission on Interracial Cooperation," 60.

15. Ecumenical Race Relations

1. John A. Hutchison, *We Are Not Divided: A Critical and Historical Study of the Federal Council of the Churches of Christ in America* (New York, 1941), 25.
2. For background information, see especially Elias B. Sanford, *Origin and History of the Federal Council of Churches of Christ in America* (Hartford, 1916); and Hutchison, *We Are Not Divided*.

3. W. B. Derrick, "The Work of Evangelization among Negroes," in *Church Federation: Inter-Church Conference on Federation* (New York, 1906), 520–24.
4. *Report of the Commission on the Church and Social Service to the Federal Council of the Churches of Christ in America* (New York, 1912), 20–21.
5. *Annual Reports of the Federal Council of the Churches of Christ in America* (New York, 1916), 219.
6. Charles S. Macfarland, *Christian Unity in the Making: The First Twenty-Five Years of the Federal Council of the Churches of Christ in America* (New York, 1948), 116–19.
7. *Annual Reports, Federal Council of the Churches of Christ in America, 1918* (New York, 1918), 7; I am indebted to John F. Piper, Jr., for much of the information in the following pages. See Piper, *The American Churches in World War I* (Athens, Ohio, 1985), 164–74.
8. The various memos and reports by Williams are in the Federal Council of Churches Papers, the Presbyterian Historical Society, Philadelphia. These form the basis for a later book by Williams entitled *Sidelights on Negro Soldiers* (Boston, 1923).
9. Charles H. Williams, "Resume of Conditions Surrounding Negro Troops" (typed report, Aug. 5, 1918), Federal Council of Churches Papers; Piper, *American Churches*, 168–70.
10. "Subjects for a Conference with War Department on Welfare of Negro Troops" (Sept. 25, 1918), Federal Council of Churches Papers.
11. William M. Tuttle, Jr., *Race Riot: Chicago in the Red Summer of 1919* (New York, 1970); Arthur I. Waskow, *From Race Riot to Sit-In, 1919 and the 1960s: A Study in the Connections between Conflict and Violence* (Garden City, N.Y., 1966); Piper, *American Churches*, 172.
12. *Annual Reports, Federal Council of the Churches of Christ in America, 1921* (New York, 1921), 79.
13. Minutes of the First Meeting of the Commission on Negro Churches and Race Relations, July 12, 1921, 1, Federal Council of Churches Papers.
14. Ibid.
15. *Minutes*, Oct. 7, 1921, CIC Papers.
16. Speer, *John J. Eagen*, 93–97.
17. Minutes of the Meeting of the Commission on Negro Churches and Race Relations, Jan. 6, 1922, 2, Federal Council of Churches Papers.
18. For a fine biographical study of Haynes, see Perlman, "Stirring the White Conscience."
19. George E. Haynes, "Memoirs," sec. V, 9b. The "Memoirs" are unpublished papers cited by Samuel Kelton Roberts, "Crucible for a Vision: The Work of George Edmund Haynes and the Commission on Race Relations, 1922–1947" (Ph.D. diss., Columbia University, 1974), 58.
20. Haynes, "Memoirs," 9c, cited in Roberts, "Crucible for a Vision," 58.
21. Addie Hunton, *William Alphaeus Hunton: A Pioneer Prophet of Young Men* (New York, 1938).
22. Perlman, "Stirring the White Conscience," 33–34.
23. "Annual Report, Aug. 31, 1906–June 17, 1907, of George E. Haynes to the International Committee of the YMCA, Colored Men's Department, rendered Aug. 30, 1907 at Silver Bay, Lake George, N.Y." (typewritten manuscript), Library of the National Council of the YMCA, cited in Perlman, "Stirring the White Controversy," 44.
24. George E. Haynes, Address delivered at Preacher's Institute, Paine College, June 14, 1927, Haynes "Memoirs," cited in Perlman, "Stirring the White Controversy," 45–46. This meeting was three years earlier than the meeting described in chapter 12 attended by Hunton, Moorland, and four others, where the final decision seems to be have been made to commission Weatherford to write the book.
25. Haynes, "Memoirs" (no page cited), quoted in Perlman, "Stirring the White Controversy," 57.
26. Perlman, "Stirring the White Controversy," 93–98.

27. Harlan Paul Douglass to President George Gates, Apr. 14, 1910, Student File of George Edmund Haynes, Fisk University, cited in ibid., 87.
28. Roberts, "Crucible for a Vision," 64–68.
29. Haynes, "Memoirs," sec. XI, 80A, cited in Perlman, "Stirring the White Controversy," 166.
30. George E. Haynes, "Tentative Report of a Preliminary Study of Specific Conditions of the Colored People of Minneapolis, and Their Relation to the Community," Commission on the Church and Race Relations, Federal Council of Churches Papers.
31. Perlman, "Stirring the White Controversy," 150–53; Roberts, "Crucible for a Vision," 100.
32. George E. Haynes, The Trend of the Races (New York, 1922), 14–15.
33. Ibid., 16–17.
34. Haynes and Staff, The Work of the Commission on Race Relations, II-1, Federal Council of Churches, 1932 (Type Script) cited in Roberts, "Crucible for a Vision," 125.
35. Materials including church bulletins, letters from pastors and parishioners, and promotional materials are in abundance in the Commission on the Church and Race Relations, Federal Council of Churches Papers.
36. Joseph R. Cotter, Jr., "And What Shall You Say?" frontpiece of numerous church bulletins for February 10, 1924, ibid.
37. Perlman, "Stirring the White Controversy," 79–80.
38. Roberts, "Crucible for a Vision," 53.
39. George E. Haynes to Dr. J. E. Moorland, June 2, 1916, Haynes Papers, quoted in ibid., 74–75.
40. "Toward Interracial Cooperation: What Was Said and Done at the First National Interracial Conference, Cincinnati, Ohio, Mar. 25–27, 1925, 167, Commission on the Church and Race Relations, Federal Council of Churches Papers.
41. Hopkins, History of the YMCA, 532.
42. "Toward Interracial Cooperation," 174–75, 177.
43. Ibid., 170–72.
44. Ibid., 5.

Epilogue

1. Martin Luther King, Jr., Stride toward Freedom (New York, 1958), 91.
2. Justice Robert H. Jackson to Ernest Cawcroft and Walter H. Edson, Apr. 4, 1950, copy in Robert H. Jackson Papers; cited in C. Vann Woodward, American Counterpoint: Slavery and Racism in the North-South Dialogue (Boston, 1976), 232.
3. Miller, Following In His Steps, 52.
4. An important contribution is Cynthia Neverdon-Morton, Afro-American Women of the South and the Advancement of the Race, 1895–1925 (Knoxville, Tenn., 1989).
5. King, Stride toward Freedom, 91.
6. Reinhold Niebuhr, The Leaves from the Notebook of a Tamed Cynic (New York, 1930), 22.
7. Barrows, First Mohonk Conference, 108.
8. Martin Luther King, Jr., Why We Can't Wait (New York, 1964), 35, 67.

Index

Abbott, Edward, 78–79

Abbott, Lyman, xxi, 10, 17, 27, 67, 77, 136, 180–81, 208, 262–63; American Freedmen's Union Commission, 25; antislavery position, 24–25; and Booker T. Washington, 15, 94; chaplain to President Roosevelt, xxiii; commends George W. Cable, 55; Capon Springs Conference, 82–83; Federal Elections Bill, 27–28; industrial education, 127; Lake Mohonk Conference on the Negro Question, 3–9; Niagara Movement, 175–76; retreat from reform to accommodation, 25–26; Southern Education Movement, 82–83, 87–88; and *Up from Slavery*, 92–93; and W. E. B. Du Bois, 137

Abolitionism, xi, xiii, 86, 131, 145, 181, 259; ancestral spirit of NAACP, 172–75

Addams, Jane, 178, 186, 212

Advance (Chicago), 6, 30–31

Africa, 22–23, 70

African Methodist Episcopal Church, xxiii, 177–78, 180, 246

African Methodist Episcopal Church Zion, xxiii, 177

Afro-American Council (formerly Afro-American League), 37, 69, 178–79, 282n.34

Alexander, Will, 66, 204, 227, 245, 259, 263; and Commission on Interracial Cooperation, 237–44; and Commission on the Church and Race Relations, 249–50; early career, 237–38

American Baptist Home Mission Society, 63–64, 85, 229

American Colonization Society, 21–23

American Freedmen's Union Commission, 25, 63

American Home Missionary Society, 64, 134

American Institute of Social Service, 211–12

American Missionary Association, ix, 58, 118, 209, 212, 242, 253; a case study, 63–67; and Harlan Paul Douglass, 214–

19, 224; and Washington Gladden, 132–41, 146

Ames, Mrs. Jesse Daniel, 244

Anderson, Matthew, 106–7

Armstrong, Samuel Chapman, 4, 79, 123

Atlanta, 13, 136–37, 240, 258–60; riot (1906), 122, 140, 142, 144–45

Atlanta Compromise Address. *See* Booker T. Washington

Atlanta Constitution, 26, 97

Atlanta University, 63, 87, 124–26, 135, 143, 173, 191; Conference on the Negro Church (1903), 118–19, 136; Trustees of, 66; and W. E. B. Du Bois, 97

Baker, Ray Stannard, 229, 235

Baldwin, Ruth Standish, 172

Baldwin, William H., 66, 124, 151; First Capon Springs Conference, 80; General Education Board, 84; influence on Urban League, 171–72; Southern Education Movement, 85–87

Baptist Church, xxiii, 173, 197; *See also* American Baptist Home Mission Society; Northern Baptist Social Service Commission

Batton, Samuel Zane, 234, 246

Beecher, Henry Ward, 4

Bennett, Belle H., 219–20, 242

The Birth of a Nation, 145, 204

Bishop, Hutchins C., 177, 236

Blacks. *See* Education; Racism; Slavery; and *specific black individuals; churches; institutions; movements; newspapers; schools*

Blair Education Bill, 11–12, 36

Bliss, W. D. P., xxi

Boston, 114, 227

Boston Evening Transcript, 91–92

Bowen, John Wesley Edward, 72, 98, 105; early career, 119–20; Congress on Africa, 121–22; Booker T. Washington, 119–22

Bowne, Borden Parker, 120

Bradford, Amory H., 66–67, 137

Bratton, Theodore D., 234, 241

Brooks, William Henry, 171, 177–78

Brown, Charlotte Hawkins, 243

ena. sp - p114

educating, primacy - p129

sacrifice principle to p143
          seques